Marriage *and* Family

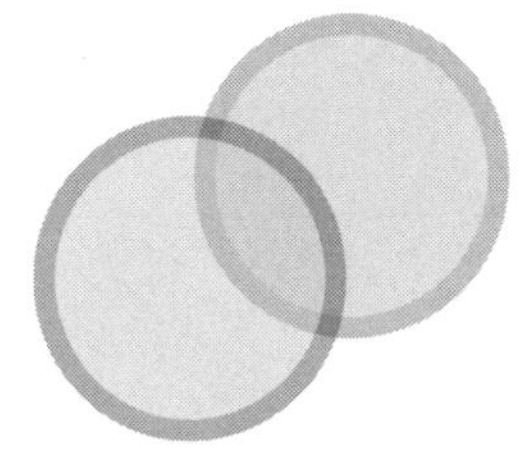

MARRIAGE *and* FAMILY

Perspectives *and* Complexities

Edited by H. ELIZABETH PETERS
and CLAIRE M. KAMP DUSH

COLUMBIA UNIVERSITY PRESS  New York

Columbia University Press
Publishers Since 1893
New York Chichester, West Sussex

Library of Congress Cataloging-in-Publication Data
Marriage and family : perspectives and complexities / edited by H. Elizabeth Peters and Claire M. Kamp Dush.
p. cm.
Includes bibliographical references and index.
ISBN 978-0-231-14408-7 (cloth : alk. paper)—ISBN 978-0-231-52002-7 (ebook) 1. Marriage—United States. 2. Family—United States. 3. Parenting—United States. I. Peters, Elizabeth, 1955– II. Kamp Dush, Claire M. III. Title.

HQ734.M3872 2009
306.850973—dc22
2008054886

Columbia University Press books are printed on permanent and durable acid-free paper.
This book is printed on paper with recycled content.
Printed in the United States of America

c 10 9 8 7 6 5 4 3 2 1

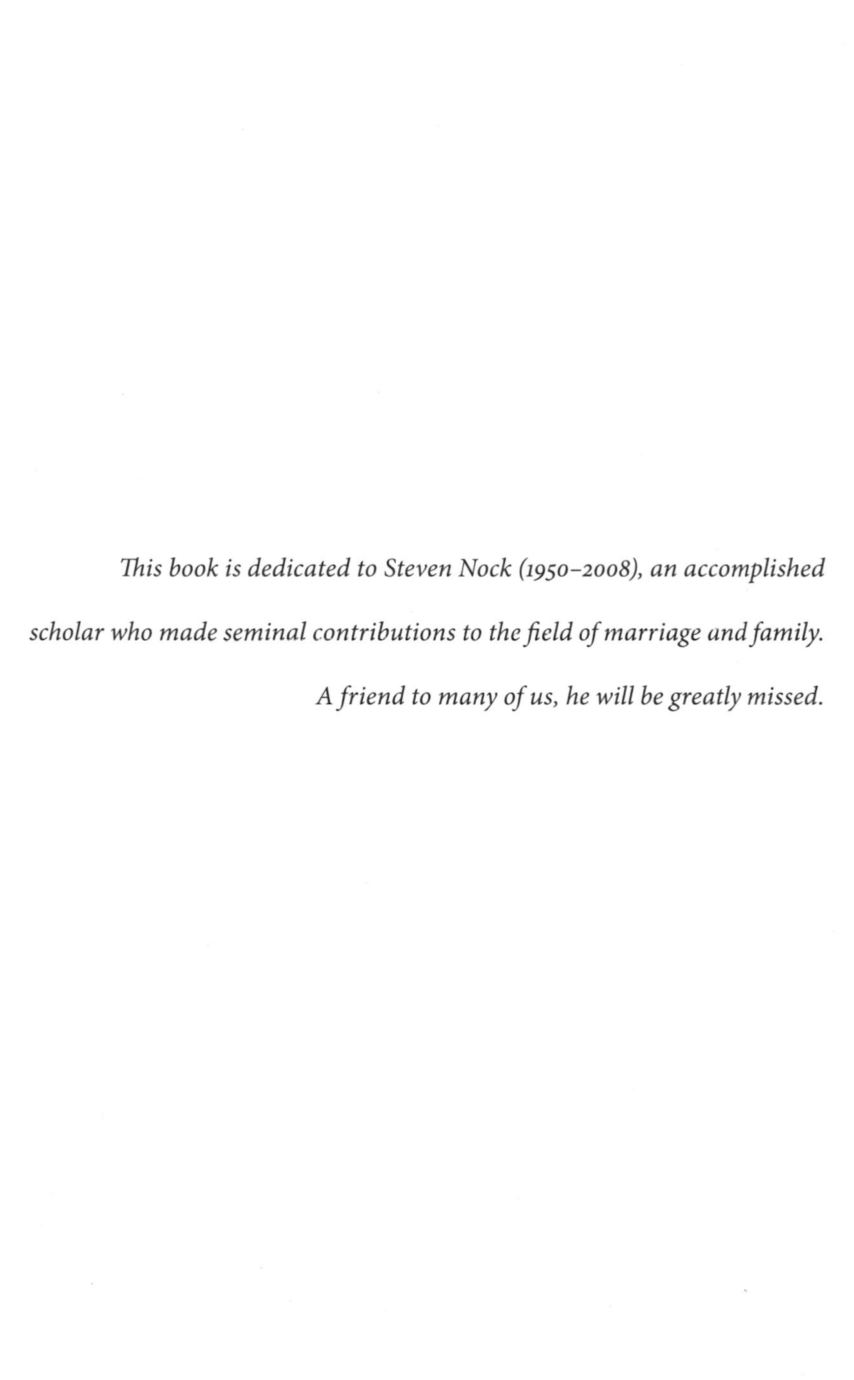

This book is dedicated to Steven Nock (1950–2008), an accomplished scholar who made seminal contributions to the field of marriage and family. A friend to many of us, he will be greatly missed.

Contents

List of Illustrations

List of Tables

Acknowledgments

The editors wish to acknowledge generous support for this project from the Evolving Family Theme Project of the Institute for the Social Sciences at Cornell University. This book is partly based on a conference that was held at Cornell University as an activity of the Evolving Family Theme Project on April 7 and 8, 2006. Evolving Family Theme Project team members contributed to the planning and execution of this project, and to them we are grateful. In addition to the editors of this volume, they included Elizabeth Adkins-Regan, Stephen Emlen, Michael Goldstein, Mary Katzenstein, Stefan Klonner, Kathryn March, Maureen Waller, Elaine Wethington, and Lindy Williams. For their support and assistance, we are also grateful to David R. Harris, director of the Institute for the Social Sciences at this project's conception, and to the administrative staff of the institute, Anneliese Truame and Judi Eastburn.

Introduction

H. ELIZABETH PETERS AND
CLAIRE M. KAMP DUSH

As the title suggests, a central theme of this book is one of diversity. We document diversity in men's, women's, and children's experiences of family and marriage—over time, across cultures, and especially today within the United States. We describe a variety of perspectives that provide different lenses on the questions of why people marry and the consequences of those choices for parents, their children, and society at large. We also present evidence suggestive of continuing and potentially increasing diversity of those experiences and consequences into the future.

This book is divided into four parts. The first includes chapters examining motivations for marriage and the role of marriage in society from a variety of disciplinary perspectives. The second presents empirical work that contrasts several emerging family types with the traditional married nuclear family. The third examines current policy efforts to promote healthy and stable marriages. The fourth discusses the future of marriage, given recent changes in the social, economic, and demographic context in the United States.

Family forms are becoming increasingly diverse. Some demographers have characterized the dramatic changes in family structure and behavior over the past forty years as the "second demographic transition" (Lesthaeghe 1995). These changes include delays in marriage and increases in divorce, nonmarital childbearing, and cohabitation. The changes have not occurred equally for all groups, however. The retreat from marriage and increases in nonmarital childbearing are concentrated among racial and ethnic minorities and the less educated, and these differences in marriage

Figure I.1 Median Age at Marriage, 1890–2005

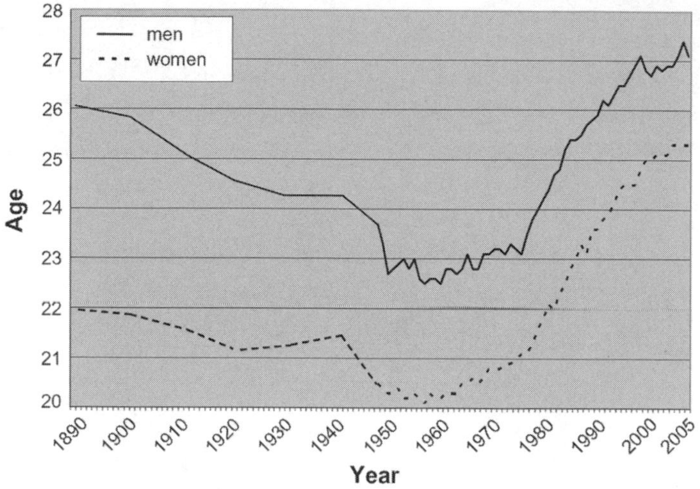

Source: U.S. Census Bureau

Note: Figures for 1947 to present are based on Current Population Survey data. Figures for years before 1947 are based on decennial censuses.

outcomes have contributed to the increase in inequality over the last thirty years (McLanahan 2004).

There has been considerable debate about whether individuals are tending forgo marriage altogether, or whether due to increases in the age of marriage and in the likelihood of divorce they are just spending less of their life cycle being married. Data clearly show that both men and women remain single for a longer period of time. In 2005 the median age of marriage in the United States was twenty-seven for men and twenty-five for women (see figure I.1). The age at marriage has increased substantially since the 1950s, when half of women married during their teen years. As the figure shows, however, the 1950s were an anomaly. At the end of the nineteenth century, the age of marriage was closer to what it is today; in 1890 the median age of marriage was twenty-two for women and twenty-six for men.

Figure I.2 sheds some light on the question of whether marriage is delayed or avoided. The figure shows the proportion of white and black women who were ever married by age 45–50 by education level over time (this is a good proxy for ever marrying, because first marriage is unlikely after these ages). The top panel shows that marriage propensities have increased for white women. Since 1950, the likelihood of ever marrying remained almost constant for those with less than a high school education, but this likelihood increased for white women with more education (by about 6 percentage points for women with a high-school degree and 10 percentage points for women with some college). In contrast, the lower panel shows that marriage propensities decreased substantially over time for black women of all education levels. The decline was largest for black women with less than a college education (from 96 percent to 62 percent),

Figure I.2 Panel A (*top*): Percent of White Women Aged 45–50 Ever Married by Educational Attainment; Panel B (*bottom*): Percent of Black Women Aged 45–50 Ever Married by Educational Attainment

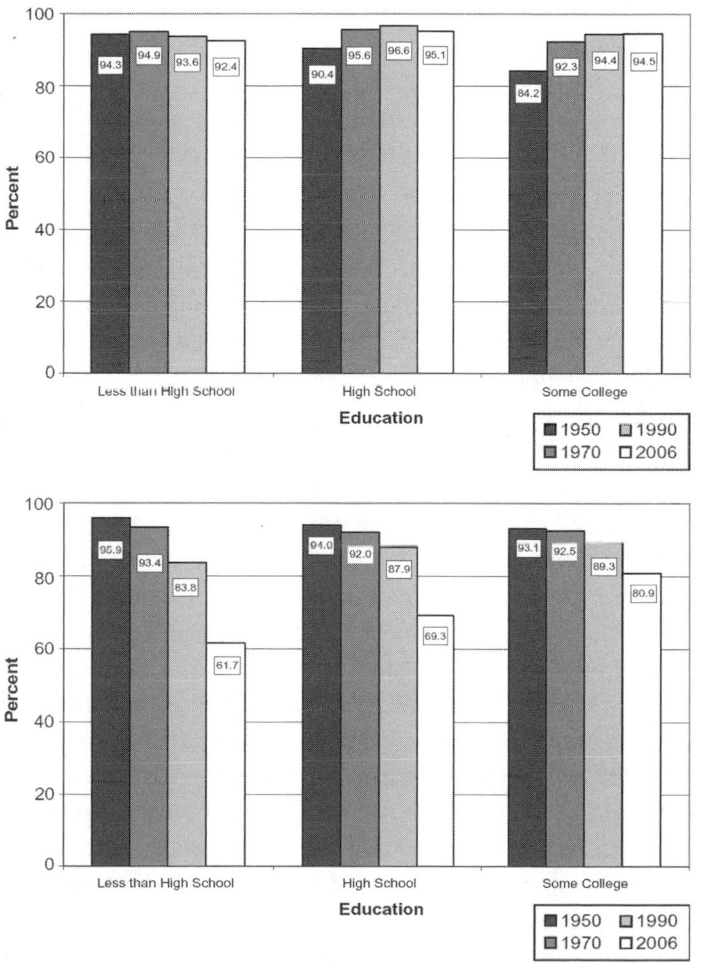

Source: Author's calculations from the IPUMS files for the U.S. decennial census and the American Community Survey

Figure I.3 Marriage and Divorce Rates per 1000 Women at Risk

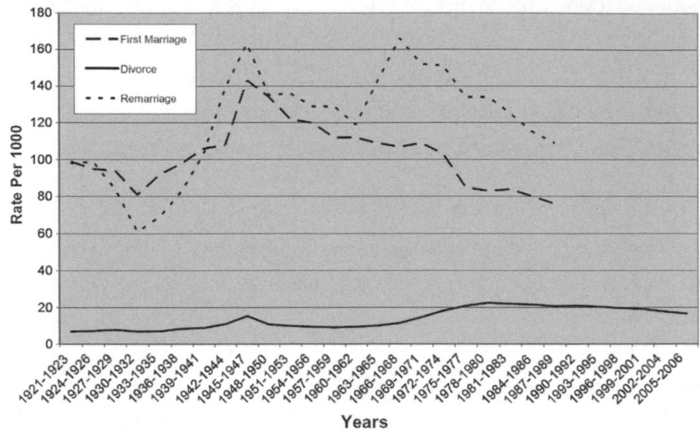

Sources: 1921–1989 from the U.S. Census Bureau (1992); 1990–2004 from the editors' tabulations of multiple years of the NCHS Vital Statistics Report and Current Population Survey March Annual Social and Economic Supplement

but there was still a 10-point decline in marriage probabilities for black women with some college. In the past, blacks and women with less education were more likely to be married than were whites or women with more education, but the opposite is true today. As several of the chapters in this book emphasize, over time marriage has become increasingly selective of those with higher socioeconomic status.

The increase in divorce rates is another factor contributing to the decline in marriage (see figure I.3). The substantial increase began in the late 1960s, but aggregate divorce rates have been fairly flat since 1980, with a small decline in recent years. Divorce propensities also reflect the divide between high and low socioeconomic groups. The likelihood of divorce has fallen slightly for non-Hispanic whites but has continued to rise for blacks (Bramlett and Mosher 2002). Figure I.3 also shows that remarriage rates have fallen over time. Again remarriage rates have fallen faster for blacks than for whites (Bramlett and Mosher 2002).

The delay in marriage has not been matched by a similar delay in fertility, especially for black women and those with lower education. Essentially marriage and childbearing are less closely connected now than in the past, resulting in an increasing number of births outside of marriage. This behavior has been the focus of much debate by policymakers and pundits alike. In 2005, almost seven in ten black children and about one in four

Figure I.4 Percent of Births to Unmarried Women: United States, 1940–2006

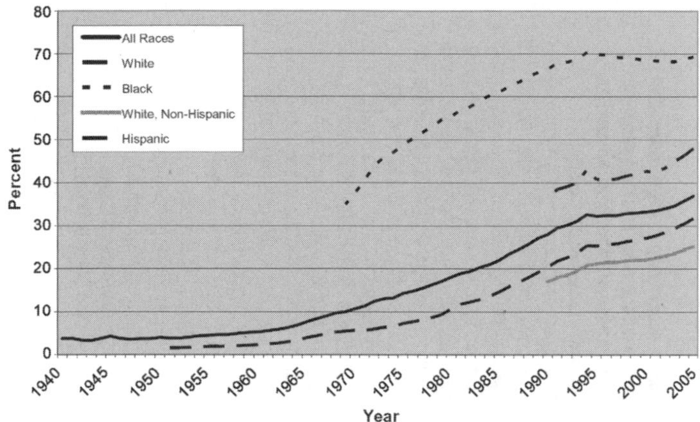

Source: Ventura and Bachrach 2000, table 4, 28–31, and multiple years of NCHS Vital Statistics Report

white non-Hispanic children were born to nonmarried parents (Figure I.4). The enormous rise in nonmarital childbearing began in the 1960s, and the percent of births that are nonmarital has almost quadrupled since 1970. Unlike the other demographic behaviors discussed earlier, however, the numbers for blacks and whites are beginning to narrow. The proportion of births outside of marriage reached a peak for blacks in 1994 and has remained fairly constant for more than a decade, while this proportion for whites continues to increase.

Another change in family structure has been the rise of nonmarital cohabitation. Estimates based on the 2000 U.S. census show that there are nearly 5.5 million cohabiting couples in the United States today, which represents a more than 1,000 percent increase since 1970. It is estimated that about 40 percent of cohabiting households include children (Fields and Casper 2001; Simmons and O'Connell 2003). This varies by race, such that 35 percent of white cohabiting couples, 54 percent of black cohabiting couples, and nearly 60 percent of Hispanic cohabiting couples have children in the household (Fields and Casper 2001). Indeed, evidence from the National Survey of Family Growth estimates that 40 percent of nonmarital births are births to unmarried cohabiting couples (Chandra et al. 2005).

Individuals also experience diversity across the life course. Today, many men and women spend their life course in various family structures, moving back and forth between being single, cohabiting, married, remarried,

Figure I.5 Family-structure experiences from ages 16 to 40: National Longitudinal Survey of Youth (NLSY) 1979 Cohort

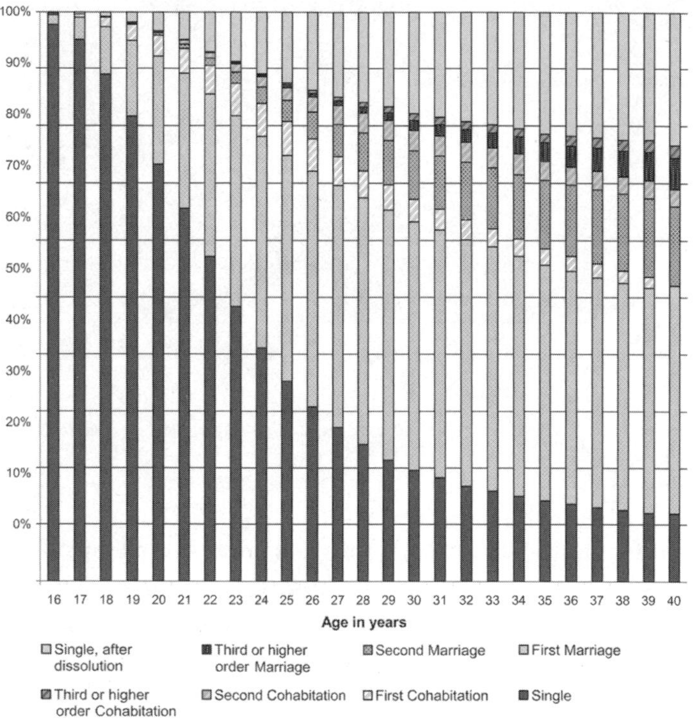

divorced, and/or widowed. Figure I.5 illustrates the dynamic nature of family life for a cohort of young men and women born between 1957 and 1964 using data from the National Longitudinal Survey of Youth 1979 (NLSY79) data. This graph depicts the family structures of these young men and women from ages sixteen to forty, using longitudinal data collected between 1979 (and retrospective data from before 1979) and 2004. The figure illustrates that by age twenty-three, half the sample had entered into a first union, most residing in their first marriage. Ten years later, by age thirty-three, only 16 percent had never entered a union. Meanwhile, 46 percent were still in their first union, yet 20 percent were single after a marital or cohabitation dissolution, and 18 percent were in their second, third, or higher-order marital or cohabiting union. Seven years later, at age forty, only 12 percent had never entered a union, 39 percent were in their first marriage, 23 percent were single after a union dissolution, and 26 percent were in their second, third, or higher-order marital or cohabiting union. At midlife, only 51 percent had yet to experience a union dissolution.

Figure I.6 Family-structure experiences from ages 16 to 26: National Longitudinal Survey of Youth (NLSY) 1997 Cohort

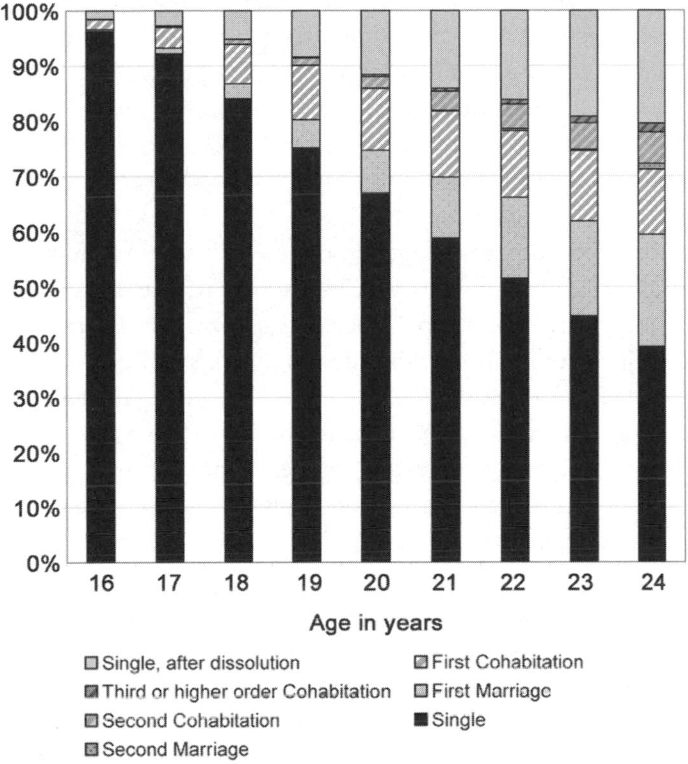

A cohort comparison of the NLSY79 and a more recent cohort of men and women who were born between 1980 and 1984 (the National Longitudinal Survey of Youth 1997) highlights how in the future these trends may be exacerbated. In figure I.6, we compare data from the NLSY97 collected between 1997 and 2004 with data from the older cohort shown in figure I.5. By age twenty-four, both cohorts have similar percentages of respondents who have yet to enter a union—41 percent of the NLSY79 cohort and 39 percent of the NLSY97 cohort. However, the rest of the family structure experiences are quite different. By age twenty-four, 43 percent of the original NLSY79 cohort was in their first union, with 86 percent of these unions being first marriages and 14 percent being first cohabitations. On the other hand, by age twenty-four only 32 percent of the NLS97 cohort members were in their first union, with 62 percent in their first marriage and 38 percent in a first cohabitation. Thus, fewer of the NLSY97 are in their first union at age twenty-four, and they are more likely to be in a cohabiting union than are men and women from the original NLSY79 cohort. In the NLSY79 cohort, only 5 percent were in a second union by age twenty-four, while in the NLSY97 cohort, 9 percent were in a second or even third union. Finally, both the number of twenty-four-year olds who were single after dissolving their union (11 percent versus 21 percent) and the number ever dissolving a union (16 percent versus 29 percent) almost doubled between the 1979 and 1997 cohorts. Given the levels of union instability already present by the age of twenty-four in the NLSY97 data, the trends outlined here are likely to continue.

Overall, the trends and changes described in this introduction highlight the considerable diversity in experiences of marriage and indicate that there remain many unanswered questions about contemporary marriage and family life. Our intention when developing this book was to have a mix of reviews of theory and the literature (see part 1 and chapter 5), original empirical research (see part 2), and thought pieces (see parts 3 and 4). This mix gives our readers both breadth and depth into the multitude of issues and perspectives that mark contemporary research on marriage and family.

The chapters in part 1, Perspectives on Marriage, examine motivations for marriage and the role of marriage in society from various disciplinary perspectives. It begins with a chapter by Arland Thornton that provides a broad overview of marriage historically and cross-culturally. Thornton points out that marriage institutions and norms for northwestern European countries and their North American overseas populations have differed from many other countries going back more than six hundred years. In particular, northwestern European countries had a more individualistic orientation, nuclear family structures, older ages at marriage and higher rates of nonmarriage, and less parental control over marriage. Thornton also describes social changes in the Western world, including industrialization, increasing wages for women, and the development of the birth-control pill, that have contributed to the decline in marriage.

Contrasting and complementing the historical and cultural approach is the sociobiological framework outlined in the chapter by Bobbi Low. She focuses on the evolutionary and ecological reasons for both similarities and differences in marriage and family institutions among humans. Low uses examples from other species to shed light on the importance of ecological constraints in explaining human mating and parenting behaviors. She points out that male-female conflicts of interest and tensions between mating and parenting efforts are universal among humans and animals. For example, polygamy is the norm for most mammals, including humans, because males generally maximize genetic fitness by mating and females maximize genetic fitness by investing in their children's survival. Because males and females are likely to succeed in mating and raising families by doing different things, the evolutionary model can also explain why parents teach boys and girls different skills.

Paula England's chapter provides another perspective on gender conflict. She approaches the question from a sociology-of-gender framework. Her chapter addresses two questions. First, she applies the gender perspective to gender inequality in marriage. Specifically, she summarizes the empirical evidence on how normative and economic factors affect power within marriage, looking at outcomes such as the distribution of housework, consumption, and violence. England then turns to her second question: whether marriage promotes or diminishes gender equity. She argues that the effect of marriage on gender equity depends on social class. For example, women with more education are more likely to delay marriage and establish careers, leading to greater gender equity. In contrast, women with less education also delay marriage, but are more likely to have children outside of marriage. Because the costs of childbearing are disproportionately born by women, nonmarriage combined with children can lead to more gender inequity.

Chapter 4, by Paul Amato, concludes this part with a social-psychological perspective. He suggests that there is less agreement about the nature of marriage now than in the past. He describes three competing marriage schema that operate today: institutional, companionate, and individualistic. Although most marriages contain aspects of each of these stylized types, Amato suggests that over time young adults have placed less importance on the structural aspects of marriage such as children, religion, and home and, increasingly, have moved closer to the individualistic model of marriage focusing on happiness and finding a "soul mate." However, these cultural shifts are not uniform across socioeconomic class, and over time more educated individuals are becoming more conservative about marriage while the less educated are becoming less conservative. This shift in attitudes mirrors the change in behavior, described above: divorce among the more educated has declined over time and the retreat from marriage is concentrated among those with less education.

Part 2, Contemporary Families, contrasts emerging family types with the traditional two-biological-parent nuclear family. Rachel Dunifon focuses on single-parent families. Over the past forty years the percent of all children living in single-parent households has increased from 12 percent to 29 percent. Consistent with one of the main points of this book, Dunifon shows that there is considerable diversity in the prevalence and experience of single-parent families across different racial, ethnic, and educational groups, and there is diversity in the route through which single parenthood occurs (divorce or nonmarital childbearing). Dunifon also points out that the household composition differs across single parent families. For example, 12 percent of children in single-parent households also live with grandparents, and 40 percent of children are predicted to spend some of their childhood living in a cohabiting family. Studies generally show that children who live in a single-parent household have worse outcomes than those living with two biological married parents, but there is little consensus about the mechanisms that lead to these worse outcomes. Dunifon concludes that understanding the role of different mechanisms is complicated by the fact that single-parent families are diverse.

Chapter 6, by Wendy Manning, Pamela Smock, and Cara Bergstrom-Lynch, looks at cohabitation. The authors analyze data about young adults' views about cohabitation as a setting in which to raise children. They found a range of attitudes. The most important advantage of cohabitation over single parenthood that respondents mentioned was being able to raise a child together, sharing financial support and other caretaking responsibilities. The comparison between cohabitation and marriage was more complex. Some respondents believed that marriage and cohabitation were not much different as a setting in which to raise children, while others believed that marriage provided benefits such as security, commitment, financial resources (e.g., access to heath insurance), and social recognition, and helped to defined social roles, especially for stepparent families.

Chapter 7, by Claire Kamp Dush, compares outcomes for children living in two family types that have never had a family structure transition: stable married-biological parent and stable single-mother families. By the age of fourteen, only half of white children and less than half of black and Hispanic children were still in the family structure in which they were born. Overall, the family structure experiences of the children varied greatly by race and other socioeconomic characteristics. Matching the two samples on a variety of characteristics, she finds mixed evidence regarding the advantage of two-married parent families over single-mother families among these stable families. Her results suggest that research on the consequences of different family structures needs to carefully distinguish family structure from family stability.

Chapter 8, by Megan Sweeney, Hongbo Wang, and Tami Videon, compares outcomes for adolescents in stepfamilies with those in single-parent families. The authors emphasize the importance of taking into account the diversity of these families, specifically focusing on whether the stepfamily is formed through cohabitation or through marriage and whether the stepfamily is preceded by a divorce or by a nonmarital birth. Their results show the complexity of the relationship between stepfamily formation and adolescent outcomes. For example, stepfamily formation following a divorce is associated with higher levels of adolescent depression and sexual risk taking, but the greater economic and parenting resources available in stepfamilies partly mitigate those negative outcomes. Stepfamily formation following a nonmarital birth is associated with the positive outcome of less involvement in selling drugs.

Chapter 9, by Gary Gates and Adam Romero, describes the characteristics of same-sex couples who are raising children, documenting considerable geographic, racial, ethnic, and socioeconomic diversity among this largely understudied population. The data show that about a quarter of same-sex couples are living with a child under age eighteen. Contrary to popular perceptions, the prevalence of these households is greater among nonwhites and more economically disadvantaged groups. These disadvantages are exacerbated by the fact that gay and lesbian couples are not eligible to receive federally mandated benefits that are linked to marriage, such as health insurance and social security. This chapter also points out the importance of the stepfamily context in understanding outcomes of children living with same-sex parents. Although much of the recent literature that examines this topic focuses on intentional parenting by lesbian couples, Gates and Romero show that many of the children living in same-sex couple households are from previous heterosexual relationships.

The chapters in part 3 focus on the policy arena. Beginning with welfare reform in 1996, which stated in its preamble the goal of encouraging the formation and maintenance of two-parent families, the federal government has shown a strong policy interest in promoting marriage. Subsequent to welfare reform, the Administration on Children and Families developed the Healthy Marriage initiative. Chapter 10, by Virginia Knox and David Fein, describes the Supporting Healthy Marriage Program, a marriage-education program targeted to low-income families. Compared to middle-income families, these couples face additional challenges (among them health issues, depression, drug abuse, poverty, and unemployment), and programs designed for middle-income families have been substantially modified to address these challenges. The model behind the Supporting Healthy Marriage Program was developed collaboratively by psychologists who were involved in earlier marriage education efforts and economists and sociologists who have expertise in antipoverty programs and the provision of other social services. The chapter describes the challenges of implementing the model across a large number of communities and rigorously evaluating outcomes. Both a process and impact evaluation will be done as the program unfolds.

Chapter 11, by Michael Johnson, focuses on a critical issue that needs to be considered as marriage education programs are developed: the problem of domestic violence. Johnson suggests that it is important to distinguish between intimate terrorism and situational couple violence, different types of domestic violence that might have different implications for marriage interventions. Intimate terrorism is used as a way of gaining control over one's partner. It is problematic for marriage-education interventions, because it is generally less responsive to interventions, and participation in the program may pose a danger to the victim. In contrast, situational violence is a result of specific conflicts between the couple, and the types of relationship skills taught by marriage-education programs may be particularly useful in reducing this type of violence. Thus the challenges marriage-education programs face are screening procedures to identify different types of violence (and protecting victims for whom participation in such programs might pose a danger) and developing targeted strategies for each type of violence.

The chapters in part 4 discuss the future of marriage, both in terms of the meaning that marriage has and could have in people's lives and the impact of racial and ethnic diversity in the United States on marriage patterns in the future. In chapter 12, Steven Nock notes that as marriage has become less universal, it has also become more selective of individuals with higher education and other socially valued characteristics. He states that as marriage rates decline, "the symbolic importance of marriage increases." In addition, he suggests that employers in the labor market also value the qualities that are signaled by being married: fidelity, commitment, maturity, independence, and responsibility. Thus, as marriage becomes more selective, its value as a signal of quality to employers increases and labor-market inequality between married and nonmarried individuals will increase. Nock argues that this is likely to be true for men, but because labor-market attachment is generally less for women with children and fertility is higher in marriage, the argument may not fully carry over to women.

In chapter 13, Tamara Metz draws from the political-science literature to ask whether marriage promotes our values of liberty, equality, and stability. She suggests that marriage, as a state-established and state-supported institution, falls short on several grounds. Specifically, she argues that supporting families is an important social goal, because one of their main functions is to provide intimate caregiving by raising children, caring for the elderly, helping family members who have fallen on hard times, and so forth. The institution of marriage privileges one type of family, which violates equality and reduces an individual's freedom to choose a nonmarital family type. Metz then proposes an alternative: to abolish the state establishment of marriage and instead create an intimate caregiving union status that protects both marital and nonmarital families.

Chapter 14, by Shirley Hill, looks at the marriage experiences of African Americans. Hill argues that both historical and current class, racial, and gender inequalities have made marriage less viable for blacks and have produced a gap between the cultural support for marriage and the reality of low marriage rates in this population. Racial discrimination not only affects employment prospects of black males but also leads to anger, which undermines emotional connections between husbands and wives. The economic reality that black women have to work outside the home also conflicts with the ideal of the male as primary breadwinner, producing additional family conflict. These issues lead to the question of whether marriage is as beneficial for black families as it is for white families. The data show, however, that there is strong ideological support for marriage among blacks, and Hill argues that addressing class, racial, and gender inequality is essential to increasing marriage among black families.

The book ends with a chapter by Daniel Lichter and Warren Brown that highlights the issue of how racial and ethnic diversity will shape the future of the family. The chapter points out that Hispanics and Asians represent an increasing share of the population in the United States, and that future patterns of marriage and fertility will reflect the changing composition of the population. Lichter and Brown first present a projection showing that if the marital behavior of each racial or ethnic group did not change over time, projected changes in the composition of the population by 2050 would have little effect on the marital distribution in the population. This result occurs because the lower marriage rates of Hispanics are offset by the higher marriage rates of Asians. The authors caution, however, that the assumption of unchanging marital behavior for each racial or ethnic group is unlikely to hold. The chapter ends with a discussion of how factors such as intermarriage, assimilation, and discrimination could alter the marriage behavior of different groups.

Overall, this book contributes to the literature on marriage and family by highlighting the diversity and complexities of modern American marital and family life. The chapters in this book point out several unanswered questions regarding marriage and family in the United States. We hope our readers are stimulated and motivated by the many interesting questions that remain.

REFERENCES

Bramlett, M. D., and W. D. Mosher. 2002. Cohabitation, marriage, divorce, and remarriage in the United States. *National Center for Health Statistics, Vital Health Statistics* 23, no. 22: 1–93.

Chandra, A., G. M. Martinez, W. D. Mosher, J. C. Abma, and J. Jones. 2005. Fertility, family planning, and reproductive health of US women: Data from the 2002 National Survey of Family Growth. *National Center for Health Statistics, Vital Health Statistics* 23, no. 25. Retrieved March 7, 2008, from www.cdc.gov/nchs/data/series/sr_23/sr23_025.pdf.

Fields, J., and L. Casper. 2001. America's families and living arrangements: Population characteristics. *Current Population Reports*, P20–537. Washington, D.C.: U.S. Census Bureau. Retrieved January 13, 2008, from www.census.gov/prod/2001pubs/p20–537.pdf.

Lesthaeghe, R. 1995. The second demographic transition in western countries: An interpretation. In K. O. Mason and A. Jensen, eds., *Gender and family change in industrialized countries*, 17–62. Oxford: Oxford University Press.

McLanahan, S. 2004. Diverging destinies: How children are faring under the second demographic transition. *Demography* 41, no. 4: 607–627.

Simmons, T., and M. O'Connell. 2003. Married-couple and unmarried-partner households: 2000. *Census 2000 Special Reports: US Census Bureau*. Retrieved January 13, 2008, from www.census.gov/prod/2003pubs/censr-5.pdf.

U.S. Census Bureau. 1992. *Current Population Reports, P23–180, Marriage, Divorce, and Remarriage in the 1990's*. Washington, D.C.: GPO.

———. 2005. Current Population Survey, March and Annual Social and Economic Supplements. Retrieved March 25, 2008, from www.census.gov/population/socdemo/hh-fam/ms2.pdf.

———. 2006. Children with grandparents by presence of parents, gender, race, and Hispanic origin for selected characteristics: 2006. Retrieved January 13, 2008, from www.census.gov/population/socdemo/hh-fam/cps2006/tabC4-all.xls.

Ventura, S. J., and C. A. Bachrach. 2000. Nonmarital childbearing in the United States, 1940–99. *National Center for Health Statistics, National Vital Statistics Reports* 48, no. 16. Retrieved January 13, 2008, from www.cdc.gov/nchs/data/nvsr/nvsr48/nvs48_16.pdf.

Marriage *and* Family

Perspectives on Marriage

PART 1

Historical and Cross-Cultural Perspectives on Marriage

ONE

ARLAND THORNTON

This chapter discusses the place of marriage and family in the lives of individuals and societies from cross-cultural and historical perspectives—considering similarities and differences across time and across culture. I begin with cross-cultural perspectives and a discussion of some of the many features of marriage and family life that have been nearly universal. I then share my awe at the incredible number of different ways in which people in different societies have organized and experienced marriage and family life. Of great importance to understanding American family life are the numerous ways in which marriage in northwestern Europe and its overseas populations have differed from experiences in other societies. Given that a single chapter is too short to discuss in detail cross-cultural differences, I focus on some of the central aspects of marriage and family life in the history of northwestern Europe—and contrast these elements with those in other regions. Readers are referred to the references cited here for more in-depth detail on cross-cultural differences.

Turning next to matters of history and marriage and family change, I observe that students of social change have always been plagued with data of insufficient quality and quantity from ordinary people to answer their questions about change in the general population. This has led scholars for hundreds of years to use data from one country in proxy for the past circumstances in another country and data from the aristocracy to describe marriage and family practices among ordinary people. I show that these practices have produced many beliefs about marriage and family change in the general population in the Western world that were later discovered to be incorrect. I then review some of the central elements of what we know from the historical archives about marriage and family change during the past two centuries in northwestern Europe and its overseas populations in the United States. The changes in marriage and family life in recent decades have been dramatic, as the introduction to this book documents, but there have also been important long-term continuities, and there have been changes that are contrary to what many assume.

I must paint with a very broad brush, providing only the briefest of details. Readers who wish a fuller discussion of these issues and additional references to the relevant literature are invited to refer to more extensive treatments of these topics elsewhere (Axinn, Emens, and Mitchell 2008; Thornton 2005; Thornton, Axinn, and Xie 2007).

UNIVERSAL IMPORTANCE OF FAMILY AND MARRIAGE AMONG HISTORICAL SOCIETIES

I begin this section with the observation that historically family units have been central organizations for all—or almost all—societies (see, for example, Lee and Wang 1999; Sanderson 1990; Thornton and Fricke 1987; Thornton and Lin 1994; Todd 1985; Wright 1899). Indeed, in most societies of the past family units were the loci of many—if not most—of the central activities of human life. The primary residential units were usually composed of family members. Babies were usually born into family units and were reared and educated by relatives. Families were the loci of companionship, love, and affection as well as quarreling, conflict, and even violence. Information and protection were largely obtained through family members. Family authority was very important in the lives of both children and adults. Family units were also the primary locus of economic activity, as most production and consumption occurred within them.

Just as the family was a central organization structuring social and economic life in most populations of the past, the husband-wife dyad and the parent-child dyad were the central units structuring family life. Companionship and love were important elements of the husband-wife relationship, but indifference and dislike could also emerge. It was husbands and wives who formed the primary unit for sexual expression and the bearing, rearing, and socialization of children. Although the roles of the marital dyad in the activities of the family and economy often varied by gender, cultural settings, and the ages of the wife and husband, this couple usually played leadership and management roles in the family economy and household.

Because of the centrality of marriage in people's lives, marriage in virtually all societies in the past was viewed as both one of the most important events between birth and death and as part of the natural progression of the life course for both women and men. Most of the world's population married, but those who did not were usually expected to live as dependents in households headed by other family members. Given the centrality of marriage, it is not surprising that its importance in virtually all societies was not limited to the individuals involved but also to their families and communities. In addition, marriage had religious or spiritual significance in many societies of the world.

Obtaining knowledge of people's motivations for marriage is difficult, and our ignorance of people's motivations for marriage in the past is extremely large. Yet, from descriptions of marriage and family life around the world, we can assume that for centuries most people of the world have married for a variety of reasons, ranging from economic well-being to affection and companionship, from religion to sex, and from the desire for social support to the bearing and rearing of children. People almost everywhere probably married because it was the "natural" thing to do, brought social prestige, and immediately or eventually turned girls and boys into women and men and mistresses and masters of their own households and family economies.

VARIATIONS IN FAMILY AND MARRIAGE AMONG HISTORICAL SOCIETIES

Despite, or perhaps because of, the centrality of family and marriage units in most societies of the past, there has historically been enormous variation in the ways in which different groups have organized marital and family units (for a more extensive discussion and references to the literature, see Thornton 2005, esp. 47–61; see also Broude 1994; Burguière and Lebrun 1986; Goody 1990). In fact, the differences across groups have been so large that it has been difficult even to define what is meant by family and marriage (Coontz 1988; Gough 1959; Yanagisako 1979). For example, marriage in some groups was strictly monogamous with one wife and one husband, in others a man could have multiple wives, and in yet others a wife could have multiple husbands. In some societies households often consisted of elderly parents, multiple married children and in-laws, and numerous grandchildren, while in other societies households usually consisted of just a married couple and their children. And, in some groups a newly married couple would live with or near the husband's parents, in other groups with or near the wife's parents, and in others away from both parents. Similarly, marital practices could vary from the marriage being decided almost entirely by the parents of the couple with no premarital contact between the prospective bride and groom to the marriage being arranged almost entirely by the prospective bride and groom, with substantial premarital courtship, companionship, affection, and sometimes even sex and pregnancy. In some places marriage occurred primarily during the teenage years or earlier, while in others marriage was postponed into the twenties or later.

There were enormous variations in family and marriage patterns between the regions of the world—for example, between Asia and Africa and between Europe and Africa and Asia. In addition, there were important differences within regions—for example, between East Asia and West Asia, and between North Africa and Africa south of the Sahara. Important differences even existed between the family systems in northwestern Europe and the family systems in eastern and southern Europe. Because of the importance of the differences between northwestern Europe (and its overseas populations in North America) and other places, it is useful to understand some of the central elements of those differences.

COMMON HISTORICAL FAMILY AND MARRIAGE PATTERNS OUTSIDE NORTHWESTERN EUROPE

Given the enormous variation in family and marriage patterns outside northwestern Europe, it is impossible to cover that variation in a brief chapter. Consequently, I provide a stylized or composite version of a complex of attributes from multiple societies rather than a description of patterns at any specific time in any particular non-Western country. At the same time, I note that many features of this stylized or composite description roughly fit the situations in many places outside northwestern Europe (for more information and references, see Thornton 2005, esp. 47–61; see also Broude 1994; Thornton and Fricke 1987; and Westermarck 1891).

One of the attributes that contrasted societies outside of northwestern Europe with those within it was the stronger reliance on family units for social organization in the former. Although many people outside of northwestern Europe had important nonfamily experiences and relationships, the family mode of organization in many of these societies was especially widespread. Emphasis on the community rather than the individual has also been particularly important in societies outside of northwestern Europe.

In many societies outside of northwestern Europe, households were frequently large and extended, consisting of grandparents, multiple married children and their spouses, and grandchildren. It was common in such societies for newly married couples to live with one set of parents, at least during the initial years of marriage. These societies also had considerable authority in the hands of parents and the elders, with older parents having extensive authority over their children well into adulthood. In addition, men frequently had extensive authority over women.

Marriage was frequently universal in these societies and was often contracted during the teenage years and earlier in some places. Arranged marriages were frequently the norm, with parents deciding who their children would marry, sometimes with the assistance of a matchmaker. In such arranged-marriage societies there was often very little, or no, opportunity for interaction, courtship, and the creation of love between the prospective husband and wife before marriage. Companionship and affection were meant to be the result of the marriage and not its precursor. The virginity of the prospective bride was often an essential qualification for marriage, a condition which early marriage and parental control of the marriage process helped to ensure.

COMMON HISTORICAL NORTHWESTERN EUROPEAN FAMILY AND MARRIAGE PATTERNS

I now turn to a discussion of the situation in northwestern Europe, with my time frame being the several hundred years preceding the nineteenth century (for more general discussions, including references, see Thornton 2005, esp. 47–61 and 81–95; Thornton, Axinn, and Xie 2007, esp. 27–44; see also Demos 1970; Fleming 2001; Gillis 1985; Gottlieb 1993; Hajnal 1965, 1982; Laslett 1984; Macfarlane 1986; McSheffrey 1995; O'Hara 2000; and Sheehan 1971, 1978). In discussing common marriage and family patterns in northwestern Europe and its overseas populations in North America, it is important to distinguish between the patterns of the aristocracy and the patterns of ordinary people because the patterns of the upper classes varied substantially from those of the common people (see Gottlieb 1993 and Ribordy 2001). My focus here is on ordinary people, not the aristocracy.

Although there were important variations within northwestern Europe, the typical patterns there varied sharply in many respects from the patterns existing in many other places. One important contrast is that although family relationships were generally important for organizing the activities and authority of society, there were especially important nonfamily organizations as well. These included schools, the market, the church, the state, and the military. Many young people also worked and lived in households where they had no family relations. In addition, at the same time that family and community solidarity was important in this region, there was also considerable emphasis on the individual.

Another crucial contrast between northwestern Europe and many other parts of the world is that households in northwestern Europe were usually not large and complex with a diverse number of relatives, but composed primarily of a married couple and their dependent children. A relatively modest number of newlywed couples shared a household with both the mother and father, although many lived in the same area and others lived with a widowed mother or widowed father. Very few married siblings shared the same household. Within these nuclear or weak-stem households, the husband and wife were usually the master and mistress of the household and its many activities, including those of economic production. Marriage also brought individuals socially across the threshold of adulthood and into manhood and womanhood.

Because northwestern European couples usually had to have their own means for providing their economic necessities, marriage could not be entered until the couple had established its own economic and household unit. This meant that marriage was very late by international standards, with women usually not marrying until they were in their early twenties and men frequently waiting until their late twenties. This system also resulted in a relatively high incidence of women and men remaining unmarried throughout life.

In addition, before marriage, large fractions of young people in northwestern Europe left their parental homes—frequently as teenagers—to live and work in the homes and economic units of unrelated families. Consequently, living apart from parents for several years prior to marriage was a common experience for many young people.

As in other societies, marriage was important not only to the couple involved, but to their parents and the larger community. However, the arranged marriage system of other societies did not exist among the ordinary people of northwestern Europe. Instead, despite parental interest and influence, young people had exceptional freedom in mate selection, with the choice of a spouse primarily being determined by the relatively mature prospective couple. Free consent of the prospective bride and groom was an essential element in marriage—a principle endorsed by the Catholic Church.

Mate selection in northwestern Europe often involved extensive periods of courtship between mature women and men who understood that marriage was based on love and companionship, as well as shared residence, economics, and children. It was in the interactions and companionship of courtship that young couples found and nurtured love and affection—in preparation for making marital promises to love, cherish, and honor each other, as the Book of Common Prayer (1552) put it.

Local communities in northwestern Europe provided considerable opportunities for couples to meet and interact with each other—including markets, fairs, religious meetings, work groups, farm buildings, and the houses of neighbors and relatives. Courting couples spent time together, visiting and going on walks or rides. The frequency of visiting increased as the courtship became more serious, with the visits often occurring at the woman's residence. Sometimes these visits involved substantial distances and the man might spend the night at the woman's house.

This courtship system involved sexual attraction and physical affection. Yet significant boundaries were drawn around sexual expressiveness, and premarital sexual intercourse was discouraged. The normative restrictions against nonmarital intercourse were apparently quite effective, although there were deviations from the norms, and sex and even pregnancy sometimes occurred. Such violations indicate that total control over a marriage system based on youthful autonomy and courtship was difficult.

The simple exchange of vows between a bride and groom pledging themselves to each other constituted the central act that joined them together as wife and husband. Although the Catholic Church considered marriage to be a religious sacrament, it endorsed the authority of individuals to marry—placing the power to form a union in the words and commitment of the couple. This meant that the prospective wife and husband administered the sacrament of marriage.

Although the required elements for becoming husband and wife in the Western past were remarkably simple, the process was often elaborated by extensive ritual and ceremony involving family and community. The church also supported the ritual and ceremonial aspects of marriage, but did not require a particular ritual form. The most common form of marriage among ordinary people was a process that involved four steps: betrothal; banns or announcement; the wedding; and sexual consummation.

Betrothal or engagement constituted the first step that transformed an unmarried man and woman into a husband and wife. It was during betrothal that the couple made the crucial vows that committed them to marriage as husband and wife. The betrothal was made public with the proclamation of banns that announced the engagement to the community through multiple oral statements during church services or by placing a written announcement at the local church. The next step was a public wedding, usually held at the church with the assistance of the clergy. The betrothal vows were repeated, with the public promise to love, cherish, and honor each other. Communal celebration to bless and support the newlyweds in their lives together frequently followed the wedding. The final step in the marriage process was consummation through sexual intercourse.

Although the system described here was the most highly sanctioned way to contract a marriage, there were simpler valid alternatives. Couples could hold a wedding without a clergyman because he was not required in the marriage process. Marriage could also be constituted by the exchange of betrothal vows for a future marriage, which was then followed by sexual consummation. Another deviation occurred in the middle of the seventeenth century, when the Puritans in England advocated against religious weddings and instituted purely civil proceedings—a policy that Puritan New England adopted.

Thus, the contraction of a valid and legitimate marriage could occur in many ways that ranged from elaborate to simple, from religious to civil, and with or without religious or governmental officiators. This is because the only required elements were the exchange of vows and sexual consummation. Although witnesses could attest that vows were, in fact, exchanged, marriages could be private, even clandestine, and still be recognized as valid. Furthermore, in many places the exchange of vows did not have to be voiced explicitly but could be inferred by the observation that a man and woman were living together as husband and wife and presenting themselves as a married couple (for more information about the history of common-law marriage, see Bowman 1996; O'Donnell and Jones 1982; and Thornton, Axinn, and Xie 2007, 58–64).

Although a couple could marry without parental involvement, marriage tended to be an intergenerational process. Parents influenced the choice of mates through their geographical and socioeconomic location, religious affiliation, and other attributes. There were also many opportunities for parents—and the household heads where children might be living apart from their parents—to be directly involved in the courtship and marriage of their children. Parents frequently made introductions and provided advice about potential partners. Parents often monitored the activities of their children, helped make economic arrangements, and planned weddings. The procurement of living quarters and the means of production often depended upon the assistance of both the bride's and the groom's parents. It also sometimes included the transfer of a house and farm, giving the parental families significant influence on the feasibility of marriage.

The transfer of economic resources that often allowed young adults to marry had implications for the older as well as the younger generation. The transfer of a house and other economic resources often marked parental retirement. This meant that the marriage decisions of children were linked integrally with the retirement and economic needs of the parents.

It was generally expected that children would ask their parents for permission to marry. This action was generally taken seriously even though it was recognized that mature people could marry without parental consent. Parental opposition could easily slow down a marriage or produce parent-child discord, but it is believed that it did not frequently prevent the marriage of a persistent mature couple.

During most of this period there were clear policies against divorce. Formal separation was permitted but normally not legal divorce and remarriage. During the Protestant Reformation, most reformers accepted divorce, but the reasons for obtaining one were exceptionally limited. Marriage continued to be viewed socially, religiously, and legally as a lifetime contract and most couples practiced this principle, with exceptionally few legal divorces being granted, although many couples probably experienced discord and some would have experienced separation.

CONFLATING FAMILY CHANGE WITH CLASS AND CROSS-CULTURAL DIFFERENCES

Efforts to describe family change among ordinary people are often constrained by the deficiencies in the available data. Data suitable for this purpose are relatively scarce even for recent centuries and as one goes back in time, both their quantity and quality decline, until the record for ordinary people almost entirely disappears (by approximately the fourteenth century in northwestern Europe).

Many scholars have tried to extend the historical record for the ordinary people of northwestern Europe back in time by substituting data from other classes and from other places for the missing data for ordinary people for earlier periods. Some scholars have used data from the European aristocracy to represent the marriage and family patterns of the ordinary people in earlier periods. And, some scholars have used data from people outside of northwestern Europe—including southern and eastern Europe—to substitute for the missing data during the earlier periods for ordinary northwestern Europeans. Because of the important differences across social classes and cultures discussed earlier, these substitutions have produced many misunderstandings—even myths—of family change among ordinary people in northwestern Europe.

History and cross-cultural perspectives have been confused in scholarly discussions (see Thornton 2005, 13–72). Many scholars from northwestern Europe and its diaspora from the late 1700s through the present have had a developmental model of history that they believed provided theoretical justification to use cross-sectional data to make conclusions about historical change. This developmental model assumed that all societies are on the same pathway, with each going through the same necessary and uniform stages of development. The model also assumed that the pace of change along this developmental trajectory varies across societies, with the result being that societies were at different stages of development in any specific period of history. To oversimplify, they labeled their own northwestern European social, economic, and family systems as modern or developed, while systems in other societies were labeled as traditional or less developed.

With this framework, scholars of the late 1700s and 1800s created a methodology for writing history that, instead of following a particular society across time, draws historical conclusions by comparing different societies. This approach assumes that the previous conditions of a more advanced society can be proxied by the situations of a different society (either at the same time or earlier) believed to be at an earlier stage of development. That is, the society perceived as less developed is used as a proxy for an earlier historical period of the society perceived as more advanced.

With this theoretical model and data from multiple societies, scholars of the late 1700s and 1800s concluded that sometime in the preceding periods northwestern Europe was characterized by large and extended households, by everyone marrying, and by young age at marriage. These scholars also believed that in the past parents had exceptionally strong control over both teenage and adult children and that parents arranged marriages. They also believed that the arranged marriage system presumed to exist in the northwestern European past provided little or no opportunity for the prospective bride and groom to interact in courtship and create bonds of companionship and affection before marriage.

Although marriages in all societies probably include instances of quarreling, conflict, and violence, it is now understood that affection is part of marriage and family relationships throughout the world (Broude 1994; Jankowiak 1995; Jankowiak and Fischer 1992; Westermarck 1891). However, many of the scholars of the late eighteenth and nineteenth centuries believed that there was no love or affection in marriage in many societies outside northwestern Europe, either before or after marriage. This inaccurate conclusion was probably the result of an extrapolation of the absence of love and affection—even interaction—before marriage to the postmarriage relationship and a misinterpretation of the quality of husband-wife relationships in these societies after marriage. Such misinterpretations are easy to make today, and scholars of the past were probably especially susceptible to them. The belief that there was no love or affection in many societies outside northwestern Europe and that northwestern Europe had previously had the same circumstances as elsewhere in the world led some scholars to conclude that there was also no love or affection within marriage in the northwestern European past.

With their developmental model and comparative methodology, these scholars believed that in the late 1700s and 1800s northwestern Europe had undergone a great family transition where society changed from having large and complex extended households to having predominately small nuclear or stem households and from having young and universal marriage to having older marriage with many people never marrying. They also believed that there had been changes from parents having very substantial control over adolescent and adult children to these children having extensive autonomy. In addition, these scholars believed that there had been a transformation from a system where parents arranged marriages for relatively young children with little or no opportunities for companionship or affection before marriage to a system where relatively mature adults engaged in a process of courtship that led to love and marriage. Furthermore, this reasoning led to the belief that a system of loveless marriages had been transformed into a situation with considerable love and affection.

The central elements of this great family transition in northwestern Europe were widely believed until the middle 1960s, when a new generation of scholars began to investigate family history before 1800 in the archives. As I discuss elsewhere (Thornton 2005, 81–102), many of these scholars extended the historical record in northwestern Europe back in time as far as the archives permitted, sometimes back as far as the 1300s, when the quality of data became especially poor. What these scholars discovered was paradigm-shifting. They found that the great family transition perceived from cross-cultural data was not supported by data from the historical archives. It was concluded that the marriage and family patterns of northwestern Europe in the 1700s that I described earlier had existed in northwestern Europe for centuries—extending as far back in time as the relevant materials in the archives.

Understanding this history of scholarship on family change is important for at least four reasons. First, the discovery that most of the elements of the supposed great family transition never happened is relatively recent. It is likely that many policymakers and members of the public today still believe that this supposed great family transition occurred in the northwestern European past, even though there is no historical support for this belief.

Second, this intellectual history reminds us of the enormous pitfalls inherent in substituting data from other cultures for data from earlier periods in northwestern Europe. It should also be a warning against substituting data from the aristocracy for data from ordinary people, inasmuch as their marriage and family patterns were so different. It is important to limit data to ordinary people from northwestern Europe (and its overseas populations) and not to confuse the history of ordinary people in this population by using data from other classes and places.

A third reason for discussing this history of family scholarship is to note that some studies of family change continue to substitute data from the aristocracy and from other cultures for missing data about ordinary people in the northwestern European past. I have documented elsewhere the continuing practice of using data from other cultures to proxy for past circumstances in northwestern Europe and its diaspora (Thornton 2005, 110–118). A more recent example is Stephanie Coontz's *Marriage, a History* (2005). Chapters 7–9 of the book conclude that from about the fourteenth through the eighteenth century there was a transformation of marriage, with the great bulk of information in these chapters coming from the ordinary people of northwestern Europe and the United States. However, the great bulk of material in the first six chapters establishing the baseline of marriage for earlier times does not come from the ordinary people of northwestern Europe but from the European aristocracy and from people outside the region. The dust jacket of the book states, "Coontz takes us on a journey from the marital intrigues of ancient Babylon to the sexual torments of Victorian lovers to the current debates over the meaning and future of marriage. She provides the definitive story of marriage's evolution from the arranged unions common since the dawn of civilization into the intimate, sexually fulfilling but volatile relationships of today." Thus, this supposed change is across class and geography—from the European aristocracy and from the people outside northwestern Europe to the ordinary people of northwestern Europe and the United States.

A fourth reason for discussing the history of substituting data from other places and other classes for missing data from ordinary people in northwestern Europe is that some important scholarly discussions still rely on theoretical frameworks and empirical baselines derived from this methodology. A relevant example is the framework provided by Ernest Burgess and Harvey Locke (1945) that marriage and family life in the Western world had been transformed "from institution to companionship." This book is of particular importance because the "institution to companionship" conclusion and framework is still used by family scholars today. It is not that scholars using the Burgess-Locke framework are substituting data from other places and other classes for missing data from northwestern Europe or its overseas diaspora, but that the Burgess-Locke framework itself is based on results that used that method.

The argument of Burgess and Locke that affection and companionship had evolved from being exceptionally limited to being widespread was based on the construction of a developmental model. They write, "The three chief historical stages in the evolution of the family are: the large patriarchal family characteristic of ancient society; the small patriarchal family which had its origin in the medieval period; and the modern democratic family which to a great extent is a product of the economic and social trends accompanying and following the industrial revolution" (18). The data concerning the large patriarchal family reported by Burgess and Locke come from such places as China, India, Japan, ancient Rome, and the Hebrews under the Law of Moses. For the next stage in their developmental sequence, the small patriarchal family, the authors move in both space and time to medieval Europe where they present data only about the nobility. For their final stage of development, the modern democratic family, Burgess and Locke focus on the ordinary people of the United States after the industrial revolution. Using this constructed developmental sequence, the authors conclude that "the family has been in historical times in transition from an institution with family behavior controlled by the mores, public opinion, and law to a companionship with family behavior arising from the mutual affection and consensus of its members" (26–27). The authors report, "Most people in the United States are unaware that their ancestors—the ancient Celts, Teutons, and Scandinavians—all lived" in the same type of family as people in such places as China, India, Japan, and ancient Israel, Rome, and Greece (34). In the book's 1963 revision (with Mary Margaret Thomes), the authors drop the explicit reliance on the developmental paradigm and the use of data from other cultures and English aristocrats, but they still suggest the trend from institution to companionship without discussing their methods.

With a history constructed by moving from places such as China and India to aristocratic England in medieval times to the United States after industrialization, it is not surprising that Burgess and Locke report change from parental arrangement and little courtship and companionship to independence, companionship, and affection. By ignoring the ordinary people of northwestern Europe in the past, it was inevitable that they would also discount the extensive companionship, love, and affection that existed among these people before the industrial revolution. In addition, without establishing what marriage was like in the general population of northwestern Europe or the United States before industrialization, it was impossible for them to describe changes associated with industrialization.

A belief in the "institution to companionship" trend also misses—and even contradicts—the observed trend toward formalization of marriage from the middle of the sixteenth century through the middle of the twentieth century—one of the most important and little-known trends in Western family history (see Thornton, Axinn, and Xie 2007, 58–74, for a more detailed discussion and references). In Europe in the sixteenth century there were substantial numbers of private unions that were recognized as valid but were not performed by either church or state. These private marriages sometimes produced disputes concerning whether the marriage had occurred. There were enough of these marital disputes litigated in the ecclesiastical courts that many of the Protestant reformers saw it as a problem and made the tightening of marriage procedures and authority a plank in several strands of the Protestant Reformation, a lead the Catholic Church followed. The result was a stream of initiatives to formalize marriage by requiring it to be a public event and by removing the authority of couples to marry themselves. The reforms also made as requirements many of the previously optional elements such as the announcement of betrothal through banns, the presence of witnesses, and the use of officials to perform the wedding. Another example of the formalization process was the effort to outlaw common-law marriage and require a formal ceremony. The reforms also moved to require a wedding ceremony rather than just betrothal to legitimate sex and cohabitation. The implementation and enforcement of such reforms varied across both time and location, but there were long-term trends from the 1500s through the middle 1900s for more formal requirements and more involvement of the church and/or state.

Although the efforts to require formal processes and authority for a valid marriage were never fully effective—as illustrated by the continuing use of common-law marriage by some—it is, nevertheless, likely that the formalization reforms had important effects on the meaning and practice of marriage. Marriage was probably increasingly seen as a formal institution that required the authority and procedures of the church and/or state, and it was viewed more as a public than a personal contract. In addition, common-law marriage was seen as less legitimate than before, and the wedding ceremony gained power relative to betrothal/engagement as a legitimator of sex and coresidence.

This long-term trend in the formalization of the meaning and process of marriage probably played an important role in the devaluation of marriage that occurred during the last half of the twentieth century. It is likely that as society experienced a dramatic movement during this period toward defining interpersonal relations, sex, and cohabitation as private matters requiring only the consent of the participants, it would have produced a conflict with the formalized, structured, and bureaucratic definition and process of marriage that had evolved over the previous centuries. This conflict probably interacted with other forces—discussed in the next section—to accelerate the decline of the centrality and power of marriage itself in the twentieth century.

This trend may also help us to understand the emergence of the phrase "marriage is just a piece of paper"—one of today's most derogative comments about the irrelevance of marriage. This assertion is often accompanied by the observation that what is important in relationships is the long-term love, sharing, companionship, and commitment between two partners. Also implied as relevant in this rhetoric is the long-term interconnection of finances, the sharing of living quarters, sexual relations, and frequently the bearing and rearing of children. According to the statement that "marriage is just a piece of paper," it is these things that are important in interpersonal relationships, and marriage with its bureaucracy of government and religious authority, regulations, ritual, and certifications can only be "just a piece of paper" with little or no relevance.

Of course, marriage certificates did not exist in the distant past in northwestern European societies, and the rules and rituals that existed were recognized as useful by many, but ultimately optional. In such a society it would not have been possible for marriage to be seen as "just a piece of paper," since there were no certificates for marriage. Instead, marriage would have consisted of the long-term love, companionship, sharing, and commitment between two partners plus the interconnection of finances, the sharing of living quarters, sexual relations, and frequently the bearing and rearing of children that some people today state as something different than marriage. It is hard to imagine this important evolution of the meaning of marriage without the long-term trend toward formalization of marriage and its definition to include and require governmental and/or religious authority, obligatory rules, and certificates. With this evolution and the sharp reemergence of freedom and individual authority in the construction of personal and partner relationships, it was easy for marriage to be defined as "just a piece of paper."

It is remarkable that the success that government and religious authorities had over hundreds of years to regulate marriage has in many respects been reversed in recent decades (Lesthaeghe 1995). Many individuals in the United States and northwestern Europe have reclaimed from government and religious bodies and societal norms control over crucial elements of the union formation process. This desire for individual control today is reflected in recent survey findings that eight out of ten young Americans believe that "marriage is nobody's business but the two people involved." In addition, nearly one-half believe that "the government should not be involved in licensing marriages" (Whitehead and Popenoe 2001, 13).

CHANGES IN NORTHWESTERN EUROPE AND NORTH AMERICA IN THE 1800S AND 1900S

Many important social and economic changes in northwestern Europe and North America occurred during the 1800s and 1900s, with implications for marriage and family life. Here I discuss several aspects of change in marriage and family life among ordinary people during this period (for more complete discussions with additional references, see Thornton 2005, 161–179, and Thornton, Axinn, and Xie 2007, 44–75).

Changing Technology and Social Organization

One of the central changes occurring during the past two centuries was the expansion of the number and significance of organizations and relationships that were not based on kinship. Factories, schools, and other nonfamilial organizations increasingly became the locations for the activities of individuals. Other nonfamilial organizations such as the government, schools, businesses, the mass media, and commercialized entertainment increasingly became the source for information and direction.

Particularly important was the industrialization of the economy that separated people's residences from their workplaces—a phenomenon that occurred for men across the nineteenth and twentieth centuries, but for women mostly in the last half-century. Whereas individuals in earlier eras primarily conducted economic production in family-organized units, afterwards nonfamilial organizations were the source of livelihoods for most women and men. The entrance of women into the paid labor force also made it more difficult for them to participate in economic production while caring for their homes and children. As women joined their husbands in paid employment, the specialization of roles associated with marriage declined, as did women's reliance on their husbands' paychecks. This also provided women more independence in forgoing marriage or dissolving an unsatisfactory marriage. In addition, both income and consumption aspirations increased substantially.

Increased industrialization and employment outside the home also affected the residential arrangements of unmarried adults—ending the practice of adolescents and young adults living and working in the households and economic units of nonfamily members. However, today, many young people experience a considerable period away from their parental homes in order to attend college or serve in the military. In addition, independent living in apartments or houses, either alone or with unrelated peers, has emerged as a common pattern in recent decades. Thus, between the time that young adults leave their parents' households and the time they first cohabit or marry, they can experience a considerable period of time as independent householders.

Educational expansion has modified the transition to adulthood. Given the historical pattern of requiring economic self-sufficiency before marriage, extended education can delay entrance into marriage. Extended school attendance can also provide exposure to new ideas and modify the authority relations between parents and children.

These changes in social organization helped to reduce the central role of marriage in structuring and defining adult life. Marriage was for centuries a requirement for independent living and directing one's own household and economic unit, but it is now easy for young adults to attain these without being married. However, while marriage is no longer required for economic independence, such independence is still required for marriage. In fact, some recent research suggests that the economic accomplishments couples require of themselves before entering marriage may have escalated in recent decades (Edin and Kefalas 2005; Smock, Manning, and Porter 2005).

Accompanying the changing social and economic conditions has been a dramatic increase in the availability of medical means of birth control. Legal abortion has also become widely available. These methods are not only very effective in preventing births, but, unlike such earlier contraceptive methods as rhythm, withdrawal, the condom, and the diaphragm, they can be separated from the sex act itself.

A particularly important consequence of the availability of medical contraception and abortion is that it gave women the confidence and ability to be sexually active without becoming pregnant. This ability to separate sex from pregnancy and childbearing may have contributed to the increase of sexual relationships outside of marriage and to the rise of unmarried childbearing and cohabitation. The knowledge and means of such effective birth control may also have facilitated the expansion of women's pursuit of careers, as women knew they could be sexually active while pursuing fulfilling careers and postponing or avoiding childbearing.

The Changing Religious Context

One of the important trends affecting marriage and family life is the increasing number and diversity of religious institutions. This proliferation of religious authority and viewpoints has diminished a common sense of morality and expanded the diversity of beliefs and values (Hunter 1991). There has also been an increased acceptance of the faiths and values of people of diverse religious persuasions. Other societal changes, such as the expansion of the claims of science and technology, have increased the legitimacy and authority of nonreligious bodies. In addition, such organizations as the state, corporations, the mass media, and schools have taken additional moral authority.

The authority of religious texts, organizations, and leaders has declined in the United States in recent decades. The Bible is now used less as a literal guide to life, less weight is placed on religious pronouncements, and religious answers are seen as less relevant for today's problems. Many indicators of religiosity have also declined in recent decades, including identification with religion, religious service attendance, church or synagogue membership, and frequency of prayer. Religion is now defined less in terms of institutional loyalty and obligation and more in terms of individual beliefs and spirituality. Religion has also become more tolerant in being less inclined toward condemnation and punishment for violations of community standards (for more extensive discussion and references, see Thornton, Axinn, and Xie 2007, 48–50).

The Enlightenment and Developmental Idealism

As I have discussed elsewhere (Thornton 2005), the ideas of development and the association of northwestern Europe with the pinnacle of progress produced a set of ideas that became a powerful source of change from the Enlightenment to the present. These ideas—that I call developmental idealism—identified individualism, youthful autonomy, high ages at marriage, high status of women, family planning, and low fertility as positive attributes. Developmental idealism also associated these same personal and family characteristics with such positive attributes as high levels of education, good health, and prosperity. In addition, equality and freedom were said to be fundamental human rights. These ideas have been disseminated widely, especially in recent decades.

The principles of freedom and equality have helped to fuel the women's movement and its advocacy for greater rights for women in virtually all areas of life, including the family. Some advocates in the women's movement have suggested that the hierarchical nature of marriage makes it a negative institution that is destructive to women. This belief has been disseminated widely for decades and has received serious challenge in the academic literature only recently (Waite and Gallagher 2000; see also England 2000 and chapter 3 in this volume).

Although the culture of northwestern Europe has for many centuries emphasized the individual more than have many other cultures, developmental idealism helped to push the pendulum even further away from families and communities and toward individualism. This occurred as developmental idealism emphasized the individual and the freedom of individuals to operate independently of the family unit, decreasing the view that marriage permanently fused family members into a single organic unit with singular interests. Family and marriage units were defined socially and legally more as voluntary groups of individuals and less as organic wholes. This individualization trend has been especially marked in the last half century when it has overridden the long-term effort discussed earlier to increase the formalization of marriage (Regan 1999; Schneider 1985; Thornton and Young-DeMarco 2001; Witte 1997).

As I discussed earlier, young people in northwestern Europe have had extensive autonomy from their parents for centuries, but this freedom has become even more marked in recent decades. Between the 1920s and the 1980s parents have increasingly endorsed the values of autonomy, independent thinking, and tolerance in their children. At the same time, parents place less importance on conformity, obedience, and loyalty to church (Alwin 1986, 1988).

Changing Status of Marriage and Being Single

These changes in social and ideological structures have probably been important forces changing the ways in which people view and approach marriage and family life. They have probably been especially powerful in suggesting that marriage and parenthood are not the only ways to happiness and fulfillment of one's destiny. They have probably also contributed to the substantial decrease that occurred in negative attitudes toward those who do not want to marry—and to the declines in the number of people who view marriage as changing a person's life for the better. In recent years only a minority of young adults say that they would be bothered a great deal if they did not marry (Thornton 1989; Thornton and Freedman 1982; Thornton and Young-DeMarco 2001).

Although marriage has become less central in the lives of Americans, most also believe that a good marriage and family life are very important, and most also expect to marry. In fact, more than four-fifths of all college women participating in a national survey in the United States in 2000 agreed that "being married is a very important goal for me" (Glenn and Marquardt 2001, 4).

Although many scholars, including the editors of this volume, appropriately emphasize the decline in marriage during the past several decades, it is also important to place this decline in the context of the marriage boom that followed World War II in most countries of Western Europe and North America. Immediately after World War II the rate of marrying increased dramatically and the age at marriage dropped—a marriage boom that continued in most of the countries through part of the 1960s. The decline in marriage in subsequent years not only reversed the marriage boom but also brought the age at marriage in the United States to its highest point in history (see the introduction to this volume).

Changes in Marital Dissolution

A general trend over the past two centuries has been the amendment of laws to make divorce easier. Especially large changes occurred in divorce laws in the 1960s and 1970s, as almost every state passed a no-fault divorce law. This represented an important switch from government support of marriage as a lifetime commitment to an endorsement of individual autonomy and freedom in marriage. There has also been a substantial softening of negative attitudes toward divorce in the general population (Thornton 1989; Thornton and Young-DeMarco 2001).

Although the increase in divorce following World War II is generally widely known, less well known is the fact that the overall American trajectory of divorce has been upward at least since 1860. However, the divorce rate increased so rapidly in the decades after World War II that by the beginning of the 1980s divorce was terminating approximately one-half of all marriages. During the 1980s and 1990s the rate declined somewhat, but was still at a high level by long-term standards (Casper and Bianchi 2002; Preston and McDonald 1979).

Having to endure a bad marriage was historically a concern for people contemplating marriage. The rising divorce rate made it possible to terminate bad marriages, but it introduced a new problem—having to deal with the trauma and difficulties associated with terminating a marriage. This concern is reflected in the fact that about one-half of young single adults in the United States in 2001 indicated that the possibility of marital dissolution was one of their biggest concerns about marriage (Whitehead and Popenoe 2001). It is likely that this concern about divorce has helped to drive the decline in marriage and the increase in unmarried cohabitation (Waller and Peters 2007). Three-fifths of all unmarried young Americans believe that marital stability will be facilitated by living together prior to marriage (Whitehead and Popenoe 2001). This belief is prominent even though cohabitation is associated with less and not more marital stability, though some scholars argue that cohabiting only with the future spouse is not associated with lower marital stability (Teachman, 2003).

Dating and Going Steady

The ways in which young women and men met, courted, and married have been changing for well over a century. The expansion of the years spent in school provided a new locus for young people to interact, helping to create a youth culture. New opportunities for interaction and courtship were also provided by the growing trend of residence in college dormitories and apartments.

A system of dating and going steady evolved during the early part of the 1900s. Modell (1983, 1989) has suggested that dating became nearly a universal experience in high schools during the 1930s and 1940s. Dating the same person would result in the couple "going steady," and going steady eventually became a status with rights previously associated with engagement and marriage.

An important trend in recent decades has been the decrease in the formality of dating and courtship. Today young people interact more informally, "hanging out" with friends and "hooking up" in less regular relationships (Glenn and Marquardt 2001). Associated with this trend is the increased sexualization of male-female interactions.

Dating and courtship may have been part of the youth culture, but it also involved a heavy dose of parental advice and consent through the middle of the twentieth century. For example, two-thirds of adolescents in Minnesota in the late 1940s believed that dates should not be made or accepted until consulting with parents (Modell 1989). In addition, about two-thirds of American high school students in 1961 said that it was very desirable for parents to approve their future spouse (Franklin and Remmers 1961).

Changing Sexual Experience and Attitudes

Although some unmarried people in steady relationships in the first part of the twentieth century undoubtedly experienced sexual intercourse, the social norms stating that marriage was the main legitimator of sexual relations generally remained in place well into the twentieth century in the United States. A national survey found that only about one-tenth of women born at the turn of the twentieth century had sexual intercourse before marriage. About one-half of those having sex before marriage in this era reported they had sex only with their future husband (Klassen et al. 1989; also see Laumann et al. 1994). The same survey reported that among ever-married women reaching marriageable ages at the middle of the century, about five-sixths married as virgins or had sex only with their future husband (Klassen et al. 1989; also see Michael et al. 1994). The proscriptions against premarital sex, however, were stronger for women than for men.

Although the requirement that sex be limited to marital relations remained strong into the early 1960s, it declined rapidly beginning in the late 1960s. By the middle of the 1970s, the general consensus that marriage had to precede sexual relations had largely been broken. In 1971, 46 percent of never-married nineteen-year-old women reported having had experienced sexual intercourse. This figure had grown to 80 percent by the end of the 1980s, and was 86 percent for nineteen-year-old unmarried men (Abma and Sonenstein 2001; Zelnik and Kantner 1980a, 1980b; also see Abma et al. 1997; Laumann et al. 1994). About eight in nine new brides in the early 1990s reported that they had had sexual intercourse before marriage. A small fraction of these sexually experienced brides reported having first intercourse after engagement, but most experienced premarital sex before engagement, including many in relatively casual relationships (Abma et al. 1997). Also significant fractions of young people now engage in sexual relations that are less relational than recreational (Glenn and Marquardt 2001; Whitehead and Popenoe 2001).

Unmarried Cohabitation

Unmarried cohabitation was still uncommon during the middle of the twentieth century, but it increased substantially during the subsequent decades. In the 1990s, more than one-half of those marrying for the first time had cohabited before marriage, and the fractions of second marriages preceded by cohabitation were even higher (Bumpass and Lu 2000). These substantial increases in cohabitation have offset much of the decline in marriage discussed earlier. The countries of northwestern Europe have experienced similar or even more pronounced increases in unmarried cohabitation. Many cohabitating unions are relatively short-lived, as they are often rapidly dissolved or transformed into marriage (Bumpass and Lu 2000).

It is useful to note that the definition, evaluation, and experience of cohabitation can vary greatly across individuals (Thornton, Axinn, and Xie 2007; see also chapter 6, this volume). Some people enter cohabitation with no thoughts about eventual marriage to the partner, with some simply deciding to spend more nights together and the relationship then turning into cohabitation. Other couples enter cohabitation as a means of fostering the relationship toward marriage or testing its suitability for marriage. Yet other couples cohabit as an alternative to marriage, sometimes with the relationship being roughly equivalent to marriage, but without the "piece of paper." For other couples, cohabitation occurs during the period between engagement and marriage—a situation that would have defined them as married several hundred years earlier.

The widespread practice of cohabitation in America today is supported by the beliefs and values of young adults. During the 1980s and 1990s, young adults accepted cohabitation by a two to one margin. Today most American young people actively endorse cohabitation, suggesting that it is usually a good idea to live together before marriage (Thornton, Axinn, and Xie 2007). However, there is a strong generation gap in values and attitudes concerning both nonmarital sex and cohabitation, with the older generation being much less approving than the younger generation.

Childbearing

During the last two centuries the linkage between marriage and childbearing has been weakened on two fronts—both in the requirement that marriage precede childbearing and that childbearing be a part of marriage. Marital childbearing in the northwestern European past was "natural" in that the conscious restriction of the number of children was uncommon, but beginning in the last half of the nineteenth century and continuing into the 1900s, increasing numbers of couples took action to restrict their childbearing. Birth control became especially easy in the latter part of the twentieth century, when medical contraceptives became available and, in the United States, the Supreme Court legalized abortion.

Birthrates declined substantially in the United States in the decades before World War II, increased again in the marriage boom years after the war, and then subsequently declined. However, for the last two decades the total fertility rate has hovered around two children per woman. This is substantially higher than the fertility rates in many European countries, where fertility has fallen to very low levels (Population Reference Bureau 2007).

The norms against voluntary childlessness in marriage remained strong into the 1960s, and most couples had at least one child. However, the belief that having children is a moral imperative in marriage has declined so dramatically in recent decades that in the 1980s and 1990s only a minority believed that all married couples ought to have children. There is, however, little evidence that personal desires for childlessness have increased (Thornton 1989; Thornton and Young-DeMarco 2001).

In the past, unmarried childbearing was both disapproved and infrequent. However, acceptance of unmarried childbearing has increased substantially, along with the acceptance of unmarried sex and cohabitation. Among American high school seniors, about 35 percent in the 1990s said that unmarried childbearing was destructive to society or violating a moral principle, compared to about 45 percent in the 1970s (Axinn and Thornton 2000; Thornton and Young-DeMarco 2001).

There have been important long-term fluctuations in nonmarital childbearing over the past several centuries. In many Western countries before the middle of the 1700s, nonmarital childbearing rates were apparently low. However, they increased from then through the last part of the 1800s, and then declined through the early 1900s. There were dramatic increases again through most of the last half of the twentieth century, as the rates increased in the United States by more than six times. Accompanying these changes was a substantial increase in the percentage of children born out of wedlock from about one in twenty in the 1950s to about one in three in the mid-1990s (Thornton, Axinn, and Xie 2007).

There were many factors behind the dramatic increase in the percentage of children born outside of marriage (Thornton, Axinn, and Xie 2007). Although some of the trend was due to increasing rates of childbearing among women outside coresidential unions, a substantial portion was due to changes in marriage itself. One of these marital changes was the decline in the likelihood of a pregnant unmarried woman marrying to "legitimize" the birth. Another important change was the decline in childbearing among married women. Yet, another contributor to this trend was a decline in the percentage of women who were married and an increase in the number cohabiting. In fact, children born to unmarried cohabiting couples make up an increasing fraction of out-of-wedlock births and explain a large part of the increase in nonmarital childbearing (Bumpass and Lu 2000). These changes are also related to the growing beliefs among many in poor neighborhoods that marriage should be postponed until later in life after economic stability is achieved, while childbearing in young adulthood—even without marriage—is highly valued.

Although it is clear that marriage no longer has a monopoly over the bearing and rearing of children in the United States, it does not mean that "marriage is irrelevant to contemporary childbearing" (Morgan 1996, 44). Birthrates for married women are still substantially higher than for both single and cohabiting women.

CONCLUSION

The first conclusion of this chapter is that in all observed societies and during all observed periods, marriage and family have been universal—or nearly universal. Second, this universality of marriage and family life has been accompanied by enormous variations in the organization of marriage and family life. Third, family life in northwestern Europe has historically been quite different from other places in the world, including other regions of Europe. This relative uniqueness of northwestern Europe has been reflected in such dimensions as nuclear (or weak-stem) households, youthful independence, affection, and courtship in marital arrangements, marriage at relatively mature ages, and substantial numbers of people never marrying. Fourth, the study of marriage and family change is often greatly constrained by significant deficiencies in the quantity and quality of data. This has encouraged some scholars to substitute data from other places and other social classes in trying to describe historical trends in northwestern Europe. Because of the great differences across cultures and across social classes, this practice has led to considerable misunderstanding of marriage and family change. And fifth, northwestern Europe and the United States have experienced substantial changes in marriage and family life during the past two centuries. These include movement from communalism to individualism, more emphasis on freedom and equality in relationships, and more youthful autonomy. These also include trends in more sexual experience outside of marriage and more unmarried cohabitation and childbearing. In addition, the centrality of marriage has declined, as has its indissolubility. The ability to control fertility has also increased, while the number of children born to married couples has declined.

REFERENCES

Abma, J. C., A. Chandra, W. D. Mosher, L. S. Peterson, and L. J. Piccinino. 1997. Fertility, family planning, and women's health: New data from the 1995 National Survey of Family Growth. In U.S. Department of Health and Human Services, *Vital and Health Statistics*, 23:1–114. Washington, D.C.: GPO.

Abma, J. C., and F. L. Sonenstein. 2001. Sexual activity and contraceptive practices among teenagers in the United States, 1988 and 1995. In U.S. Department of Health and Human Services, *Vital and Health Statistics*, 23:21. Washington, D.C.: GPO.

Alwin, D. F. 1986. Religion and parental child-rearing orientations: Evidence of a Catholic-Protestant convergence. *American Journal of Sociology* 92, no. 2: 412–440.

———. 1988. From obedience to autonomy: Changes in traits desired in children, 1924–1978. *Public Opinion Quarterly* 52, no. 1: 33–52.

Axinn, W. G., A. Emens, and C. Mitchell. 2008. Ideational influences on family change in the United States. In R. Jayakody, W. G. Axinn, and A. Thornton, eds., *International Family Change: Ideational Perspectives*, 119–150. Mahwah, N.J.: Erlbaum.

Axinn, W. G., and Thornton, A. 2000. The transformation in the meaning of marriage. In L. Waite, C. Bachrach, M. Hindin, E. Thomson, and A. Thornton, eds., *Ties that bind: Perspectives on marriage and cohabitation*, 147–165. Hawthorne, N.Y.: Aldine de Gruyter.

Book of Common Prayer, Church of England. 1552 (repr. 1888). London: Griffith, Farran, Okeden, and Welsh.

Bowman, C. G. 1996. A feminist proposal to bring back common law marriage. *Oregon Law Review* 75:709–780.

Broude, G. J. 1994. *Marriage, family, and relationships: A cross-cultural encyclopedia.* Santa Barbara, Calif.: ABC-CLIO.

Bumpass, L., and H-H. Lu. 2000. Trends in cohabitation and implications for children's family contexts in the U.S. *Population Studies* 54, no. 1: 29–41.

Burgess, E. W., and H. J. Locke. 1945. *The family.* New York: American Book Company.

Burguière, A., and F. Lebrun. 1986. The one hundred and one families of Europe. In A. Burguière, C. Klapisch-Zuber, M. Segalen, and F. Zonabend, eds., *A history of the family*, 2:11–94. Cambridge, Mass.: Harvard University Press.

Casper, L. M., and S. M. Bianchi. 2002. *Continuity and change in the American family.* Thousand Oaks, Calif.: Sage.

Coontz, S. 1988. *The social origins of private life: A history of American families, 1600–1900.* New York: Verso.

———. 2005. *Marriage, a history: From obedience to intimacy, or how love conquered marriage.* New York: Viking Penguin.

Demos, J. 1970. *A little commonwealth: Family life in Plymouth colony.* Oxford: Oxford University Press.

Edin, K., and M. J. Kefalas. 2005. *Promises I can keep: Why poor women put motherhood before marriage.* Berkeley: University of California Press.

England, P. 2000. Marriage, the costs of children, and gender inequality. In L. Waite, C. Bachrach, M. Hindin, E. Thomson, and A. Thornton, eds., *Ties that bind: Perspectives on marriage and cohabitation*, 320–342. New York: Aldine de Gruyter.

Fleming, P. 2001. *Family and household in medieval England.* New York: Palgrave.

Franklin, R. D., and H. H. Remmers. 1961. *Youth's attitudes toward courtship and marriage.* Lafayette, Ind.: Purdue University Press.

Gillis, J. R. 1985. *For better, for worse: British marriages, 1600 to the present.* New York: Oxford University.

Glenn, N., and E. Marquardt. 2001. Hooking up, hanging out, and hoping for Mr. Right: College women on dating and mating today. *An Institute for American Values report to the Independent Women's Forum.* New York: Institute for American Values.

Goody, J. 1990. *The oriental, the ancient and the primitive: Systems of marriage and the family in the pre-industrial societies of Eurasia.* Cambridge: Cambridge University Press.

Gottlieb, B. 1993. *The family in the western world from the black death to the industrial age.* New York: Oxford University Press.

Gough, E. K. 1959. The Nayars and the definition of marriage. *Journal of the Royal Anthropological Institute* 89:23–34.

Hajnal, J. 1965. European marriage patterns in perspective. In D. V. Glass and D. E. C. Eversley, eds., *Population in History,* 101–143. Chicago: Aldine.

———. 1982. Two kinds of preindustrial household formation system. *Population and Development Review* 8, no. 3: 449–494.

Hunter, J. D. 1991. *Culture wars: The struggle to define America.* New York: Basic Books.

Jankowiak, W. 1995. *Romantic passion.* New York: Columbia University Press.

Jankowiak, W., and E. F. Fischer. 1992. A cross cultural perspective on romantic love. *Ethnology* 31, no. 2: 149–155.

Klassen, A. D., C. J. Williams, E. E. Levitt, L. Rudkin-Miniot, H. G. Miller, and S. Gunjal. 1989. Trends in premarital sexual behavior. In C. F. Turner, H. G. Miller, and L. E. Moses, eds., *AIDS: Sexual behavior and intravenous drug use,* 548–568. Washington, D.C.: National Academy of Sciences.

Laslett, P. 1984. *The world we have lost: England before the industrial age.* 3rd ed. New York: Charles Scribner's Sons.

Laumann, E. O., J. H. Gagnon, R. T. Michael, and S. Michaels. 1994. *The social organization of sexuality: Sexual practices in the United States.* Chicago: University of Chicago Press.

Lee, J. Z., and F. Wang. 1999. *One quarter of humanity: Malthusian mythology and Chinese realities, 1700–2000.* Cambridge, Mass.: Harvard University Press.

Lesthaeghe, R. 1995. The second demographic transition in Western countries: An interpretation. In K. O. Mason and A.-M. Jensen, eds., *Gender and family change in industrialized countries,* 17–62. Oxford: Clarendon Press.

Macfarlane, A. 1986. *Marriage and love in England: Modes of reproduction, 1300–1840.* Oxford: Basil Blackwell.

McSheffrey, S. 1995. *Love and marriage in late medieval England.* Kalamazoo: Medieval Institute Publications, Western Michigan University.

Michael, R. T., J. H. Gagnon, E. O. Laumann, and G. Kolata. 1994. *Sex in America: A definitive survey.* Boston: Little, Brown.

Modell, J. 1983. Dating becomes the way of American youth. In L.P. Moch and G.D. Stark, eds., *Essays on the family and historical change*. College Station: Texas A&M University Press.

———. 1989. *Into one's own: From youth to adulthood in the United States, 1920–1975*. Berkeley: University of California Press.

Morgan, S.P. 1996. Characteristic features of modern American fertility. *Population and Development Review* 22:19–63.

O'Donnell, W.J., and D. A. Jones. 1982. *The law of marriage and marital alternatives*. Lexington, Mass.: D. C. Heath.

O'Hara, D. 2000. *Courtship and constraint: Rethinking the making of marriage in Tudor England*. Manchester: Manchester University Press.

Preston, S.H., and J. McDonald. 1979. The incidence of divorce within cohorts of American marriages contracted since the Civil War. *Demography* 16, no. 1: 1–25.

Population Reference Bureau. 2007. World population highlights. *Population Bulletin* 62, no. 3: 1–12.

Regan, M.C., Jr. 1999. Marriage at the millennium. *Family Law Quarterly* 33, no. 3: 647–661.

Ribordy, G. 2001. The two paths to marriage: The preliminaries of noble marriage in late medieval France. *Journal of the Family History* 26:323–336.

Sanderson, S.K. 1990. *Social evolutionism: A critical history*. Oxford: Basil Blackwell.

Schneider, C.E. 1985. Moral discourse and the transformation of American family law. *Michigan Law Review* 83, no. 8: 1803–1879.

Sheehan, M.M. 1971. The formation and stability of marriage in fourteenth-century England: Evidence of an Ely Register. *Medieval Studies* 33:228–263.

———. 1978. Choice of marriage partner in the middle ages: Development and mode of application and a theory of marriage. In S.A.S. Evans and R.W. Unger, eds., *Studies in Medieval and Renaissance history*, 1–33. Vancouver: University of British Columbia Press.

Smock, P.J., W. Manning, and M. Porter. 2005. "Everything's there except money": How money shapes decisions to marry among cohabitors. *Journal of Marriage and Family* 67:680–696.

Teachman, J. 2003. Premarital sex, premarital cohabitation, and the risk of subsequent marital dissolution among women. *Journal of Marriage and Family* 65:444–455.

Thornton, A. 1989. Changing attitudes toward family issues in the United States. *Journal of Marriage and the Family* 51, no. 4: 873–893.

———. 2001. The developmental paradigm, reading history sideways, and family change. *Demography* 38, no. 4: 449–465.

———. 2005. *Reading history sideways: The fallacy and enduring impact of the developmental paradigm on family life*. Chicago: University of Chicago Press.

Thornton, A., W. G. Axinn, and Y. Xie. 2007. *Marriage and cohabitation.* Chicago: University of Chicago Press.

Thornton, A., and D. S. Freedman. 1982. Changing attitudes toward marriage and single life. *Family Planning Perspectives* 14, no. 6: 297–303.

Thornton, A., and T. Fricke. 1987. Social change and the family: Comparative perspectives from the West, China, and South Asia. *Sociological Forum* 2, no. 4: 746–772.

Thornton, A., and H.-S. Lin. 1994. *Social change and the family in Taiwan.* Chicago: University of Chicago Press.

Thornton, A., and L. Young-DeMarco. 2001. Four decades of trends in attitudes toward family issues in the United States: The 1960s through the 1990s. *Journal of Marriage and the Family* 63, no. 4: 1009–1037.

Todd, E. 1985. *The explanation of ideology: Family structures and social systems.* Oxford: Basil Blackwell.

Waite, L. J., and M. Gallagher. 2000. *The case for marriage.* Cambridge, Mass.: Harvard University Press.

Waller, M., and H. E. Peters. 2007. The risk of divorce as a barrier to marriage among parents of young children. Unpublished paper, Cornell University.

Westermarck, E. A. 1891. *The history of human marriage.* London: Macmillan.

Whitehead, B. D., and D. Popenoe. 2001. *The state of our unions: The social health of marriage in America, 2001.* New Brunswick, N.J.: National Marriage Project.

Witte, J., Jr. 1997. *From sacrament to contract: Marriage, religion and law in the western tradition.* Louisville, Ky.: Westminster John Knox.

Wright, C. D. 1899. *Outline of practical sociology.* New York: Longmans, Green.

Yanagisako, S. J. 1979. Family and household: The analysis of domestic groups. *Annual Review of Anthropology* 8:161–205.

Zelnik, M., and J. F. Kantner. 1980a. Sexual activity, contraceptive use and pregnancy among metropolitan area teenagers: 1971–1979. *Family Planning Perspectives* 12, no. 5: 30–36.

———. 1980b. Sexual and contraceptive experience of young unmarried women in the United States, 1976 and 1971. In C. S. Chilman, ed., *Adolescent pregnancy and childbearing: Findings from research*, 43–82. Washington, D.C.: GPO.

Marriage and Family

The Evolutionary Ecological Context

TWO

BOBBI S. LOW

Mating occurs in all sexual species, but marriage is specific to human societies. Although we often seek cultural explanations for variations in human marriage and mating systems, hidden biological/ecological underpinnings help shape these patterns. Some phenomena are virtually universal among mammals (such as the tensions between effort in mating versus effort in parenting, and male-female conflicts of interest); some things vary with ecological conditions (such as fertility and degree of parental investment); and some things seem to vary with the social system independent of ecological pressures (such as rules about age at marriage and whether/which cousins may marry). Even rules about marriage may have ecological influences (e.g., the occurrence of polyandry), as I will discuss in this chapter, which focuses on how ecological constraints interact with social norms to produce the varied patterns we see in marriage and family forms. I use an evolutionary approach, which emphasizes something we rarely think of in human societies: how environmental factors shape what behaviors will be reproductively successful. I use examples from other species to shed light on the importance of biological and ecological constraint in explaining human mating and parenting behaviors.

How are we similar and how are we different from other mammals in our mating and parenting? In modern nation-states, we see remarkably little variation in marriage and family: typically we see open mate choice rather than arranged marriages; we find neolocal families (the couple lives apart from the parental generations) with only one spouse of each sex, and the children live with their parents. But as I will explain, across human history and prehistory, these were rare, and throughout most of our evolution, our mating arrangements were more ecologically influenced, more "typically" mammalian, and they more directly reflected potential conflicts of interest in mating and parenting: between males and females and between parents and children.

In other sexual species, it is usual for only one mating arrangement to predominate. For entirely biological reasons (reviewed in Low 2000a, chapters 3 and 4), polygyny is the most common system, the default system, across vertebrates and invertebrates. Unless there are specific countervailing ecological pressures favoring some other arrangement, polygyny will predominate. Although we typically see polygyny as a "one-male-several-females" system, biologists define the mating system by the relative variance in reproductive success displayed by males versus females. Polygyny thus defined is a system in which male variance in reproductive success exceeds female variance in success (e.g., Clutton-Brock 1983; reviewed in Low 2000a, 53–56). In most species, males spend calories and take risks as mating effort (and many fail; hence the typically high variance). Females tend to spend much of their parental effort (Low 1978) on specific offspring in ways that mean it cannot be invested in other offspring (tending, feeding, and so forth; Trivers 1972); the reproductive returns for these activities are more linear, failure is less frequent, and variance tends to be less than for male mating effort. Thus the impacts of sexual selection—what strategies will succeed and which will fail—tend to differ for males and females, and there is diversity in strategies for each sex at a number of levels (Clutton-Brock 2007). At the simplest, common, level, there are male-female conflicts of interest: reproductive success tends to favor males who focus on mating and females who focus on parenting. This is particularly true in mammals (including humans), in which females are specialized, as the very name "mammal" suggests, to feed infants. One result in human populations is the existence of biases in marriage and family residence arrangements. For example, polygyny is the "default" marriage system across traditional societies. However, monogamy and polyandry tend to be associated with scarce resources—men have more surviving children when they help provide and care for those children, rather than simply seeking many matings (though there are many ways, as we will see, for men to accomplish both in some circumstances).

It is important to distinguish between genetic mating systems (actual genetic maternity and paternity), and social mating systems (who feeds, protects, and the like). Genetic polyandry and genetic monogamy are almost unknown among mammals, but the genetic mating system may not (indeed probably seldom does) match the social mating system (e.g., Reichard 2003). That is why, across species, socially monogamous systems are characterized by EPCs (extra-pair copulations), and thus extra-pair paternity (e.g., Westneat and Stewart 2003). The principle genetic mating system of most human societies is clearly polygynous in biological terms.

We humans are unusual in having multiple mating systems: we have polygynous societies, (socially) monogamous societies, and even a few polyandrous societies—all in our one species. Perhaps only the dunnock (*Prunella modularis*), a little brown British bird, exhibits within a single species (sometimes within a single population) mating diversity comparable to that of humans. There are monogamous pairs, polyandrous females with their mates, polygynous males with their mates, and polygynandrous groups of males and females, each of which has multiple mates (Davies 1992). This is a species in which males help feed the chicks, and in which food and survivorship vary owing to ecological factors. Females who raise chicks alone fledge fewer chicks than couples or trios; females clearly prefer having males behave parentally. But feeding chicks is expensive. When a male gets less sexual access (is less likely to have fathered chicks), he reduces his feeding rate; males who spend considerable effort feeding other males' chicks spend more effort caring for offspring who are not theirs, and father fewer offspring than those who are able to discriminate. This complexity arises from an interaction of ecological forces and conflicts about reproductive success among individuals.

Beyond biological complexity, we are far more complicated than other species in the *social* aspects of our reproduction. Achieving mating is only one step toward reproductive and lineage success. As parents know all too well, successful children, who marry and raise families of their own, typically require years of expensive parental investment—feeding, nurturing, teaching, and more. Marriage as a social institution is important in many ways, over and above mating; it serves far more purposes than the simple reproductive interests of male and female across societies. Alliance formation and the exchange of goods and services are both important. Marriage typically involves the giving or exchange of goods (in some societies from the bride's family to the groom's; in others vice versa), and sometimes of women or of services. In most societies, arrangements are not simply the outcome of one man's and one woman's desires, but rather the culmination of negotiations by members of the older generation; an individual might be betrothed before puberty, or even both, for example.

Human marriage as a social institution further involves rules about allowed number of spouses at any one time, allowable consanguinity in pair bonds, allowable ages of mates, allowable residence of the couple, goods or services to be exchanged, and so on. We vary in, and have social rules about, mating outside marriage, as well. Nonmarital mating arrangements may be relatively open, and children acknowledged, or may be entirely clandestine.

The approaches of biologists, anthropologists, and sociologists to family life are complementary. Biological definitions of monogamy and polygyny predict much about parental care patterns, as well as the relative intensity of sexual selection on males versus females. In contrast, anthropological definitions of marriage systems are about social, property, and inheritance rights. In most socially monogamous societies, wealthy and powerful men have always had more sexual access (and until very recently, higher fertility as a result) than other men. In polygynous societies, these forces interact. For example, in polygynous systems, resource control contributes to the great variance in men's reproductive success; whenever men can acquire resources, men use them to enhance reproduction (e.g., by buying more wives). In contrast, women in polygynous societies typically control few resources; further, resources have less impact on women's reproduction than on men's in any marriage system. The result is that inheritance across polygynous cultures tends to be male-biased: families concentrate resources into the children who can most effectively convert resources into reproductive success (see Dickemann 1979, 1997; Hartung 1982, 1983, 1997; Hrdy 2005). Here, I explore such interactions, seeking both common threads, and understanding of the patterns of variation.

CROSS-CULTURAL PATTERN AND DIVERSITY IN RESIDENCE AND MARRIAGE ARRANGEMENTS

Across traditional societies, the major sources of data (Murdock 1957, 1967, 1981; Murdock and White 1969) suggest that although most major nation-states are socially monogamous, about 83 percent of societies, even today, have marriage rules that permit (or even mandate) polygyny. (Note that a majority of *societies* are formally polygynous; however, the majority of the world's *people* live in large, socially monogamous nations.) This simply positions human reproduction as typically mammalian in some ways: almost all mammals are polygynous, and it should be no surprise that a majority of marriage systems reflect our mammalian mating system. Nonetheless, polygynous marriage systems often have social constraints (for example, the allowed number of wives for men of different status).

For ecological reasons (see Low 1990a, 1990b, 2005; Flinn and Low 1986), most human societies studied by anthropologists are patrilocal: a man lives near his male relatives and works in coalitions with them, and a woman comes to live with her husband's kin group. There are, of course, complexities: the rule may involve either patrilocality or virilocality (these are equivalent except for the details of how the man's kin are distributed spatially), and may also have different rules for the first years of marriage.

In most Western nations today, couples live neolocally: in a new place, rather than with either the husband's or wife's family. In the traditional societies of the Standard Cross-Cultural Sample (Murdock and White 1969), only about 5 percent of societies show this neolocal residence pattern we tend to take for granted. Because of the value of resources to men in reproductive terms discussed above, and the value to men of working and fighting together to control resources, couples in most traditional societies (118 of 185, or 63.7 percent) live with the husband's kin (patrilocally or virilocally). In fact, patrilocal residence is associated with the presence of internal warfare (such as feuding or raiding by different groups within a political unit; Ember and Ember 1971, 1992). Other marriage residence patterns are also rare: matrilocal or avunculocal residence (with the wife's kin) occurs in 38 of 185 societies (20 percent), and ambilocal (with either husband's or wife's kin allowed) in 12 of 185 (6.5 percent). Matrilocality is associated with a combination of external warfare and high women's contribution to subsistence (Ember and Ember 1971). In larger samples such as Murdock's (1967) *Ethnographic Atlas*, fully two-thirds of the 862 societies mandate living with the husband's kin. Though the rules are clearly social, the drivers of the rules are ecological.

The rarity of monogamy across mammals (and across human societies) also derives from the impact of resources on reproductive success. Monogamy is associated with a small set of conditions—a major one is high male investment in offspring. The ecological conditions that favor greater male expenditure on offspring-specific true parental investment (what is given to one offspring is not available for any other use; Trivers 1972), resulting in genetic monogamy, are rare for all mammals (Low 2007; Reichard 2003). These conditions include: (1) relatively safe adult life (low mortality), combined with conditions that (2) allow adults to extend that safety to their offspring (e.g., species such as geese), resulting in (3) greatly enhanced offspring success with care by more than one parent. Human males have largely been able to circumvent these constraints, and monogamy—even social monogamy—is really rare.

Although social monogamy is the rule for modern nation states, fewer than 16 percent of human societies that anthropologists call "traditional" societies (such as hunter-gatherers, pastoralists, and agriculturalists) are socially monogamous. Because social monogamy seldom reflects genetic monogamy (Reichard 2003), this means that polygyny is even more common than the coding would lead one to suspect. In fact, the anthropological codings usually specify "monogamy or mild polygyny"—meaning simply that men who can garner sufficient resources for second and subsequent wives marry polygynously. Even "purely" socially monogamous societies—societies with one-spouse-at-a-time rules—are thus polygynous in a biological definition: more men than women fail to marry, and more men than women remarry after death or divorce, producing families in these later unions. The United States today fits this definition.

Polyandry is even less common than monogamy in human marriage arrangements (about 0.5 percent of societies cross-culturally), not surprisingly. It is almost always fraternal (brothers marry a single woman), and it appears to result from one of two strategies: brother-brother coalitions to combat resource scarcity, or attempts to control the distribution of resources such as land, which is immobile and loses its value when too finely divided (Low 2000a). Polyandry is rare for several reasons, including the fact that men who share sexual access to one woman will have fewer descendants under most circumstances than men who have either sole access to one woman or access to more than one woman. However, as Mace (1997, 1998) points out, such men may fare no worse than younger brothers in systems with primogeniture, in which the oldest son inherits but younger sons do not. Polyandry simply throws these conflicts into sharp relief.

Marriage and family forms in Western nations today provide a number of sharp contrasts compared to our past, and to traditional societies. As noted above, for example, most mammals, and most marriage systems in small-scale societies, are polygynous. Another difference is that of "who chooses." In most mammals, males compete for resources and or status, and display to females, who choose among them; women in Western nations today are largely able to choose their own mates, although arranged marriages persist today in parts of the world (India, Japan, parts of the Middle East). However, overt female choice is uncommon in traditional societies. Parents (typically fathers and male relatives) in many societies choose their children's marital partners, sometimes, as among the Arunta, before at least the girl's birth. In some societies, capture of women as either wives or concubines, is common; this is associated with the ecological pressures of high parasite stress, which made exogamy (out-marrying), with its production of genetically diverse children, advantageous (Low 1988, 1989a, 1990a). Reported occurrences may be changing with medicine and the pacifying influence of developed nations.

MARRIAGE, FAMILY, AND CHILDCARE VARIATIONS CROSS-CULTURALLY

Within the United States today, thirty-one states have some cousin-marriage restrictions; nineteen states have none (Ottenheimer 1996). No European nations prohibit cousin marriages, and recent data suggest that fertility is higher in some levels of cousin marriages than in outbred marriages. This implies no particular genetic disadvantages (Helgason et al. 2008). Indeed, cross-culturally cousin marriage was the rule in traditional societies, rather than the exception. The patterns in cousin marriages have clear ecological influences. There are four types of first-cousin marriages: two are "parallel" (a man marries his father's brother's daughter or his mother's sister's daughter) and two are "cross" (a man marries his father's sister's daughter or his mother's brother's daughter). The degree of relatedness, if there are no relevant hidden EPCs, is identical for all four—but the resource implications for men are not. Because marriage rules and preferences will be manipulated in the reproductive interests of those who control them, the ecology of resource concentration—who gets how much of what—leads to a complex set of predictions (Flinn and Low 1986). For example, societies with symmetrical cross-cousin marriage rules (children of opposite-sex siblings—either father's-sister's-daughter (FZD) or mother's-brother's-daughter (MBD) allowed) tend to exchange women (rather than goods or resources). These societies are characterized by poor resource bases—there is little besides women to exchange. Not surprisingly, these societies also tend to lack inheritance rules (Flinn and Low 1986), since there is also little to inherit.

In richer resource areas, asymmetrical cousin marriage rules reflect men's coalitions around resource control. The common rules (father's-brother's-daughter, or FBD; mother's-brother's-daughter, MBD; and father's-sister's-daughter, FZD) all enhance the power of coalitions among *male* relatives, and are associated with residency patterns that enhance the particular kind of male coalition (e.g., FBD is associated with patrilocal residency so that both senior males are close by, while MBD is associated with avunculocal residency—the mother's brother is close by). Even the social rules of descent, in contrast to kinship analyses per se, appear to function in ways that allow men to work together well, control resources, and sometimes even solve collective action problems (Cronk and Gerkey 2007). The most striking example, perhaps, is that MZD (mother's-sister's-daughter), which would enhance nepotism and reciprocity among *female* kin, is virtually unknown, regardless of other factors—women in most societies simply cannot control significant resources so that female interests can dictate marriage alliance patterns.

So far, it is clear that across human societies (just as in other mammals), males and females are likely to succeed in mating and raising families by doing different things—male and female "strategies" differ. It is not surprising, therefore, that across societies, men and women tend to teach different skills to different audiences of children (older/younger boys and girls). Women tend to have responsibility for "younger" children (<7); after that, men and women train children in different skills. Across all societies, boys are taught, in early and late childhood, to show more fortitude and be more self-reliant than are girls (Barry et al. 1971; Low 1989b). Girls are taught, in early and late childhood, to be more industrious, responsible, obedient, and sexually restrained than boys. Training is more intense in later childhood than in early childhood for most traits. In nonstratified traditional societies, in which striving can raise men's status, there is an interesting interplay (Low 1989b): the more polygynous the society (the greater the potential reproductive rewards for striving), the more intensely boys are taught to strive. The traits expressed as desirable in wives in stratified societies are chastity and obedience; the more stratified the society, the more older girls are taught to be sexually restrained and obedient, and the less they are urged to be self-reliant (Low 1989b). Similarly, in stratified societies, the pattern of exceptions is asymmetrical: a man can almost never marry a woman from a higher-status family than his own, but hypergyny ("marrying up" of women from lower classes) is common. A woman who can marry up may not have more children than a woman marrying within her class, but her children are likely to be better invested and survive better.

Modern nations present an interesting set of contrasts and confluences with the patterns of traditional societies. As noted above, most modern nations have rules requiring social monogamy—but they are effectively biologically polygynous in terms of men's remarriage and the relative variance in men's versus women's reproduction. Furthermore, effective contraception is widely available. Nonetheless, it appears that wealthier men, if they choose, have greater sexual access than poorer men (Pérusse 1993, 1994). In modern India, we may see an unfortunate interplay between hypergyny and parental success. The dowry required for a lower-caste woman to marry up is greater than the dowry required from the families of higher-caste women (all else equal), and hypergynously married women may suffer marital mistreatment (Rao 1993a, 1993b, 1997). The relationships among dowry, caste, son preference, and domestic violence are complex (Shenk 2006), but it is worth noting that there are geographic associations, and that dowry-associated violence is more common in urban areas (where status competition is more intense and women are more separated from their kin networks) than in rural areas, and among lower-status groups (where there is knowledge of the worth of resources, but little ability to get them in abundance).

Today, we have broad definitions of "family" (see Low 2005, 2007), but there is increasing evidence that background ecological and evolutionary forces, about which we seldom think, still influence our family patterns today. As noted earlier, among mammals, human males are extraordinarily paternal. However, patterns of paternal investment vary greatly across societies, apparently independent of the marriage system—but not of paternity certainty. In polygynous societies with low confidence of paternity (for example, where men and women live apart), it is common for children's maternal uncles to invest in the children, rather than their (putative or nominal) father, for example. Because children are expensive in terms of parental investment, men tend to discriminate, giving more to their sisters' children, whose genetic relationship is more certain, than to their "own" children. This discrimination is cost-sensitive—much more likely when the investment is something like money, rather than time spent with children. Similarly, social fathers are likely to discriminate between genetic children and stepchildren. I suspect that variation in kinds of stepparenting, like other aspects of family life, has resource correlations. A testable hypothesis is that stepparents should view their role positively and take on the role most willingly when investment is low and generalizable (for example, men's teaching of skills to young boys in some traditional societies), or costs are defrayed (for example, by children's labor in agricultural societies). In contrast, when children are costly to rear for both parents, we should not be surprised if step- and foster-parents typically invest less than genetic parents.

We see more neolocal blended families today than in past Western societies, and in modern conditions children do not defray much of their costs (see Bumpass, Raley, and Sweet 1995; Cherlin and Furstenburg 1994; Hewlett 1992). The implication of this differential investment by stepparents is likely to be of more concern today than in the past. In traditional societies with few heritable resources, stepfathers may invest as much time and training in stepchildren as in their genetic children (see Hewlett 1992; Hewlett et al. 2000). In modern socially monogamous (but genetically polygynous) societies with remarriage, there exist both high resource stakes and considerable stepparenting. In these conditions, stepchildren are, in many societies, more vulnerable than genetic children to lowered investment (Anderson et al. 1999; Anderson, Kaplan, and Lancaster 1999; Hofferth and Anderson 2003; Lancaster and Kaplan 2000), child abuse, and infanticide (Daly and Wilson 1980, 1981, 1984, 1985, 1987, 1988, 1989; reviewed in Low 2000a, chapter 6).

HUMAN LIFE HISTORY, REPRODUCTIVE ECOLOGY, AND FAMILY PATTERNS

In some ways, we humans are "typical" primates: we are polygynous, and the physical differences between the sexes reflect our mating system. But in other ways, our life histories are unusual (Kaplan 1997; Low 1997; Low 2000a, chapter 6; Lummaa 2007; Mace 2000a, 2000b). We wean our infants far earlier than predicted, and we reach sexual maturity far later than expected, for a primate of our size. Our infants' brains at birth are larger than predicted—and, in contrast to the infant brains of other primates, the brain keeps growing rapidly for the first year of life. Most scholars relate these life history differences to our highly developed intelligence (especially social intelligence), and our complex sociality (see Byrne 1995; Byrne and Whiten 1988). Another life history difference is important: in most other primates, and other mammals in general, females live about 10 percent of their lifespan after their last birth. Humans are unusual in spending approximately 30 percent of their lifespan postreproductively. These ecological and life-history differences might seem of little interest today, but in fact, as I discuss in the next section, it is their interactions with our cultural diversity that appears to shape fertility shifts, and both enhance and limit that diversity (Mace 1998, 2000a, 2000b, 2007; Mace, Jordan, and Holden 2003; Voland 1998, 2007; Voland and Dunbar 1995).

Because of such complexities, we struggle today to understand which family patterns are adaptive (have current reproductive utility for parents), and which are maladaptive (see Voland 2007). Finally, some patterns that are adaptive for parents and result in greater lineage success and persistence can have perverse effects at the population level. We need to understand more about the ecology of modern human reproduction.

WOMEN'S LIFE PATHS TODAY: HIDDEN ECOLOGICAL INFLUENCES ON MARRIAGE

To understand modern reproduction, why look to other species and to the past? It is easy to imagine that our evolutionary past is remote, unconnected to our lives today, and of interest only when we think of traditional societies or ancient history. Can nonhuman, cross-cultural, and historical data really tell us anything about life today? The old established correlations, for males versus females, between resources and reproductive success: have they not disappeared? As the earlier examples suggest, resource correlations and sex differences have persisted, and, I suggest, remain important today. Our evolved tendencies interact with today's environments, novel though they may be; today's cities, no less than yesterday's rain forests and savannas, *are* our environments. Both physical and social aspects of our current environments can be evolutionarily novel, largely the result of our own actions; yet they still interact with our evolved tendencies.

Resources affect even basic life history variables—demographic traits such as age-specific fertility and mortality (for instance, well-nourished individuals in most vertebrates mature earlier than poorly nourished individuals and are less likely to die early). These, in turn, shape not only individual lifetimes but also social factors, such as age at marriage and probability of remarriage. Typically, the pattern for the two sexes differs. In most modern and historical societies, widows remarry far less frequently than widowers, with no obvious demographic or economic explanation. Furthermore, widowers tend to marry younger women when they remarry, not widows of their own age; women remarry at earlier ages than men when they do remarry; and women's probability of remarriage declines with age. Classical demographic analyses have found such patterns puzzling, for women's economic value, like men's, does not decline with age. But biologically, these patterns make sense: women's reproductive value (RV; Fisher 1958) does decline, with certainty, after the late teens and early twenties.

New work connects family and environment at an even more fine-grained level. Across species, when life expectancy is short, reproduction begins early. This is a well-known pattern to biologists; it holds true whether one is asking about wildebeest, chipmunks, or meadow voles (see Harvey and Zammuto 1985; Roff 1992, 2001; Stearns 1992, figure 5.10), and it holds across primate species. Today, this remains true in transnational comparisons (Low et al. 2008). Across approximately 170 nations, life expectancy is a better predictor of women's age at first birth than either women's workforce participation or women's schooling. For some subgroups of nations, however, women's schooling and/or women's workforce participation are important, and it is clear that cultural influences, from religion to expectations and norms about women's education and social roles, also affect this very basic biological phenomenon.

Analyses within societies find the same pattern, even when other conditions (such as socioeconomic status) are controlled for (see Anderson and Low 2003; Low, Simon, and Anderson 2002, 2003; Wilson and Daly 1997). Furthermore, in a number of modern nation-states, early first births under conditions such as short life expectancy are likely to be nonmarital, and single motherhood is common, particularly if men have little to offer in terms of security and resources (see Geronimus 1996, 2001; Geronimus et al. 1996; Wilson and Daly 1997). This seems puzzling from a purely social science analysis; but from a biological analysis, it is adaptive (in fact, the much-delayed and often below-replacement fertility of wealthier women is the puzzle from a biological perspective; see Low, Simon, and Anderson 2002, 2003).

The widely discussed difficulties attending single parenthood raise another complication. People's perceptions of difficulties matter: when people perceive that life is risky or uncertain, they are more likely to take life-threatening risks (after all, the potential gains from risk-taking may be worth it, if one is likely to die anyway); they are also less likely to "attach" securely to a mate or child (see Hill 1994; Hill, Ross, and Low 1997; Kruger, Wang, and Wilke 2007; Wilke, Hutchinson, and Todd 2003; Wilke et al. 2006). The clear drivers are resource richness and predictability of resources (Anderson and Low 2003; Low et al. 2008; Luker 1996). Life expectancy (and perceived life expectancy) can predict much about patterns of age at first marriage, risk-taking (including in some cases drug and alcohol abuse), family form (such as proportion of single motherhood), and even, perhaps, psychological attachment style.

MODERN MARRIAGE AND FAMILY PATTERNS

Marriage arrangements can, and do, serve several purposes. For example, interfamilial alliances can provide resource protection for women and their children. In some ways, both marriage arrangements and family forms vary more today than in traditional societies. Although it varies across nations, women today typically marry whom they choose, live where they wish, and have independent access to formal education and resources.

Throughout our prehistory and history, subsistence (hunting/gathering, intensive/extensive agriculture, animal husbandry, fishing) and marital locality have influenced family forms. From medieval times in Europe, land was a central resource, and structured much of family life (see Gies and Gies 1989; Mitterauer and Sieder 1982; Netting 1993; Rotberg and Rabb 1980). Male kin in land-owning families tended to stay nearby, so most families again lived patrilocally. Extended families tended to live together; the family was an economic unit both for working the land and for protoindustrial production. Inheritance developed geographical patterns, apparently related to the type and (reproductive) utility of heritable resources. In the "Mediterranean" pattern, one child (typically the oldest living son) inherited virtually everything, while later-born children more or less fended for themselves, but the "European" pattern had more equal inheritance (Goody 1988). Even within regions, variation could occur. In Sweden during the nineteenth century, for example, families in southern Sweden (with small, productive farms, and high market penetration) tended to divide land among children, while in the central regions and the north, most land tended to go to the oldest son (Clarke and Low 1992; Low and Clarke 1992). Family forms, as well as inheritance patterns, changed further with the coming of the industrial revolution, and its impact on children's resource-garnering value.

During the nineteenth century in Europe and North America, a major shift occurred, from reliance on agricultural work and small-scale cottage industries to reliance on major industrial enterprises. Concurrently, fertility fell significantly (see Coale and Watkins 1986; Schofield and Coleman 1986). Family size and form shifted in significant ways: families became smaller and children remained dependent on parental resources for much longer than previously; women attended school longer and worked for pay outside the home to a greater extent than previously, with attendant delays in fertility. A reasonable hypothesis, the focus of much demographic work for much of the past thirty years, was that in some (largely unspecified) way, industrialization was at least a proximate cause of fertility decline. The results have been disappointing to many demographers (see Coleman and Schofield 1996), and new data from the developing world also suggest that "industrialization" was a theoretical red herring. Today it appears that the broader theoretical approach of life history theory better predicts the patterns we see.

Today in Western developed nations, "family" denotes a variety of household organizations (see Low 2005). Where once variation appeared to exist primarily across cultures (for example, in the cross-cultural databases such as those in Murdock 1957, 1967, and 1981), variation within large societies may predominate today. This variation in family form both within and across societies has attracted attention, in part, because it is associated with variation in resource dependence, urbanization, and population growth.

THE EVOLUTIONARY NOVELTY OF MODERN FAMILY LIFE

Problems of wealth, health, and fertility for men and women are not just of academic interest to a few evolutionary anthropologists and behavioral ecologists. These questions, and these data, are important in a highly applied context—the global issues often called "population and environment"—as well as for their own intellectual merit. Both the number of people alive and consumption per person today are higher than at any time in the past. Population patterns—birth and death patterns—are the sum of what individual men and women do: they mate and marry, have children, and die, consuming resources along the way.

The disappointing search for a singular cause of nineteenth-century fertility declines nonetheless has been illuminating. Rather than "the" demographic transition with a singular sociocultural cause, there is good reason to expect ecologically influenced fertility trends with local, reversible, patterns—and that is, when we look carefully, what we see (see Low 2000b; Low and Clarke 1992). That is, when resources are abundant and competition is moderate, we see high fertility.

The primary components of population change—fertility, mortality, and migration—respond to ecological conditions *at the individual family level* in ways that are predictable and familiar to students of nonhuman populations. As noted before, what we call "the" demographic transition was once thought to be a by-product of industrialization, a hypothesis that proved relatively unsatisfactory (see Coleman and Schofield 1996). But it appears, to biologists, to be an example of the impacts of heightened competition (see MacArthur and Wilson 1967)—when offspring face serious competition to get established, parents who invest more per offspring are more successful. The cost, of course, is that these parents are able to produce fewer offspring. Thus we see smaller, but more resource-consumptive, families, with broad ecological implications. Which families respond, and how, depends on local resource conditions and the nature of competition, even though we typically see the results at the population level. For example, in Thailand, fertility fell dramatically because employers began preferring to hire workers with (costly) secondary-school education; in response, couples began to plan how many children, given their resources, they could afford to put through secondary school (Knodel and Wongsith 1991; Knodel, Havanon, and Sittitrai 1990).

At least through demographic transitions, certain predictable ecological rules underlie patterns of fertility, mortality, and migration, although these may be constrained by a variety of cultural complexities and interactions. For example, in traditional and historical societies, men's reproductive patterns vary in concert with resource control to a much greater extent than women's patterns; this difference between the sexes is greatest when resources are abundant in these societies. There are hints of this pattern even in aggregate data (marriage rates and fertility rates in England and Sweden rose and fell with crop and grain prices; see Wrigley and Schofield 1981 and the studies reviewed in Low and Clarke 1992), although it is difficult to analyze aggregate data to answer the resource-fertility question. Analyses of lineage, rather than aggregate, data strongly suggest that marriage decisions and fertility of both men and women were influenced by resource access during the demographic transition (Low 1993; Low, Clarke, and Lockridge 1992; Low 2002, ch. 8).

In many traditional and historical societies, these differences are apparent because men controlled major resources; women depended on their fathers or husbands for resources to raise children successfully. Patterns in modern nations provide an interesting contrast: women have, in Western developed nations at least, much greater autonomous access to resources. This evolutionarily novel phenomenon has several unexpected consequences. One consequence is that, as in other species, when a female and her offspring can do well without a male, males tend not to enter permanent bonds; thus the low marriage rates in some countries (for example, Sweden, with broad social support systems), and high divorce rates are not surprising. Even at relatively low socioeconomic levels, it appears to be common that if men can bring little in the way of substantial resources to a partnership, lineages are likely to be centered on women and their children (see Geronimus 1996).

Does a shift from high fertility to lower fertility and high consumption make ecological and evolutionary sense? At first glance, reduced fertility combined with increased per capita investment seems evolutionarily reasonable in environments of heightened competitiveness for offspring. In other species, this often simply means that density is high and the environment is packed with competitors (MacArthur and Wilson 1967); mates and nest sites, for example, are limiting. But in modern human populations, far more than simple density matters (see Knodel 1994; Knodel and Chayovan 1990; Low et al. 2002, 2003). Key to understanding cultures of declining fertility is the issue of wealth inheritance and its role in producing competitive, successful children (Mace 1998, 2000a, 2000b).

The fertility shifts we call *the* demographic transition generated an unexpected consequence for modern Western women. We are more likely to work, and to have careers rather than, for example, part-time jobs. We tend to marry later than women in the rest of the world. A change in women's strategies from "reproductive value" to a mixture of reproduction and resource-garnering makes sense in a competitive environment in which only well-invested children do well—up to a point. What we find, however, is that women face harsher constraints than do men in spending effort to get resources versus investing resources in children. At lower socioeconomic levels, we see women who must pay almost as much in childcare in order to work, as they can make working. At the high end of the scale, a recent Harvard Business School study found that of individuals who had completed their fertility in the United States making over $100,000 per year, 49 percent of women were childless, versus 19 percent of men.

There is a further dilemma at a larger scale; what is favored by selection at the family level may have unexpected effects at the population level, and we have been slow to realize this. In the Rio Conference of 1992 and its ten-year follow-up conference, "Northern" (developed) and "Southern" (developing) nations squared off. The central issues, with little progress and no resolution, boiled down to conflicts over resources and fertility multiplied up from individual to population levels.

A difficult problem arises if fertility declines are accompanied by consumption increases—as is predicted by life history theory, as has been the case in past demographic transitions, and as appears to be the case in most developing-nation transitions today. Fertility decline today is promoted by many successful family-planning programs around the world with the clear message that fewer children means wealthier families. Wealthier families consume more resources than poorer families, and if one asks about the interplay of population and consumption, fewer-but-more-consumptive families do not lead to decreased or stabilized resource consumption (Low 2000a, chapter 15; 2000b). This is why ecologists and environmentalists in the 1960s began to popularize the relationships between resource use and population growth. Titles such as *The Population Bomb* (Ehrlich and Ehrlich 1968) and "Doomsday: Friday, 13 November, 2026" (Von Foerster, Mora, and Amiot 1960) appeared in scientific journals and as popular-science books. In contrast, today the press is full of articles about below-replacement fertility in the West. These seemingly opposite phenomena are, I suspect, responses to the general principle that there is, as the demographer Richard Easterlin suggested, a trade-off between numbers of children and the per capita investment in those children (Easterlin 1978; Easterlin and Crimmins 1985). The nature of family life has shifted: raising successful children in modern Western nations takes far more resources than raising a child in the third world—so Western families are smaller (say, two children rather than eight or ten) than families in the third world, but Western families consume perhaps ten to fifteen times (or more) the resources per capita of third-world families.

Policy is being made or proposed without the knowledge we need. Understanding both the evolved patterns, and the proximate cues that drive our behavior (for example, why we tend to seek "more" even when we know rationally it does not improve our lives) might help us devise more useful approaches to population-environment issues. For example, it should be relatively easy to get individuals and corporations to change behavior if the changes are immediately "profitable"; simply making the information available should help (such as installing energy-efficient light bulbs). In contrast, problems that are immediately costly (not only economically, but also in terms of time, attention, or effort, for example) will be more difficult to solve. These dynamics are crucial, but we are just beginning to analyze modern populations in this light.

REFERENCES

Anderson, K. G., H. Kaplan, D. Lam, and J. B. Lancaster. 1999. Paternal care by genetic and stepfathers II: Reports by Xhosa high school students. *Evolution and Human Behavior* 20:433–451.

Anderson, K. G., H. Kaplan, and J. B. Lancaster. 1999. Paternal care by genetic fathers and stepfathers I: Reports by Albuquerque men. *Evolution and Human Behavior* 20:405–431.

Anderson, K. G., and B. S. Low. 2003. Non-marital first births and women's life histories. In J. Rogers and H.-P. Kohler, eds., *The biodemography of human fertility and reproduction*, 57–86. Boston: Kluwer.

Barry, H., III, L. Josephson, E. Lauer, and C. Marshall. 1971. Agents and techniques for child training: Cross-cultural codes 6. *Ethnology* 10, no. 4: 191–230.

Bumpass, L., R. Raley, and J. A. Sweet. 1995. The changing character of stepfamilies: Implications of cohabitation and nonmarital childbearing. *Demography* 32:425–436.

Byrne, R. 1995. *The thinking ape: Evolutionary origins of intelligence.* Oxford: Oxford University Press.

Byrne, R., and A. Whiten. 1988. *Machiavellian intelligence: Social expertise and the evolution of intellect in monkeys, apes, and humans.* Oxford: Clarendon Press.

Cherlin, A., and F. Furstenburg Jr. 1994. Stepfamilies in the United States: A reconsideration. *Annual Review of Sociology* 20:359–381.

Clarke, A. L., and B. S. Low. 1992. Ecological correlates of human dispersal in 19th-century Sweden. *Animal Behaviour* 44, no. 4: 677–693.

Clutton-Brock, T. H. 1983. Selection in relation to sex. In D. S. Bendall, ed., *Evolution from molecules to men*, 457–481. London: Cambridge University Press.

———. 2007. Sexual selection in males and females. *Science* 318:1882–1885.

Coale, A. J., and S. C. Watkins. 1986. *The decline of fertility in Europe.* Princeton: Princeton University Press.

Coleman, D., and R. Schofield, eds. 1996. *The state of population theory: Forward from Malthus.* London: Basil Blackwell.

Cronk, L., and D. Gerkey. 2007. Kinship and descent. In R. L. M. Dunbar and L. Barrett, eds., *The Oxford handbook of evolutionary psychology*, 463–478. Oxford: Oxford University Press.

Daly, M., and M. Wilson. 1980. Discriminative parental solicitude—A biological perspective. *Journal of Marriage and the Family* 42, no. 2: 277–288.

———. 1981. Abuse and neglect of children in evolutionary perspective. In R. D. Alexander and D. W. Tinkle, eds., *Natural selection and social behavior*, 405–416. New York: Chiron.

———. 1984. A sociobiological analysis of human infanticide. In G. Hausfater and S. B. Hrdy, eds., *Infanticide: Comparative and evolutionary perspectives*, 487–502. New York: Aldine de Gruyter.

———. 1985. Child abuse and other risks of not living with both parents. *Ethology and Sociobiology* 6:197–210.

———. 1987. Children as homicide victims. In R. J. Gelles and J. Lancaster, eds., *Child abuse and neglect: Biosocial dimensions*, 201–214. New York: Aldine de Gruyter.

———. 1988. *Homicide.* Hawthorne, N.Y.: Aldine de Gruyter.

———. 1989. Evolution and family homicide—Reply. *Science* 243, no. 4890: 463–464.

Davies, N. 1992. *Dunnock behaviour and social evolution.* Oxford: Oxford University Press.

Dickemann, M. 1979. Female infanticide, reproductive strategies, and social stratification: A preliminary model. In N. Chagnon and W. Irons, eds., *Evolutionary biology and human social behavior: An anthropological perspective*, 321–367. North Scituate, Mass.: Duxbury Press.

———. 1997. Paternal confidence and dowry competition: A biocultural analysis of purdah. In Laura Betzig, ed., *Human nature: A critical reader*, 297–330. Oxford: Oxford University Press.

Easterlin, R. 1978. The economics and sociology of fertility: A synthesis. In C. Tilly, ed., *Historical studies of changing fertility*, 57–134. Princeton: Princeton University.

Easterlin, R., and E. Crimmins. 1985. *The fertility revolution: A supply-demand analysis.* Chicago: University of Chicago Press.

Ehrlich, P. R., and A. Ehrlich. 1968. *The population bomb.* New York: Ballantine.

Ember, M., and C. R. Ember. 1971. The conditions favoring matrilocal versus patrilocal residence. *American Anthropologist* 73:571–593.

———. 1992. Resource unpredictability, mistrust, and war: A cross-cultural study. *Journal of Conflict Resolution* 36, no. 2: 242–262.

Fisher, R. A. 1958. *The genetical theory of natural selection.* New York: Dover.

Flinn, M. V., and B. S. Low. 1986. Resource distribution, social competition, and mating patterns in human societies. In D. Rubenstein and R. Wrangham, eds., *Ecological aspects of social evolution*, 217–243. Princeton: Princeton University Press.

Geronimus, A. T. 1996. What teen mothers know. *Human Nature* 7, no. 4: 323–352.

———. 2001. Inequality in life expectancy, functional status, and active life expectancy across selected black and white populations in the United States. *Demography* 38, no. 2: 227–251.

Geronimus, A. T., J. Bound, T. A. Waidmann, M. M. Hillemeier, and P. B. Burns. 1996. Excess mortality among blacks and whites in the United States. *New England Journal of Medicine* 335:1552–1558.

Gies, F., and J. Gies. 1989. *Marriage and the family in the Middle Ages.* New York: Harper Perennial.

Goody, J. 1988. *The development of family and marriage in Europe.* Cambridge: Cambridge University Press.

Hartung, J. 1982. Polygyny and inheritance of wealth. *Current Anthropology* 23:1–11.

———. 1983. In defense of Murdock: A reply to Dickemann. *Current Anthropology* 24, no. 1: 125–126.

———. 1997. If I had it to do over. In L. Betzig, ed., *Human nature: A critical reader*, 344–348. Oxford: Oxford University Press.

Harvey, P., and R. M. Zammuto. 1985. Patterns of mortality and age at first reproduction in natural populations of mammals. *Nature* 315:319–320.

Helgason, A., S. Palsson, D. F. Guabjartsson, B. Kristjansson, and K. Stefansson. 2008. An association between the kinship and fertility of human couples. *Science* 319:813–816.

Hewlett, B.S. 1992. *Father-child relations: Cultural and biosocial contexts.* Chicago: Aldine de Gruyter.

Hewlett, B.S., M. E. Lamb, B. Leyendecker, and A. Scholmerich. 2000. Parental strategies among Aka foragers, Ngandu farmers, and Euro-American urban-industrialists. In L. Cronk, N.A. Chagnon, and W.G. Irons, eds., *Adaptation and human behavior: An anthropological perspective*, 155–178. New York: Aldine de Gruyter.

Hill, E.M. 1994. Childhood adversity, attachment security, and adult relationships: A preliminary study. *Ethology and Sociobiology* 15:323–338.

Hill, E.M., L. T. Ross, and B. Low. 1997. The role of future unpredictability in human risk-taking. *Human Nature* 8, no. 4: 287–325.

Hofferth, S.L., and K. G. Anderson. 2003. Are all dads equal? Biology versus marriage as basis for paternal investment. *Journal of Marriage and Family* 65:213–232.

Hrdy, S.B. 2005. *Mother nature: Maternal instincts and how they shape the human species.* New York: Ballantine.

Kaplan, H. 1997. The evolution of the human life course. In K.W. Wachter and C.E. Finch, eds., *Between Zeus and the salmon: The biodemography of longevity*, 175–210. Washington, D.C.: National Academy Press.

Knodel, J. 1994. Gender and schooling in Thailand. *Population Council* 60:1–60.

Knodel, J., and N. Chayovan. 1990. Contraceptive initiation patterns in Thailand. *Population Studies* 44:257–271.

Knodel, J., N. Havanon, and W. Sittitrai. 1990. Family size and the education of children in the context of rapid fertility decline. *Population and Development Review* 16, no. 1: 31–62.

Knodel, J., and M. Wongsith. 1991. Family size and children's education in Thailand: Evidence from a national sample. *Demography* 28:119–131.

Kruger, D., X. T. Wang, and A. Wilke. 2007. Toward the development of an evolutionarily valid domain-specific risk-taking scale. *Evolutionary Psychology* 5:555–568.

Lancaster, J.B., and H. S. Kaplan. 2000. Parenting other men's children: Costs, benefits and consequences. In L. Cronk, N.A. Chagnon, and W.G. Irons, eds., *Evolutionary biology and human behavior: 20 years later*, 179–201. New York: Aldine de Gruyter.

Low, B. 1978. Environmental uncertainty and the parental strategies of marsupials and placentals. *American Naturalist* 112:197–213.

———. 1988. Pathogen stress and polygyny in humans. In L.L. Betzig, M. Borgerhoff Mulder, and P.W. Turke, eds., *Human reproductive behaviour: A Darwinian perspective*, 115–128. Cambridge: Cambridge University Press.

———. 1989a. Human responses to environmental extremeness and uncertainty: A cross-cultural perspective. In E. Cashdan, ed., *Risk and uncertainty in tribal and peasant economies*, 229–255. Boulder, Colo.: Westview.

———. 1989b. Cross-cultural patterns in the training of children: An evolutionary perspective. *Journal of Comparative Psychology* 103, no. 4: 311–319.

———. 1990a. Marriage systems and pathogen stress in human societies. *American Zoologist* 30:325–339.

———. 1990b. Sex, power, and resources: Ecological and social correlates of sex differences. *International Journal of Contemporary Sociology* 27, nos. 1–2: 49–74.

———. 1993. Ecological demography: A synthetic focus in evolutionary anthropology. *Evolutionary Anthropology* 2:176–187.

———. 1997. The evolution of human life histories. In C. Crawford, ed., *Handbook of evolutionary psychology: Behavior: Ideas, issues, and applications*, 131–161. Mahwah, N.J.: Erlbaum.

———. 2000a. *Why sex matters: A Darwinian look at human behavior.* Princeton: Princeton University Press.

———. 2000b. Sex, wealth, and fertility—Old rules, new environments. In L. Cronk, N. A. Chagnon, and W. G. Irons, eds., *Adaptation and human behavior: An anthropological perspective*, 323–344. New York: Aldine de Gruyter.

———. 2005. Families: An evolutionary ecological approach. In J. Roopnarine and U. Geilen, eds., *Families in global perspective*, 14–32. Boston: Allyn & Bacon.

———. 2007. Ecological and sociocultural influences on mating and marriage systems. In R. Dunbar and L. Barrett, eds., *The Oxford handbook of evolutionary psychology*, 449–462. Oxford: Oxford University Press.

Low, B., and A. L. Clarke. 1992. Resources and the life course: Patterns through the demographic transition. *Ethology and Sociobiology* 13, nos. 5–6: 463–494.

Low, B., A. L. Clarke, and K. A. Lockridge. 1992. Toward an ecological demography. *Population and Development Review* 18, no. 1: 1–31.

Low, B., A. Hazel, N. C. Parker, and K. Welch. 2008. Influences on women's reproductive lives: Unexpected ecological underpinnings. *Cross-Cultural Research* 42:201–219.

Low, B., C. P. Simon, and K. G. Anderson. 2002. An evolutionary ecological perspective on demographic transitions: Modeling multiple currencies. *American Journal of Human Biology* 14:149–167.

———. 2003. The biodemography of modern women: Tradeoffs when resources become limiting. In J. L. Rodgers and H. P. Kohler, eds., *The biodemography of human reproduction and fertility*, 105–134. Boston: Kluwer Academic.

Luker, K. 1996. *Dubious conceptions: The politics of teenage pregnancy.* Cambridge, Mass.: Harvard University Press.

Lummaa, V. 2007. Life-history theory, reproduction and longevity in humans. In R. L. M. Dunbar and L. Barrett, eds., *The Oxford handbook of evolutionary psychology*, 397–413. Oxford: Oxford University Press.

MacArthur, R., and E. Wilson. 1967. *The theory of island biogeography.* Princeton: Princeton University Press.

Mace, R. 1997. Commentary on Levine and Silk. *Current Anthropology* 38:386.

———. 1998. The coevolution of human fertility and wealth inheritance strategies. *Philosophical Transactions of the Royal Society of London, Series B* 353:389–397.

———. 2000a. An adaptive model of human reproductive rate where wealth is inherited. In L. Cronk, N. A. Chagnon, and W. G. Irons, eds., *Adaptation and human behavior: An anthropological perspective*, 261–281. Hawthorne, N.Y.: Aldine de Gruyter.

———. 2000b. Evolutionary ecology of human life history. *Animal Behaviour* 59:1–10.

———. 2007. The evolutionary ecology of human family size. In R. L. M. Dunbar and L. Barrett, eds., *The Oxford handbook of evolutionary psychology*, 4449–4462. Oxford: Oxford University Press.

Mace, R., F. Jordan, and C. Holden. 2003. Testing evolutionary hypotheses about human biological adaptation using cross-cultural comparison. *Comparative Biochemistry and Physiology—Part A: Molecular and Integrative Physiology* 136, no. 1: 85–94.

Mitterauer, M. and R. Sieder. 1982. *The European family*. Oxford: Blackwell.

Murdock, G. P. 1957. World ethnographic sample. *American Anthropologist* 59:195–220.

———. 1967. *Ethnographic atlas*. Pittsburgh: University of Pittsburgh Press.

———. 1981. *Atlas of world cultures*. Pittsburgh: University of Pittsburgh Press.

Murdock, G. P., and D. White. 1969. Standard cross-cultural sample. *Ethnology* 8:329–369.

Netting, R. M. 1993. *Smallholders, householders: Farm families and the ecology of intensive, sustainable agriculture*. Palo Alto, Calif.: Stanford University Press.

Ottenheimer, M. 1996. *Forbidden relatives: The American myth of cousin marriage*. Champaign: University of Illinois Press.

Pérusse, D. 1993. Cultural and reproductive success in industrial societies: Testing the relationship at proximate and ultimate levels. *Behavior and Brain Sciences* 16:267–322.

———. 1994. Mate choice in modern societies: Testing evolutionary hypotheses with behavioral data. *Human Nature* 5, no. 3: 255–278.

Rao, V. 1993a. Dowry "inflation" in rural India: A statistical investigation. *Population Studies* 47:283–293.

———. 1993b. The rising price of husbands: A hedonic analysis of dowry increases in rural India. *Journal of Political Economy* 101:666–677.

———. 1997. Wife-beating in rural south India: A qualitative and econometric analysis. *Social Science and Medicine* 44:1169–1180.

Reichard, U. 2003. Introduction. In U. Reichard and C. Boesch, eds., *Monogamy: Mating strategies and partnerships in birds, humans, and other mammals*, 3–23. Cambridge: Cambridge University Press.

Roff, D. A. 1992. *The evolution of life histories: Theory and analysis*. New York: Chapman and Hall.

———. 2001. *The evolution of life histories: Theory and analysis.* New York: Chapman and Hall.

Rotberg, R., and T. Rabb. 1980. *Marriage and fertility. Studies in interdisciplinary history.* Princeton: Princeton University Press.

Schofield, R., and D. Coleman. 1986. Introduction: The state of population theory. In D. Coleman and R. Schofield, eds., *The state of population theory,* 1–13. Oxford: Basil Blackwell.

Shenk, M. K. 2006. Dowry and public policy in contemporary India. *Human Nature* 18, no. 3: 242–263.

Stearns, S. C. 1992. *The evolution of life histories.* Oxford: Oxford University Press.

Trivers, R. L. 1972. Parental investment and sexual selection. In B. Campbell, ed., *Sexual selection and the descent of man, 1871–1971,* 136–179. Chicago: Aldine.

Voland, E. 1998. Evolutionary ecology of human reproduction. *Annual Review of Anthropology* 27:347–374.

———. 2007. Evolutionary psychology meets history: Insights into human nature through family reconstruction studies. In R. L. M. Dunbar and L. Barrett, eds., *The Oxford handbook of evolutionary psychology,* 415–432. Oxford: Oxford University Press.

Voland, E., and R. Dunbar. 1995. Resource competition and reproduction: The relationship between economic and parental strategies in the Krumhörn population. *Human Nature* 6:33–49.

Von Foerster, H., P. M. Mora, and L. W. Amiot. 1960. Doomsday: Friday, 13 November, A.D. 2026. *Science* 132, no. 3436: 1291–1295.

Westneat, D. F., and I. R. K. Stewart. 2003. Extra-pair paternity in birds: Causes, correlates, and conflict. *Annual Review of Ecology, Evolution, and Systematics* 34:365–396.

Wilke, A., J. M. C. Hutchinson, and P. M. Todd. 2003. Human mate preference for risky behavior: Male risk-taking as an indicator of mate quality. Paper presented at the 15th Annual Human Behavior and Evolution Meeting, Lincoln, Nebraska.

Wilke, A., J. M. C. Hutchinson, P. M. Todd, and D. Kruger. 2006. Is risk-taking used as a cue in mate choice? *Evolutionary Psychology* 4:367–393.

Wilson, M., and M. Daly. 1997. Life expectancy, economic inequality, homicide, and reproductive timing in Chicago neighbourhoods. *British Medical Journal* 314, no. 7089: 1271–1274.

Wrigley, E. A., and R. Schofield. 1981. *The population history of England, 1541–1871.* Cambridge: Cambridge University Press.

A Gender Lens on Marriage

THREE

PAULA ENGLAND

What are the ways in which marriage is "gendered," and what are the implications of this for gender inequality? To answer this, I first describe a broad perspective on gender that has many adherents among sociologists of gender—a view of gender as operating at multiple levels from individual to institutional. I use this view to consider how normative and economic factors determine inequality of power within marriage—the ability to get what one wants even when the partner's wishes conflict. I consider how norms and partners' earnings affect who does more housework, whose wants determine purchases, and who is a victim of violence. I then reflect on how "the retreat from marriage," which includes increases in divorce, but especially later age at marriage, has affected gender inequality in power and well-being. I consider this separately by class, because delayed marriage much more frequently comes with nonmarital childbearing among the poor than the affluent. I suggest that women have more autonomy in a society in which many individuals spend a good share of their adult life unmarried, but that, in such a low-marriage regime, women also bear more of the costs of childrearing, especially among the poor.

A MULTILEVEL GENDER PERSPECTIVE

An emerging consensus among sociologists is that gender operates at multiple levels. The sociology of gender has as its starting point the claim that sex differences are not entirely innate or "hard-wired." One view is that early socialization in the family and elsewhere leads to internalization of norms, preferences, skills, and habits that differ by gender. This view features a social process that affects individuals early in life, leading to gendered individual selves, from which gendered roles in marriage and work flow. However, the last two decades of the sociology of gender could be summarized as a diatribe against this position for being "too individual."

The criticism of overly individualistic views of gender is associated with phrases such as "doing gender" (West and Zimmerman 1987), "gender as social structure" (Risman 2004; see also Risman 1987), and "gender as institution" (Martin 2004). Part of the claim is that the causative social processes extend beyond youth in the life cycle, that is, that gender differences keep getting reinforced from sources external to the individual at all ages. The related claim is that larger cultural, institutional, and macrostructural forces are involved. Sociologists are sometimes downright murky about what they mean by "institution" or "structure," as Risman (2004) has pointed out. Moreover, some statements of these positions have surely erred in the extent to which they minimize the impact of gendered individual selves as part of the mix, as England and Browne (1992) have observed. After some debate, the field is converging on a theoretical view that sees gender differences and inequalities to be sustained at multiple levels and all across the life cycle, with the relative weight of each factor an empirical question, possibly differing by topic and time period.

In this multilevel view, biology and early socialization have effects, but they are not the whole story. At the interactional level, we all continually confront others' gender stereotypes that form prescriptions or expectations for our behavior. Interactional social psychologists have documented that encountering such expectations affects beliefs and behavior in ways that perpetuate gender inequalities (Ridgeway and Correll 2004). Others focusing on the interactional level coined the term "doing gender" to denote actions taken to display our gendered selves in order to "make sense" to others presumed to hold dominant gender norms (West and Zimmerman 1987). The organizational level comes in when, even if explicit organizational policies do not disadvantage women, cultural beliefs about what men and women can and should do lead to discrimination by decision makers in the workplace (Ridgeway and England 2007). The multilevel view of gender also posits effects of organizational and state policies that explicitly dictate gender-differentiated rewards. More subtly, but more frequent in modern societies, institutions are "gendered" when their rules are explicitly gender neutral but have disparate impacts by gender given a history that positions men and women in different situations. For example, state policies that collectivize costs of child rearing (through education, health care, child care, and so on) help women relative to men since otherwise women bear more of the costs of raising children. To take another example, Acker (1990) argued that expectations in high-level jobs were formed around the image of a male worker with a homemaker wife. This leads to work/family overload for both male and female professionals with employed partners, but especially for women where a culture of intensive childrearing focuses expectations on women more than men (Hayes 1996).

The multilevel view of gender includes consideration of power as well as norms. Sociologists' definitions of power vary (and are sometimes murky), but generally they consider actors or groups to have power to the extent that they can get what they want even against the wishes of another actor or group. Power can flow from structural position, from networks, or from money.

APPLYING THE GENDER PERSPECTIVE TO GENDER INEQUALITY IN MARRIAGE

In this section, I use the multilevel sociological gender perspective to explain gender inequality within marriage, focusing on the role of partners' earnings and of norms, and their interaction. I start with a view that comes from economists but can be seen as part of the broader multilevel view. In Becker's (1991) view of specialization and gains from trade, there is nothing seen as disadvantageous for women's utility. Becker posits that specialization of spouses, with one more in market and one more in household work, is undertaken because it is efficient. When combined with an assumption about the altruism of the head, the fact that one person brings in and thus controls the money is not seen to affect outcomes adversely for the other (generally the woman).

A different economic approach is taken by bargaining models, which come from game theory (Lundberg and Pollak 1996). Here spouses' relative wage rates, or, more generally, "threat points" are seen to matter. Bringing in more money (relative to what your partner brings in) is seen to increase one's bargaining power in the marriage. In external-threat-point models, this is because one's own earnings affect what one would have to fall back on if the marriage dissolved. In this view, a person's bargaining power is also affected by any wealth or state payments she or he would have access to if the marriage dissolved, as well as by one's attractiveness on the remarriage market. The better off one would be outside marriage, the better a deal from the partner one requires to stay in the marriage. In internal-threat-point models, the importance of who earns money is that they can decide whether to pool it with the partner in joint funds or use it for one's own wishes and this provides some leverage over expenditures and other decisions.

Contrasting the bargaining models with the Beckerian specialization and gains to trade model, the latter emphasizes the gains to both spouses of specialization (through efficiency), while the former theories imply that, whatever the possible efficiency advantages of a traditional gender division of labor, it clearly disadvantages the ability of those with lower earnings, usually women, to bargain for what they want in their relationships.[1] Bargaining models illuminate a possible source of gender inequality better and are very similar to the sociological view of power proposed by exchange theory. It, too, proposes that the economic resources one contributes to a marriage affect how much one's spouse will have to accommodate to one's wishes (see Bittman et al. 2003 for a review). It can thus be seen as part of a multilevel model of the sources of gender inequality.

As described earlier, sociologists also see cultural norms as important but generally eschew a view that sees norms as deeply internalized in childhood and thereby carried exclusively on the individual. The preferred view is that various social forces keep reproducing gendered norms and behavior (Ridgeway and Correll 2004; Risman 1998), although few studies of couples give us good purchase on how much or how early norms are internalized, versus how much they are followed in deference to others' contemporaneous expectations even when the actor does not agree with their prescriptions. Thus, when I discuss evidence that suggests a role of norms, I am agnostic on how deeply internalized are the norms being followed. While the multilevel view also stresses the causal role of public policy and other institutions' policies, the specific literature I review here will narrow the scope to examine the roles of earning power and norms, and not analyze the many ways that earnings and norms are affected by institutions and public policy. For example, relative earnings of husbands and wives may be affected by how much public policy encourages women's employment and how aggressively it roots out gender discrimination by employers, but I will not go into these causal pathways here.

Studies that are interpretable in terms of power are those where the outcome studied is one for which it is reasonable to assume we know what people want. It seems a safe assumption that most people (1) prefer to do less housework (which may mean having partners do more), (2) prefer expenditures on items they will use (so, for example, women will prefer expenditures on women's relative to men's clothes), and (3) prefer not be beaten or hit.[2] Thus, I will consider studies of these outcomes, looking at effects of relative earnings and indirect evidence of the role of norms.

How do or should studies measure relative earnings? Economists use wage rates, not weekly or annual earnings, which are affected by labor supply as well as the wage rate. In their view, what is relevant to threat points is what one *could* earn. They also make the simplifying assumption that individuals have a wage rate and can increase their hours at that rate at will. Sociologists usually use relative annual earnings, presumably assuming that it is money actually brought "to the table" that brings power in the relationship. Of course, if spouse A is employed full time and B part-time or not at all, when A does less housework this may have little to do with money-based power but be a matter of available time within an agreed-upon division of labor. Thus, it is important for analyses to control for each spouse's hours worked for pay in models purporting to show effects of relative earnings.

HOUSEWORK

Exchange/bargaining theory predicts that as Partner A has higher relative earnings, A will do less and B will do more housework.[3] Consistent with this, in the range between husbands providing all the earnings and spouses having equal earnings, net of hours worked in the market, several studies covering the United States, Sweden, and Australia show that as women gain earnings they do less housework (Brines 1994; Bittman et al. 2003; Evertsson and Nermo 2004). The same studies show that as women earn relatively more, men do a bit more housework, but the increment is small and nonsignificant in Australia.

However, there is substantial indirect evidence for a role for norms, whether internalized or of the "doing gender" variety. Something other than economic dependence is leading women to do more housework, because women typically do more than is fully explained by the earnings differential (Bittman et al. 2003).

Sometimes norms and economic power interact. Recent literature focuses on a particular prediction about gendered norms or doing gender—a tendency of women or men to engage in *compensatory* gender display in one area, housework, when they are violating gender norms in another area, relative earnings. (The norms are not observed but inferred in these studies.) If this is true, then in some parts of the distribution of relative earnings, where women earn more than their male partners, the prediction is the opposite of what exchange/bargaining theory predicts. Recall that in the range between equality and men earning all a couple's annual income, relative earnings reduce a spouse's housework (especially for women). But the same three studies show that in the range between equality and women earning it all, in the United States and Australia, housework gets more traditional, either through men doing less as their relative earnings decrease in this range, or through women doing more as men's relative earnings decrease. Norms are kicking in to increase gender traditionality as if in compensation for the gender deviance of the woman earning more than the man. This phenomenon, while fascinating theoretically, has received more attention than its magnitude merits. First, commentators sometimes forget that the relationship opposite to that predicted by exchange theory exists only for the small percentage of cases where women earn more than their husbands; in the rest of the range, the more women earn, the less housework they do. Moreover, the impact of relative earnings or any other variables on men's housework is quite small, and the evidence for men's compensatory gender display is very reliant on a small proportion of outliers (Gupta 1999; Bittmann et al. 2003; Evertsson and Nermo 2004).

Gupta (2006, 2007) has recently reoriented thinking about what affects women's housework. He argues that it is not women's relative but their absolute earnings that dictate their housework. After experimenting with many specifications, his results suggest that it is women's absolute earnings (up to at least to a threshold of about $30,000 a year) that affect their housework, not their earnings relative to their spouses. If both relative earnings and women's absolute earnings are put in the same equation, women's absolute earnings persist while relative earnings show no significant effect on women's housework. A husband's earnings do not reduce a woman's housework as much as her own earnings do (controlling for both spouses' hours of employment), so the issue is not merely family income. Why, when employment hours are held constant, do women do less housework as their absolute earnings go up? One possibility is that as women earn more money, they replace more of their own services with services bought in the market—for example, by buying takeout food instead of cooking.[4] Perhaps earnings give her the bargaining power to do less housework by spending on things that replace housework, but greater bargaining power does not get the husband to do more housework. This suggests that norms ridiculing men for doing "female" housework constrain what money-based bargaining can achieve.

EXPENDITURES AND CONSUMPTION

The same bargaining power flowing from women's earnings that reduces their housework may also permit them to make household expenditures on items they want. In a similar vein, Lundberg, Pollak, and Wales (1997) show that a change in British law toward making the child allowance payable to wives rather than be included in a husband's paycheck led to an increase in the purchase of both women's and children's clothing relative to men's clothing in the affected households. Assuming that women are more interested in women's (and possibly children's) clothing than are men, the results are consistent with bargaining theory in that the change increased women's relative personal income, but also consistent with the possibility (as Gupta has found for housework) that it is women's absolute rather than relative income that matters, since the policy change at issue in this analysis also entailed an increase in the absolute income of women.[5]

VIOLENCE

Let us assume that some proportion of people are tempted to be violent, at least occasionally, and that most people would prefer not to be hit; then the prediction of exchange/bargaining theory is that one's relative resources decrease one's victimization. One study (Anderson 1997) uses a national probability survey to examine the effect of relative earnings of partners on his and her domestic violence, as reported by either the victim or both partners. She is probably largely tapping what Michael Johnson (see chapter 11 in this volume) calls "situational couple violence." While this type of violence is generally less severe and controlling than what Johnson has dubbed "intimate terrorism," it surely reduces the well-being of victims. For example, one study found that 29 percent of women who had experienced situational couple violence had sustained a serious injury.[6] After controlling for household income, age, race, and whether it is a cohabitation or marriage, Anderson (1997) finds that increases in married or cohabiting women's relative earnings have little or no effect on his or her violence in the range between her complete dependence and equality, contrary to what I suggested as an exchange/bargaining prediction. In contrast, in the range between equality and women earning much more than men, as the woman's relative earnings go up, both men's and women's violence increases. While the increase in women's violence in this range is consistent with bargaining/exchange theory (although it begs the question of why there is no effect in the range below her earnings being equal), the increase in men's violence is not consistent with bargaining/exchange theory. Rather, men's violence increasing as their female partners' earnings go more above theirs could be interpreted in terms of compensatory gender display; men compensate for their violation of gender norms dictating that they should earn more than women with violence. Another possible interpretation is that men use violence to get power when they cannot get it through their earnings, and women's violence in these couples is defensive.

Christina Gibson-Davis and her colleagues (2005) use experimental data from a number of welfare to work random-assignment experiments. Findings for these low-income mothers are of interest because of the high rates of victimization by violence they report. The study's causal inference is especially strong because employment is measured with an instrumental variable predicted from the respondent's random assignment into control or treatment group, and thus is probably exogenous. Women's employment, instrumented from random assignment into experimental conditions, reduced women's reports of domestic violence.[7] In some states the effect of employment probably came through increased earnings, although we do not know if it was her absolute earnings or hers relative to her partner's. In other states, the gains from women's employment did not lead to enough earnings to offset losses from welfare, so the program should not have increased women's threat point, but still their experience of violence was reduced. In these cases, the authors suggest that employment effects came through increasing women's expectation of their future earning power. These results are not consistent with those of Anderson (1997), since her analysis suggested that women's economic superiority increases violence. Gibson-Davis et al. 2005 use experimental data, so that the authors' causal claim is more solid; however, they did not test for the nonlinearity found by Anderson, in which women's earnings only hurt when above their partner's. Thus, the question of how partners' relative earnings affect violence is unresolved.

IS A HIGH-MARRIAGE OR LOW-MARRIAGE SYSTEM BETTER FOR GENDER EQUALITY?

The alternative to marriage is being single, but individuals have a whole life course over which they may be married or single, possibly in alternation. Changes in recent decades toward less marriage are really changes in the proportion of the average person's life cycle spent married, especially to one coparent. While such change has affected all social classes, the changes have wrought qualitatively different life-cycle patterns for those of higher and lower socioeconomic status (SES).

College graduates are marrying later, often cohabiting before marriage, and having their first child later, but they show little change since 1960 in either the probability of ever marrying or in waiting till after marriage for childbearing (Ellwood and Jencks 2004). While there is debate about the causal order, the combination of birth control, later marriage, completing more education, and starting a career is associated with more continuous labor-force participation and earnings for women. Indeed, married college-educated mothers are more likely to be employed than less educated mothers, despite their higher-earning husbands, and because of their higher employment, their annual earnings are closer to those of their male partners (England, Gornick, and Schafer 2007). The bargaining/exchange perspective suggests that this makes their marriages more equal. Hence, delayed marriage, where the delay is associated not with nonmarital childbearing but with increased education, probably increases gender equality in the labor market and the family.[8] Indeed, mothers with high education are much more likely to be employed than those with less education, presumably because they can get better jobs. But it is notable that their higher employment is despite being more apt to be married to high earning men (Cotter, Hermsen, and England 2008). Thus, to the extent that women's earnings help their power within marriage, marriages may be more egalitarian among the more highly educated.

The decline of marriage has played out differently in less privileged segments of the population. All classes have moved to later marriage, but for those without a college degree this change has been accompanied by elevated rates of nonmarital childbearing (Ellwood and Jencks 2004). While about four-fifths of nonmarital births are to couples still romantically involved at the birth (half to cohabitors), and many express hopes of marrying the coparent, most do not marry, and many break up. About half of those born to cohabitors and about three-quarters of those born to parents in a relationship but not coresiding are broken up within five years (England and Edin 2007, chapter 1). Many then go on to have a child with one or more partners in future unions. Thus, lower on the class hierarchy, the retreat from marriage is associated with a life-course pattern of early childbearing outside marriage within partnerships that often break up. Women alternate between spending time as single parents and in coresidential unions with new men who are not the father of their first child or children. Men alternate between living in households without female partners or children and coresidential unions in households that include other men's children, as well as their own child or children by the current partner. For low SES individuals, this is the most frequent *actual* counterfactual to the previous higher marriage regime.

Is this move from a higher to lower marriage regime for those at lower SES levels good or bad for gender inequality? That is, holding constant the social class background disadvantages they bring into adulthood,[9] are women better off (relative to men) in a system where they are married to the father of their children during childbearing, or alternating periods of single motherhood and cohabitation with men, who, after the first, are stepfathers to some or all of their children?[10] This question has multiple parts (see also England 2000).

Since the lower SES decline in marriage involves a higher ratio of cohabitation to marriage, particularly after childbearing, one part of examining its implications for gender equality entails a comparison of cohabitation and marriage. Unfortunately, most studies comparing cohabitation and marriage do not make the comparison separately for those with and without children. One recent qualitative study, the TLC3 (Time, Love, and Cash Among Couples with Children) study does limit itself to unmarried parents who had a child in 2000 and were still romantically involved at the birth (England and Edin 2007). De facto, most were cohabiting and had low incomes. The study included questions about whether or not they wanted to marry, the conditions under which they would marry, and what they thought would change if they married (Gibson-Davis 2007; Reed 2006). Gibson-Davis shows that, as long as they are still romantically involved, unmarried parents almost always see marriage to the other parent as something they aspire to, but they do not want to marry until a certain economic bar is met.[11] It is as if marriage is simply not respectable without a certain economic level attained first, a threshold higher than is applied to decisions about whether to have sex that might risk a pregnancy. Parents also said that moving from cohabitation to marriage requires being really sure about the quality of the relationship; many are not sure enough to make this commitment, despite having a child together. There was little sense of one sex wanting to move to marriage more than the other. On the issue of gender equality, while not a major theme in their narratives, some women feared men would expect to have more authority over them if they married, and they put this on the negative side of the ledger.[12] Despite this association in their minds between patriarchal rights and marriage, I do not believe that fears of gender inequality are a major reason that low-income women put off marriage. Rather, the sexual revolution made marriage more optional, and cultural standards for marriage have changed to create a higher relational and economic bar to marriage, one that lower SES Americans often cannot meet (Cherlin 2004; England and Edin 2007, chapter 1).

Even if gender inequality does not *explain* reluctance to move to marriage, it is important to consider whether or not marriage is *actually* more patriarchal than cohabitation. Too few of the cohabiting parents in the TLC3 study married to give us any purchase on the question. Existing quantitative evidence suggests that marriage is probably neither less nor more egalitarian than cohabitation, although such studies combine parents and nonparents of all social classes, so we cannot be sure how much it applies to low-income parents who experience nonmarital births. One study shows little difference between cohabitation and marriage in how housework is shared, using within-person comparisons to remove the effects of selectivity of the more gender-liberal into cohabitation. Gupta (1999) shows that men's housework declines and women's increases upon entering a coresidential union, but the change is about the same whether they are entering a marriage or a cohabitation, and the change for either sex when moving from cohabitation to marriage is nonsignificant. What about violence? Anderson (1997) shows that cohabitations involve more violence than marriage. However, Kenney and McLanahan (2006), using the same data set, make it clear that cohabitational status does not *cause* a relationship to be more violent. Rather, the best relationships move most quickly to marriage, and because these couples had the least probability of violence whether they were married or not, their transition to marriage leaves the more violent relationships in the pool of cohabitors we observe in any cross-sectional comparison.[13] If women are hurt more by violent relationships than men are, then the implication of the study is that moving violent cohabiting couples to marriage would neither reduce nor increase women's risk of being hurt from violence.

An important difference between a high-marriage and low-marriage regime is how much men help women with the time and money costs of rearing children. In a low-marriage regime, the mother spends much more of her childbearing years in a household that does not include the father of some or all of her children. In such cases, even with good child support enforcement, the father provides less money and childcare time than when they live in the household. Even if new social fathers provide for her children, she is likely to spend considerable time between relationships, during which she provides most all of the care and the money for rearing her child. So, overall, the retreat from marriage decreases men's monetary and time contributions to the costs of childrearing. In this sense it increases gender inequality. This is particularly true in the United States, where the state has collectivized fewer of the costs of childrearing. Where societies have state provision of childcare, medical care for children, family allowances, and parental leave, paid for through progressive taxation, this shifts some of the costs of childbearing from poor to rich and women to men.

CONCLUSION

I have applied a multilevel gender perspective to marriage and considered how cultural meanings and unequal earnings create unequal power in marriages. Studies suggest that as women move from very low relative earnings to some threshold, they decrease their housework, even holding market work hours constant. Whether this threshold is equal relative earnings or about $30,000 in absolute earnings is under debate, but above the threshold women's earnings do not reduce their housework. In the range where earnings reduce women's housework, it is not that they increase men's housework much, suggesting that what earnings give women is the power to buy substitutes for their own housework. Other evidence also suggests that when income comes in through a check to a woman, expenditures reflect her interests more. Evidence on whether women's earnings reduce or increase their exposure to domestic violence is contradictory. Overall, the findings suggest that earning power and norms interact such that the more gender-nonnormative the situation is, the less women's money can "talk" in a way that advances her interests, especially if this entails changing men's behavior in a more traditionally female direction.

I have also considered here which is better for gender equality, a high-marriage or low-marriage regime, finding that the answer is not clear. Moving the same couple from cohabitation to marriage does little to help or hinder women's freedom from either housework or violence. The lower marriage regime has the advantage for women of all classes of entailing more socially acceptable exits from—and alternatives to—troubled relationships. Of course, by the same token, it legitimizes men leaving women who do not want to be left.

At higher SES levels, the retreat from marriage has mainly entailed cohabitation before marriage while education and careers are solidified, and later marriage followed by childbearing. The move to later marriages has probably increased the gender equality that ensues after marriage. This is partly because the late marriage enhances the chance that the relationship will last and fathers will share the costs of childrearing. It is also because late marriage allows higher education, which contributes to women's employment, thus allowing well-educated women to reap some of power-equalizing fruits of earning power within marriage. At lower SES levels, childbearing is now in less stable unions, and a woman's life cycle includes cohabitation with fathers and stepfathers of her children as well as spells of single motherhood. Here, the low-marriage regime has the disadvantage for gender equality of leading women to bear a higher proportion of the costs of childrearing, especially given how little the United States has collectivized those costs.

NOTES

1. One might wonder why women's domestic work, at least that on behalf of the children, does not count for anything in this game-theoretic calculus. England and Kilbourne (1990) argue that it will lead to no bargaining power if it is assumed that women will do it even if the marriage dissolves or the bargaining breaks down. One could argue that the fact that men know they will lose the ability to live with their children in the event of breakup increases women's bargaining power, but this may not be true in most of the existing range of variation in how parents divide care.
2. One example of the analytical difficulty in inferring power from outcomes in the absence of clear evidence on what individuals want is that, if norms create gender differences in preferences, then gendered outcomes may reflect these different preferences rather than unequal bargaining power. So, for example, while it seems safe to assume that most of us would rather have someone else clean the toilet, it is less clear how much time caring for children people prefer, and how much gender differences in such time reflect preferences versus power.

3. Becker's specialization and gains from trade model is sometimes depicted as having this same prediction that relative wage rates drive how the couple will decide that it is jointly optimal to divide household and market work. Here, however, relative wage rates are seen to determine whether the next hour will be spent in household versus market production. Bargaining/exchange models speak, rather, to leisure versus housework, conditional on a given number of employment hours.
4. The fact that the effect begins at 0 and levels out below the median suggests that it is not driven by housecleaning or nanny services, which require high incomes to purchase.
5. The finding is consistent with internal but not external threat point models from bargaining theory. The change in which spouse was sent the family allowance did not change women's or men's threat-point situations; women received the allowance in the event of divorce if they had child custody both before and after the policy change.
6. The comparable figure for men was 6 percent. Michael Johnson, personal communication, September 2007. See also chapter 11 in this volume.
7. The authors argue that the effects are not entirely through earnings allowing women to leave violent relationships, since control/experimental group differences in partnership status were small at either baseline or follow-up.
8. Increases in divorce are also part of a lower marriage regime, and divorce, while always higher at lower education and income levels, increased dramatically in all classes in the 1960s and 1970s. In marriages contracted since then, it appears that divorce rates have declined again for women with college degrees, bringing them back down almost to their 1960s levels, while they have stayed high for those with less education (Martin 2006). Thus, as with nonmarital childbearing, the trends have increased discrepancies by class in how much women are either single mothers or in unions with someone other than the father of all or some of their children.
9. Of course, many argue that marriage causes individuals' incomes to be higher. It is probably true that if women forgo early nonmarital childbearing, their chance of higher later earnings and marriage to a higher-earning man go up, although the extent of any such causal effect is surely much less than the observed association of early childbearing and later disadvantage; much of the later disadvantage of women who have early nonmarital births is rooted in their early family disadvantage.
10. Kamp Dush suggests that stable single parent families may be better for children than a succession of two-adult partnerships, in part because transitions are stressful. One could analyze these two distinct patterns for gender equality differences as well. But I do not do so here, inasmuch as I think that what is common among those with nonmarital births is moving between these statuses.
11. My reading of these transcripts convinces me that the counterfactual most individuals had in their minds to getting married to this partner was remaining in a

cohabiting union with this partner, not breaking up to search for a better partner (although some ended up doing this). The economic bar did not appear to be about mate selection but about the meaning of marriage.

12. Edin's (2000) qualitative-interview study with poor single mothers, only some of whom were cohabiting, found this theme even more strongly.
13. Violent cohabitations break up more than other cohabitations, which biases cross-sectional comparisons from marriage the opposite way, but the transitions to marriage among those low on violence bias the cross-sectional comparison more (Kenney and McLanahan 2006). Kenney and McLanahan (2006) and Anderson (1997) used the National Survey of Families and Households.

REFERENCES

Acker, J. 1990. Hierarchies, jobs, and bodies: A theory of gendered organizations. *Gender and Society* 4:139–159.

Anderson, K. L. 1997. Gender, status, and domestic violence: An integration of feminist and family violence approaches. *Journal of Marriage and the Family* 59:655–669.

Becker, G. 1991. *A treatise on the family.* Rev. ed. Cambridge, Mass: Harvard University Press.

Bittman, M., P. England, L. Sayer, N. Folbre, and G. Matheson. 2003. When does gender trump money? Bargaining and time in household work. *American Journal of Sociology* 109:186–214.

Brines, J. 1994. Economic dependency, gender and the division of labor at home. *American Journal of Sociology* 100:652–688.

Cherlin, A. 2004. The deinstitutionalization of American marriage. *Journal of Marriage and Family* 66:848–861.

Cotter, D., J. Hermsen, and P. England. 2008. Moms and jobs: Trends in mothers' employment and which mothers stay home. In S. Coontz, M. Parson, and G. Raley, eds., *American families: A multicultural reader*, 379–386. New York: Routledge.

Edin, K. 2000. What do low-income single mothers say about marriage? *Social Problems* 47:112–133.

Ellwood, D. T., and C. Jencks. 2004. The spread of single-parent families in the United States since 1960. In D. P. Moynihan, T. M. Smeeding, and L. Rainwater, eds., *The future of the family*, 25–65. New York: Russell Sage Foundation.

England, P. 2000. Marriage, the costs of children, and gender inequality. In L. Waite, C. Bachrach, M. Hindin, E. Thomson, and A. Thornton, eds., *The ties that bind: Perspectives on marriage and cohabitation*, 320–342. New York: Aldine.

England, P., and I. Browne. 1992. Internalization and constraint in theories of women's subordination. *Current Perspectives in Social Theory* 12:97–123.

England, P., and K. Edin. 2007. *Unmarried couples with children.* New York: Russell Sage Foundation.

England, P., J. Gornick, and E. Shafer. 2007. How women's employment and the gender earnings gap vary by education: Common patterns across affluent nations. Presented at the annual meeting of the Population Association of America, New York.

England, P., and B. Kilbourne. 1990. Markets, marriage, and other mates: The problem of power. In R. Friedland and S. Robertson, eds., *Beyond the marketplace: Society and economy,* 163–188. New York: Aldine.

Evertsson, M., and M. Nermo. 2004. Dependence within families and the division of labor: Comparing Sweden and the United States. *Journal of Marriage and Family* 66:1272–1286.

Gibson-Davis, C. M. 2007. Expectations and the economic bar to marriage among low income couples. In P. England and K. Edin, eds., *Unmarried couples with children,* 84–103. New York: Russell Sage Foundation.

Gibson-Davis, C. M., K. Magnuson, L. A. Gennetian, and G. J. Duncan. 2005. Employment and the risk of domestic abuse among low-income women. *Journal of Marriage and Family* 67:1149–1168.

Gupta, S. 1999. The effects of transitions in marital status on men's performance of housework. *Journal of Marriage and the Family* 61:700–711.

———. 2006. Her money, her time: Women's earnings and their housework hours. *Social Science Research* 35:975–999.

———. 2007. Autonomy, dependence, or display? The relationship between married women's earnings and housework. *Journal of Marriage and Family* 69:399–417.

Hays, S. 1996. *The cultural contradictions of motherhood.* New Haven: Yale University Press.

Kenney, C., and S. McLanahan. 2006. Why are cohabiting relationships more violent than marriage? *Demography* 43, no. 1: 127–140.

Lundberg, S., and R. A. Pollack. 1996. Bargaining and distribution in marriage. *Journal of Economic Perspectives* 10:139–158.

Lundberg, S., R. A. Pollak, and T. J. Wales. 1997. Do husbands and wives pool their resources? Evidence from the UK child benefit. *Journal of Human Resources* 32, no. 3: 463–480.

Martin, P. Y. 2004. Gender as social institution. *Social Forces* 82:1249–1273.

Martin, S. P. 2006. Trends in marital dissolution by women's education in the United States. *Demographic Research* 15, no. 20: 537–560.

Reed, J. 2006. Not crossing the "extra line": How cohabitors with children view their unions. *Journal of Marriage and Family* 68:1117–1131.

Ridgeway, C., and P. England. 2007. Sociological approaches to sex discrimination in employment. In F. J. Crosby, M. S. Stockdale, and S. A. Ropp, eds., *Sex discrimination in the workplace,* 189–211. Oxford: Blackwell.

Ridgeway, C., and S. J. Correll. 2004. Unpacking the gender system: A theoretical perspective on cultural beliefs and social relations. *Gender and Society* 18:510–531.

Risman, B. 1987. Intimate relationships from a microstructural perspective: Mothering men. *Gender and Society* 1:6–32.

———. 1998. *Gender vertigo: American families in transition.* New Haven: Yale University Press.

———. 2004. Gender as social structure. *Gender and Society* 18: 429–450.

West, C., and D. H. Zimmerman. 1987. Doing gender. *Gender and Society* 1:125–151.

FOUR

Institutional, Companionate, and Individualistic Marriage

A Social Psychological Perspective on Marital Change

PAUL R. AMATO

After fifty years of profound change in marriage and family life in the United States, this is an appropriate time to look back and ask, "What happened?" As other chapters in this volume point out, during the last half of the twentieth century, the divorce rate increased, the percentage of children born outside of marriage rose, cohabitation became common as a prelude (or as an alternative) to marriage, the age at marriage increased, the percentage of people remarrying after divorce decreased, and the percentage of people projected to ever marry declined. Taken collectively, these changes indicate that marriage has become a less central part of the life course for many Americans. Yet, paradoxically, the great majority of young adults plan to marry, and marriage continues to have important symbolic value within our culture.

As family scholars, our ability to explain these changes has been underwhelming. The full explanation is likely to be complex, and it will be necessary to draw on a variety of disciplines to understand the extraordinary shifts that occurred during the last half-century. In this chapter, I contribute some ideas on marital change from a social-psychological perspective. My perspective is meant to complement rather than compete with other perspectives presented in this volume. Historical, demographic, economic, and sociological viewpoints all have a role to play in clarifying the past, current, and future status of marriage.

SOCIAL PSYCHOLOGICAL PERSPECTIVE ON MARITAL CHANGE

Social psychology is a broad field that contains many theories. Some of them, such as exchange theory (Levinger 1976), cognitive dissonance theory (Amato and Rogers 1999), and social network theory (Sprecher et al. 2002), have been used to study marriage. Rather than rely on one particular theory, however, I draw on a variety of constructs that appear commonly in the social psychological literature and attempt to weave them into a micro-level perspective on recent shifts in marriage.

I begin with the assumption that marriage as a social institution—a fundamental element of social organization—has been affected by a large number of historical, social, demographic, and economic factors. A short list of these factors would include increasing urbanism, greater geographical dispersion of kin networks, the rising labor force participation of wives, the introduction of the birth-control pill in the 1960s, changes in patterns of immigration, and government policies, such as the provision of mass education for children and social security for the elderly. These large-scale changes shape micro-level processes, including the daily face-to-face interactions of spouses and the cognitions and emotional states experienced by individuals. New social arrangements make possible the rise of new ideas—ideas that would not have made sense in an earlier era. Changes in the perceptions, beliefs, and feelings of millions of individuals, when aggregated, represent change in marriage at the societal level. In general, social psychological processes underlie and mediate shifts in the organization and functioning of large-scale social institutions.

A social-psychological perspective gives a prominent role to culture. Although many social scientists think of culture as a macro-level construct, culture is primarily intrapsychic. That is, culture consists of beliefs, attitudes, values, meanings, and expectations that exist in the minds of individuals. Because the contents of culture are shared among large numbers of people, culture is also inherently social. The *culture of marriage* involves shared beliefs, attitudes, values, meanings, and expectations about marriage. These elements usually come together to form a logically consistent understanding (or gestalt) of marriage. The culture of marriage has shifted over time, but a particular cultural ideal has been dominant in the United States during most historical periods. Not all members of a society, however, share all cultural constructs, and specific aspects of culture can differ—often sharply—between particular groups in the population. At present, a variety of groups with opposing views are contesting the culture of marriage, and there is probably less consensus about the nature of marriage now that at any time in our country's past.

THREE TYPES OF MARRIAGE

Family scholars have described three types of marriage that were dominant at different times in American history. Ernest Burgess, a sociologist who wrote extensively on marriage and family life in the middle of the twentieth century, argued that marriage was gradually transforming from a social institution to a private relationship based on companionship (Burgess, Locke, and Thomes 1963; Burgess and Wallin 1953). By *institutional marriage*, Burgess meant a formal union that was strictly regulated by social norms, law, and religion. In contrast, the emerging form of marriage, which he referred to as *companionate marriage*, was based primarily on the emotional bonds between spouses.

Until the late nineteenth century, the United States was predominantly rural, and most people lived and worked on family farms. During this era, marriage was essential to the welfare of family members and the larger community. Family members relied on one another to meet basic needs, including economic production, childcare, education, and elder care. Marriage also created ties between families that facilitated the sharing of resources. For example, a good match might involve a daughter from one family and a son from a second family that shared adjacent farmland. Although the United States did not have a system of arranged marriages (like those in other agricultural societies such as India), parents had a great deal of influence over their children's marital choices. Because cohesive and interconnected families were necessary for survival, the community had an interest in ensuring the stability of the family unit. Consequently, society was strongly opposed to divorce unless it was absolutely necessary (for example, in cases of serious physical abuse). The stability of the family was more important than the needs of individual family members. Indeed, spouses in institutional marriages were expected not only to conform to traditional standards of behavior, but also to sacrifice their personal needs, if necessary, for the sake of their marriages. Because marriages were patriarchal, wives typically sacrificed more than did husbands. Nevertheless, through marriage, men and women participated in an arrangement that was essential for their own survival and for the continuation of society itself.

By the beginning of the twentieth century, the United States had become an industrialized nation, and urban two-parent breadwinner-homemaker families replaced farm families as the dominant family form (Hernandez 1993). During this time, several factors allowed individuals to have greater control over their marriages, including the geographical mobility of young adults (which freed them from the control of parents and the kin group) and a decline in religious control (which resulted in more freedom to adopt unconventional views and behaviors). Moreover, during the twentieth century, the growth of economic opportunities for women gave adult daughters more economic independence from their parents and wives more economic independence from their husbands. Spouses continued to value marital stability, but they also recognized that divorce was sometimes a necessary (although unfortunate) solution to a seriously troubled relationship.

As the rules surrounding marriage relaxed, a new idea gained prominence. Instead of a code of strict obligations to others, marriage was now based on ties of mutual affection between spouses. People have always expected marriage to contain elements of affection and emotional support. But the notion that marriage should be based primarily on love is relatively recent (Coontz 2005). This vision of marriage reached its zenith with the homemaker-breadwinner marriages of the 1950s—a time when almost all Americans, irrespective of social class, accepted the companionate model of marriage as the cultural ideal (Mintz and Kellogg 1988). Although emotional bonds held these marriages together, spouses also obtained satisfaction from the fulfillment of complementary marital roles, such as breadwinner, homemaker, and parent. Husbands and wives worked together to achieve common goals, such as owning a home, attaining a decent standard of living, raising children, and maintaining mutually supportive unions. Although companionate marriages were less patriarchal than institutional marriages, husbands retained the role of "senior partner" in the relationship. Despite the continuation of gender inequality, successful teamwork was the hallmark of a good marriage.

Repeated cross-sectional surveys of university students provide evidence for a continuing shift away from institutional marriage. Beginning in 1939, college students ranked the importance of eighteen characteristics assumed to be important for marriage. In that year, love was ranked fifth by women and fourth by men. But by the 1970s (and continuing thereafter), women and men ranked love as the most important characteristic. For women and men, mutual attraction, education, intelligence, sociability, and good looks also increased in importance. Correspondingly, men attached less importance to their future wives being good housekeepers and cooks, and women attached less importance to their future husbands being ambitious or industrious (Buss et al. 2001). Another study of college students' expectations for marriage revealed a similar pattern (Barich and Bielby 1996). Between 1967 and 1994, students' expectations for "healthy and happy children," "moral and religious unity," and "maintenance of a home" declined in importance. In contrast, students' expectations for "companionship," "personality development," and "emotional security" increased in importance. These trends suggest that young adults today, compared with young adults in the recent past, attach less importance to the structural aspects of marriage (children, religion, and home) and more importance to the personal rewards and individual development that marriage makes possible.

Andrew Cherlin (2004) argued that the *deinstitutionalization* of marriage continued throughout the second half of the twentieth century. As a result, a third type of marriage, *individualistic marriage*, came to challenge the dominant companionate model. During the 1960s and 1970s, American culture shifted toward an ethic of "expressive individualism" (Bellah et al. 1985). These ideas were popularized by members of the Human Potential Movement, as reflected in the writings of psychologists such as Carl Rogers (1961) and Abraham Maslow (1962). This perspective assumes that people have an intrinsic need to express their innermost feelings, and that close relationships exist primarily to enhance individual happiness and maximize psychological growth. As these ideas grew in popularity, self-development and personal fulfillment came to replace mutual satisfaction and successful team effort as the basis of marriage. In individualistic marriage, love is necessary to form a union, but these unions are successful only to the extent that they meet each partner's innermost psychological needs. Indeed, personal fulfillment is the raison d'être for individualistic marriage. Consequently, if the union fails to meet one or both spouses' needs, then divorce is viewed as inevitable and necessary. Because it is difficult to attain a deep level of intimacy and foster self-development in an unequal relationship, these unions also tend to be relatively egalitarian with respect to gender.

Corresponding to the rise of individualistic marriage was a tendency for married couples to value privacy and disengage from other social groups and networks. Robert Putnam (2000) documented a trend during the last several decades for people to be less involved in community organizations, including civic organizations, political parties, recreational groups (for example, bowling teams), and church social groups. Consistent with this trend, Paul Amato, Alan Booth, David Johnson, and Stacy Rogers (2007) found that between 1980 and 2000, married individuals reported having fewer close friends and belonging to fewer organizations. Moreover, people reported having fewer close friends and group memberships *in common with their spouses.* The same study also found that spouses were less likely than in the past to eat dinner together, go out for recreation or leisure activities together, go shopping together, work on projects around the home together, or visit friends together. These trends are consistent with the notion that American culture in general—and marriage in particular—became increasingly individualistic during the second half of the twentieth century.

Table 4.1 summarizes how institutional, companionate, and individualistic marriages differ across a variety of characteristics. Although these types represent a historical progression, not all marriages during a given era fit the dominant model. For example, in the nineteenth century, when most marriages were institutional, some people married primarily for love. Similarly, it would be a mistake to assume that all spouses currently hold individualistic views on marriage. Many contemporary couples (especially those who are highly religious) continue to believe that the marriage contract is sacred and inviolable, and that a stable marriage is more important than personal happiness. Moreover, many marriages, now and in the past, contain a mixture of institutional, companionate, and individualistic features. Nevertheless, the three forms of marriage outlined in table 4.1 represent a useful heuristic for analyzing marital change.

These three forms of marriage can be conceptualized as "marriage schemata." Cognitive psychologists define a schema as a mental framework through which individuals perceive and interpret the world (Fiske 1984). People with an institutional schema believe that marriage exists to meet the practical needs of family members, value marriage as a source of security and community respectability, and expect to sacrifice their own needs to maintain the stability of the union. People with a companionate schema see marriage as a team of two individuals working to achieve common goals, value affection and companionship from their spouses, and expect their marriages to last for a lifetime—unless the ability to work together as a team breaks down irrevocably. Finally, people with an individualistic schema believe that marriage is a vehicle for achieving personal growth and development, value the opportunity to share intimacy with a soul mate, and expect their marriages to last as long as their personal needs are met. Seen in this light, the three marriage types are primarily mental in nature—organized structures of cognitions, values, meanings, and expectations that reside within people's minds. Because people are motivated to make their behavior consistent with their implicit understandings of the world, they attempt to construct marital relationships that reflect these understandings.

TABLE 4.1 Characteristics of Institutional, Companionate, and Individualistic Marriage

MARITAL CHARACTERISTICS	TYPE OF MARRIAGE		
	Institutional	Companionate	Individualistic
Social regulation (law, religion, norms)	Strict	Moderate	Minimal
Main purpose of marriage	Survival of family members and community	Successful teamwork to achieve goals	Individual happiness
Role of romantic love	Valued but not a prerequisite	Love as the basis of marriage	Spouse as soulmate
Expectations for personal fulfillment	Minimal	Moderate	Strong
Importance of marital stability	Necessary	Desirable	Optional
Commitment to union	Strong	Moderate	Weak
Social integration	Strong	Moderate	Weak
Couple power	Strict patriarchal	Husband as senior partner	Egalitarian

CLASHING CULTURES OF MARRIAGE

During the last few decades, a debate has occurred among family scholars over the status of marriage. Some family scholars are concerned that marriage has become too individualistic, weak, and unstable (e.g., Blankenhorn 1990; Glenn 1996; Popenoe 1996; Wilson 2002).

Although these observers do not agree on all issues, they believe that the excessive individualism of American culture has undermined marital quality and stability. For example, the emphasis on finding a soul mate to meet one's deepest needs for personal growth has raised people's expectations—unrealistically—for a spouse. In addition, because people enter relationships for personal gain, they are reluctant to make the self-sacrifices and investments necessary to maintain a marriage over the long run. Individualism also has led many people to believe that marriage is not always the best route to happiness, and that one's life goals can be achieved through individual effort rather than cooperative teamwork. As a result, they postpone or avoid marriage, cohabit rather than marry, and think that it is possible (or even desirable) to raise a child as a single parent, especially when a suitable spouse does not appear on the horizon. According to these scholars, the weakening of marriage has had generally negative consequences for adults, children, and society in general. Consequently, they argue that we should increase the social regulation of marriage (by, for example, introducing legal restrictions on no-fault divorce) and strengthen the values of commitment, obligation, and sacrifice in marriage. In other words, we need to *reinstitutionalize* many aspects of marriage.

Other family scholars are more sanguine about the current status of marriage (e.g., Coontz 1992, Scanzoni 2001; Skolnick 1991; Stacy 1996). These observers do not believe that people have become excessively individualistic or selfish, and they do not view recent changes in marriage as having been harmful, overall. Moreover, they point out that the companionate, team-oriented marriages of the 1950s relegated women to a lower status in the relationship. These scholars value the freedom, egalitarianism, and possibilities for self-growth inherent in contemporary marriage. They also note that children can be raised successfully by single parents, and that many married-couple households are not necessarily good environments for children's development. Rather than try to reverse recent changes in the culture of marriage, these scholars believe, policies should support all types of families, not just married heterosexual couples.

Despite the widespread acceptance of individualistic marriage, there is no society-wide consensus at the moment on the ideal form of marriage. Consequently, many spouses are torn between clashing values and expectations for their unions. For example, consider a wife who has affection for her husband and experiences little overt conflict with him. Nevertheless, she comes to the conclusion that her husband is not her true soul mate, and that the marriage is not meeting her expectations for personal growth. Although the marriage is not bad, she feels that something important is missing from her life, that opportunities are passing her by, and that she would be happier with an alternative partner. If the wife adopts an individualistic schema, she will be motivated to leave the marriage to meet her needs with a new partner. But if she shifts to a companionate or institutional schema, she is likely to be concerned about the consequences of divorce for her children, her husband, their extended families, and the community in general.

Because people can shift from one schema to another, elements of uncertainty and tension are introduced into marriage. Should spouses make decisions that maximize their personal gain, or should they sacrifice their own outcomes to maintain the stability of their unions?

During the last two decades, policymakers, practitioners, and members of the public have become increasingly concerned about continuing high levels of marital instability and nonmarital childbearing. In the 1990s, the Marriage Movement—a loose affiliation of academics, therapists, educators, policymakers, and religious leaders—gained momentum (Institute for American Values 2000; Smart Marriages 2007). The central goal of the marriage movement is to strengthen the institution of marriage in the United States. Many state governments also have taken steps to support marriage. Three states (Louisiana, Arizona, and Arkansas) implemented the option of Covenant Marriage—a form of marriage in which spouses attend premarital counseling, vow to seek counseling if their marriages are in trouble, and refrain from seeking a no-fault divorce. In 2000, Oklahoma established the Oklahoma Marriage Initiative and trained hundreds of individuals to provide free premarital education to thousands of couples. Other states adopted alternative strategies to strengthen marriage, such as incorporating relationship skills and conflict resolution courses into high school curricula, distributing information on marriage to newlyweds, and funding public education campaigns to promote the value of healthy marriage (Parke and Ooms 2002).

The federal government became involved in marriage with the 1996 Personal Responsibility and Work Opportunities Reform Act (PRWORA). This act replaced the older Assistance to Families with Dependent Children (AFDC) program with Temporary Assistance to Needy Families (TANF). Although most of the media attention at the time focused on the new rules for single mothers on public assistance (stringent work requirements and time limits for public assistance), the act also had much to say about marriage. In particular, the act allowed states to spend some of their TANF funds on programs to promote marriage, reduce the incidence of nonmarital births, and encourage the formation and maintenance of two-parent families (Ooms 2001). A decade later, the Deficit Reduction Act of 2005 (signed in 2006), reauthorized TANF. The new Act allocates $100 million a year for five years for programs to strengthen healthy marriage and another $50 million for programs to promote responsible fatherhood (many of which contain a relationship skills component).

Most currently funded programs focus on teaching communication and conflict-resolution skills to couples (see chapter 10, this volume). In addition, many programs teach couples to have realistic expectations for their relationships, to value long-term commitment, and to practice self-sacrifice and forgiveness. These elements are inconsistent with the individualistic model of marriage and represent attempts to shift our cultural view of marriage toward a more companionate or institutional model. The approach is based on the assumption that changing people's beliefs, attitudes, values, expectations, and behaviors—one couple at a time—will eventually create new and widely shared understandings of the meaning and role of marriage. Although many advocates assume that lower SES families will be the main beneficiaries of these programs, the overarching goal is to change the culture of marriage across the entire population. In this sense, these programs are not unlike the feminist consciousness raising groups of the 1960s and 1970s.

Many people are skeptical about the value of these steps (e.g., Cherlin 2003; Huston and Melz 2004). Some observers are opposed to these measures because they fear that people will become trapped in unhappy marriages. Others argue that these programs are likely to be ineffective and a waste of money. Still others believe that marriage is a private rather than a public matter—a perspective consistent with an individualistic view of marriage. Finally, some fear that promarriage policies imply a return to a patriarchal authority structure and a traditional gender division of labor.

Despite these concerns, there is a growing recognition among policymakers, as well as the general public, that marriage is not a strictly private relationship between two individuals, and that the broader community has an interest in increasing the proportion of healthy and stable marriages, especially those with children. Some conservative religious groups want to return to the patriarchal marriages of the past. (For examples, see www.focusonthefamily.com.) Other marriage advocates, however, believe that contemporary unions should practice gender equality, and that couples should be free to choose a division of homemaking, breadwinning, and child care responsibilities that best meets their particular needs (Blankenhorn 2007). There is no inherent contradiction in adopting a companionate schema for marriage but replacing the older "husband as senior partner" option with an "equal partner" alternative.

SOCIOECONOMIC DIFFERENCES IN MARRIAGE PATTERNS

As noted earlier, different models of marriage coexist in American society. Recent research suggests that these models vary by socioeconomic status. Although the overall level of marital dissolution in the population continues to be about 50 percent, the rate of divorce decreased between 1980 and 1994 among college-educated individuals but increased among individuals with less than a high-school degree (Raley and Bumpass 2003).

Two explanations can account for this divergence. With respect to economic factors, many studies demonstrate that low SES couples have a greater risk of divorce than do high SES couples (e.g., Bramlett and Mosher 2002). Between 1980 and 2000, married couples in which the husband did not have a college degree experienced a slight decline in standard of living, whereas married couples in which the husband had a college degree experienced a substantial increase in standard of living (Amato et al. 2007). Consequently, the growing divergence in economic well-being associated with educational attainment may have led to a corresponding divergence in divorce rates.

A second explanation refers to cultural shifts in the meaning of marriage. Paul Amato and his colleagues (2007) report that between 1980 and 2000, married individuals' scores on an instrument that measured support for the norm of lifelong marriage rose by about one-fourth of a standard deviation, overall. A further analysis of these data indicates, however, that virtually all of this increase occurred among spouses with college degrees. In other words, a shift toward a less individualistic view of marriage increased among the middle class, but not among the working class or poor.

The General Social Survey (GSS) represents a second source of evidence for the cultural explanation. The GSS has been conducted in most years between 1974 and 2004 (annually until 1994 and biannually after that year). Most surveys have included the following item: "Should divorce in this country be easier or more difficult to obtain than it is now?" Replying that divorce should be easier reflects an individualistic view of marriage, whereas relying that divorce should be more difficult reflects a companionate or institutional view. Between 1974 and 2004, individuals with a college education were increasingly likely to state that divorce should be more difficult to obtain. In contrast, individuals with less than a college education were increasingly likely to state that divorce should be easier to obtain. These results are presented in figure 4.1. To minimize year-to-year fluctuations, the figure is based on a five-year moving average. (That is, for a given year, I used the mean response for that year, the preceding two years, and the following two years. Also, for years in which the survey did not take place, I relied on linear interpolation to maintain a continuous trend line.)

This figure reveals that in 1974, people without a high school diploma tended to be relatively conservative on this issue, whereas people with a college degree tended to be relatively liberal. Over time, the two groups

Figure 4.1 Percentage of respondents stating that divorce should be more difficult to obtain (by year and education). (Source: General Social Survey)

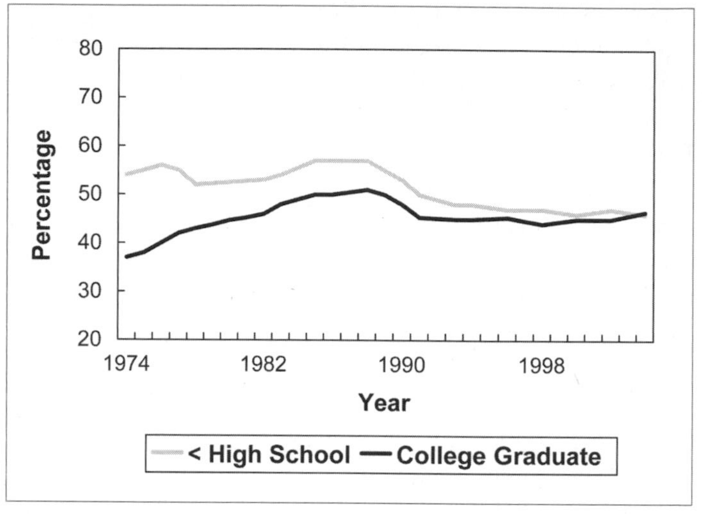

converged. Although the trend lines were not strictly monotonic, a regression analysis indicated that among less-educated individuals (n=6,735), support for the belief that divorce should be more difficult to obtain declined over time (B=–.004, SE=.001, p<.001). In contrast, among college-educated individuals (n=5,632), support for this position increased (B=.011, SE=.002, p<.001). The overall interaction between level of education and year was significant (p<.001).

Taken together, these data suggest that since the mid-1970s, many middle-class individuals have shifted away from an individualistic view of marriage and toward a more companionate or institutional view. In contrast, less educated individuals appear to have increasingly accepted an individualistic model of marriage—a model that is linked with higher levels of divorce as well as nonmarital births. Further support comes from recent qualitative studies of poor unmarried mothers, who appear to hold particularly high expectations, not only for economic security prior to marriage, but also for the ability of their male partners to be emotionally expressive and responsive—expectations previously associated primarily with middle class women (England and Shafer 2007). The reasons for these trends are not well understood, although future research may cast some light on this topic. Nevertheless, cultural changes, along with the economic trends noted earlier, may explain why rates of divorce are declining among the well educated but increasing among the poorly educated.

CONCLUSIONS

A social-psychological perspective focuses on the beliefs, attitudes, values, meanings, and expectations of individuals. Because these intrapsychic contents are shared widely, this perspective is also a cultural perspective. This perspective does not clash with historical, demographic, economic, or sociological viewpoints. Instead, as described earlier, social psychological processes can be viewed as mediators of macro-level social forces. Large-scale social change makes possible the rise of new ideas, meanings, and behaviors at the individual level. The aggregation of these individual changes creates new social arrangements at the societal level. New cultural forms also can affect other social institutions. For example, the shift toward individualistic marriage (and the resulting increase in divorce and nonmarital births) has affected the economy (through the increase in employment among single mothers), the law (through the expansion of family courts and legislation governing divorce, child support, and custody arrangements), and public policy (through changes in the rules relating to the support of single mothers and their children). Moreover, the high expectations that accompany individualistic marriage have led many people to delay or avoid marriage. The perspective I have adopted in this chapter highlights the role of culture because it is through cultural change that new marriage patterns are eventually adopted or jettisoned. The study of culture and its social psychological underpinnings, therefore, is fundamental to understanding recent patterns of marital change.

We live in a time in which the culture of marriage is contested and consensus does not exist about the ideal form of marriage. Currently, the marriage movement, state governments, and the federal government are attempting to shift the culture of marriage from an individualistic model to a more companionate or institutional model. Through public education campaigns, relationship education, and other methods, these actors are hoping to change people's beliefs, attitudes, values, expectations, and behaviors. Although difficult to measure, these attempts may have had some success, because attitudes about marriage and divorce have become more conservative in recent years, at least among well-educated individuals.

A need exists to develop research tools and instruments that will allow us to measure, describe, and explain marital change more effectively. In particular, no research instruments exist for measuring the extent to which couples endorse and practice institutional, companionate, and individualistic forms of marriage. Given the categories in table 4.1, it should be relatively straightforward to design questionnaire items that tap these different orientations for inclusion in large-scale surveys. Preliminary qualitative work with individuals or focus groups would strengthen this effort. Currently, we do not know how many marriages are best classified as institutional, companionate, or individualistic; the extent to which mixed or hybrid types exist; and the extent to which husbands and wives hold similar or clashing schemata for marriage.

If a reliable and valid method of classification were available, it would be possible to address questions about the individual correlates and predictors of these marriages types. Examples of these questions include:

1. Do people with individualistic marriages tend to be more or less educated than people who hold alternative views? As suggested earlier, less educated individuals may be embracing individualistic marriage at the same time that increasing numbers of well-educated individuals are rejecting it.

2. Are highly religious individuals more likely than other individuals to hold institutional or companionate views of marriage? If yes, then which aspects of religion (denomination, strength of beliefs, attendance at religious services) are most strongly associated with this orientation?

3. Do women and men differ in the extent to which they hold institutional, companionate, or individualistic views about marriage? The fact that wives are more likely than husbands to initiate divorce suggests that women may be more individualistic than men (the reverse of our common views about gender). Alternatively, women may be more likely than men to initiate divorce because they are frustrated by the reluctance of some husbands to share household labor and childcare, thus violating the expectation of cooperative teamwork that characterizes companionate marriage.

4. How do marriages change over time? Do they tend to become more individualistic, with couples developing different interests and perhaps becoming bored with one another? Or do they become more companionate, with older couples learning to appreciate more fully the importance of mutual support, cooperation, sacrifice, and forgiveness? (Of course, selection issues are relevant to this question, because individualistic marriages are more likely to end in divorce than are other forms of marriage.)

If appropriate instruments were available, it would be possible to see if a particular combination of institutional, companionate, and individualistic elements is associated with optimal levels of marital happiness and stability, as well as child well-being. If such a configuration could be identified, it would be extremely useful to policymakers, practitioners, and advocates who wish to strengthen marriage.

REFERENCES

Amato, P.R., A. Booth, D. Johnson, and S. J. Rogers. 2007. *Alone together: How marriage in America is changing.* Cambridge, Mass.: Harvard University Press.

Amato, P.R., and S. Rogers. 1999. Do attitudes toward divorce affect marital quality? *Journal of Family Issues* 20:69–86.

Barich, R.R., and D. D. Bielby. 1996. Rethinking marriage: Change and stability in expectations, 1967–1994. *Journal of Family Issues* 7:139–169.

Bellah, R.N., R. Madsen, W. N. Sullivan, A. Swidler, and S. N. Tipton. 1985. *Habits of the heart: Individualism and commitment in American life.* Berkeley: University of California Press.

Blankenhorn, D. 1990. American family dilemmas. In D. Blankenhorn, S. Bayme, and J.B. Elshtain, eds., *Rebuilding the nest: A new commitment to the American family,* 3–25. Milwaukee: Family Service Association.

———. 2007. *The future of marriage.* New York: Encounter Books.

Bramlett, M.D., and W. D. Mosher. 2002. Cohabitation, marriage, divorce, and remarriage in the United States. *Vital Health Statistics,* series 23, no. 22. Washington, D.C.: National Center for Health Statistics.

Burgess, E.W., H. J. Locke, and M. M. Thomes. 1963. *The family: From institution to companionship.* New York: American Book Company.

Burgess, E.W., and P. Wallin. 1953. *Engagement and marriage.* Chicago: Lippincott.

Buss, D.M., T.K. Shackelford, L. A. Kirkpatrick, and R. J. Larsen. 2001. A half century of mate preferences: The cultural evolution of values. *Journal of Marriage and the Family* 63:491–503.

Cherlin, A.J. 2003. Should the government promote marriage? *Contexts* 2:22–29

———. 2004. The deinstitutionalization of American marriage. *Journal of Marriage and Family* 66:848–861.

Coontz, S. 1992. *The way we never were: American families and the nostalgia trap.* New York: Basic Books.

———. 2005. *Marriage, a history: From obedience to intimacy, or how love conquered marriage.* New York: Viking.

England, P., and E. F. Shafer. 2007. Everyday gender conflicts in low-income couples. In P. England and K. Edin, eds., *Unmarried couples with children,* 55–83. New York: Russell Sage.

Fiske, S. T. 1984. *Social cognition*. New York: Random House.

Glenn, N. D. 1996. Values, attitudes, and the state of American marriage. In D. Popenoe, J. B. Elshtain, and D. Blankenhorn, eds., *Promises to keep: Decline and renewal of marriage in America*, 15–33. Lanham, Md.: Rowman & Littlefield.

Hernandez, D. J. 1993. *America's children: Resources from family, government, and the economy*. New York: Russell Sage Foundation.

Huston, T. L., and H. Melz. 2004. The case for (promoting) marriage: The devil is in the details. *Journal of Marriage and Family* 66:943–958.

Institute for American Values. 2000. *The marriage movement: A statement of principles*. New York: Institute for American Values.

Levinger, G. 1976. A socio-psychological perspective on marital dissolution. *Journal of Social Issues* 52:21–47.

Maslow, A. 1962. *Toward a psychology of being*. New York: Van Nostrand.

Mintz, S., and S. Kellogg. 1988. *Domestic revolutions: A social history of American family life*. New York: Free Press.

Ooms, T. 2001. The role of the federal government in strengthening marriage. *Virginia Journal of Social Policy and the Law* 9:163–191.

Parke, M., and T. Ooms. 2002. More than a dating service: State activities designed to strengthen and promote marriage. Center for Law and Social Policy, Publication 02–64.

Popenoe, D. 1996. *Life without father*. New York: Martin Kessler.

Putnam, R. D. 2000. *Bowling alone: The collapse and revival of American community*. New York: Simon & Schuster.

Raley, R. K., and L. Bumpass. 2003. The topography of the divorce plateau: Levels and trends in union stability in the United States after 1980. *Demographic Research* 8:246–258.

Rogers, C. 1961. *On becoming a person*. Boston: Houghton Mifflin.

Scanzoni, J. 2001. From the normal family to alternate families to the quest for diversity with interdependence. *Journal of Family Issues* 22:688–710.

Skolnick, A. S. 1991. *Embattled paradise: The American family in an age of uncertainty*. New York: Basic Books.

Smart Marriages. 2007. www.smartmarriage.com/diane.sollee.html.

Sprecher, S., D. Felmlee, R. L. Orbuch, and M. C. Willetts. 2002. Social networks and change in personal relationships. In A. L. Valgelisti, H. T. Reis, and M. A. Fitzpatrick, eds., *Stability and change in relationships*, 257–284. New York: Cambridge University Press.

Stacey, J. 1996. *In the name of the family: Rethinking family values in the postmodern age*. Boston: Beacon.

Wilson, J. Q. 2002. *The marriage problem: How our culture has weakened families*. New York: HarperCollins.

Contemporary Families

PART 2

Single Parenthood and Child Well-Being

FIVE

Trends, Theories, and Evidence

RACHEL DUNIFON

The number of children living with a single parent has increased dramatically in the past decades. In 2006, 29 percent of all U.S. children under the age of eighteen were living with an unmarried parent (17 percent of these children were living with a single father and the rest were living with a single mother). These statistics vary dramatically by race and ethnicity. In 2006, 21 percent of all non-Hispanic white children lived with a single parent, compared to 56 percent of black children and 29 percent of Hispanic children (U.S. Census Bureau 2006a).

Children's living arrangements have received a great deal of interest from researchers and policymakers. Researchers have sought to understand the factors leading to the large increase in single parenthood, as well as the subsequent consequences for children. Policymakers too have focused attention on the issue, culminating in the enactment of policies designed to reduce single parenthood and increase marriage.

This chapter begins by reviewing the trends in single parenthood for the population as a whole as well as for various subgroups of children, separately by race and ethnicity, by mothers' marital history, and by the presence of other household members. I next discuss theories regarding which factors could be contributing to the dramatic increase in single parenthood, followed by an examination of the policy context in which such changes have occurred. The chapter continues with a review of the literature on the associations between living in a single-parent family and child well-being, and it concludes with a discussion of what is yet to be learned about single parenthood and child well-being.

TRENDS IN SINGLE PARENTHOOD

Figure 5.1 shows the percentage of all U.S. children under the age of eighteen who lived with an unmarried parent from 1968 through 2006. Data come from the U.S. Census Bureau's Current Population Survey. As shown in the figure, the percent of children living with a single parent has increased dramatically in the past decades, from 12 percent in 1968 to 29 percent in 2006. The sharpest increase occurred during the 1970s and early 1980s, and the trend has remained relatively flat during the 1990s and through 2006. Figure 5.1 also separates children living with a single parent into those who live with a single mother vs. those living with a single father. As the figure indicates, the vast majority (83 percent in 2006) of children living with a single parent live with a single mother; however, the percentage of children living with a single father has increased over the past thirty years, reaching nearly 5 percent of all U.S. children in 2006.

Figure 5.2 presents trends in the percentage of children living with a single parent separately for white, black, and Hispanic children (data for Hispanic children became available only in 1980). As this figure shows, the increase in single parenthood has occurred among all groups. However the prevalence of single parenthood differs greatly by race; in 2006 black children were 2.5 times more likely to live with a single parent than white children (21 percent vs. 56 percent). Hispanic children fall between black and white children in terms of the prevalence of this living arrangement.

Figure 5.1 Percentage of all children living with a single parent (1968–2006)

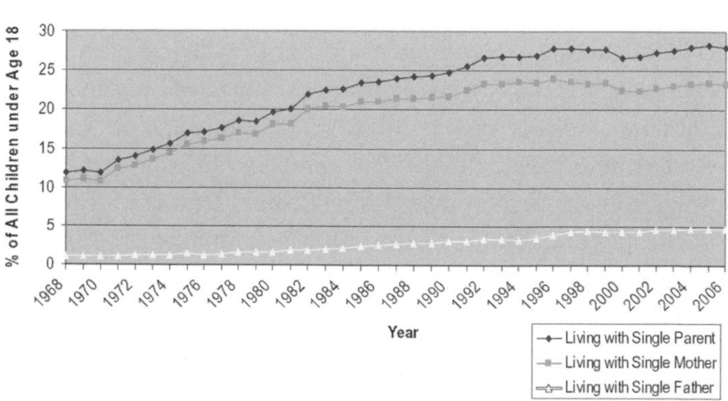

Source: U.S. Census Bureau

Figure 5.2 Percentage of all children living with a single parent, by race and ethnicity (1968–2006)

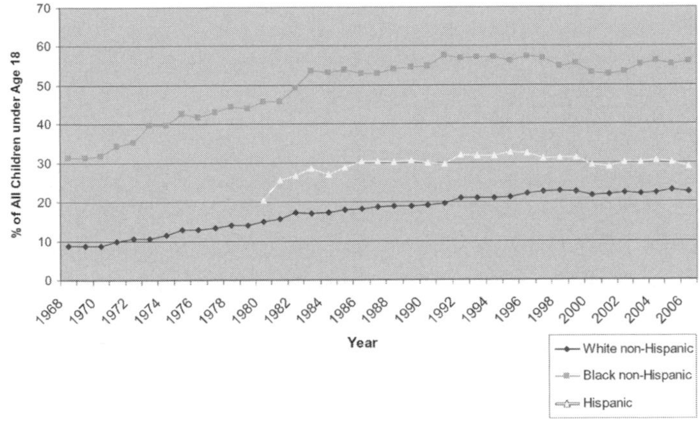

Source: U.S. Census Bureau

Figures 5.1 and 5.2 present snapshots of the percentage of children living with a single parent at various points in time. However, children living with a single parent are a diverse group, representing a variety of experiences. Some children living with a single parent were born to and continue to live with an unmarried mother; others had lived with married parents but experienced a divorce or separation; others have experienced the death of a parent. Figure 5.3 presents trends over time in the percentage of all children living with a single mother, detailing whether the child was living with a never-married, divorced or separated, or widowed mother. As this figure shows, from the 1960s through the mid-1980s, the vast majority of children living with a single mother entered this arrangement due to a divorce or separation. In more recent years, however, the population of children living with a single mother is increasingly comprised of children born to never-married mothers. In 2006, 43 percent of all children living with a single mother lived with a never-married mother, vs. 53 percent living with a divorced or separated mother and 3 percent living with a widowed mother.

It is also important to note that many "single" parents live in households with other adults. Many unmarried parents are cohabiting, or living with unmarried romantic partners. As Susan Brown (2004) notes, 5 percent of all U.S. children live with a cohabiting parent, and almost 40 percent of such children will experience some time in a cohabiting household during their

Figure 5.3 Percentage of all children living with a single mother, by mother's marital history (1968–2006)

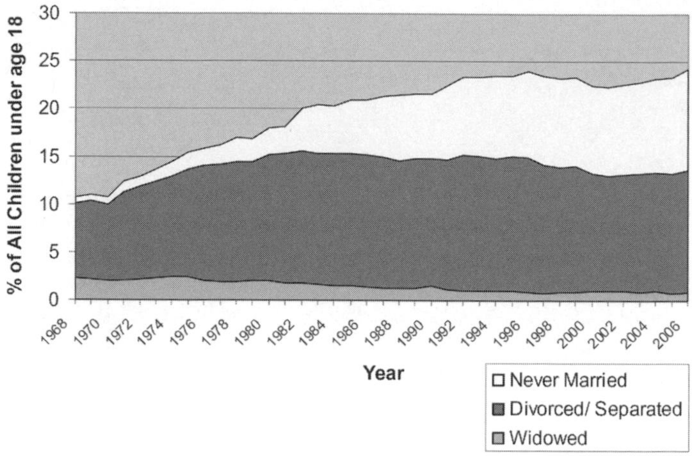

Source: U.S. Census Bureau

lifetime (Bumpass and Lu 2000). The next chapter in this volume discusses issues of cohabiting parents more thoroughly.

Other children living in single-parent households also live with their grandparents in multi- or three-generational households. As shown in figure 5.4, 9.8 percent of white children, 12.4 percent of black children, and 15.3 percent of Hispanic children in single-parent families also live with one or more grandparents in the household. As discussed later in this chapter, it is possible that the presence of additional adults in the household could offset some of the often-observed detriments to child well-being associated with single parenthood.

As noted by both David Ellwood and Christopher Jencks (2004) and Sara McLanahan (2004), the increase in single parenthood discussed above differs not only by race, but also by women's educational status. As Ellwood and Jencks show, the increase in single-motherhood shown in figure 5.1 has occurred almost entirely among less-educated women, particularly those without a college degree. Among college-educated women, the percentage of children living in a single-mother household has risen only slightly, from 6 percent to 10 percent between 1965 and 1980, and has remained quite level since. In contrast, for children with mothers who did not complete high school, the percentage living with an unmarried mother more than tripled,

Figure 5.4 Percentage of all children living with a single parent who also live with a grandparent (2006)

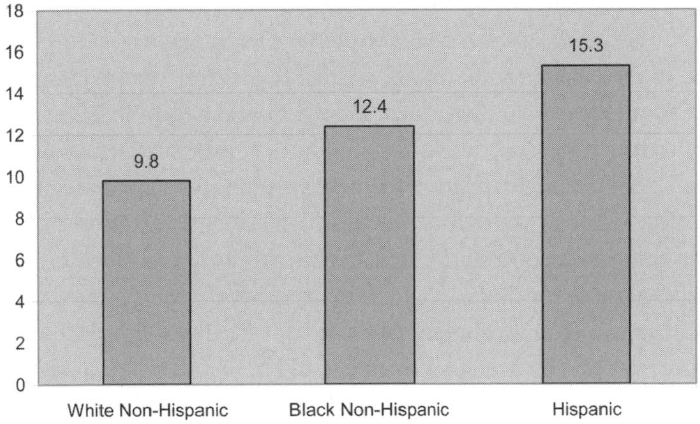

Source: U.S. Census Bureau

increasing from 13 percent to 40 percent; for those whose mothers finished high school but not college the numbers increased from 6 percent to 25 percent (Elwood and Jencks 2004). These changes are driven primarily by the fact that nonmarital childbearing has increased dramatically among less-educated women during this period, as well as the fact that divorce rates have fallen for more-educated but not less-educated women. It is important to note that race differences in the prevalence of single parenthood remain, however; even within educational categories, black children are more likely to live with a single parent than are white children (Ellwood and Jencks 2004).

POSSIBLE REASONS FOR THE INCREASE IN SINGLE PARENTHOOD

The preceding discussion emphasizes several key points: single parenthood increased, particularly during the 1970s and 1980s; this increase has primarily taken place among less-educated and minority women; and increasing numbers of single parents are never-married mothers, as opposed to those who are divorced and separated. What are some of the causes behind such dramatic demographic shifts? Because the changes in family structure that have been observed differ so dramatically by race and by maternal education, any explanation of such changes must be able to explain why some groups have experienced large increases in single parenthood while others have not.

Across racial and educational backgrounds, women have experienced a delay in marriage, and several factors have been theorized to play an important role, including changing norms regarding sexual behavior that make sex outside of marriage more common and acceptable; the introduction of birth-control techniques which allow women to control their fertility; rising female wages relative to men; and changes in male and female expectations about the responsibilities of men both economically and in the household (Ellwood and Jencks 2004; McLanahan 2004). For more-educated women this delay in marriage has been accompanied by a delay in childbearing, as such women have the tools to delay childbearing as well as the motivation for doing so in terms of increased rewards in the labor market (Ellwood and Jencks 2004). For less-educated women, a delay in childbearing has not accompanied the delay in marriage. The review that follows focuses on two key factors that are particularly salient for less-educated or minority women and therefore can shed particular light on the divergent trends in living arrangements by race and education—specifically, the availability of public assistance programs and the availability of marriageable men in low-income communities.

A large literature has examined the influence of welfare programs on family structure, spurred in large part by Charles Murray (1984), who argues that cash-assistance programs serve to encourage single motherhood. Specifically, Murray argues that, because such assistance has traditionally been made available only to single mothers, it is possible that more generous benefits may increase single parenthood by making such a living arrangement more attractive relative to marriage. Numerous studies have tested this hypothesis. A review of the literature relating welfare benefits to marriage and nonmarital fertility shows mixed results, with a slight majority indicating a positive influence of welfare benefits on fertility and a negative influence on marriage; these effects were more pronounced for white, rather than black, women (Moffitt 1998). Welfare benefits alone may not explain the increase in single parenthood that occurred during the 1970s and 1980s, though, as this was a time during which welfare benefits actually declined in real terms. However, as Sara McLanahan (2004) points out, the overall value of in-kind transfers to single mothers increased over this period, as programs such as Food Stamps and Medicaid were expanded.

The passage of welfare reform legislation in 1996 sought to eliminate some of the feared perverse incentives of the former welfare system by ending the entitlement to welfare, and requiring that welfare recipients to go work, among other things. It was hoped that such changes would make welfare less attractive, thereby reducing single parenthood and potentially increasing marriage. Additionally, if such reforms mean that women leave welfare and obtain jobs that provide them with greater financial stability, marriage rates could increase if women become more attractive marriage partners (on the other hand, increased financial independence may reduce the likelihood of marriage).

Several studies have examined how such policy changes have influenced family living arrangements. Lisa Gennetian and Virginia Knox (2003) review data from fourteen random assignment studies testing the impact of policies designed to promote work and reduce welfare. Meta-analysis results indicate no consistent relationship between any of these policies and changes in marriage or cohabitation among the single mothers who participated in the programs. In another study, Kristen Harknett and Lisa Gennetian (2003) analyzed data from welfare reform experiments that took place in two Canadian sites in which single mothers were offered generous earnings supplements if they worked at least thirty hours per week. Importantly, for women participating in the program, earnings of spouses or cohabiting partners were not included when determining their eligibility for public assistance; this was in contrast to traditional welfare programs, which did take such earnings into account. Analyses of the experiment showed contradictory results: in one location, the program increased marriage, while in the other marriage decreased. The authors conclude that impacts of welfare policies may be moderated by local labor market and other conditions.

Other data comes from the New Hope project, an experimental study of an antipoverty program in Milwaukee in the mid-1990s. Using data from this project, Anna Gassman-Pines, Hirokazu Yoshikawa, and Sandra Nay (2006) found that participation in New Hope led to an increase in marriage among previously single mothers. Using both qualitative and quantitative data, the authors reveal that this was primarily due to increased earnings and subsequent improvements in relationship quality among those participating in the program. Finally, an evaluation of the Minnesota Family Investment Program (MFIP), an experimental intervention that required work and helped to increase income, found that the program led to an increase in marriage (Gennetian and Miller 2004). Overall, then, results from studies examining whether welfare-reform programs have the potential to increase marriage among lower-income mothers are mixed.

An additional potential factor in the rise in single parenthood, cited by many scholars, is a lack of marriageable men (that is, those earning enough and willing to support a family). As William Julius Wilson (1987) noted, economic changes over the past decades have led to the erosion of wages among less-educated men, making their financial situations more precarious and leaving them less desirable as marriage partners, with the ultimate result being a decline in marriage. However, among less-educated and minority populations, the reluctance to marry is often not accompanied by a decline in parenthood (Ellwood and Jencks 2004; McLanahan 2004). Whereas more educated women often delay or avoid childbearing in order to pursue their careers or education, less-educated women, whose job prospects are often meager, see fewer benefits in doing so. Thus, marriage and childbearing can become unlinked, with the end result being a rise in nonmarital births.

Scholars have examined the potential influence of "marriage market" factors in influencing family structure decisions. Kristen Harknett and Sara McLanahan (2004) use Fragile Families data to examine the factors that predict the likelihood that a couple will marry after having a nonmarital birth, seeking to explain why white and Hispanic parents are more than two times more likely to do so than blacks. They test a variety of factors including fathers' education and employment, the quality of the couple's relationship, and attitudes towards marriage, as well as measures of the local marriage market—specifically the ratio of men to women in the couples' city of residence. They find that a lack of employed (that is, marriageable) men explains a great deal of the lower rates of marriage among African American women in their sample. Francine Blau, Lawrence Kahn, and Jane Waldfogel (2000) use census data spanning 1970–1990 and relate local labor and marriage markets and welfare benefits to the marriage rates of women aged 16–24. For whites, as well as older black women (ages 25–34), the results show that better labor markets increase marriage, while worse marriage markets decrease marriage. These studies provide evidence that the availability of acceptable partners may play a role in explaining some of the racial differences in marriage behavior.

The literature reviewed here makes clear that, while researchers have explained some of the recent increase in single parenthood by factors such as the availability of marriageable men and, to a lesser extent, changes in public-assistance policies, a great deal remains to be learned about how and why such a dramatic change in children's living arrangements occurred. Because living arrangements are the result of complicated decisions regarding relationships and fertility, ethnographic data can play a useful role in identifying themes and important factors that are not easily measured in larger-scale surveys. Indeed, several recent ethnographic studies shed light on patterns of childbearing and marriage behavior in low-income communities.

In the book *Promises I Can Keep*, Kathryn Edin and Maria Kefalas (2005) report findings from qualitative interviews of 162 low-income single mothers living in New Jersey and Philadelphia. The study shows that, although women place a high value on marriage, they are reluctant to marry until several criteria are met, including securing their own financial independence and meeting a responsible and trustworthy man, criteria that women recognize could take a long time to achieve. A study by Christina Gibson-Davis, Kathryn Edin, and Sara McLanahan (2005) suggests that lower-income women have high financial standards for marriage, and often report delaying marriage until aspects of a middle-class lifestyle, such as home ownership, are attained. At the same time, Edin and Kefelas (2005) report that women express a strong desire for children, which many feel give purpose and meaning to their lives. The women interviewed by Edin and Kefelas place a high value on having children, and express confidence in their ability to perform the role of motherhood. This is often in contrast to the lack of confidence they have in the labor market, or even in marriage. Thus, although marriage is seen as an important and hoped-for goal, it is somewhat elusive. Children, on the other hand, are seen as an essential part of life, with the end result that women often delay marriage, but not childbearing.

Women in Edin and Kefalas's book also report that fear of eventual divorce led them to delay or avoid marriage. This idea is validated in a study by Maureen Waller and Elizabeth Peters, who, using data on a sample of unmarried parents of newborns, find that a couple's predicted propensity for divorce (which includes the percentage of divorced women in a respondent's city) predicted their later likelihood of marriage to the child's father. The authors conclude, "our results are consistent with the argument that the high prevalence of divorce has produced a fear of divorce, leading some unmarried parents of young children to delay or avoid marriage" (Waller and Peters 2007, 22).

In summary, while research points to some potential factors that may have led to the increase in single parenthood throughout the past decades, including the economic condition of less-educated men, it is clear that no one factor played a determinative role in shaping the complex relationship and fertility behaviors that produced such changes. As Ellwood and Jencks note, "it is only a slight exaggeration to say that quantitative social scientists' main contribution to our understanding of this change has been to show that *nothing* caused single-parent families to become more common" (2004, 3). Ethnographic work tells us that marriage and childbearing decisions in lower-income communities are nuanced and based on factors related to the value of children; parents' self-confidence as parents, as spouses, and in the labor market; and the frustrations of trying to attain a middle-class lifestyle under difficult economic circumstances. Future research that is able to incorporate these concepts into larger, longitudinal datasets may be able to shed light on some of the more complex reasons behind these recent demographic trends.

THE POLICY CONTEXT

Single parenthood has become a topic of interest not only among researchers, but also among policymakers. This was made clear in the landmark 1996 welfare reform legislation, which eliminated low-income single mothers' entitlement to cash assistance programs, and replaced it with short-term, time-limited assistance programs that mandated work. Although the main impact of this legislation has been to decrease welfare use and increase employment among single mothers (Blank 2002), the legislation was motivated in large part by a desire to reduce single parenthood and promote marriage. It was thought that, by making public assistance programs less attractive, the incentive to become a single parent would be reduced as well. However, as shown in the experimental studies described above, and as noted by Rebecca Blank (2007) the overall research suggests that the impact of welfare reform on marriage has been minimal.

In recent years, further legislation has been enacted which more directly promotes marriage among lower-income families through activities such as public advertising, financial education for youth, programs for pregnant women who are not married, programs for couples thinking about getting married, programs for married couples, and programs designed to reduce the disincentives for marriage through public assistance programs. Chapter 10 in this volume describes one marriage-promotion program in detail.

Why do policymakers care so much about single parenthood? They care in part because of the high correlation between living in a single-parent family and poverty (Hogan and Lichter 1995). In 2005, 43 percent of female-headed families with children lived below the federal poverty line, compared to only 8.5 percent of married-couple families with children (U.S. Census Bureau 2006b). Poverty is not only associated with risks to child well-being (Duncan and Brooks-Gunn 1997), but is also associated with participation in government assistance programs.

However, poverty alone does not account for the negative outcomes often associated with single parenthood. A large body of research indicates detrimental associations between growing up with a single parent and child well-being. While about half of this is estimated to be due to differences in economic circumstances between children in single vs. married-parent families, the rest is unexplained (McLanahan and Sandefur 1994). By making dramatic changes to public assistance programs policymakers hoped that, by decreasing single parenthood and increasing marriage, outcomes for children would improve, and the number of families participating in government programs would decrease. In order to understand whether and how recent changes in welfare policies might influence the lives of children, it is important first to understand the links between single parenthood and child well-being.

SINGLE PARENTHOOD AND CHILD WELL-BEING

A great deal of research has examined whether living with a single parent is detrimental for children. In general, this research finds that growing up with a single parent is associated with more behavior problems, higher rates of teenage pregnancy, and lower academic achievement (McLanahan and Sandefur 1994). Others show associations between living with a single mother and behavior problems (Thompson, Hanson, and McLanahan 1994), and early childbearing (Wu 1996). The influence of living with a single parent appears to extend into adulthood as well. For example, a recent study found that men who grew up in father-absent households had higher rates of incarceration than those who lived with both biological parents (Harper and McLanahan 2004), while Sara McLanahan and Gary Sandefur (1994) found that living with a single parent is associated with higher rates of unemployment and public assistance use in adulthood.

However, understanding the relationship between single parenthood and children's adjustment is complicated by the fact that "living in a single-parent family" means many different things. In recent years, researchers have moved beyond simple comparisons of children who do and do not live with a married parent, and instead are using more complex measures that better reflect the diversity of living arrangements children experience. For example, researchers have begun to define better what is meant by "single" and "married." Children in "married" families are a diverse group; some live with their own biological parents, while others live in a stepfamily. It is likely that children's well-being will vary depending on each of these factors. Generally, research shows that children living with a stepparent fare worse than those living with married biological parents (see Brown 2004; Peters and Mullis 1997).

Additionally, many "single" parents live with other adults. Some live with cohabiting partners. Overall evidence suggests that children living in cohabiting families fare worse than those living with married parents (Brown 2004).

Other single parents live in three-generational households with the child's grandparent. As shown in figure 5.4, a significant percentage of children in single-parent families also live with one or more grandparents in the household. Some research shows that children fare better when living with a single mother and grandparent than when living with a single mother alone (DeLeire and Kalil 2002; Dunifon and Kowaleski-Jones 2007). The latter authors, however, examine subgroups and find that the benefits to living with a grandparent occur for white, but not black, children. The authors cite a variety of factors to explain this finding. Their descriptive analyses show that grandparents of black children have less education and provided a less stimulating learning environment for their own children than did grandparents of white children. Because of these discrepancies, it is possible that black grandparents may have fewer of the skills necessary to promote children's development than white grandparents. There remains much to be learned about the roles that grandparents may play in single-parent families.

Further diversity among children living with single parents arises from the fact that the pathways to living in a single-parent family differ among children. Some were born to unmarried mothers (who may or may not have been cohabiting with the child's father), while others were born to married parents who later divorced or separated, a change that may have occurred at any of the various developmental stages in that child's life. It is likely that children will fare differently depending on how they came to live in a single-parent family and how recently and at what age they entered that arrangement. Chapter 8 in this volume examines differences in outcomes for youth in stepfamilies, distinguishing between those who were born to an unmarried mother vs. those who experienced a divorce, finding that children's previous experiences do make a difference when examining their later well-being.

At any point in time, children living in a single-parent family represent a variety of experiences in terms of the amount of time they have lived in that arrangement. Some children were born to a single parent and will remain in that arrangement (that is, with a mother who never marries or cohabits) until they leave home; others have experienced one or more unions and dissolutions. It is possible that it is family structure change that is detrimental for children, not the living arrangement itself. This hypothesis would suggest that the relevant factor is not whether a mother is married or single, but rather the number of changes a child has experienced. For example, Lawrence Wu (1996) highlights the detrimental effects of family instability by documenting significant positive effects of family structure changes experienced in childhood on the likelihood that a woman has a premarital birth.

It is also possible that different subgroups of children may experience single parenthood very differently. As noted, single parenthood is much more prevalent among African Americans than among other racial and ethnic groups. Robert Hill (1972) argues that one of the greatest strengths of African American families is the existence of strong kinship ties. Similarly, Anne Roschelle (1997) observes that caring for other people's children, whether kin or not, has historically been a salient role for African American women. This suggests that African American families may have access to a set of parenting resources outside the context of a traditional marriage; this may mean that single parenthood could be associated with less detrimental outcomes for African American children, compared to white children. A study by Rachel Dunifon and Lori Kowaleski-Jones (2002) supports this hypothesis, finding that living in a single-parent family is associated with worse outcomes (in terms of delinquent behavior and lower test scores) for white, but not for black, children.

Finally, when relating children's living arrangements to measures of child functioning, it is important to keep in mind the challenges social science researchers face when attempting to determine whether living with a single parent is causally related to child outcomes. Children living with a single parent, however defined, are likely different from those living with married parents in a variety of ways. Without being able to hold constant all of the possible differentiating factors, it is difficult to disentangle whether living with a single parent *causes* a child to have a certain outcome, or whether that outcome is due, at least in part, to some other, unmeasured, factor. In an ideal world, from a research perspective, children would be randomly assigned to live with either a married or single parent and followed over time. Any differences in outcomes observed between the two groups could be definitively attributed to that child's living arrangements. Given the impossibility and undesirability of carrying out such an experiment, researchers have made a great deal of progress in attempting to more carefully discern the relationship between family structure and children's outcomes. With a variety of rich datasets at their fingertips, researchers can measure as many of the possible factors that differentiate children in single and married-parent households as possible, including income, maternal mental health, and maternal ability and family background. Some studies find that, after controlling for an extensive range of such characteristics, differences in outcomes between children in single- and married-parent families become insignificant (Carlson and Corcoran 2001; Ginther and Pollak 2004). Other studies (Dunifon and Kowaleski-Jones 2002; Foster and Kalil 2007; Gennetian 2005) examine how children's outcomes change in conjunction with changes in family living arrangements, thereby comparing children to themselves over time, rather than contrasting between children with different backgrounds and experiences. Studies using such methods often find small or insignificant associations between living arrangements and children's outcomes.

With the complexities reviewed here in mind, researchers have begun to test different theories regarding how and why children may be influenced by their living arrangements. Different theories lead to various predictions about which types of arrangements might be particularly beneficial or detrimental for children. Several theories explaining how growing up with a single parent may influence children are discussed later in this chapter (see Sigle-Rushton and McLahanan 2002 for a thorough review of the evidence of each of the theories). Although these theories are not mutually exclusive, determining which are supported by research and which are not is important in order to gain a better understanding of whether family structures are associated with children's well-being and, if so, how. Gaining this understanding is important not just from a research perspective, but also essential in informing policies For example, if income is the main reason that children living with single parents fare worse than others, then giving single parent families more income would be a possible way to assist such children. Similarly, if having fewer adults to monitor the child were the primary mechanism, then marriage, even to someone other than the father (or doubling up with any other adult) would be a better way to improve children's well-being.

The economic deprivation theory suggests that children living with single parents fare worse than other children because of the high rates of poverty and subsequent correlates, including sporadic or low-wage employment, among many single-parent families. As noted, children in single-mother families are more than five times as likely to live in poverty as those living with married parents. This is in part because such households only have one earner, and also because single parents tend to be less well-educated, and have lower-wage jobs, than married parents. A well-established literature has documented the adverse effects of poverty on children (Duncan and Brooks-Gunn 1997). These economic circumstances are also associated with living in worse neighborhoods and attending lower-quality schools, each of which could independently contribute to child outcomes. Therefore, it is possible that it is not single parenthood per se but the lack of economic resources associated with it that lead to the worse child outcomes observed among children living with a single parent.

In their summary of the evidence on this topic, Wendy Sigle-Rushton and Sara McLanahan (2002) suggest that 30–50 percent of the association between single parenthood and child outcomes can be explained by economic differences between children in various living arrangements. Thus, while income explains a large part of the observed differences in child outcomes across family structures, significant differences still remain. If income explained most family structure differences among children, then one would expect children in stepfather families to fare as well as those living with biological married parents, inasmuch as stepfamilies tend to have higher incomes than single-mother families. However, most research finds this is not the case, suggesting that income differences do not tell the whole story in differentiating children in single- vs. married-parent families.

A second theory is the socialization perspective, which suggests that the presence of only one adult in the household leads to worse child outcomes among children living with a single parent, as such parents may have less time to monitor and engage with their children. Single parents may also experience stress or isolation as a result of trying to parent a child single-handedly, which in turn could impact their parenting behaviors. Finally, because single-parent families consist of parents of only one gender, children in such families may lack role models of appropriate gender behavior or relationship skills (Sigle-Rushton and McLanahan 2002). Research has documented family structure differences in parenting behaviors, such that single parents spend less time with their children (Astone and McLanahan 1991; Sandberg and Hofferth 2001), exert weaker control and make fewer demands on their children (Amato 1987; Astone and McLanahan 1991; Thomson, McLanahan, and Curtin 1992), and provide less support (Thomson,

Hanson, and McLanahan 1994). However, most studies find that such differences in parenting do not explain differences in outcomes between children living with single vs. married parents (Dunifon and Kowaleski-Jones 2002; Thomson, Hanson, and McLanahan 1994).

If the socialization perspective is correct, then the presence of another adult in the household should benefit children living in single-parent families if that adult serves as an additional person to monitor or engage with the child, to serve as a role model, or reduce the stress and isolation of the single parent. The evidence on this is mixed. As noted, children do not appear to benefit when living with a stepparent. Additionally, living with a cohabiting parent, even if it is the child's biological parent, does not confer benefits (Brown 2004); this may be due to the finding that cohabiting biological fathers are less involved with their children than married biological fathers (Hofferth and Anderson 2003). As discussed earlier, though, there is some evidence that grandparent coresidence can benefit children in single-parent households. Thus, it appears that the mere presence of an additional adult in the household does not confer benefits in and of itself, but that living with a grandparent may be beneficial for children.

The stress-and-instability perspective suggests that children living in single-parent families fare worse than other children because of the disruptions they have experienced. As noted, some children come to live with a single parent after experiencing a divorce, which has been linked to increased distress among adults, with possible implications for their effectiveness as parents, as well as stress among children (Amato 2000). Some children of single parents may also experience one or more instances of remarriage or cohabitation during their lives. Such changes could lead to disruptions in family routines, could strain the parent-child relationship, or be accompanied by other disruptive changes such as residential moves. It is possible that it is not the family structure per se but the disruptions associated with changes in family structure that could lead to detrimental outcomes among children. This would help to explain why children living with stepparents fare worse than those living with biological married parents (Brown 2004; Sigle-Rushton and McLanahan 2002); such children have experienced a remarriage as well as the introduction of one or more new family members into their homes, which could lead to stress. Lawrence Wu (1996), looking at factors predicting premarital births, documents large and significant detrimental effects of family structure changes. If it is instability rather than family structure per se that is important for children, then children living with a stable single parent (one who never marries or cohabits) may fare better than others. This topic has not received much research attention (but see chapter 7 in this volume).

In summary, understanding the relationship between single parenthood and child well-being is complicated by the fact that family structures are nuanced, change over time, and may have different meanings for different children. With this in mind, researchers have tested several theories to try to explain why a relationship between family structure and children's functioning may exist, and under what conditions. Research to date suggests that economic factors account for some of the differences in well-being often observed between children in single vs. married-parent families, but that these factors do not tell the whole story. Evidence also suggests that parenting practices do not appear to play a large role in explaining such differences. There is some research showing that living with a grandparent may benefit children, while living with a cohabiting partner or stepparent generally does not. Finally, instability has been shown to be harmful for children, suggesting that it may not be the living arrangement per se, but rather the stability of the arrangement that is important.

CONCLUSION

This chapter has reviewed the data, theories, and research evidence that address how children fare when they live with a single parent. Single parenthood has increased dramatically in the past decades, but has remained relatively flat in recent years. As noted by David Ellwood and Christopher Jencks (2004), this may be attributable to a rise in the real wages of less-skilled men as well as expansions in the Earned Income Tax Credit that also occurred around this time, each of which has increased the economic resources available to lower-income parents. The increase in single parenthood has occurred primarily among less-educated and minority women. Although evidence suggests that children living with a single parent fare worse than those who live with married parents, this conclusion is tempered by the complexities in the ways in which family living arrangements may be defined as well as the numerous ways in which single- and married-parent families may differ from each other. Researchers have risen to this challenge and have begun to examine the multidimensional ways in which family structure can be defined, testing several theories regarding how children fare when living with a single parent.

Despite the difficulties inherent in understanding the relationship between family structure and child well-being, doing so is important, particularly at a time when policies designed to influence children's living arrangements are being implemented. Understanding whether and how children succeed is critical in informing the development and evaluation of these policies. For example, the research reviewed here suggests that income plays a role in explaining the well-being of children living with a single parent. Additionally, it appears that the economic standing of less-educated men has played a role in the recent rise in single parenthood. These findings suggest that economic policies, particularly those that raise the wages of less-skilled men, may influence children's living arrangements and their ultimate well-being. Additionally, other research suggests that multigenerational living arrangements may benefit children. This suggests that programs designed to promote marriage may also want to consider promoting multigenerational living arrangements as well.

However, while much progress has been made in understanding the rise in single parenthood and the ways in which living arrangements influence child well-being, this review also highlights how much is not known. Despite the extensive body of research on this topic, the use of detailed datasets and robust methods, and the attention to the complexities of the issues, researchers still have much to learn about these demographic trends and their implications for children.

Going forward, several issues would benefit from particular attention. One need is for more mixed-methods analyses. Such analyses could provide a more nuanced understanding of how and why parents make childbearing and marriage decisions and how these decisions play out in the lives of their children. Results from such studies could be incorporated into the collection and analyses of larger, longitudinal datasets that allow researchers to most robustly examine the associations between family structure and child well-being. Other research needs include a more thorough examination of the roles of other adults, such as grandparents or other relatives, in single parent families; the use of longitudinal data to examine the patterns of living arrangements children experience over their lifetimes and the subsequent associations with child well-being; and a better understanding of the factors that have led to divergent living arrangements, and implications of such arrangements, for children of various races and ethnicities. Finally, it is important that research be translated to policymakers and practitioners so that programs designed to promote marriage or address the needs of children living with single parents can be informed by the best possible evidence.

REFERENCES

Amato, P. 1987. Family processes in one-parent, stepparent, and intact families: The child's point of view. *Journal of Marriage and the Family* 49:327–337.

———. 2000. The consequences of divorce for adults and children. *Journal of Marriage and Family* 62:1269–1287.

Astone, N. M., and S. S. McLanahan. 1991. Family structure, parental practices, and high school completion. *American Sociological Review* 56:309–320.

Blank, R. 2002. Evaluating welfare reform in the United States. *Journal of Economic Literature* 40:1105–1166.

———. 2007. What we know, what we don't know, and what we need to know about welfare reform. National Poverty Center Working Paper 2007–19. Retrieved February 22, 2008, from www.npc.umich.edu/publications/working_papers.

Blau, F., L. Kahn, and J. Waldfogel. 2000. Understanding young women's marriage decisions: The role of labor and marriage market conditions. *Industrial and Labor Relations Review* 53, no. 4: 624–647.

Brown, S. 2004. Family structure and child well-being: The significance of parental cohabitation. *Journal of Marriage and Family* 66:351–367.

Bumpass, L., and H. Hsu. 2000. Trends in cohabitation and implications for children's family contexts in the United States. *Population Studies* 54:29–41.

Carlson, M. J., and M. E. Corcoran. 2001. Family structure and children's behavioral and cognitive outcomes. *Journal of Marriage and the Family* 63, no. 3: 779–792.

DeLeire, T., and A. Kalil. 2002. Good things come in 3s: Mutigenerational coresidence and adolescent adjustment. *Demography* 39:393–413.

Duncan, G. J., and J. Brooks-Gunn. 1997. *Consequences of growing up poor.* New York: Russell Sage Foundation.

Dunifon, R., and L. Kowaleski-Jones. 2002. Who's in the house? Race differences in cohabitation, single parenthood, and child development. *Child Development* 73, no. 4: 1249–1264.

———. 2007. The influence of grandparents in single-mother families. *Journal of Marriage and Family* 69:465–481.

Edin, K., and M. Kefalas. 2005. *Promises I can keep: Why poor women put motherhood before marriage.* Berkeley: University of California Press.

Ellwood, D., and C. Jencks. 2004. The spread of single-parent families in the United States since 1960. John F. Kennedy School of Government Faculty Research Working

Paper Series RWP04–008. Retrieved December 2007 from http://ksgnotes1.harvard.edu/research/wpaper.nsf.

Foster, E. M., and A. Kalil. 2007. Living arrangements and children's development in low-income white, black and Latino families. *Child Development* 78:1657–1674.

Gassman-Pines, A., H. Yoshikawa, and S. Nay. 2006. Can money buy you love? Dynamic employment characteristics, the New Hope Project, and entry into marriage. In H. Yoshikawa, T. Weisner, and E. Lowe, eds., *Making it work: Low-wage employment, family life and child development*, 206–232. New York: Russell Sage Foundation.

Gennetian, L. 2005. One or two parents? Half or step siblings? The effect of family structure on young children's achievement. *Journal of Population Economics* 18:415–436.

Gennetian, L., and V. Knox. 2003. Staying single: The effects of welfare reform policies on marriage and cohabitation. MDRC Working Paper Series No. 13. Retrieved January 2008 from www.mdrc.org.

Gennetian, L., and C. Miller. 2004. How welfare reform can affect marriage: Evidence from an experimental study in Minnesota. *Review of Economics and the Household* 2, no. 3: 275–301.

Gibson-Davis, C., K. Edin, and S. McLanahan. 2005. High hopes but even higher expectations: The retreat from marriage among low-income couples. *Journal of Marriage and Family* 67:1301–1312.

Ginther, D., and R. Pollak. 2004. Family structure and children's educational outcomes: Blended families, stylized facts and descriptive regressions. *Demography* 41, no. 4: 671–696.

Harknett, K., and L. Gennetian. 2003. How an earnings supplement can affect union formation among low-income single mothers. *Demography* 40, no. 3: 451–478.

Harknett, K., and S. McLanahan. 2004. Race and ethnic differences in marriage after the birth of a child. *American Sociological Review* 69, no. 6: 790–811.

Harper, C., and S. McLanahan. 2004. Father absence and youth incarceration. *Journal of Research on Adolescence* 14, no. 3: 369–397.

Hill, R. B. 1972. *The strengths of black families*. New York: Emerson Hall.

Hofferth, S., and K. Anderson. 2003. Are all dads equal? Biology versus marriage as a basis for paternal investment. *Journal of Marriage and Family* 65:213–232.

Hogan, D., and D. Lichter. 1995. Children and youth: Living arrangements and welfare. In R. Farley, ed., *State of the union*, 93–138. New York: Russell Sage Foundation.

McLanahan, S. 2004. Diverging destinies: How children are faring under the second demographic transition. *Demography* 41, no. 4: 607–627.

McLanahan, S., and G. Sandefur. 1994. *Growing up with a single parent: What hurts, what helps?* Cambridge, Mass.: Harvard University Press.

Moffitt, R. 1998. The effect of welfare on marriage and fertility. In R. Moffitt, ed., *Welfare, the family and reproductive behavior*, 50–97. Washington, D.C.: National Research Council.

Murray, C. 1984. *Losing ground: American social policy, 1950–1980.* New York: Basic Books.

Peters, H. E., and N. Mullis. 1997. The role of family income and sources of income in adolescent achievement. In G. Duncan and J. Brooks-Gunn, eds., *Consequences of growing up poor,* 340–381. New York: Russell Sage Foundation.

Roschelle, A. 1997. *No more kin: Exploring race, class, and gender in family networks.* Thousand Oaks, Calif.: Sage.

Sandberg, J. F., and S. L. Hofferth. 2001. Changes in children's time with parents: U.S. 1981–1997. Research Report No. 01–746. Ann Arbor, Mich.: Population Studies Center.

Sigle-Rushton, W., and S. McLanahan. 2002. The living arrangements of new unmarried mothers. *Demography* 39, no. 3: 415–433.

Thomson, E., T. Hanson, and S. McLanahan. 1994. Family structure and child well-being: Economic resources vs parental behaviors. *Social Forces* 73, no. 1: 221–242.

Thomson, E., S. McLanahan, and R. Curtin. 1992. Family structure, gender, and parental socialization. *Journal of Marriage and the Family* 54, no. 2: 368–379.

U.S. Census Bureau. 2006a. Household relationship and living arrangements of children under 18 years, by age, sex, race, Hispanic origin, 2006. Retrieved August 2007 from www.census.gov.

———. 2006b. People in families by family structure, age, and sex, iterated by income-to-poverty ratio and race: 2005. Retrieved August 2007 from http://pubdb3.census.gov

Waller, M., and H. E. Peters. 2007. The risk of divorce as a barrier to marriage among parents of young children. Center for Research on Child Wellbeing Working Paper #2005–03-FF. Retrieved February 25, 2008, from http://crcw.princeton.edu/working-papers.

Wilson, W. J. 1987. *The truly disadvantaged: The inner city, the underclass, and public policy.* Chicago: University of Chicago Press.

Wu, L. 1996. Effects of family instability, income and income instability on the risk of a premarital birth. *American Sociological Review* 61:386–406.

SIX

Cohabitation and Parenthood

Lessons from Focus Groups and In-Depth Interviews

WENDY D. MANNING, PAMELA J. SMOCK, AND CARA BERGSTROM-LYNCH

Cohabitation has become a family form that increasingly includes children (Bumpass and Lu 2000; Graefe and Lichter 1999). Most of the work on cohabiting parent families has focused on trends and patterns with an emphasis on who has children while cohabiting, the stability of cohabiting parent families, and the implications of cohabitation for child well-being (Brown 2000, 2006; Lichter, Qian, and Mellott 2006; Manning 2001; Manning, Smock, and Majumbar 2004). Yet, relatively little is known about the decision-making process surrounding becoming a cohabiting parent (biological or stepparent). The limited research interprets behavioral patterns (marriage before the birth of the child) (e.g., Loomis and Landale 1994; Manning 1993) or retrospective reports of planning status to interpret the context of cohabitation as a family form to have and raise children (e.g., Manning 2001; Musick 2002).

This chapter moves beyond prior studies by directly assessing how young adults view cohabitation and parenthood and comparing the advantages of having children while cohabiting rather than in marriage or living alone. We draw on focus groups and in-depth interviews to address two issues. First, we examine how young adults evaluate cohabitation as an arena for childbearing and raising children. Currently available surveys only include general attitudinal items on nonmarital childbearing, and not nonmarital childbearing in the context of cohabitation. Second, we investigate perceptions of cohabitation versus marriage as well as cohabitation versus single motherhood as settings for childrearing. These findings will assess the potential value of marriage among cohabiting parents and benefits of cohabitation among single parents. We also examine whether perceptions and experiences of parenting roles vary depending on the child's biological relationship (stepchild or biological child) to the cohabiting partner.

This chapter is purposefully exploratory and discovery-oriented, geared to provide description. Cohabiting families are a rapidly changing and growing phenomenon; at this stage of scientific knowledge, qualitative exploratory investigations are not only useful but also arguably essential (Bumpass and Sweet 2001; Smock 2000).

BACKGROUND

Although most people still marry at some point (Goldstein and Kenney 2001), and the vast majority of Americans desire to marry, unmarried cohabitation represents a potential challenge to marriage, dramatically transforming the marriage process (Smock and Gupta 2002). The percentage of marriages preceded by cohabitation rose from about 10 percent for those marrying between 1965 and 1974 to well over 50 percent for those marrying between 1990 and 1994 (Bumpass and Lu 2000; Bumpass and Sweet 1989).

Recent growth in children's experience in cohabiting families has presented new challenges to the dominance of marriage as the arena for raising children. Increasingly, children are born into cohabiting-parent families or raised by parents who are cohabiting; cohabitation is thus playing an increasingly important role in fertility and child raising processes (Manning 2001; Raley 2001). Nearly 4 million children currently live in cohabiting households, and about one-fifth of children living with an unmarried parent are living in cohabiting households (Fields 2001). The estimated proportion of children who will live in a cohabiting household at some point during childhood is a striking 40 percent (Bumpass and Lu 2000).

Moreover, contrary to common beliefs about single motherhood, a substantial proportion of nonmarital births are occurring to cohabiting couples (Bumpass and Lu 2000; Harknett and McLanahan 2004)—almost 40 percent overall, roughly 50 percent among white and Latina women, and 25 percent among African American women. Even the widely cited increase in nonmarital childbearing over the past few decades is largely accounted for by cohabitation rather than women living without a partner (Bumpass and Lu 2000).

In addition, growth in cohabitation has led to shifts in our understanding of stepfamilies (Bumpass, Raley, and Sweet 1995; Stewart 2007; see also chapter 8, this volume). Approximately half of children living with cohabiting parents are living with one biological parent and his or her cohabiting partner (Fields 2001). Cohabiting families that include children from prior unions may face a "double-institutional" jeopardy because of the lack of both marital and biological ties. We expect that cohabiting stepparents may report more potential advantages of marriage than cohabiting biological parents.

Recent trends have led to questions about whether cohabitation is an increasingly acceptable arena to have and raise children (Sigle-Rushton and McLanahan 2002; Raley 2001). The evidence is largely indirect and mixed. Researchers have studied fertility intentions and behavior of cohabitors, contrasting them to their single and married counterparts, an approach providing indirect clues about the acceptability of cohabitation as an appropriate and even desirable family form in which to have and raise children. The evidence suggests that marriage is the preferred context for childbearing and that cohabitation and marriage are not viewed as equivalent locations for family building. First, cohabiting women have higher odds of having children than noncohabiting, single women and lower odds of having children than married women (Heaton, Jacobson, and Holland 1999; Loomis and Landale 1994; Manning and Landale 1996). At the same time, and not surprisingly, greater proportions of married than cohabiting men and women intend to have a child (Rindfuss and Vanden Heuvel 1990). Second, children born to cohabiting couples are more often unplanned than children born to married couples (Manning 2001; Musick 2002). Nonetheless, the former are substantially more often reported as planned than children born to single women (Manning and Landale 1996). Third, children are associated with higher marriage rates among cohabitors. Cohabiting women who become pregnant move into marriage faster than cohabiting women who are not pregnant (Brown 2000; Manning 2001). Also, cohabitors with children (not necessarily born within cohabitation) have higher odds of marriage (Manning and Smock 1995). At the same time, there is some evidence suggesting that cohabitation may be evolving into a desirable location for having and raising children. In recent years, childbearing in cohabitation has become more common. For example, there have been dramatic increases in the percentage of children born into cohabiting unions: 12 percent of children born in the early 1990s were born to cohabiting mothers, representing a striking 100 percent increase from levels reported just 10 years earlier (Bumpass and Lu 2000). Additionally, pregnant single women are less frequently marrying in response to their pregnancies than in prior decades. In fact, pregnant single women are almost as likely to decide to cohabit as they are to marry before the birth of the child. Cohabiting couples are also decreasingly marrying in response to a pregnancy and are instead giving birth during cohabitation (Raley 2001).

A more direct way to address the topic would be to rely on attitudinal reports. However, as noted above, national surveys have not included questions about attitudes towards childbearing or parenting during cohabitation. Changes in the linkage between cohabitation and parenthood could be measured by shifts in attitudes toward childbearing and parenting children while cohabiting.

CURRENT INVESTIGATION

To date, research on attitudes and views about childbearing, childrearing, and cohabitation is sparse. Part of the reason for lack of attention to this topic is the development of cohabitation as a new family form. "No matter how widespread the practice, nonmarital unions are not yet governed by strong consensual norms or formal laws," writes Steven Nock (1995:74). In a sense, couples have to "create" their relationships because they are not heavily anchored and scripted by society. Given that cohabitation is less "institutionalized" than marriage (Cherlin 2004), it is important to identify how individuals define their relationships in terms of parenting and building families. The limited research on parenting and cohabitation and the emergence of cohabitation as a family form suggests that a qualitative assessment of parenting in cohabiting unions is a key step to moving our understanding forward.

We adopt a mixed-method approach relying on focus groups and in-depth interviews. Each method contributes to our understanding, and together they provide insight that would not be possible with a single approach. We address two research questions. First, we gain insight about cohabitation as an arena for childbearing and raising children by exploring variation in views and perceptions about the advantages and disadvantages of cohabitation as a location for children compared to marriage. To our knowledge, there is no empirical evidence about attitudes toward childbearing in cohabitation from a broad group of young adults. We draw primarily on focus group data to assess broad attitudes about cohabitation for childbearing and the conditions under which having and raising children in cohabitation is considered acceptable or unacceptable. Our focus group findings establish some of the important conceptual categories necessary to understand views of childbearing and childrearing in cohabitation versus marriage.

Second, we use focus groups to assess attitudes and in-depth interviews to ask cohabitors *directly* about their perceptions of the advantages and disadvantages of cohabiting parenthood rather than single or married parenthood. We draw heavily on the in-depth interviews to allow us to make links between feelings and perceptions and actual behavior. We begin with a focus on the advantages and disadvantages of having children while cohabiting rather than raising children alone. We examine what is gained by cohabitation (rather than remaining single) and whether marriage is perceived as an option for cohabiting unmarried parents. Our data thus provide insight into the question of why pregnant single mothers are increasingly transitioning into cohabitation rather than marriage (Raley 2001). Next, we evaluate perceptions of the value of marriage by analyzing respondents' replies to questions about the advantages of marriage rather than cohabitation. Cohabitors' reports about the value or gains (or lack of gains) to marriage will enhance understanding of the reasons why cohabitors who are pregnant or have children may or may not make transitions to marriage. We specifically differentiate between stepparent and two biological parent families.

DATA AND METHODS

In-Depth Interviews

In 2002 we conducted 115 in-depth interviews with young adults who had recent cohabitation experience. The age range is 18–36, and the average age of the sample is 26. Respondents were either cohabiting at the time of interview or had cohabited in the last three years. The interviews on average lasted about two hours, and the mean length of a single transcribed interview is thirty-nine pages. Our sample consists of at least fifteen interviews with each gender and race or ethnic group (white, black, Latino).

The study is based on respondents living in the vicinity of Toledo, Ohio. The population of Toledo and that of the nation as a whole are quite similar with regard to education, marital status, race, and income. This is a purposive sample and was recruited via newspaper advertisements, posted signs in grocery stores, break rooms at work, laundries, and libraries, personal contacts, and encounters with potential respondents in the community (for example, restaurants, shops, and the neighborhood). While some work on contemporary families focuses on particular social classes (see Edin and Kefalas 2005; Sassler 2004; Winston et al. 1999), our study reaches a broader spectrum of social classes.

Table 6.1 shows the distribution of the sample according to whether children (biological or step) were living in the home or not. Our analyses includes responses of individuals who do not live with children as well as those who do, but this table provides some sense of the composition of parents in our sample. Generally, respondents who have children in the home are Hispanic or black, have at least twelve years of education, and report low incomes. These respondents were on average quite young when they started cohabiting. In contrast, respondents without children were more advantaged (education and income). These findings echo national census estimates: cohabiting parents are more disadvantaged than cohabitors who do not have children. For example, according to PUMS data, 28 percent of cohabiting parents have less than a high-school education, and 25 percent of our sample of cohabiting parents do not have a high-school diploma or GED.

The interviews rely on semistructured interview techniques. The interviewer used an interviewer guide and followed up and probed on key themes. The questions that directly inquired about children, marriage, and cohabitation include the following. "If X/you got pregnant how would you react? How would X react? [Probe: get married?] How do you think decisions about children and parenting influenced your relationship with X? [Probe: stepchildren] Would you ever consider getting married for your children's sake? Why or why not? How do you think parenting differs when you are married than when you are cohabiting? What would be/is easier about parenting if/when you were married?" Responses from other portions of the interview also provide information used to help us understand children and cohabitation. In-depth interviews are well suited to this project because they are an excellent method for exploring perceptions, behavioral patterns, and their cognitive justifications. We are able to obtain a much richer and more nuanced understanding of perceptions and behaviors than closed-ended survey questions provide. In addition, this method helps to reveal linkages among meanings, decision making, and behavior, and it ultimately helps to illuminate the causal processes that quantitative social science seeks to uncover (Weiss 1994).

TABLE 6.1 Socioeconomic Characteristics of In-depth and Focus-group Interviews

	IN-DEPTH INTERVIEWS[1]		FOCUS GROUPS[2]
	Children (%)	Childless (%)	
Race			
Black	33.8	22.0	34.8
White	33.8	58.0	34.8
Hispanic	32.3	20.0	30.4
Gender			
Male	38.5	56.0	42.7
Female	61.5	44.0	57.3
Education			
Less than high school	13.8	8.0	2.2
High school or GED	24.6	26.0	21.0
Technical school or some college	46.1	42.0	42.8
College graduate	15.4	22.0	34
Personal income			
Less than $20,000	65.5	38.0	—
$20,000–40,000	22.4	30.0	—
More than $40,000	12.1	12.0	—
Union status at time of interview			
Ever cohabit	100.0	100.0	47.8
Never cohabit	—	—	52.2
Children			
No	—	100.0	37.7
Yes	100.0	—	62.3
N	65	50	138

[1] In-depth interview respondents all have some cohabitation experience.

[2] Focus group respondents have a range of union-status experiences, including those who never cohabited.

Focus Groups

A total of 138 young adults participated in eighteen focus groups (6–10 individuals each). These focus groups were conducted between October 2003 and July 2004 in the Detroit metropolitan area. Separate focus groups were run for race/ethnic and gender subgroups (Latino, black, and white young men and women). We interviewed twenty-six white women, twenty-two white men, twenty-five Latinas, seventeen Latinos, twenty-six black women, and twenty-two black men. Our strategy of relying on gender and race-ethnic homogenous groups allowed us to determine diversity and range in perceptions within and across groups. The focus groups included respondents in all union statuses and experiences (single, dating, married, currently cohabiting).

Each focus group had a lead moderator who introduced topics, encouraged respondent interaction and participation, kept the discussion on track, and limited the length of discussion. Training sessions and a prepared interview guide helped ensure uniformity across sessions. The focus group sessions typically ran a full two hours. We used three male and three female moderators who were Latino (one), black (one), or white (four). Two of the white moderators were fluent in Spanish. We were always able to match moderators for groups on gender, but we could only partially do so on race and ethnicity.

We used several methods to recruit participants, including advertisements in local papers; flyers posted at posted at strategic locations in the Detroit metropolitan area such as community centers, churches, bus stations, gyms, grocery stores, restaurants, community and colleges; emails to group listings; and face-to-face recruitment at organizations serving specific populations (e.g., Latinos). Potential respondents were provided a toll-free number to call and screened on age, gender, race/ethnicity, and educational attainment. Respondents received $40 to participate.

For this chapter we focus on questions in the moderator guide that were asked about children and cohabitation. The moderator guide includes the following questions: “First, we just want to get your thoughts on having children in a relationship where the parents are living together but not married. What do you think about couples having kids when they’re living together and not married? Is it a good idea for the child’s sake? Would it be better to have and raise children while married rather than when living together?” In addition, data are used from respondents who offer opinions about childbearing during other points of the interview.

Table 6.1 shows the characteristics of the focus groups. The average age of focus group participants is from the middle to late twenties for all groups.

Our goal was to gather data from largely working and middle-class young men and women—neither the very poor nor the privileged. Most (66 percent) of the sample did not have a college degree, and 23 percent had only a high-school education or less. As desired, there is variation in terms of union statuses and experience. The percentage of currently married participants was 25 percent. The percentage *ever* cohabiting is on target with nationally representative estimates (Bumpass and Lu 2000); 48 percent had ever cohabited, ranging 40 percent to 54 percent across groups.

Analysis

Our coding led to categories that were derived as they emerged from the data. We used the Atlas/ti computer program to aid in our data management and analyses. The program assists with coding and analysis of qualitative data (Weitzman 1999), and provides tools to manage, store, extract, compare, explore, and reassemble meaningful pieces of our data flexibly and systematically. The development of our coding scheme was an intensive, evolving, iterative analytic task. Essentially, coding applies a meaning or interpretation to a segment of data—in our case, textual data from the interviews. It consists of creating categories and marking segments of the data with these codes. A single paragraph or sentence may have one code or several, and these may be overlapping with other text segments.

In the quotes that appear in the following sections, proper names have been given aliases to protect the identities of the participants. At the end of each focus group quote, the date of the focus group appears after a two-letter code indicating the gender and racial composition of the focus group. The first letter represents the racial composition: B stands for black, L stands for Latino/Latina, and W stands for white. The last letter indicates the gender composition of the focus group: M for men, F for women.

RESULTS

Attitudes About Parenting and Cohabitation

Respondents in both focus groups and in-depth interviews provide a variety of responses about the acceptability of having and raising children while cohabiting. The consensus seems to be that it is preferable to have children while married, but having children while cohabiting is acceptable as long as the parents are loving and caring.

Marriage is preferable to cohabitation. We rely on the focus-group data to tap into general attitudes and beliefs about parenting in cohabitation. Our focus groups were asked to reflect upon whether it would be better to have and raise children while married rather than when living together. Most focus groups expressed concerns about cohabitation, because it means that you are more likely to get pregnant and have to care for children. Thus, a potentially negative aspect of cohabitation is the heightened risk of getting pregnant and starting a family outside of marriage. As one man put it, "I wouldn't move in 'cause I don't wanna have no kids, start havin' sex, every night, and me, I want to just keep my money right, you know, I don't want to get entangled" (BM 4–24–04). Every focus group discussed concerns about children as a reason that parents should get married instead of cohabit, and they all discussed pressure from society (e.g., family, religion) to marry when one has children. Even though individuals think it is acceptable, there is recognition of societal influence: "Society does not necessarily think it is acceptable for you to have a child and not be married . . . . We all have friends and we personally may be in that situation, but it's a lot of pressure from the outside" (LF 11–15–03). Marriage seems to offer the promise of security, legitimacy, and provides a good example for children.

The in-depth interviews indicate that cohabitors without children have the most negative views about childbearing during cohabitation; this group of respondents successfully avoided having children. Most of the cohabitors who did not have children expressed the desire not to have children while they were unmarried or "out of wedlock" and wanted to wait to have children in marriage. Imogene, a white, full-time-employed young woman who remained childless while cohabiting, stated, "What was my view of cohabiting and having children? Out of wedlock? Wasn't going to happen." Berta, a pregnant Hispanic married mother of one who cohabited before she had children, agreed: "I don't want to have a child out of wedlock. I want to be married. I don't want to get married because I'm pregnant . . . . If we were going to bring a kid into it, it would, I would have a ring on my finger and we'd be married." Male cohabitors echoed these views. Ben, a white, full-time-employed, childless young man, stated, "You should be married before you have kids. Like, ya know, you could live with somebody and everything, that's fine, but like before you have kids you should be married." It was quite rare for cohabitors who had children while cohabiting to report that it was a bad decision for them, even though they recognized the benefits of marriage. Peter, a white, full-time-employed father of two children, said that he "felt guilty that we were having a child and we weren't married. Even though we knew we both loved each other."

Cohabiting couples are also forming stepfamilies. Focus-group respondents expressed concern about cohabitation as a place to raise other people's children, that is, in stepfamilies. Male focus groups in particular expressed concerns about becoming responsible (financial and caretaking) for their partner's children. Female focus groups expressed concerns about bringing other men into the family. One woman expressed disapproval with a friend's decision to cohabit with a partner who was not her daughter's father: "I have a friend who was dating a guy for a short period and she had a daughter who's, she's seven now, at the time she was five. . . . She moved in with him and I totally, you know, 'What do you think you're doing?'—I think when kids are involved you don't want to [cohabit]" (WF 11–14–03). A woman expressed similar discomfort with the idea of cohabiting with another man: "I'm single and I'm almost to the point to where I want to date but then I'm not—'cause when you have kids, especially little girls, you don't want anybody around to . . . set an example, you don't want to bring different guys over all the time" (BF 3–27–04).

Parenting in cohabitation is acceptable, as long as partners have a good relationship. Every focus group had at least one participant who said that cohabitation is fine for children or believed that there is no difference between cohabitation and marriage for children. The in-depth interviews reveal that even though the majority of cohabitors (even those with children) would prefer to have children while married, they report that having children while cohabiting is acceptable.

The respondents' support for childbearing in cohabitation seems to be conditioned on the couple having a good relationship. This definition of a good relationship varies and often includes at least one of the following qualities: love, respect, trust, and communication. One male focus-group participant referred to his own experience growing up: "I think if you have two people who love each other and love that child, it's better, you know. I was from a divorced family, my parents were divorced and I'd much rather have two people who live together who aren't necessarily married, and have a good relationship and so I think its fine" (WM 10–23–03). In a female focus group, one participant said, "I feel like as long as they are both . . . trying to be good parents and like they are trying to do the same thing as people would do when they were [married], it doesn't make a difference in my opinion" (BF 10–11–03). A man who participated in the focus-group discussions said, "I feel like as long as there is a healthy relationship between them both, you know what I am saying, between the two people—I think it would be ideal for there to be marriage. But I think that most importantly as long as it's something that's stable, you know what I am saying? So that the child knows there's two people there that love them" (BM 12–6-03).

The in-depth interviews show that many cohabitors with children report that marriage and cohabitation are similar and cohabiting parents can raise children as well as married parents. As a white, part-time worker and mother of three children, Emma, said, "I don't think the label marriage has anything to do with how the parents are." Even some cohabitors without children report seeing nothing wrong with having children while cohabiting. Marilou, a white, full-time-employed woman, was currently cohabiting, and neither she nor her partner had children. She did not believe that people have to be married if they have kids together. "I mean, the kids are going to be affected by anything that happens, but as long as the two people that are living there love them and take care of them, and aren't fighting in front of the kid, then no I don't think it's any different [than marriage]." Thus, not all cohabiting respondents without children held a negative view of having children in cohabitation.

Cohabiting Parenthood Is Better Than Single Parenthood

The in-depth interviews reveal what is gained for parents who are cohabiting rather than living alone. The primary advantage appears to be that cohabitation provides an opportunity for biological parents to raise their child together and create a bond with the child's father. Nearly half of cohabitors with biological children cohabited in response to a pregnancy. In some cases the pregnancy may speed up the timing of the cohabitation. Cohabitation provides an opportunity, especially for dads, to be part of the baby's life and participate in the child's life everyday. Laura, a currently employed, Hispanic mother of one child, said they wanted to live together so they could both help out. Flor, a currently pregnant, Hispanic mother, wanted "to be together and so we could be in the baby's life." Leonel, a Hispanic, part-time-employed young man, had one child and was happy he could "see my kid everyday, you know, spend as much time as I want with my kid." Cohabitation allows children to be with their parents; "he knows his mommy and daddy, we both try to be there for him." Patricio, an unemployed, Hispanic father of one child, felt that living together was a "morally right" activity because the child was living with both parents and "makes me feel like we're a family"; other respondents agreed.

An advantage of cohabitation for single parents is that there is another parent to help raise children by providing instrumental support: providing childcare, helping with financial support, or taking responsibility. Women who are single when they get pregnant view cohabitation as an opportunity to have help providing for the child. Evidence above shows the support provided by biological fathers, however, stepfathers also provide support. Gregory, a white, full-time-employed young man who had no biological children, lived with a woman who had children from a prior relationship. He felt that his cohabiting partner was looking for a father figure and someone to help with her children: "She wanted, she basically wanted a father figure in her kids' lives, and she saw that I pretty much, saw that I fit the description because I am the only one that ever actually took care of her kids and cared for their needs." Edward, a white, full time-employed man with no biological children, provided childcare for his partner's children: "I was working nights, she was working days, I was taking the kids during the day, because it started being their Christmas vacation break, for the kids. So I started taking them during the mornings, and afternoon. She would come and get them after work, then we would hang together until I went to work."

Cohabiting women (stepmothers) also helped their partners as parents. Often children lived with their biological mothers but visited frequently. Erin, a white woman who was working and attending college, had lived with the same person for four years. She had no biological children of her own. Her partner had two children from previous relationships; one daughter visited every other weekend, the other less frequently. Erin said, "I think I have a responsibility as far as accepting them into my household and recognizing them as family too." Similarly, Nadine, a white, full-time-employed woman, helped her partner Marty with his daughter from another relationship, who seemed to spend a lot of time at Marty and Nadine's home. Nadine claimed that Marty "didn't know really how to care for her. I mean, there is a lot of things that he tells me that he would never be able to do without me or would have never known how to handle . . . . Yeah I mean getting sick and you know just giving her a bath, doing her hair, just all kinds of things that." Marty appreciated her parenting his daughter because he felt he did not know how to take care of a girl.

Consistent with the focus groups, men in particular recognized that cohabiting with a woman who already had children meant extra responsibilities. Edward had in a prior relationship lived with someone with a child, and he said, "if I did another relationship like that with kids, it would be a while before I moved in." Joseph, a white, full-time-employed young man who moved in with his cohabiting partner and her children, viewed this as a serious commitment because "she had enough trust in me to bring in her kids and involve me with her kids." Wesley, a black, full-time-employed man, lived with a woman who had children from a prior relationship: "I mean, you take on that responsibility if you, you're a responsible person you take on that responsibility. Um . . . if you meet somebody and they have a kid then you've got to decide if you gonna go further than just dating or whatever then not only does she become part of the responsibility, well it's her kid too."

In fact, some cohabiting men and women reported that they would not date a woman who had children because they wanted to avoid having to take care of children. Edgar, a black, part-time-employed male with no biological children who was cohabiting, stated, "I would never [have] dated somebody with a kid . . . 'cause I wouldn't want the role of being a father."

Children are an impetus to cohabit. Increasingly, young adults are cohabiting with pregnant partners (Raley 2001). The focus-group data show strong consensus. Every focus group noted that pregnancy or having children with your partner can be a reason to cohabit. One woman said, "I know someone that got pregnant and moved in because she didn't want to be married. She was wanting the father to . . . feel like he was part of living with his child and be a part of that child's life" (WF 10–11–03).

Similarly, in the in-depth interviews the pregnancy or birth of the child was typically cited as a reason that pregnant cohabitors started living together. Nearly two-fifths of in-depth interview respondents who had a child with a cohabiting partner were pregnant when they started cohabiting. For example, Peter and Susan had been dating. They were not planning on moving in together, but Susan got pregnant. Peter claimed, "We moved in for the baby." A young Hispanic mother who was employed part-time, Crystal, stated that she initiated the cohabitation: "I figured we had a kid and we shouldn't be living at home with our parents no more." She was tired of going back and forth across households. In fact, some couples get back together because of a child. Terri, a white, currently employed mother of one child, moved back in with her ex-cohabiting partner in response to getting pregnant. She said her partner "insisted on moving back in because he wasn't going to leave me or the child." Most of these couples considered cohabiting for the sake of the child and did not consider marriage an option. They stated they were not ready for marriage because of their age, economics, or relationship stage. Even though the respondents moved in together because of a baby, some explicitly stated they did not want to get married just because of a baby.

Cohabiting vs. Married Parenthood

Our data indicate that about half of the parents believe that marriage does not provide clear benefits over cohabitation. They reported that cohabitation is essentially equivalent to marriage. The other half of parents in the in-depth interviews view marriage as more beneficial for children than cohabitation. They reported some specific ways in which they believe that marriage benefits children.

Cohabitation is equivalent to marriage. Cohabiting respondents who have children often do not see clear advantages to being married. They believe that children are just as well off if their parents are living together as married. As discussed earlier, they sometimes express a general opinion that children are better off if their parents are married, but do not necessarily see any advantage to marriage for *their* children.

The notion that cohabitation is equivalent to marriage is especially true among couples where both partners are biologically related to the child. We find this view more common among parents who only have biological children (71 percent) rather than those who have stepchildren (45 percent). Often respondents claim that children are happy if their parents are living together (married or not) or if the cohabiting partner really loves and cares for the biological or stepchild. A young Hispanic mother, Petra, who was currently in school and employed, did not think that marriage would change her relationship: "I don't think anything would be different if we just got married." Crystal, who had a child while cohabiting, stated, "Not around here. I don't think he, I don't think it would even matter. As long as mom and dad are together and they love each other."

Some parents do not believe their children know whether their parents are married or just cohabiting. We find support for this in our focus groups and in-depth interviews. A focus-group participant said, "The children, they don't see the difference between the mother and father married and the mother and father single. They don't see the difference because they see only mother and father—they don't question 'Are you married?'" (LF 10–23–03). Calvin, a black, unemployed father who had a child while cohabiting, believes that children are not better off in marriage and the children do not care: "I think the kids are better off as long as they have two parents in the same home. Whether being married or whatever, they don't um, kids don't even care about none of that. They don't care if their daddy married or not. [I: Are kids better off if their parents marry?] Me, personally, I don't think it matters if they married or not." Vincent, a Hispanic, full-time-employed father who had one child while cohabiting, reported that marriage does not matter to children: "The children don't really, don't even know you know what's the difference between married and not being married. They just know mommy and daddy are always there together, they kiss each other." Kerry, a white, unemployed, young woman, made similar statements about their child not understanding differences in meaning of marriage or cohabitation: "He doesn't understand what marriage means I don't think. He's too young and we've always been you know, his mom and dad, and that was it. I don't know if he's never really told people 'that's my dad's girlfriend' or nothing like that. I don't think he's ever acted like that because we've always been together, and been with him. So, he probably to this day he still doesn't understand what it means because we've been together. Maybe if we didn't live together when he was born."

In-depth interviews show that parents believe that little would change with marriage or little had changed in their lives as a result of marriage. A mother with a young son feels that her cohabiting partner did a lot to help with her son and that marrying him would not change his responsibilities. A mother with a child from a previous relationship stated that she thought nothing would change if they married: "It's almost like we are living the married life, is what it feels like." Similarly, Grace, a white mother of one living with a cohabiting partner, said, "It's almost like we're married now it's just not legal." Leonel, a father who has had children with his cohabiting partner, stated, "Nothing would really change, 'cause we already have kids, we have kids and we live together." Basically, some parents reported that they feel like they might as well be married and do not see how getting married is going to change their relationship. One mother, Heather, a white, full-time-employed mother of two, stated, "I don't think I would be more committed because I just, my life revolves around him and my kids, you know." Luz, a currently employed Hispanic male who actually married the child's mother, also claimed that he saw "no difference," while Susan claimed their relationship "hasn't changed, to be honest."

Cohabiting parents recognize that some of the same parenting issues exist if you are married or cohabiting. Shirley, a black, full-time-employed, young woman, stated, "You can have the same problems if you were married to the person as compared to not living with that person, it all depends on what type of person they are you know." A black, unemployed, and pregnant respondent, Emily, who is a cohabiting stepparent, claimed that no matter if you are cohabiting or married, you "still gotta deal with the exes . . . . You still gotta deal with the attitude, you still gotta deal with the smart remarks." Thus, marriage is not always perceived as a solution to potential relationship and parenting problems.

Part of the reason that some cohabitors with children did not see many benefits from marriage may be that their definitions of family do not have to include legal marriage. Individuals defined their families in terms of relationships rather than by legal or institutional criteria. For example, both Tomas, an unemployed Hispanic man, and Wanda, cohabiting partners living with children from prior relationships, reported that they were living together as a family. Annie, a part-time employed, black woman, said that she did not see much distinction between cohabitation and marriage: "There's nothing that we don't do now that is not like being married, I mean our finances together . . . we do for our daughter, he has a little boy that's four by someone else before we got together, we do, I do for him like you know, he's part of the family, even though we're not married." Even Martin, a Hispanic, full-time-employed young man, did not have any children while cohabiting but believed "you don't have to be married to be a family."

Cohabitors who do not see advantages of marriage view childbearing and marriage as separate activities. Julio, an unemployed Hispanic male with three children who was cohabiting, distinguished between parenthood and marriage: "Anybody can have a kid but not everybody can get married . . . . When you get married both people have to love each other. When you have a kid you can just one night stand and that's it." Some cohabiting parents view their love and commitment for their child as long-lasting and durable; however, their ties to the cohabiting partners are not as strong. Cohabitors who view no benefits to marriage frequently mentioned that marriage provides no guarantee that their relationship will last.

Marriage ensures security. All of the female focus groups reported that marriage creates security and provides benefits for the children (legal and medical). A woman explained why she prefers to be married before she has children: "I think it is that security thing. And so it is just like, it is a logical step. You know, like getting secure in certain things before. I just believe that should happen, you know. You need to secure that last name and that insurance. Then making sure that he is accountable for that child" (BF 11–4–03). Focus-group respondents also noted that marriage can protect the couple from breaking up. A Latina woman explained her experience: "I wasn't married, had a child, and then her dad got up and left. It was a lot harder for me, you know. It's really tough for her—I mean, he comes around once in a while but now that I'm married, you know, he's her dad. She calls him daddy and then for my son, yeah, I do feel a lot securer—like I feel like, gosh, you know, we are a family now, he can't just get up [and leave]" (LF 11–15–03).

The in-depth interviews reveal that many cohabiting parents feel that marriage provides a greater bond or commitment than cohabitation. Yasmina, a black, full-time-employed mother of two, stated, "Marriage makes it easier for the two parents to be united." Debbie, a full-time-employed, white cohabiting woman without any children reported that with "being married comes the expectation that you are going to be around and that you are participating." A white mother of one, Kerry, stated that children would be better off if parents married: "The parents are probably gonna stay together . . . . They're tied together, and if they weren't it is a lot easier for just one of them to leave." Yasmina echoed this statement: "If we were just living together then it would be easier for me to say, 'I quit,' whether we have kids or not." Peggy, a white, full-time-employed, married mother, had a child during cohabitation and felt that marriage provides stability by creating a family, which would become even more important when the children were older: "I think that marriage is important. I think that marriage especially when you have kids is important. I think that provides stability. It gives everybody a unit. A unit to focus on. It's important for kids. They don't realize it until they get older." Peggy was pregnant when she started cohabiting but was not ready for marriage because of her own childhood experiences with parental divorce. She married her cohabiting partner when her oldest daughter was five. Marriage is also a way of showing a male is committed to the family. Leonel, a father of one child during cohabitation, stated, "The father should show his commitment to the family by marrying their mom." He did not want to have more children during cohabitation. Similarly, focus-group women reported that marriage makes men "accountable," and without marriage, "I really don't have the security nets that the father is going to be necessarily be there" (LF 11–15–03).

Even in the event of a breakup, cohabiting respondents believe that marriage serves children better. Henry, a full-time-employed, cohabiting white male without children, said, "There's a great risk with cohabitation that things are going to turn sour and, then badly than there is with marriage. And, when you got a kid involved, that makes it, the damage all the greater." He went on to state that a breakup of a marriage is bad for a child but that for cohabitation it is even worse because the parents were never committed via marriage. In a sense, the lack of institutionalization of cohabitation makes a parental breakup worse because there are no formal parental ties. He viewed cohabitation as more unstable and creating more problems for children. Marriage seemed to guarantee some connection to the father: "If you're married and with that person [parent] for a while, at least the kids will know who the parent is and how the parent is."

Marriage provides financial benefits by ensuring that children have access to the benefits of their parent's workplace, such as insurance and medical benefits. No cohabiting respondents spoke about any other financial benefits of marriage. Wesley, a full-time-employed, black father, felt that it doesn't matter whether or not the parents of a child are married; the only advantage of marriage in his mind is medical insurance. A young, full-time-employed white man without children, Owen, thought that the only disadvantage of having a child while cohabiting rather than being married was "financial because my insurance wouldn't cover it." He had a good insurance plan and wanted to avoid the financial burden. Janet, a full-time-employed white woman who got married before her child was born, mentioned medical insurance as a benefit of being married.

Marriage clarifies social roles. The legal act of marriage is one way to solidify family roles. A fundamental way that marriage may clarify roles is by sharing a name. A few in-depth interview respondents referred to importance of marriage as a way to create a "real" family that shared one last name. Inquires by children about last names seemed to crystallize the importance of marriage to parents. From a child's perspective, sharing a last name is a clear indicator of marriage. Luz's children asked their parents why they do not have the same last name. Patricio stated that kids know whether their parents are married by "the rings and by what the last names are." He claimed that it makes a difference to children because they can be proud they know their parents. Terri, a white woman who was not working but was attending beautician school, was concerned because her daughter sometimes said, "Mommy has a different name than my daddy; they're not married yet, they just live together." She claimed this was hard on her daughter. Focus-group respondents echoed these same concerns. A woman who participated in the focus-group conversations decided to get married so that her future children would share the same surname: "My stepsister growing up with a different last name than my mom, she had issues about that. And I know that . . . it is kind of idealistic but if I wanted to have kids I wanted to do it in a marriage and, you know, have all of us have the same last name and be a family. That was just my—that is what I wanted that was my goal. So and you know my husband felt the same way" (BF 10–11–03). Fran, a white, full-time-employed young mother of one, who was single and living alone when she had her child, stated that she would want to be married so the child would have the father's last name and he could not dispute fatherhood: "It would be automatically his . . . and he automatically would have a responsibility and it wouldn't have to go down to a blood test."

Marriage is a clear way to solidify family roles, especially in stepfamilies. Among stepfamilies, marriage guarantees a new title—stepmother or stepfather—and this new title may make it easier to parent children. For example, some cohabitors expressed some confusion about their relationship with their partner's children. Carlos, a full-time-employed Hispanic man who was living with his partner's child, struggled when trying to explain his role in his partner's child's life: "I'm just, you know, like a father figure. Step, almost. Like, not a stepfather, 'cause he has a father. But just being there to support." Sometimes the roles varied with families and depended on the age or gender of the children. Erin, a twenty-two-year-old who was cohabiting with a partner who had two children from a prior relationship, reflected on her stepmother role: [I: Do you act like you're these kids' mother?] "The oldest I do. The youngest, no. Her mama's in her life and real active. So I try to be a role model for the oldest. That's it basically. I try to be a role model for both of them . . . . I think I have a responsibility as far as accepting them into my household and recognizing them as family, too." Marriage is expected to help the family work together. Judy, a cohabiting stepparent, said, "When you're married everyone kind of has their set roles and place, I think it's easier to function as a family."

Some cohabitors realized that their parenting roles would change with marriage. Nadine was interested in getting married so she could gain a new official role as stepmother. "You know, another thing I wanted to hurry the marriage up was his daughter. I just wanted to be the stepmother, not just the girlfriend, you know." Marriage also improved her relationship with the child's biological mother, because she was no longer "just the girlfriend." Wanda had her cohabiting partner's child visit on weekends. She claimed she felt like an aunt. "I'm not trying to be, I don't know, it's kind of weird. I'm not trying to be a stepmother figure. I just treat her like a child in the household like I do my niece or nephew." She then went on to state that she would view herself as a stepmother if she were married to her partner. Grace thought her cohabiting partner would "feel like a parental figure . . . more important to him or more serious" if they got married.

Children also use the fact their parent is not married as a means to get their way. Teresa, a full-time-employed Hispanic woman, said her partner's children would use the phrase "You're not my dad's wife" as a way to show disrespect. Similarly, other blended families struggled with discipline and felt that marriage might be one way to solidify authority in the family. Bob, a full-time-employed white man, grappled with how to handle discipline while living in a "Brady Bunch" family, with his own children and his partner's children. "I just thought it, uh, neither of us really had the authority to say so other than the fact that I'm the parent and they're the child." He stated that marriage would help to better define the parenting roles.

Some cohabitors did not take on stepparenting roles because they were not married. Once they got married, they felt more responsible for the children. In some cases they distanced themselves from decisions related to parenting and discipline. Melany, a part-time-employed, black mother of one biological child, stated, "I'm not married so why should I treat him like a step child?" She went on to say that if she were married then she would take on greater roles: "If we were married I would be wrong not to act as a as stepmother because I've gotten married in the situation knowing that he has a child and I married him. I married him and his luggage. So, whatever, whatever comes with him, I should also you know accept and I'll be wrong if I don't do that."

Marriage provides social recognition. One of the functions of marriage is to demonstrate publicly commitment to another person. Some cohabiting parents realize that they may be viewed negatively because they have children outside of marriage. Daniela, an unemployed, Hispanic mother of two children born while cohabiting, felt pressured to say she was married or engaged. "Probably because you don't want them to look down on you." Cohabitors made statements about the importance of following society's expectation to have children in marriage.

Marriage is expected to influence children by making it easier for them at school and in other social situations. Nadine, who had children while cohabiting, thought it would have been better to be married because "you're actually a family, you know and people see it that way when you are married."

Similarly, Malcolm, a full-time-employed, black father, felt that children would prefer if their parents were married: "It's easier to explain at school or at a function with other people." Kerry, who married after the birth of her child, felt it was socially awkward to refer to her boyfriend when she was around other parents: "It just didn't feel right." Keith, who married before the birth of his child, mirrored Kerry's statement: "When you're married it says something. There's a big difference introducing somebody as your wife than just somebody as your girlfriend." Judy, a full-time-employed white woman who married her cohabiting partner, felt that it was easier to be a stepparent when married because she had more authority: "I can go into their school; I'm their stepmother so I can take them out of school."

Marriage teaches the value of marriage. One of a parent's important roles is to socialize his or her children. A young woman who participated in the in-depth interviews and did not have children while cohabiting felt that raising children in cohabitation might result in socializing children away from marriage. She felt that one way to teach children about commitment was to be married rather than cohabiting. Marc, a full-time-employed white man, claimed that parents wanted to "set the best example possible" for their children by showing that marriage is the ideal situation. Dorothy, a white, full-time student who worked part-time and had no biological children, stated, "I think if kids are raised with a parent and a boyfriend/girlfriend then they don't put as much stock into marriage as they would if they were raised by married parents."

Indeed, having children while cohabiting may make it difficult to encourage your own children to wait until marriage to have children. A focus-group participant explained, "I did live with a female prior to getting married, but if I had thought it through I probably wouldn't have because you want to set an example for future, so when you have your offspring, your children, and they want to live with someone, you really don't have the place to say well, 'You shouldn't' when you already did it" (LM 12–13–03). Myron, a black, full-time-employed man who had been living with his partner's child, was concerned about being hypocritical about marriage and childbearing: "Your kids see you living together and you're not married and everything else then you try to push them about getting married and being a wife you know what I'm saying. You can't say one thing and do another, you can't tell your kids to do one thing and they see you doing the totally different than that . . . . That makes you hypocritical. I can't tell my child that she can't live with a man and she be like 'Well, you lived with mama for three years.' You know what I'm saying, we're not married, you can't do that, you have to set examples." A mother, Yasmina, who had a child while cohabiting, felt that having children could lead to larger social problems: "Because in the society that we live in now if you were raised right then you would know it's not cool to have kids out of wedlock, so if you see, if my kids see me you know living with this man and we're pretending to be married then she'll grow up and do the same thing and that's where the patterns start." Thus, these parents show ways that there may be intergenerational processes influencing decisions to cohabit.

CONCLUSIONS

Our chapter demonstrates a range of responses about attitudes and views toward having and raising children while cohabiting. One motivation for this work is that it is difficult with quantitative research alone to understand how parenting within cohabitation fits in current family patterns and norms about family formation. Our first aim was to explore how young adults felt about cohabiting and parenting. Their responses generally reflect the larger societal norm of marriage as the ideal or best place to have children. In fact, some of the acceptance of cohabitation rests on whether or not children are present; in some cases, cohabitation is supported only if children are not involved. Of particular concern seemed to be the formation of cohabiting stepparent families. As found in prior studies, women in focus groups expressed caution about living with men who are not the children's biological father (Edin and Kefalas 2005), and men in focus groups reported concern about taking on responsibility for other men's children.

At the same time, every focus group and many cohabiting respondents also expressed the opinion that cohabitation and marriage can be similar when it comes to having and raising children. They also recognized that cohabitation is more socially acceptable than it used to be. Men and women both agreed that children are being raised successfully in cohabiting as well as marital relationships. Respondents believed that having children while cohabiting can be no different than having children while married, as long as the relationship is "consistent," "thriving," "stable," and "healthy" and children are in a "loving environment."

Few researchers have asked about the potential advantages of cohabitation for having and raising children. When the alternative is raising children alone, cohabitation appears to serve at least two needs. Cohabitation was reported to provide a sense of security and ensure the involvement of a male (biological father or not). In fact, cohabitation allows men to demonstrate their responsibility for children—even when those children are not their biological children and even when they do not feel ready for marriage. Men believe that they are demonstrating commitment by raising and being there for their child; moving in with a partner allows the father to be involved and active in the child's life. Researchers frequently have overlooked that cohabitation may be operating as alternative way to legitimate a pregnancy. The majority of cohabitors who were pregnant at the start of their union did not consider marriage an option for them.

Young adults provided several diverse responses to queries about the potential gains to marriage rather than cohabitation. These reports help to explain why cohabitors who are pregnant or have children may or may not make transitions to marriage. First, respondents referred to the security, largely emotional, and maintenance of the father-child relationship that marriage provides. Financial benefits were rarely mentioned. For example, while marriage could guarantee medical and health benefits for family members, this was not frequently reported as a strong motivation for marriage. Some respondents may not have had jobs that included good benefit packages. Second, respondents highlighted the importance of marriage for social learning. Concerns were expressed that cohabitation may teach children that it is acceptable to have children outside of marriage and diminish the importance of marriage. Third, marriage provides legitimacy to the relationship in social situations. Marriage may become more important to parents as their children enter school and are forced to be more public about the nature of their relationship. Finally, marriage serves to define social roles. One way is via observable shifts such as sharing the same last name and using marital relationship terms—wife rather than girlfriend.

Cohabiting stepparents saw clear advantages to marriage. They face the double institutional jeopardy by not being biologically related to their partners' children as well as not being married to the children's mother. This seems to create parenting stress and challenges to parental roles. Marriage among cohabiting stepparents is viewed as an opportunity to solidify their status in the family and guarantee parenting authority. This finding may help to explain poorer child well-being in cohabiting-parent stepfamilies versus married stepparent families (see Manning and Lamb 2003; see also chapter 8, this volume).

There is also a strong sentiment that marriage is not necessary for having and raising children. About half of cohabiting parents saw little or no advantage to marriage. Many cohabiting couples with children already felt as if they were married and that marriage would not change their relationship or parenting. Some respondents with young children noted that their children did not know the difference in their legal status. Our findings suggest that the perceived advantage to marriage is stronger among stepparents than biological parents.

Overall, we do not have one consistent storyline, but instead several narratives about cohabitation as a family form in which to have and raise children. This variation should not be ignored, and it may be part of a larger flux in all unions or the "deinstitutionalization of marriage" (Cherlin 2004).

Our qualitative data speak to some methodological issues. In terms of measurement, general-attitude questions about parenting in cohabitation may reflect a simplified social norm that childbearing should occur within marriage. For example, most Americans say marriage is desirable, but they still are delaying and facing barriers to marriage. Thus, some family forms, such as cohabitation, may be acceptable but are not the most highly desired or preferred family form. New surveys that include family-attitude questions should incorporate these nuances by framing questions that tap into accepting cohabitation under certain conditions as well as preferences for marriage over cohabitation and cohabitation rather than single parenthood. In addition, new questions that ask specifically, "What would be different if *you* married?" would provide a wider range of responses that may more directly uncover motivations to cohabit and marry.

Our sample was quite heterogeneous in terms of gender as well as race and ethnicity. Certainly, this is a small sample in one region of the nation, which may lead to questions about the generalizability of our results. While we understand the limitations of this type of sample, we do not believe that respondents' replies are unique to our interview setting.

Substantively, we have learned more about why the behavioral patterns social scientists observe exist and a range of potential explanations for observed behavior. For example, marriage before the birth of a child cues the researcher that there must be some perceived benefits of marriage. Yet questions about the benefits of marriage do not appear in surveys. We have found some potential reasons why marriage occurs: security, socialization of children, social recognition, and clarification of family roles. Similarly, we have discovered some reasons why pregnant single women may move into cohabitation. Researchers have noted growth in cohabitation in response to pregnancy (Raley 2001), but they have not investigated the reasons for this growth. Our results suggest that cohabitation is an opportunity to raise a child together and provides security. Finally, some research on child well-being indicates that children in cohabiting stepfamilies fare worse than children living with married-stepparent families (see Manning and Lamb 2003; chapter 8, this volume). Our findings suggest that this may stem in part from the ambiguity of parenting roles in cohabiting-stepparent families.

Our research has implications for marriage policy and the focus on marriage as a strategy to improve the fortunes of children. If many young adults do not perceive a distinction between parenting in cohabitation and marriage, this poses a considerable challenge to encouraging marriage. Cohabitors have provided us with important reasons why cohabitation and marriage may matter, and these motivations have not been extensively discussed in the literature. Ultimately, we believe that our results can be used to broaden the base of knowledge about the value of marriage and inform efforts targeted at supporting healthy marriages and relationships.

NOTE

This chapter originated as a paper presented at the Twenty-Sixth Annual APPAM Research Conference, 28–30 October, 2004, Atlanta, Georgia. The research was supported by grants from the National Institute of Child Health and Human Development (NICHD) to the first and second authors (R03 HD039835 and R01 HD040910). It was also supported in part by the Center for Family and Demographic Research at Bowling Green State University and the Population Studies Center at the University of Michigan, which both receive core funding from NICHD (R21 HD042831 and R24 HD41028). We thank Claudia Vercellotti for her excellent interviewing skills, and Meredith Porter, Julie Downing, Gayra Ostgaard, and Jessica Cohen for their capable research assistance.

REFERENCES

Brown, S. L. 2000. Union transitions among cohabitors: The significance of relationship assessments and expectations. *Journal of Marriage and Family* 62:833–846.

———. 2006. Family structure transitions and adolescent well-being. *Demography* 439:447–461.

Bumpass, L. L., and H. H. Lu. 2000. Trends in cohabitation and implications for children's family contexts in the United States. *Population Studies* 54:29–41.

Bumpass, L. L., R. K. Raley, and J. A. Sweet. 1995. The changing character of stepfamilies: Implications of cohabitation and nonmarital childbearing. *Demography* 32:425–436.

Bumpass, L. L., and J. A. Sweet. 1989. National estimates of cohabitation. *Demography* 26:615–625.

———. 2001. Marriage, divorce, and intergenerational Relationships. In A. Thornton, ed., *The well-being of children and families: Research and data needs*, 295–313. Ann Arbor: University of Michigan Press.

Cherlin, A. J. 2004. The deinstitutionalization of American marriage. *Journal of Marriage and Family* 66:848–861.

Edin, K., and M. Kefalas. 2005. *Promises I can keep*. Berkeley: University of California Press.

Fields, J. 2001. Living arrangements of children: Fall 1996. *Current population reports*, 70–74. Washington, D.C.: Census Bureau.

Goldstein, J. R., and C. T. Kenney. 2001. Marriage delayed or marriage forgone? New cohort forecasts of first marriage for U.S. women. *Demography* 66:506–519.

Graefe, D. R., and D. L. Lichter. 1999. Life course transitions of American children: Parental cohabitation, marriage, and single motherhood. *Demography* 36:205–217.

Harknett, K., and S. McLanahan. 2004. Racial and ethnic differences in marriage after the birth of a child. *American Sociological Review* 69:790–811.

Heaton, T. B., C. K. Jacobson, and K. Holland. 1999. Persistence and change in decisions to remain childless. *Journal of Marriage and Family* 61:531–539.

Lichter, D. T., Z. Qian, and L. M. Mellott. 2006. Marriage or dissolution? Union transitions among poor cohabiting women. *Demography* 43:223–240.

Loomis, L. S., and N. S. Landale. 1994. Nonmarital cohabitation and childbearing among black and white American women. *Journal of Marriage and Family* 56:949–962.

Manning, W. D. 1993. Marriage and cohabitation following premarital conceptions. *Journal of Marriage and the Family* 55:839–850.

———. 2001. Childbearing in cohabiting unions: Racial and ethnic differences. *Family Planning Perspectives* 33:217–223.

Manning, W. D., and K. A. Lamb. 2003. Adolescent well-being in cohabiting, married, and single-parent families. *Journal of Marriage and Family* 65:876–893.

Manning, W. D., and N. S. Landale. 1996. Racial and ethnic difference in the role of cohabitation in premarital childbearing. *Journal of Marriage and Family* 58:63–77.

Manning, W. D., and P. J. Smock. 1995. Why marry? Race and the transition to marriage among cohabitors. *Demography* 32:509–520.

Manning, W. D., P. J. Smock, and D. Majumdar. 2004. The relative stability of cohabiting and marital unions for children. *Population Research and Policy Review* 23:135–159.

Musick, K. 2002. Planned and unplanned childbearing among unmarried women. *Journal of Marriage and Family* 64:915–929.

Nock, S.L. 1995. A comparison of marriages and cohabiting relationships. *Journal of Family Issues* 16:53–76.

Raley, R.K. 2001. Increasing fertility in cohabiting unions: Evidence for the second demographic transition in the United States? *Demography* 38:59–66.

Rindfuss, R.R., and A. Vanden Heuvel. 1990. Cohabitation: A precursor to marriage or an alternative to being single? *Population and Development Review* 16:703–726.

Sassler, S. 2004. The process of entering into cohabiting unions. *Journal of Marriage and Family* 66:491–505.

Sigle-Rushton, W., and S. McLanahan. 2002. Living arrangements of new unmarried families. *Demography* 39:415–433.

Smock, P.J. 2000. Cohabitation in the United States: An appraisal of research themes, findings, and implications. *Annual Review of Sociology* 26:1–20.

Smock, P.J., and S. Gupta. 2002. Cohabitation in contemporary North America. In A. Booth and A.C. Crouter, eds., *Just living together: Implications for children, families, and public policy*, 53–84. Mahwah, N.J.: Erlbaum.

Stewart, S. 2007. *Brave new stepfamilies: Diverse paths toward stepfamily living*. Thousand Oaks, Calif.: Sage.

Weiss, R.S. 1994. *Learning from strangers: The art and method of qualitative interview studies*. New York: Free Press.

Weitzman, E. 1999. Analyzing qualitative data with computer software, Part II. *Health Services Research* 34, no. 5: 1241–1263.

Winston, P., R. Angel, L. Burton, L. Chase-Lansdale, A. Cherlin, R. Moffitt, and W. Wilson. 1999. *Welfare, children, and families: Overview and design*. Baltimore: Johns Hopkins University Press.

SEVEN

An Examination of Child Well-Being in Stable Single-Parent and Married Families

CLAIRE M. KAMP DUSH

Several studies have documented that children in single-mother families fare worse than their counterparts in married two-parent families (see Chase-Lansdale, Cherlin, and Kiernan 1995; Cherlin, Chase-Lansdale, and McRae 1998; McLanahan and Sandefur 1994). Academics and policymakers alike have argued, based on evidence such as the studies cited here, that married two-parent families are the ideal place for both adults and children to reside (Popenoe 1995; Waite and Gallagher 2000). However, there is one missing piece in the single-mother family literature that, if examined, could challenge this view. There is a dearth of longitudinal research on single-mother families, and in particular, stable single-mother families. Could it be that the stability of a family structure is just as important as the type of family structure for child development? This chapter examines how children living with stable single mothers fare compared to children from stable married families, using data from merged mother-child files of the National Longitudinal Survey of Youth 1979 (NLSY79) cohort.

Specifically, I compare a variety of outcomes for children ages eight to fourteen who were born to either two married biological parents or one single mother and who have not experienced a family-structure transition such as divorce, remarriage, or entry into cohabitation. To gauge child functioning, I focus on two facets of children's academic achievement: measures of the amount of cognitive stimulation and emotional support provided in the home and measures of children's social and emotional adjustment. Making distinctions among various types of family structures is important at a time when a variety of new federally funded programs designed to promote marriage have been enacted (Dion 2005). Such programs are based on the assumption that living with a married parent is better for children than living with a single mother. The results from this study will allow a test of whether this assumption holds for stable single mothers.

BACKGROUND

Single Parents and Other Family Structure Types

The number of children living in single-parent families has increased dramatically in the past thirty years (see chapter 5, this volume). In 2005, 23 percent of all U.S. children under the age of eighteen were living with a single mother; examined separately by race, data show that 16 percent of white children were living with a single mother in 2005, compared to 50 percent of black children. Single parenthood is of concern to policymakers in part because of the high prevalence of poverty among children in such families. In 2005, 41 percent of families headed by a single mother were in poverty, compared to 9 percent of families with married parents (U.S. Census Bureau 2005).

A great deal of research has explored the connections between family structure and child development. In general, growing up in a single-parent household is associated with greater behavior problems, higher rates of teenage pregnancy, and lower academic achievement among children and youth (McLanahan and Sandefur 1994), compared to living with married parents. Dunifon and Kowaleski-Jones (2002) found that the influence of single parenthood on children differed by race, with most detrimental influences of single parenthood occurring for white, but not black, children. More recent research by Foster and Kalil (2007) finds little evidence that family structure is associated with child well-being in a very low-income sample. Other scholars have also been able to eliminate the significant difference between children in married and single-mother families by controlling for a variety of variables (Carlson and Corcoran 2001; Ginther and Pollak 2004). These results would suggest that at least part of the association between family structure and child well-being can be explained by the selection of less-educated, poorer women into single motherhood over married motherhood. These studies highlight the continued need for more research on family structure.

Few studies have examined the effects of living in a stable (never-married, never-cohabited) single-parent family on child outcomes. Of note is that most previous research simply looked at nonmarital mothers (see McLanahan and Sandefur 1994), and only recently have scholars begun to distinguish cohabiting parents from single mothers (see Brown 2004). In a notable exception, Teachman (2004) found that women who spent their entire childhoods in never-married mother-headed families had the lowest levels of education at marriage, married husbands with less education, and were the most likely to have a premarital birth. However, his analysis did not distinguish between women who lived with only their mothers versus women who lived with their mothers and their cohabiting partners during childhood.

There have been two main theories posited in the literature to explain differences between children in single-parent and married-parent families. Economic deprivation in single-mother families has been suggested as the primary mechanism by which children living with single mothers fare worse than those with two-married parents. Children raised in families with more economic resources have more positive cognitive and social outcomes (Duncan and Brooks-Gunn 1997; McLanahan and Sandefur 1994). However, controls for income have not completely eliminated the effect (Duncan and Brooks-Gunn 1997; Hill, Yeung, and Duncan 2001; McLanahan and Sandefur 1994; though see Carlson and Corcoran 2001; Foster and Kalil 2007). An alternative theory concerns differences in parenting. Parental practices, which may be compromised in single-parent families due to stress, less parental time available for supervision, or because single mothers who do not marry function less well on a variety of dimensions including personality, has been posited to explain the differences between children in single-parent families and married-parent families. Single-mother families may find it more difficult to supervise the activities of their children than do two-parent families (Astone and McLanahan 1991; McLanahan and Sandefur 1994; Thomson, McLanahan, and Curtin 1992). Single-mother families have also been found to be more socially isolated and have less parental support (Weinraub and Wolf 1983). Though I do not test these assumptions directly, I do attempt to carefully account for economic differences between single-parent and married-parent families. By carefully accounting for economic differences, I am also able to isolate a sample that may be experiencing similar levels of stress due to economic or neighborhood circumstances.

The family structure experiences of children in the United States vary widely by race. Using the National Survey of Family Growth 1995, Bumpass and Lu (2000) found that 72 percent of black children were born to single mothers, and only 22 percent of these single mothers were cohabiting at the birth. In contrast, only 18 percent of white mothers were single at birth, and of these, 50 percent were cohabiting at birth. Hispanic mothers fall somewhere in between black and white mothers such that 32 percent were single at the birth of their child, but similar to white mothers, 53 percent were cohabiting at the birth of their child. These differences persist across the life course of children. Blau and van der Klaauw (2006) found that children of black mothers spent on average only 34 percent of their childhoods living with their biological mother and father, while white children spent 73 percent and Hispanic children spent 64 percent of their childhoods on average with their biological mother and father. Owing to the differences in family structure by race and to previously cited research that has found racial differences in the implications of family structure for children (Dunifon and Kowaleski-Jones 2002), I run all models separately by race.

Sample

The National Longitudinal Survey of Youth 1979 is a survey designed to gather information at multiple points in time on the labor market experiences of groups of men and women. The 1979 cohort was a nationally representative sample of 12,686 men and women between the ages of fourteen to twenty-two in 1979. Data were collected annually from 1979 through 1994, and biannually thereafter. I rely on data collected through 2004, the most recent year available. Sample design procedures oversampled blacks, Hispanics, and economically disadvantaged nonblacks and non-Hispanics. Starting in 1986, the children of the women of the NLSY79 (CNLSY79) have been assessed every two years. The children as of 2004 were mostly below the age of twenty-nine, and it is estimated that the sample includes about 90 percent of the children who will ever be born to the NLSY79 women (Center for Human Resource Research 2004). In my analyses I use detailed information on the home environment as well as their cognitive and socioemotional development, gathered biennially for children aged 4–15 between 1986 and 2004.

A key limitation of the NLSY mother-child data is the lack of information on children's fathers. The structure of the data means that children are only followed when they live with their mothers. Therefore, the sample does not contain any children living only with their fathers, or with fathers and stepmothers. Additionally, because all data reports come from the child's mother, the data contain limited information about the child's father. Despite these shortcomings, the NLSY has several strengths making the data well suited for the analyses in this chapter. The main strength lies in the fact that children in this study have been followed since birth, giving us extensive background information on the living arrangements, income, employment status, and other important aspects of the lives of children and their mothers over a child's entire lifespan.

To create the data used for this project, I created a stacked person-year file for the mothers, with a line of data for each interview year between 1979 and 2004. I used this stacked person-year file to create a family structure history for each mother. After the coding of the family structure histories was completed, I merged a stacked version of the children's data into the mother's data. Children were dropped if the child's birth year was missing ($n=3$) or if the relationship status of the mother at birth was missing ($n=1$). Hence my sample included data from 4,910 mothers and 11,428 children.

MEASURES

Independent Variables

After selecting the sample, I coded each child's family structure history using a series of constructed variables available in the NLSY79 data that assess the total number of partners the mother had ever had by a given wave, as well information on her current relationship, if any (whether married, cohabiting, or single after a union). Using these measures, I created family structure histories at each year, which were then merged with the child data. Hence, for all years between 1970 (the earliest date of birth in the NLSY79 Children and Young Adult dataset) and 2004, I coded family structure in 181,481 person years of data, 28 percent of which were coded using retrospective data. After completing these steps, I created exclusive dichotomous measures of family structure capturing the child's lifetime family structure experiences at each year that a child was assessed: stable married parents (has always lived with married parents), stable single parent (has always lived with a single mother), stable union parents (child was born to cohabiting parents and who either continue cohabiting or marry), and unstable family structure (child has experienced at least one family-structure transition).

Dependent Variables

To capture children's cognitive achievement, I used the math, reading comprehension, and reading recognition achievement assessments, which are taken from the Peabody Individual Achievement Tests (PIAT). Children ages five and older were administered these tests at each of the biennial assessments. The mathematics assessment consisted of eighty-four multiple-choice items of increasing difficulty. My analysis is of the age and gender standardized scale.

The PIAT reading recognition assessment measured word recognition and pronunciation ability. This assessment contained eighty-four items, each with four options, which increased in difficulty from preschool to high-school levels. The NLSY's PIAT reading comprehension test measured a child's ability to understand sentences that he or she reads silently. The scoring and scaling procedures for both reading tests were similar to that of the PIAT math assessment and the age and gender standardized scales were used. Both the PIAT mathematics and reading assessments are considered to be highly reliable and valid and their widespread use is evident in the psychological and sociological literature (Baker et al. 1993). I combined the two reading subscales to be an overall measure of reading skills. The reading recognition and reading comprehension subscales were correlated at 0.74 and had an alpha reliability of 0.84.

Behavioral adjustment was measured in the NLSY79-C by the Behavioral Problem Index (BPI), a measure of the frequency, range, and type of childhood behavior problems (Peterson and Zill 1986). The measure was completed by the mothers, and the Behavior Problems total score was based on responses from the mothers to twenty-eight questions. I used the age and gender standardized Behavior Problem Index.

I also used the family structure measures to predict measures of the cognitive stimulation and emotional support provided in the child's home. In the NLSY, assessments of children's home environments were derived from the Home Observation for Measurement of the Environment (HOME) scales (Bradley and Caldwell 1984a, 1984b). I used the age standardized total HOME score, which captures both the degree of appropriate cognitive stimulation and emotional support directed toward the child. The HOME scales were developed to identify and describe homes of infants and young children who were at significant developmental risk; they have been effectively used to identify home environments associated with impaired mental development and poor school performance (Bradley 1985).

Control Variables

Analyses controlled for child age, gender, race and ethnicity, and time-varying covariates for mother's education (highest grade completed), employment status (using a dummy indicating whether the mother was employed at the time of the interview), total annual family income, and the number of children of the mother in the household. I also took advantage of the rich nature of the NLSY79 data to capture characteristics of mothers and their backgrounds that largely preceded their fertility and union-formation behavior. These measures included the mother's Armed Forces Qualifying Test (AFQT) score (a measure of IQ taken in 1980), a dummy indicating whether the mother lived with both parents when she was fourteen, a scale indicating whether the mother's own parents provided a stimulating learning environment when the mother was fourteen (specifically, whether they subscribed to newspapers and magazines and/or had a library card), and a scale indicating whether the mother participated in two or more delinquent behaviors at age fourteen. Controlling for these measures allowed me to capture a mother's own family background, as well as some maternal characteristics, all preceding the family-structure and child-outcome measures I examine here.

METHOD

I ran all models separately by race, since the prevalence of the various family structures in the data varies greatly by race. I begin the analyses by running a series of regressions where the outcomes include the HOME, BPI, and the PIAT math and reading skills subscales separately by race and two-year age groups. The main independent variable in these analyses was a dummy variable for whether the child was in a stable married family (the excluded group) or a stable single parent family. For all models, I use children aged seven to fourteen. Therefore, those children who experience a family structure transition prior to age seven are not included in these analyses. I controlled for child's age and gender, mother's AFQT, family structure at age fourteen, learning environment at age fourteen, delinquency at age fourteen, and time-varying covariates for mother's education, employment status, total annual family income, and the number of mother's children in the household. However, even with these controls, regression estimates in analyses where selection may play an important role has been found to lead to biased estimates (see Morgan and Winship 2007 for an excellent discussion). Therefore, I used propensity score matching to confirm the robustness of my findings.

The first step in conducting the propensity score matching was to conduct a series of probit regressions. Separately by race and two-year age groups, I predicted a dummy indicator where 1=the child lived with his or her single parent, and 0=the child lived with his or her biological parents. Once children experienced a family structure transition, they were dropped from the sample. The predictors in the probits were child's gender, mother's AFQT, family structure at age fourteen, learning environment at age fourteen, delinquency at age fourteen, mother's education, employment status, total annual family income, and the number of mother's children in the household. After running the models, I saved the predicted probability that a child of a particular race and age would be in a single parent family based on the observed characteristics and these predicted probabilities were used as propensity scores.

After obtaining a propensity score for each age and race category, I used Leuven and Sianesi's (2003) matching estimator for Stata, *psmatch2*.[1] The propensity scores calculated from the probit regression models were used in analyses using single nearest-neighbor matching with replacement. Thus, the children in the "treatment" group, the children of stable-single mother families, were matched to their nearest neighbor in the stable-married group, that is, the child in the stable-married group with the closest propensity score (propensity to live with a stable single mother) to the treated child's own.[2] Note that the propensity-score matching analyses were run separately by race and two-year age groups, hence constituting an exact match on race and age.

RESULTS

Descriptive Statistics

I first begin by describing the family structure experiences of all children in the NLSY 79 children and young adult cohort by race. As seen in figure 7.1, by the age of fourteen, half of white children were still in the family struc-

Figure 7.1 Family structure experiences from birth to age 14 for White children by family structure status at birth

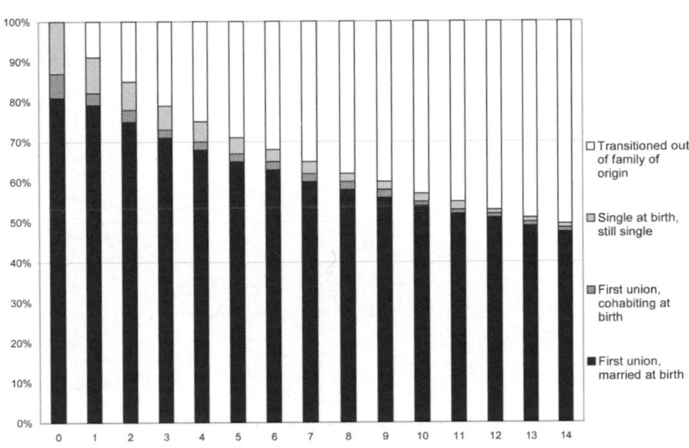

ture that they were born into, while half had transitioned out of their family structure of origin at some point in the past fourteen years. In particular, 58 percent of white children born to married parents remained with their married parents (about 47 percent of the sample of white children at age fourteen), while 8 percent of white children born into a single-mother family had never experienced a family structure transition (about 1 percent of the sample of white children at age fourteen). Similarly, 17 percent of white children born to cohabiting parents had yet to experience a family structure transition (about 1 percent of the sample of white children at age fourteen).

Turning to results for black children in figure 7.2, by the age of fourteen, 63 percent of black children had experienced a family structure transition while only 37 percent had never experienced a family structure transition. In the reverse of the pattern for white children, 32 percent of black children born to married parents remained with their married parents (about 11 percent of the sample of black children at age fourteen). In contrast, 42 percent of black children born into a single-mother family had never experienced a family structure transition (about 25 percent of the sample of black children at age fourteen). In black families, the single-mother families of origin were actually more stable than were the married families of origin. Finally, similar to the data for white children, 17 percent of black children born to cohabiting parents had yet to experience a family structure transition (about 1 percent of the sample of black children at age fourteen).

Finally, results for Hispanic children seen in figure 7.3 indicate that these children lived in more stable families than did black children but in less

Figure 7.2 Family structure experiences from birth to age 14 for Black children by family structure status at birth

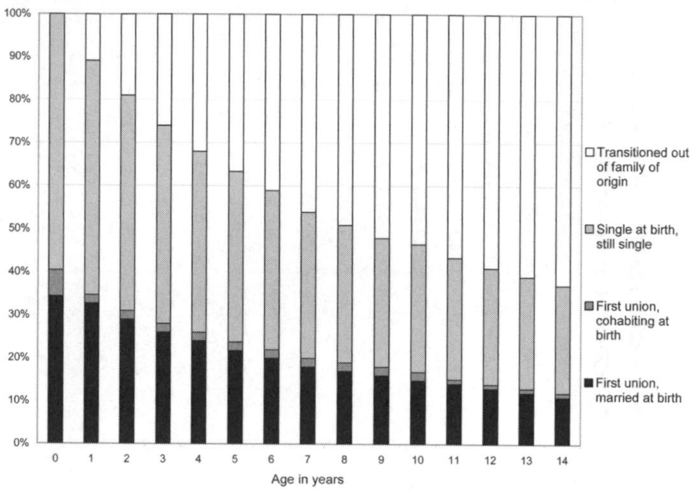

stable families than did white children. By the age of fourteen, 58 percent of Hispanic children had experienced a family-structure transition while 42 percent remained in their family of origin without having experienced a family-structure transition. Again falling between the black and white children, 50 percent of Hispanic children born to married parents remained with their married parents by the age of fourteen (about 34 percent of the sample of Hispanic children at age fourteen). While not as stable as black single-mother families, 21 percent of Hispanic children born to single mothers had never experienced a family-structure transition (about 5 percent of the Hispanic children at age fourteen). Finally, 25 percent of Hispanic mothers who were cohabiting at birth remained in a union with their cohabiting partner when the child was fourteen (about 2 percent of the sample of Hispanic children at age fourteen), making Hispanic cohabitors the most stable cohabitors of the three groups. Overall, the three most stable families of origin were, in order, married parent families of white children, married parent families of Hispanic children, and single-mother families of black children.

As shown in table 7.1, there are some interesting differences in variable means by family structure type. Regardless of race, children living with their married parents from birth reported higher HOME, lower BPI, and higher math and reading scores than did children living with only their single-mother from birth. In terms of race, white children reported higher HOME, lower BPI, and higher math and reading scores than black and

Figure 7.3 Family structure experiences from birth to age 14 for Hispanic children by family structure status at birth

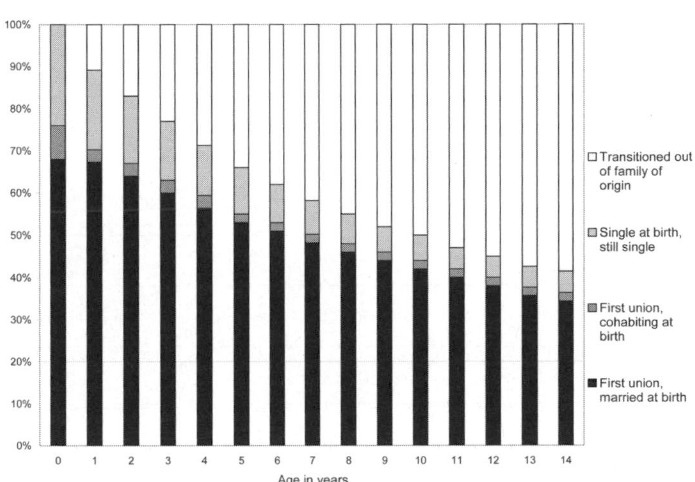

Hispanic children. I discuss the results for the rest of the control variables as they are used to construct the propensity scores in the probit models that follow.

Ordinary Least Squares Regression Results

I begin presenting the results by presenting the ordinary least squares (OLS) regression results with controls by race. Because of space limitations, I present only the results for nine- and ten-year olds in table 7.2. Specifically, I run OLS regressions among only children living in stable families, using as an independent variable the indicator of living in a stable single-mother family versus with stable married parents (the excluded group). The dependent variables in these models were the HOME, BPI, and the PIAT subscores: math and reading skills. I controlled for a variety of child gender and mother and family-background and economic characteristics.

Beginning with results for white children, I found that nine- and ten-year-old children living with a stable single-mother had poorer home environments than did children living with their married parents. This result was replicated across all age groups for white children. I also found that nine- and ten-year-old children living with a stable single mother had more behavior problems than nine- and ten-year-old children living with married parents. This finding was replicated for white children aged thirteen to

TABLE 7.1 Means and Standard Deviations of Dependent and Control Variables by Race and Family Structure for Children Aged 7–14

	WHITE CHILDREN			
	Married Parent		Single Parent	
Variable	*M*	*SD*	*M*	*SD*
Home	1,064.04	114.93	890.04	152.06
BPI	102.73	13.81	110.66	16.45
Math	106.68	13.05	99.36	13.39
Reading skills	107.08	12.11	101.97	13.24
Male	0.52	0.50	0.47	0.50
Mother's age	35.81	4.87	32.65	6.10
Mother's highest grade completed	13.35	2.33	11.69	2.37
Mother lived with her mother and father at age 14	0.82		0.51	
Mother's literacy environment at age 14	2.41	0.81	1.95	1.06
Mother's AFQT score in 1980	55.54	26.69	31.64	23.02
Mother reported two or more delinquent activities at age 14	0.29		0.47	
Mother's children in the household	2.58	1.00	1.87	1.29
Total family income ($1,000)	63.76	80.96	25.13	92.36
Mother employed	0.71		0.53	
N	16,150		575	

Note: Table 7.1 continues on opposite page

BLACK CHILDREN				HISPANIC CHILDREN			
Married Parent		Single Parent		Married Parent		Single Parent	
M	*SD*	*M*	*SD*	*M*	*SD*	*M*	*SD*
993.85	133.76	848.73	161.40	989.82	148.81	853.48	153.27
103.99	14.24	109.20	15.36	104.55	14.63	105.72	14.62
98.92	13.84	93.43	12.83	98.55	13.58	96.15	11.97
101.30	13.21	95.26	13.01	100.91	13.30	97.01	12.86
0.54	0.50	0.53	0.50	0.51	0.50	0.54	0.50
35.61	4.54	32.40	5.53	35.14	4.91	32.40	5.03
13.53	2.07	11.90	1.94	11.62	3.18	10.63	2.47
0.59		0.38		0.70		0.56	
1.61	1.09	1.40	1.02	1.47	1.09	1.14	0.96
27.09	20.03	15.25	15.08	26.44	22.60	13.61	14.40
0.23		0.31		0.23		0.22	
2.69	1.05	2.49	1.33	2.95	1.20	2.34	1.46
50.18	70.92	13.57	31.88	49.45	69.72	12.30	11.33
0.78		0.46		0.62		0.41	
3,084		6,101		5,751		816	

Note: The sample in this table included all children in each of the two family structures pooled across the ages of 7–14. Children may appear in this table more than once if the child did not experience a family structure transition between waves.

TABLE 7.2 Ordinary Least Squares Regression Results Predicting HOME, BPI, and PIAT Subscales from Family Structure and Controls by Race for Children Aged 9–10

	WHITE							
	Home		BPI		Math		Reading skills	
Variable	β	*SE*	β	*SE*	β	*SE*	β	*SE*
Stable single parent family	−162.25***	16.89	4.21*	2.14	−0.47	1.95	−2.28	1.74
Male	−16.67**	5.76	2.61***	0.71	2.52***	0.67	−1.36*	0.59
Mother's age	−4.24***	0.74	−0.30***	0.09	0.25**	0.09	0.02	0.08
Mother's highest grade completed	7.88***	1.70	−0.60**	0.21	0.79***	0.20	0.58***	0.17
Mother lived with her mother and father at age 14	−3.90	7.45	−3.23***	0.93	0.40	0.87	1.45+	0.77
Mother's literacy environment at age 14	21.42***	3.97	−0.69	0.49	−0.04	0.46	−0.11	0.41
Mother's AFQT score in 1980	0.67***	0.14	0.02	0.02	0.13***	0.02	0.13***	0.01
Mother reported two or more delinquent activities at age 14	−9.64	6.34	0.52	0.78	0.69	0.74	0.93	0.65
Mother's children in the household	−9.29**	2.98	−0.88*	0.36	−0.79*	0.34	−1.08***	0.31
Total family income ($1,000)	0.07	0.04	−0.01	0.01	0.01	0.00	0.00	0.00

Note: Table 7.2 continues on opposite page

	WHITE							
	Home		BPI		Math		Reading skills	
Variable	β	*SE*	β	*SE*	β	*SE*	β	*SE*
Mother employed	−4.70	6.86	1.35	0.84	−0.23	0.80	−0.97	0.71
Constant	1,054.76***	26.86	124.88***	3.33	80.19***	3.13	94.64***	2.78
N	1,456		1,449		1,409		1,411	
R-squared	0.18		0.06		0.17		0.15	
F	28.74		8.52		25.24		22.21	

	BLACK							
	Home		BPI		Math		Reading skills	
Variable	β	*SE*	β	*SE*	β	*SE*	β	*SE*
Stable single parent family	2.29+	1.36	−1.02	1.22	−2.39*	1.13	−2.39*	1.13
Male	3.59**	1.13	−0.41	1.01	−4.27***	0.94	−4.27***	0.94
Mother's age	−0.24*	0.12	0.25*	0.11	−0.04	0.10	−0.04	0.10
Mother's highest grade completed	0.01	0.36	0.24	0.32	0.71*	0.30	0.71*	0.30
Mother lived with her mother and father at age 14	−1.13	1.16	−0.44	1.04	−1.63+	0.97	−1.63+	0.97

(continued)

TABLE 7.2 *(continued)*

	BLACK							
	Home		BPI		Math		Reading skills	
Variable	β	*SE*	β	*SE*	β	*SE*	β	*SE*
Mother's literacy environment at age 14	−0.27	0.58	1.27*	0.52	1.02*	0.48	1.02*	0.48
Mother's AFQT score in 1980	−0.02	0.04	0.20***	0.04	0.22***	0.03	0.22***	0.03
Mother reported two or more delinquent activities at age 14	2.33+	1.28	0.22	1.13	0.59	1.06	0.59	1.06
Mother's children in the household	0.26	0.50	−1.14*	0.44	−1.42***	0.41	−1.42***	0.41
Total family income ($1,000)	−0.01	0.01	0.01	0.01	0.01	0.01	0.01	0.01
Mother employed	−0.93	1.28	−0.87	1.14	0.13	1.06	0.13	1.06
Constant	113.09***	5.62	83.77***	5.04	93.18***	4.67	93.18***	4.67
N	706		702		704		704	
R-squared	0.05		0.16		0.24		0.24	
F	3.64		11.51		19.47		19.47	

Note: Table 7.2 continues on opposite page

Variable	HISPANIC							
	Home		BPI		Math		Reading skills	
	β	*SE*	β	*SE*	β	*SE*	β	*SE*
Stable single parent family	−69.63**	21.27	−5.90**	2.24	1.92	2.15	1.56	2.14
Male	−29.62*	12.36	2.56+	1.30	1.77	1.23	−1.78	1.21
Mother's age	−3.38*	1.55	−0.29+	0.16	0.50**	0.16	0.05	0.15
Mother's highest grade completed	10.79***	2.73	−0.60*	0.29	0.40	0.27	0.48+	0.27
Mother lived with her mother and father at age 14	34.04*	14.05	−0.04	1.47	0.83	1.37	0.39	1.36
Mother's literacy environment at age 14	15.49*	6.40	0.72	0.68	0.32	0.64	0.59	0.63
Mother's AFQT score in 1980	0.97**	0.34	0.02	0.04	0.14***	0.03	0.12***	0.03
Mother reported two or more delinquent activities at age 14	−0.26	14.97	1.99	1.56	2.72+	1.48	0.74	1.46
Mother's children in the household	−13.08*	5.50	0.51	0.59	−0.46	0.54	−0.45	0.54
Total family income ($1,000)	0.03	0.06	−0.02*	0.01	0.00	0.01	0.01	0.01
Mother employed	2.14	14.21	−2.18	1.51	−1.71	1.41	−0.48	1.39

(continued)

TABLE 7.2 *(continued)*

	HISPANIC							
	Home		BPI		Math		Reading skills	
Variable	β	*SE*	β	*SE*	β	*SE*	β	*SE*
Constant	953.98***	57.58	119.91***	6.03	73.03***	5.83	90.23***	5.68
N	474		469		457		460	
R-squared	0.23		0.08		0.15		0.12	
F	12.22		3.62		7.02		5.56	

Note: *** $p < 0.001$, ** $p < 0.01$, * $p < 0.05$, $+p < 0.10$

fourteen, but was nonsignificant for white children aged seven to eight and eleven to twelve. I found no significant differences between white children by family structure for the PIAT math or reading skills subscales. The non-significant finding for reading skills was replicated across all observed ages for white children. However, I found that white children living with single mothers had significantly lower math scores at ages seven to eight and thirteen to fourteen years old. Overall, I found consistent evidence that white children living with a single mother had poorer home environments than white children living with married parents. I found some evidence that white children living with single mothers had more behavior problems and poorer math skills at some ages. Overall, I found no evidence of any disadvantage for reading skills by stable family-structure type for white children.

Similar to results for white children, I found that nine- and ten-year-old black children living with stable single mothers again had poorer home environments than nine- and ten-year-old children living with married parents. This finding held across all age groups for black children. Also similar to results for white children, I found that nine- and ten-year-old black children living with single mothers had marginally significant more behavior problems than black children living with married parents. This finding held only for black children aged eleven to twelve. I also found that black children aged nine to ten living with a single mother had poorer reading skills than black children living with married parents. However, this finding did not hold for any other age groups, consistent to results for white children. I found no significant differences in math scores for black children by type of stable family structure. Thus, overall I found for black children consistent evidence that black children living with single mothers had poorer home environments than black children living with married parents. I also found some evidence that black children living with single mothers had more behavioral problems than black children living with married parents.

Consistent with results for white and black children, I again found that nine- and ten-year-old Hispanic children living with stable single mothers again had poorer home environments than Hispanic children living with married parents. This finding held across all age groups. In contrast to the findings for behavior problems for white and black children, I found that Hispanic children living with stable single mothers had fewer behavior problems than Hispanic children living with married parents. This finding was not replicated in any other age range. I found no differences on math or reading skills across all age groups between Hispanic children living with single mothers and Hispanic children living with married parents. Thus, overall, I found consistent evidence that Hispanic children living with single mothers had poorer home environments than Hispanic children living with married parents.

Propensity Score Matching Results

Table 7.3 presents the probit models examining selection factors and time-varying factors that predict whether a child lives with a stable single mother or married parent family. Presented are the results for nine- to ten-year-olds. The results indicate that among white families, families with boys had 31 percent greater odds of being in a married-parent family as compared to a single-parent family at ages nine to ten. Gender was not a significant predictor of stable family structure for either black or Hispanic families. Black children with mothers who were older and more educated had greater odds of being in a married parent family as compared to a single-mother family at ages nine to ten, but this effect did not hold for white or Hispanic children. Turning to background characteristics, children of mothers who lived with her mother and father at age fourteen had 41 percent greater odds and 33 percent greater odds for white and black children respectively of being in a married parent family than in a single-mother family at ages nine to ten. The coefficient was not significant for Hispanic children. Black and white children of mothers with lower AFQT scores had greater odds of living in a single-mother family, but again the coefficient was not significant for Hispanic children. White and black children whose mothers reported two or more delinquent activities in adolescence had 67 percent and 22 percent greater

TABLE 7.3 Probit Regression Results Predicting Family Structure Membership from Controls by Race for Children Aged 9–10

	WHITE		BLACK		HISPANIC	
Variable	OR	SE	OR	SE	OR	SE
Male	0.69***	0.08	1.03	0.08	0.99	0.13
Mother's age	0.98	0.01	0.96***	0.01	0.99	0.02
Mother's highest grade completed	1.02	0.04	0.93***	0.02	1.04	0.03
Mother lived with her mother and father at age 14	0.59***	0.07	0.67***	0.06	0.87	0.13
Mother's literacy environment at age 14	0.96	0.06	0.96	0.04	1.07	0.08
Mother's AFQT score in 1980	0.99***	0.00	0.99***	0.00	1.00	0.00
Mother reported two or more delinquent activities at age 14	1.67***	0.19	1.22**	0.11	1.11	0.18
Mother's children in the household	0.72***	0.04	0.80***	0.03	0.79***	0.05
Total family income ($1,000)	1.00**	0.00	0.99***	0.00	0.95***	0.01
Mother employed	0.61***	0.07	0.59***	0.05	1.10	0.17
Constant	2.29*	1.05	70.04***	26.88	1.93	1.17
N	2265		1330		822	
Chi-square	178.20		396.30		190.50	

Note: *OR* refers to the exponentiated coefficient, or odds ratio.
***$p<0.01$, **$p<0.05$, *$p<0.1$

odds respectively of living in a stable single-mother family as opposed to a stable married-parent family at ages nine to ten.

For all children, regardless of race, more siblings and higher income was associated with greater odds of living with married parents as compared to a single mother. Finally, black and white children with an employed mother in the household had 39 percent and 41 percent respectively greater odds of living in a married-parent family. Results for other age groups were similar to the pattern of results observed for nine- to ten-year olds.

After running each of the probit models in table 7.3 for all age groups, I saved the predicted probabilities that a child was living in a single-parent family as opposed to a married-parent family for each age group as the propensity scores to be used in the propensity score matching analysis. These propensity scores had a minimum of almost zero, indicating a very low probability that a child, based on the observed characteristics in the models in table 7.3, was living in a single-mother family at a particular age. A very high propensity score near 1 indicated a high probability that a child, again based on the observed characteristics in the models in table 7.3, had a very high probability of living in a single single-parent household at a particular age. I next describe the propensity scores using the propensities obtained from table 7.3.

About 73 percent of white children who were living with married parents at ages nine to ten had an almost zero probability of living in a single-parent family based on their observed characteristics. In contrast, 22 percent of white children who were living with a single mother at age nine to ten had an almost zero probability of living in a single-parent family based on their observed characteristics. Black children had a higher predicted probability of being in a single-parent family than white children, regardless of family structure. About 10 percent of black children ages nine to ten and living with married parents had a 0.9 or greater probability of living in a single-parent family, while 52 percent of black children living in a single parent family had 0.9 or greater probability. Overall, the mean propensity score for black children aged nine to ten in married-parent families was 0.43, almost nine times the propensity score mean for white children in married families (0.05). The mean propensity score for black children aged nine to ten in single-mother families was 0.78, close to five times the propensity score mean for white children in single-parent families (0.17).

The results for Hispanic children again illustrated that Hispanic children tended to fall somewhere in between white and black children. A smaller proportion than that of white children, 46 percent and 3 percent of

Hispanic children living with married parents and single parents respectively had probabilities of almost 0 of living with a single mother. The overall mean propensity score for Hispanic children aged nine to ten living with married parents was 0.08, higher than the mean propensity score for white children and lower than the mean propensity score for black children living with married parents. Hispanic children aged nine to ten living with a single mother had a mean propensity score of 0.40, and similar to the results for children of married parents, white children of single mothers had a lower mean propensity score while black children of single mothers had a higher propensity score. Thus, overall, these results indicate the density and mean of the propensity scores based on observed characteristics was quite different by race and family structure. It highlights the importance of the careful consideration of selection processes in making distinctions between single mothers and married parents.

As described earlier, I used single nearest-neighbor propensity score matching with replacement with a caliper of 0.01.[3] I begin with results for white children illustrated in table 7.4. For white children, similar to the OLS regression results, I found a consistent advantage in the home environment and no apparent advantage for the PIAT math and reading skills for white children in married parent families over white children in single-mother families. Contrary to the OLS regression results, I found no support for a difference between white children in married parent families and in single mother families for behavior problems. Turning to black children in table 7.5, I again found a consistent advantage in the home environment for children living with married parents over single mothers. I found little evidence of any differences in behavior problems, and indeed, the one significant difference between the groups indicated that between ages thirteen to fourteen, black children with married parents had more behavior problems than did black children with single mothers. In contrast to results for white children and the OLS regression results, which found no differences in PIAT math scores by family structure, I found consistent evidence across age groups that black children living with a single mother had consistently lower math scores than did black children living with married parents. Further, I also found that three out of four t-tests were also significant for PIAT reading skills. Black children who were living with married parents had consistently higher reading skills than did black children living with a single mother.

Results for Hispanic children, found in table 7.6, indicated that the home environment advantage may not be as apparent as the OLS regression estimates indicated, or consistent with results for white and black children, though small sample size could play a role. At ages seven to eight and nine to ten, I did not find a significant difference in the HOME scores of the matched sample. However, at ages eleven to twelve and thirteen to fourteen, I saw significant and marginally significant differences in the HOME scores such that Hispanic children in married parent families have better HOME environments on average than Hispanic children in single mother families. With regard to behavior problems, consistent with OLS regression results, nine- and ten-year-old Hispanic children living with a single mother reported fewer behavior problems than do nine- and ten-year old Hispanic children living with married parents. Also consistent with the OLS results, I found no other evidence of this pattern. I also found no consistent family-structure differences regarding PIAT math scores and no evidence of family-structure differences in reading skills. Overall then, in comparing results for white, black, and Hispanic children in the propensity score matched models, family structure appeared to matter for math and reading skills for black children, while family structure appeared to distinguish the home environment regardless of race, though the results for Hispanic children were not as consistent as those for black and white children.

DISCUSSION

This chapter attempts to make a distinction in the family-structure literature by divorcing family-structure type from family-structure instability. Current policy initiatives in the United States assume that marriage should be promoted to unmarried parents, even though the marriages of poor, less-educated couples tend to be more unstable (Amato 2000). If children in stable families, regardless of the type of family, tend to fare equally well, then policy initiatives that promote marriage without corresponding programs to increase marital stability may not benefit children and may actually harm them.

Descriptively, I have found that most white children are born to married parents, while only a minority of black children are born to married parents. By the age of fourteen, half of white children and less than half of black and Hispanic children were still in the family structure that they were born into. For whites and Hispanics, more children born to married parents were still in their family of origin at age fourteen, while a higher proportion of black children born to single mothers were in their family of

TABLE 7.4 Propensity Score Matching Results for Mean Differences on HOM[E], BPI, and PIAT Subscales for White Children from Stable Single-Mother and Stable Married-Parent Families by Child Age

	UNMATCHED		MATCHED	
	Single-mother	Married	Single-mother	Marrie[d]
Age	M	M	M	M
Home				
7 to 8	896.3	1,057.3	894.6	1,036.9
9 to 10	879.0	1,064.2	880.2	1,018.9
11 to 12	914.8	1,078.5	912.6	1,055.6
13 to 14	898.3	1,052.0	898.3	1,009.6
BPI				
7 to 8	107.6	102.6	107.3	104.0
9 to 10	109.1	103.0	108.4	105.2
11 to 12	108.1	103.0	108.2	106.3
13 to 14	112.0	104.0	112.0	111.6
Math				
7 to 8	97.3	105.7	97.3	102.1
9 to 10	101.6	107.1	102.0	98.9
11 to 12	102.4	107.2	102.6	105.6
13 to 14	94.5	106.0	94.5	99.1
Reading skills				
7 to 8	101.9	107.5	101.8	107.5
9 to 10	102.2	107.9	102.4	102.3
11 to 12	103.7	106.5	104.1	102.7
13 to 14	96.8	105.3	96.8	99.7

Note: Table 7.4 continues on opposite page

Difference[1]	t	Treated on Support[2]	Treated on Support[3]
−142.3	−5.74***	89.5%	51
−138.7	−4.57***	97.8%	45
−142.9	−4.80***	96.7%	29
−111.2	−2.60*	100.0%	23
3.3	1.23	91.4%	53
3.3	1.07	97.7%	42
2.0	.49	96.8%	30
0.5	.10	100.0%	23
−4.8	−1.83+	89.3%	50
3.1	1.23	97.8%	44
−3.0	−.96	96.7%	29
−4.6	−1.11	100.0%	20
−5.7	−2.24*	90.9%	50
0.1	.05	97.8%	44
1.4	.46	96.7%	29
−2.9	−.66	100.0%	20

Note: Reported are the unmatched means and the matched means obtained from the propensity score matching.

1. The difference reported is $M_{children\ in\ single\text{-}mother\ families} - M_{children\ in\ married\ families}$ for the matched sample only. ***$p<0.001$, *$p<0.05$, $^{+}p<0.10$
2. Treated on support indicates the percent of children in the single-mother group (not missing on variable) who were used in the matching analysis; that is, for whom matches were found.
3. The treated on support n indicates the n of the subsample of children of single mothers who found matches.

TABLE 7.5 Propensity Score Matching Results for Mean Differences on HOME, BPI, and PIAT Subscales for Black Children from Stable Single-Mothe[r] and Stable Married-Parent Families by Child Age

	UNMATCHED		MATCHED	
	Single-mother	Married	Single-mother	Married
Age	M	M	M	M
Home				
7 to 8	834.7	976.1	832.9	982.7
9 to 10	847.3	993.0	850.1	969.4
11 to 12	859.6	1,006.2	859.4	960.8
13 to 14	852.5	987.5	845.5	1,004.1
BPI				
7 to 8	108.9	104.4	109.0	109.7
9 to 10	109.3	104.4	109.0	108.0
11 to 12	109.0	104.4	109.0	108.9
13 to 14	109.2	105.1	108.6	114.3
Math				
7 to 8	94.8	98.6	94.9	96.3
9 to 10	94.6	99.4	94.7	96.9
11 to 12	92.6	99.3	92.7	99.9
13 to 14	91.5	98.1	92.0	94.1
Reading skills				
7 to 8	100.1	104.0	100.2	102.4
9 to 10	96.4	102.5	96.5	99.2
11 to 12	92.6	99.0	92.7	101.5
13 to 14	91.2	98.5	91.6	93.6

Note: Table 7.5 continues on opposite page

Difference[1]	t	Treated on Support[2]	Treated on Support n[3]
−149.8	−13.63***	87.6%	410
−119.4	−10.76***	87.2%	389
−101.4	−9.30***	85.8%	331
−158.7	−11.93***	68.5%	215
−0.7	−0.65	87.4%	389
0.9	0.79	87.2%	383
0.0	0.03	86.1%	317
−5.7	−3.51**	68.5%	215
−1.4	−1.71+	87.8%	403
−2.2	−2.30*	87.4%	387
−7.2	−6.87***	89.7%	525
−2.1	−1.70+	66.3%	207
−2.2	−2.63**	87.4%	402
−2.6	−2.67**	87.1%	385
−8.8	−9.11***	85.6%	321
−2.0	−1.61	66.2%	208

Note: Reported are the unmatched means and the matched means obtained from the propensity score matching. $^{***}p<0.001$, $^{**}p<0.01$, $^{*}p<0.05$, $^{+}p<0.10$

1. The difference reported is $M_{children\ in\ single\text{-}mother\ families} - M_{children\ in\ married\ families}$ for the matched sample only.
2. Treated on support indicates the percent of children in the single-mother group (not missing on variable) who were used in the matching analysis; that is, for whom matches were found.
3. The treated on support n indicates the n of the subsample of children of single mothers who found matches.

TABLE 7.6 Propensity Score Matching Results for Mean Differences on HOME, BPI, and PIAT Subscales for Hispanic Children from Stable Single-Mother and Stable Married-Parent Families by Child Age

	UNMATCHED		MATCHED	
	Single-mother	Married	Single-mother	Married
Age	M	M	M	M
Home				
7 to 8	855.9	983.8	872.9	900.1
9 to 10	898.7	997.5	898.4	931.9
11 to 12	869.5	1,002.2	856.6	938.2
13 to 14	857.8	1,000.8	805.7	1,028.7
BPI				
7 to 8	107.7	104.3	105.1	108.2
9 to 10	101.7	105.4	100.1	107.4
11 to 12	105.3	105.3	102.9	108.1
13 to 14	109.8	105.3	106.0	105.1
Math				
7 to 8	97.6	98.9	98.3	96.5
9 to 10	97.5	99.5	97.3	96.5
11 to 12	92.0	98.8	91.0	96.8
13 to 14	94.3	98.0	89.8	99.6
Reading skills				
7 to 8	99.0	103.3	100.8	96.8
9 to 10	99.7	100.9	101.0	99.5
11 to 12	94.5	99.1	93.3	91.6
13 to 14	94.9	100.0	93.6	99.6

Note: Table 7.6 continues on opposite page

Difference[1]	*t*	Treated on Support[2]	Treated on Support n[3]
–27.2	–0.7	65.6%	40
–33.5	–0.94	80.9%	38
–81.6	–1.92+	69.2%	27
–223.0	–4.35***	48.1%	13
–3.1	–1	68.3%	41
–7.4	–2.03*	80.9%	38
–5.2	–1.18	66.7%	26
0.9	0.14	46.2%	12
1.8	0.72	64.3%	36
0.9	0.33	79.5%	35
–5.8	–1.62	68.4%	26
–9.9	–2.26*	51.9%	14
3.9	1.51	64.9%	37
1.5	0.50	79.1%	34
1.7	0.39	68.4%	26
–6.0	–1.08	53.8%	14

Note: Reported are the unmatched means and the matched means obtained from the propensity score matching., $^{***}p<0.001$, $^{*}p<0.05$, $^{+}p<0.10$

1. The difference reported is $M_{children\ in\ single\text{-}mother\ families} - M_{children\ in\ married\ families}$ for the matched sample only.
2. Treated on support indicates the percent of children in the single-mother group (not missing on variable) who were used in the matching analysis; that is, for whom matches were found.
3. The treated on support *n* indicates the *n* of the subsample of children of single mothers who found matches.

origin. Overall, the family-structure experiences of the children of the NLSY79 sample varied greatly by race.

Overall, I found mixed evidence regarding the superiority of marriage as a family structure for child outcomes. In the ordinary least squares regression framework, I found evidence that stable marriage was associated with improved home environments compared to living with a single mother who never entered a union, even after taking into account a variety of child, mother, family, and economic characteristics and regardless of age or race. However, in terms of behavior problems, I found only limited evidence that white and black children living with single mothers had more behavior problems than white and black children living with married parents at some ages. For academic abilities, I only found limited evidence that white children living with single mothers had poorer math skills than white children living with married parents at some ages. Overall, regardless of race, I only found consistent evidence that the HOME environment was poorer in single-mother as compared to married-parent households.

Propensity score analysis was used to test the robustness of these findings. Results from the propensity score analysis confirmed that children in stable married parent families reported better home environments than children living in stable single-parent families, particularly for black and white children. In comparing results for the propensity score matched models, family structure appeared to matter for math and reading skills for black children only, contrary to previous evidence (Dunifon and Kowaleski-Jones 2002). Consistent with the ordinary least squares regression results, I found little evidence of a difference in math, reading recognition, and reading comprehension scores between Hispanic and white children of stable married parents and stable single parents when I carefully isolated the comparison sample of stable married parents using a propensity score. Thus, I conclude that there is strong evidence overall that children living in stable unions are advantaged in terms of their home environments as compared to children living with stable single mothers. However, I found mixed evidence regarding a marital advantage in terms of test scores and behavior problems, suggesting that perhaps the stability of family structure matters more for children's academic skills and conduct than does the type of family structure in which a child resides, at least for white and Hispanic children. For black children, family structure may play a stronger role in shaping their math and reading skills, but not behavior problems.

LIMITATIONS

There are limitations to this study. First, due to the design of the NLSY79, I underestimate short-term cohabitations that occur prior to 2002. Second, I am not able to ascertain why the mothers remain single. There are many reasons why a mother may remain single, including a lack of available partners, personality or mental health issues, or a belief that remaining single will benefit the child. Third, given the low prevalence of stable single mothers for whites and Hispanics, I have a small sample size with which to test for differences. If I had a larger sample, some of the nonsignificant differences may have been significant, particularly for these groups.

Another limitation of this study is the use of methods to control for selection characteristics. By using income as a matching characteristic in the propensity score matching models, in essence, the models match the "best" of the single mothers to the "worst" of the married parents. It is a legitimate question to ask whether I am comparing Murphy Brown to a lower-middle-class, two-parent family. This is an important issue, and some might argue that controls for income in these models would be overcontrolling. If income accounts for family-structure differences, the policy implications are very different from a causal link between family structure and child well-being. It is important to keep this limitation in mind in the interpretation of these results.

Despite these limitations, this study has many strengths, lying mainly in its ability to capture stability and change in children's living arrangements over their entire childhoods, and to relate these to a wide range of important child-developmental outcomes. Overall, this study suggests that there are mixed advantages to marriage when stable marriage is compared with stable single parenthood. This chapter calls on family and marriage scholars to make careful distinctions in family-structure research through identifying appropriate comparison groups and to consider carefully the two distinct issues of family stability and family structure. A growing body of research on family-structure transitions (Craigie 2008; see chapter 8, this volume) indicates that family stability may be more important than or at least as important as family type. This chapter contributes to the literature by presenting more evidence of the importance of family stability as well as family structure.

NOTES

Parts of this paper were presented at the annual meetings of the Population Association of America, New York, March 2007. I am grateful for comments from Rachel Dunifon, Dan Lichter, Liz Peters and seminar participants in the Family Life Development Center/ Bronefenbrenner Life Course Center seminar series. I am grateful for support for this research from the National Institute of Child Health and Human Development (NICHD) (1K01HD056238). This paper and its contents are solely the responsibility of the authors and do not necessarily represent the official views of NICHD.

1. Other estimators also exist for Stata (see Morgan and Harding 2006 for a review), but psmatch2 is one of the more popular and user-friendly of the matching estimators available, and comparisons among matching estimators has not shown a clear advantage for one estimator over another.
2. In the event of ties, or when children in the nontreated group had identical propensity scores, the matched child nearest to the treated child was selected. Therefore, I ensured that my data were in random order before I ran the procedure. Each child in the "treatment" group was allowed to find his or her best match; hence, children in the "control" group, or the children of married parents, were allowed to match to more than one child in the "treatment" group. Finally, I also set a limit, or caliper, on the distance from which the matched child's propensity score could fall from the treated child's propensity score. I used a caliper 0.01, where between 46 percent and 100 percent of the sample is "on common support," or, to put it another way, where between 62 percent and 93 percent of children from stable single-mother families find a match.
3. I also ran these models with a more liberal caliper of 0.03, and the pattern of results did not change.

REFERENCES

Amato, P. R. 2000. The consequences of divorce for adults and children. *Journal of Marriage and Family* 62:1269–1287.

Astone, N. M., and S. S. McLanahan. 1991. Family structure, parental practices, and high school completion. *American Sociological Review* 56, no. 5: 309–320.

Baker, P., C. Keck, F. Mott, and S. Quinlan. 1993. *NLSY child handbook, revised edition.* Columbus, Ohio: Center for Human Resource Research.

Blau, D. M., and W. van der Klaauw. 2007. A demographic analysis of the family structure experiences of children in the United States. Institute for the Study of Labor (IZA) Discussion Paper No. 3001. Retrieved March 3, 2008, from ftp://repec.iza.org/RePEc/Discussionpaper/dp3001.pdf.

Bradley, R.H. 1985. The HOME inventory: Rationale and research. In J. Lachenmeyer and M. Gibbs, eds., *Recent research in developmental psychopathology*, 191–210. New York: Gardner.

Bradley, R. H., and B. M. Caldwell. 1984a. The HOME inventory and family demographics. *Developmental Psychology* 20:315–320.

———. 1984b. The relation of infants' home environments to achievement test performance in first grade: A follow-up study. *Child Development* 55:803–809.

Brown, S.L. 2004. Family structure and child well-being: The significance of parental cohabitation. *Journal of Marriage and Family* 66:351–367.

Bumpass, L.L., and H. Lu. 2000. Trends in cohabitation and implications for children's family contexts. *Population Studies* 54:29–41.

Carlson, M.J., and M. E. Corcoran. 2001. Family structure and children's behavioral and cognitive outcomes. *Journal of Marriage and the Family* 63, no. 3: 779–792.

Center for Human Resource Research. 2004. *NLSY79 Children and young adult data users guide*. Retrieved September 15, 2007, from www.nlsinfo.org/pub/usersvc/Child-Young-Adult/2002Child-YADataUsersGuide.pdf.

Chase-Lansdale, P.L., A. J. Cherlin, and K. E. Kiernan. 1995. The long-term effects of parental divorce on the mental health of young adults: A developmental perspective. *Child Development* 66:1614–1634.

Cherlin, A.J., P. L. Chase-Lansdale, and C. McRae. 1998. Effects of divorce on mental health throughout the life course. *American Sociological Review* 63:239–249.

Craigie, T. 2008. Effects of paternal presence and family stability on child cognitive performance. Center for Research on Child Well-being Working Paper 2008–03-FF. Retrieved March 5, 2008, from www.fragilefamilies.princeton.edu.

Dion, H.R. 2005. Healthy marriage programs: Learning what works. *The Future of Children* 15:139–156.

Duncan, G., and J. Brooks-Gunn, eds. 1997. *Consequences of growing up poor*. New York: Russell Sage Foundation.

Dunifon, R., and L. Kowaleski-Jones. 2002. Who's in the house? Race differences in cohabitation, single parenthood, and child development. *Child Development* 73:1249–1264.

Foster, E.M., and A. Kalil. 2007. Living arrangements and children's development in low-income white, black, and Latino families. *Child Development* 78, no. 6: 1657–1674.

Ginther, D.K., and R. A. Pollak. 2004. Family structure and children's educational outcomes: Blended families, stylized facts, and descriptive regressions. *Demography* 41, no. 4: 697–720.

Hill, M., W. Yeung, and G. Duncan. 2001. Childhood family structure and young adult behaviors. *Journal of Population Economics* 14:271–299.

Leuven, E., and B. Sianesi. 2003. PSMATCH2: Stata module to perform full Mahalanobis and propensity score matching, common support graphing, and covariate imbalance testing. Retrieved February 15, 2007, from http://ideas.repec.org/c/boc/bocode/s432001.html.

McLanahan, S., and G. Sandefur. 1994. *Growing up with a single parent: What hurts, what helps?* Cambridge, Mass.: Harvard University Press.

Morgan, S. L., and D. J. Harding. 2006. Matching estimators of causal effects: Prospects and pitfalls in theory and practice. *Sociological Methods and Research* 25:3–60.

Morgan, S. L., and C. Winship. 2007. *Counterfactuals and causal inference: Methods and principles for social research.* New York: Cambridge University.

Peterson, J. L., and N. Zill. 1986. Marital disruption, parent-child relationships, and behavioral problems in children. *Journal of Marriage and the Family* 48:295–307.

Popenoe, D. 1995. The American family crisis. *National Forum* 75:15–19.

Teachman, J. D. 2004. The childhood living arrangements of children and the characteristics of their marriages. *Journal of Family Issues* 25:86–111.

Thomson, E., S. S. McLanahan, and R. B. Curtin. 1992. Family structure, gender, and parental socialization. *Journal of Marriage and the Family* 54:368–378.

U.S. Census Bureau. 2005. America's families and living arrangements, 2005. Retrieved February 15, 2005, from www.census.gov/population/www/socdemo/hh-fam/cps2003.html.

Waite, L., and M. Gallagher. 2000. *The case for marriage: Why married people are happier, healthier, and better off financially.* New York: Doubleday.

Weinraub, M., and B. M. Wolf. 1983. Effects of stress and social supports on mother-child interactions in single and two-parent families. *Child Development* 54:1297–1311.

EIGHT

Reconsidering the Association Between Stepfather Families and Adolescent Well-Being

MEGAN M. SWEENEY, HONGBO WANG, AND TAMI M. VIDEON

Historical growth in rates of divorce, nonmarital childbearing, and cohabitation have increased the proportion of young people in the United States who live with a stepparent. Indeed, almost one-third of recent cohorts of American children are expected to spend some portion of their youth living in a stepfamily (Bumpass, Raley, and Sweet 1995). The association between stepfamilies and youth well-being, however, is still not well understood.

Most attention among family scholars has focused on comparisons between youth living in stepfamilies and those living with both biological parents. These studies generally find living in a stepfamily to be associated with relatively lower well-being than living with two biological parents, as indicated by a wide range of child outcomes including educational attainment, emotional well-being, and behavioral outcomes (for a recent review see Ganong and Coleman 2004). Most children enter stepfamilies after spending some time living with a single parent, however, making comparisons of outcomes in stepfamilies and two-biological-parent families difficult to interpret. Comparisons between stepfamilies and single-parent families would seem more appropriate if one's goal is to understand how stepfamily formation influences youth well-being. This more limited body of research suggests that youth in stepfamilies tend to fare no better than those in single-parent families with respect to many domains of well-being and may be at somewhat greater risk of outcomes such as poor psychological adjustment and early sexual behavior or childbearing (see Amato and Keith 1991; Musick and Bumpass 1999; Wu 1996; Wu and Martinson 1993; but see also Chase-Lansdale, Cherlin, and Kiernan 1995).

Yet fundamental sources of heterogeneity in stepfamily experiences are overlooked in much stepfamily scholarship. More than a decade ago, Bumpass and colleagues (1995) argued for the importance of taking two basic sources of stepfamily variation into account: the *mode of entry* into stepfamilies (cohabitation or marriage) and the *route into single parenthood* preceding stepfamily formation (divorce or nonmarital birth). A small but rapidly expanding body of research has focused on the first source of stepfamily heterogeneity. These studies tend to find that youth in cohabiting families do not fare as well, on average, as do those living with two married parents (Brown 2004; Manning and Lamb 2003; Nelson, Clark, and Acs 2001; Thomson, Hanson, and McLanahan 1994). Several recent studies also directly compare the emotional and behavioral well-being of youth in cohabiting stepfamilies to those living with a single parent, although few significant differences between these groups are found (see Brown 2004; Manning and Lamb 2003; Nelson, Clark, and Acs 2001).

Considerably less work has carefully considered heterogeneity across routes into single parenthood preceding stepfamily formation (Ganong and Coleman 2004). Most prior research has either examined only stepfamilies formed after divorce or has pooled together stepfamilies formed after divorce with those formed after a nonmarital birth. The lack of attention to nonmarital-birth stepfamilies is particularly surprising given that more than one-third of recent births in the United States occurred outside of marriage (Martin et al. 2005), and approximately one-third of children entering stepfamilies do so after a nonmarital birth (Bumpass et al. 1995). Taking preceding state into account seems particularly important for understanding how transitions into stepfamilies affect the well-being of young people. No child can transition from living with a divorced biological mother to living with his or her never married mother and a stepfather, making these types of counterfactual comparisons of questionable value. Furthermore, to the extent that children who enter single-parent families after a nonmarital birth are a particularly disadvantaged group, even when compared to those who have experienced divorce, ignoring preceding state may paint a misleading picture of how stepfamily formation affects youth well-being. Although involvement with a biological father is an important aspect of life for many children in stepfamilies, contact with a nonresident parent is also known to be considerably less among children born outside of marriage (Seltzer and Bianchi 1988). From a family-transitions perspective, the most theoretically relevant counterfactual comparisons would seem to be between youth in stepfamilies and those in single-parent families who share a common history of (non)divorce.

The current study investigates multiple domains of adolescent well-being using data from a large and nationally representative sample. We highlight two important sources of stepfamily diversity: mode of entry into a stepfamily (cohabitation versus marriage) and route of entry into the preceding single parenthood state (divorce versus nonmarital birth). We emphasize comparisons between youth outcomes in stepfather families and those in single-mother families among groups of adolescents who share a common prior history of (non)divorce. We consider multiple indicators of youth well-being, including symptoms of depression, having unprotected sex, riding in a car without a seat belt (an indicator of risk-taking behavior), and selling drugs. Because of adolescence's unique status as a "launching pad" into adulthood, emotional and behavioral outcomes during this period can have important implications for trajectories of well-being and socioeconomic attainment throughout the life course. Finally, we consider both the potential costs and benefits for offspring of stepfamilies relative to single-parent families and explore whether preexisting characteristics of mothers can explain well-being differentials between these groups.

THEORETICAL BACKGROUND

The family-structure literature points to multiple pathways through which stepfamilies may affect offspring. Some of these might be expected to improve youth well-being, while others might tend to bear some cost for young people. There are several reasons to expect stepfamilies to be associated with relatively better youth outcomes than single-parent families. For example, moving from a single-mother family to a stepfather family is associated with an increase in family economic resources, although remarriage after divorce is associated with better long-run economic prospects for children than is postmarital cohabitation (Morrison and Ritualo 2000). A socialization or social control perspective suggests that a stepfather may also contribute directly to parenting, may allow a mother to spend more time parenting by taking over other responsibilities, or may provide an additional positive adult role model within the household. Empirical evidence is inconsistent, however, as to whether stepfamily formation in fact tends to increase the supervision of children (Amato 1987; Needle, Su, and Doherty 1990; Thomson, McLanahan, and Curtin 1992; Thomson et al. 2001).

There are also reasons to expect that adding a stepfather to a household previously headed by a single mother may be associated with some *reduction* in offspring well-being. For example, a stress and instability perspective suggests that changes in family structure may disrupt the equilibrium of the family environment, leading to conflict within families or interrupting effective parenting behaviors. Frequent changes in childhood family structure are associated with an increased risk of adverse emotional and behavioral outcomes (Capaldi and Patterson 1991; Wolfinger 2000; Wu 1996; Wu and Martinson 1993), and children in newly remarried families tend to display more adjustment problems than those in single-parent families or remarried families that have not experienced a recent family structure transition (Hetherington and Clingempeel 1992; Hetherington and Jodl 1994). Remarried families may also experience stress and instability due to a lack of social support and unclear norms regarding expectations and behavior, creating complicated and uncertain family dynamics (Cherlin 1978). Stepfamily dynamics may be particularly complex when step- or half-sibling relationships are involved (Ganong and Coleman 2004; Mekos, Hetherington, and Reiss 1996).

A community-connections perspective also suggests that stepfamily formation may be associated with some reduction in youth well-being. To take full advantage of resources in a community, social capital theory argues that children and families must know and trust their neighbors, teachers, and peers (McLanahan and Sandefur 1994). Stepfamily formation may weaken children's access to such resources, primarily through increased rates of residential mobility (Anderson et al. 1999; Astone and McLanahan 1994; McLanahan and Sandefur 1994; South, Crowder, and Trent 1998). Residential instability is linked to a variety of poor child outcomes (see Hagan, MacMillan, and Wheaton 1996; Wood et al. 1993).

Finally, children and parents in stepfamilies may tend to differ from those in other family structures, with unobserved characteristics creating a spurious association between family structure and children's well-being (Chase-Lansdale 1994; Hogan 1994). For example, if a mother's health status is not controlled in a model and mother's health is associated both with family structure and with child well-being, estimates of the effects of family structure on children's outcomes may be biased. Several recent studies attempt to identify whether such preexisting selectivity can explain observed associations between stepfamilies and children's well-being. Evenhouse and Reilly (2004), for example, use fixed effects models to estimate within-family effects of being a stepchild rather than a joint biological child of both residential parents. They conclude that unobserved family characteristics cannot fully explain the relatively lower well-being of stepchildren. Although such efforts improve our understanding of whether stepfamilies affect the well-being of offspring, they provide little insight into what specific mechanisms might be responsible for these effects.[1]

DATA AND METHODS

The current research relies on data from the National Longitudinal Study of Adolescent Health (Add Health). The Add Health provides a wide variety of assessments of adolescent well-being and also contains extensive parental marital and union histories. In 1995 (Wave 1) in-home interviews were conducted with a core nationally representative sample of more than twelve thousand adolescents in grades 7 through 12 and with oversamples of selected populations, including 1,038 black youth from well-educated families (Harris, Duncan, and Boisjoly 2003). Interviews were also conducted with a parent of the adolescent respondent. The response rate for the survey was relatively high, with 78.9 percent of eligible adolescents responding. We also draw on data from the 1996 follow-up survey of these adolescents (Wave 2), in which 88.2 percent of eligible respondents were interviewed again.[2] Appropriate sampling weights are applied to all analyses and standard errors are corrected for design effects using STATA's survey estimators.

We place several restrictions on the analytical subsample. First, the sample is limited to adolescents who completed the Wave 1 in-home interview and who had valid sampling weights. Second, we limit the sample to non-Hispanic white and black adolescents, and to those born after 1976 because parents are only asked about their marital histories since 1977. We limit the sample to adolescents whose biological mothers completed a residential parent questionnaire, as children who live apart from their mothers are still a select group (Cancian and Meyer 1998; Seltzer 1994). Because parental death is shown to have different effects on child outcomes than other types of parental loss (Amato and Keith 1991; McLanahan 1997), we also limit the sample to adolescents who have not experienced the death of their biological father or their mother's widowing. Finally, we limit the primary analytic sample to respondents with no missing data on items used to measure well-being outcomes and on most explanatory and control variables, leaving a total of 7,643 adolescent respondents. For selected outcomes (described below), we further limit the sample to respondents to the Wave 2 interview, leaving a total of 5,803 adolescent respondents.

DEPENDENT VARIABLES

Symptoms of Depression

We rely on a modified version of the Center for Epidemiologic Studies Depression Scale (CES-D) to assess symptoms of depression, which has high reliability in populations of adolescents (Radloff 1977, 1991). This measure is based on responses to nineteen questions regarding experience of depressive symptomatology in the past week, including how often respondents felt "bothered by things that don't usually bother you," "didn't feel like eating, your appetite was poor," "that you could not shake off the blues, even with help from your family and friends," "you were just as good as other people," "had trouble keeping your mind on what you were doing," "depressed," "you were too tired to do things," "hopeful about the future," "thought your life had been a failure," "fearful," "happy," "talked less than usual," "lonely," "people were unfriendly to you," "you enjoyed life," "sad," "people disliked you," "it was hard to get started doing things," and "life was not worth living." After reverse coding four items, as described by Radloff (1977), each item was coded as follows: 0 "never or rarely," 1 "sometimes," 2 "a lot of the time," and 3 "most of the time or all of the time." The nineteen items were then summed to compute each adolescent's total CES-D score. The internal consistency of this measure in the current analytic sample was high (Cronbach's alpha=.86). Because the CES-D instrument refers to symptoms experienced *in the past week*, and thus is unlikely to capture symptoms before family structure was determined, we use the Wave 1 (1995) measure of depressive symptomatology.[3]

Unprotected Sex

To assess adolescents' experiences of unprotected sex, we construct a measure of whether respondents report having had sexual intercourse in the past twelve months without using a method of birth control. If they have not had sex in the past twelve months or report having used birth control "all of the time," they are coded zero on this measure. If they report ever having had sex in the past year without using birth control they are coded 1. Because this measure refers to behavior *over the past year,* we rely on the adolescent's response from the Wave 2 (1996) interview.

Use of Seat Belts

We next construct a measure of infrequent seat-belt use, which is a useful indicator of adolescent risk-taking behavior. Respondents are coded 0 on this measure if they report usually wearing a seat belt when riding in a car most or all of the time, and coded 1 if they report less frequent use of seat belts. This measure is based on information from the Wave 1 (1995) interview.

Selling Drugs

Finally, drug selling is an important indicator of more serious risk-taking behavior (see also Harris, et al., 2002). We construct a binary measure of whether the adolescent reports having sold marijuana or other drugs in the past twelve months, coded 1 if they report any such behavior and 0 otherwise. Because this measure refers to behavior *over the past year,* we rely on the adolescent's report from the Wave 2 (1996) interview.

INDEPENDENT VARIABLES

Family Structure

To measure family structure at the time of the Wave 1 interview, we rely on mothers' reports about marital transitions that occurred after the birth of the adolescent respondent and pay careful attention to whether "nonintact" families were formed after a nonmarital birth or after divorce.[4] Considering only those transitions that the child actually experiences seems particularly important, given that almost one-quarter of nonmarital births occur after a marital disruption (Bumpass et al. 1995). We classify current family structure into the following categories: (1) two biological parent family, (2) single-mother family, no divorce or separation[5] experienced by child, (3) cohabiting-stepfather family, no divorce experienced, (4) married-stepfather family, no divorce experienced, (5) single-mother family, divorce experienced, and (6) cohabiting-stepfather family, divorce experienced, and (7) married-stepfather family, divorce experienced by child.

Other Measures

We also construct measures to test specific hypotheses about the nature of the relationship between family structure and adolescent well-being. To test the economic-deprivation hypothesis, we construct a measure of the income-to-needs ratio, defined as total gross family income in the 1994 calendar year relative to the official poverty threshold for a given family composition (U.S. Census Bureau 1996). In order to allow for nonlinear effects of family income, we employ a categorical specification of this variable, with categories for income-to-needs ratios of less than one, greater than or equal to one but less than two, greater than or equal to two but less than four, and greater than or equal to four. We also construct a dummy variable indicating whether any household member received AFDC, food stamps, or a housing subsidy during the past month. Family income in the past year and receipt of public assistance in the past month were ascertained during the parental interview.

Next, we create several measures of parenting to test the social control/socialization hypothesis, based on information provided by the adolescent respondent. First, we construct a measure of whether a resident parent is usually present when the child leaves for school, returns from school, eats dinner, and goes to bed. We define this as more than five days per week in the case of eating dinner and "most of the time" or "always" responses to questions about the other three activities.[6] Scores on this measure of parental presence range from 0 to 4, with the highest score indicating a parent is usually present at all of these times. Second, we construct a measure of a reasoning-based parenting style, based on the adolescent's self-reported level of agreement with the statement: "When you do something wrong that is important, your mother talks about it with you and helps you understand why it is wrong." This measure ranges from 1 to 5, with higher scores indicating a higher level of agreement. Third, we construct a measure of family rules, which is based on adolescent self-reports of how many of seven possible different types of decisions adolescents are allowed to make for themselves with respect to issues such as weekend curfews and how much television to watch. The family rules measure ranges from 0 to 7, with higher scores indicating a greater number of rules (and fewer decisions made by the adolescent). Fourth, we construct measures of the biological mother's and father's involvement with the adolescent. These measures are based on a composite index of whether the adolescent has engaged in each of a total of nine activities with his or her mother or father in the past month, such as shopping, attending a religious service, or talking about school work or grades. These measures of involvement range from 0 to 9, with the higher end of the scale indicating a relatively greater level of involvement.

To test the stress and instability hypothesis, we consider the total number of family structure transitions experienced by the child. Because prior work suggests that measures of martial transitions alone may substantially underrepresent instability experienced by children (Raley and Wildsmith 2004), we consider transitions involving either marriages or "marriage-like" relationships.[7] We also construct a measure of the duration (in years) of stability of the current family structure.[8] Measures of family structure instability are based on the detailed relationship history provided during the parent interview. We also construct measures of the sibship composition of the adolescent's household, distinguishing households with only full siblings from those involving more complex sibling relationships (e.g., step- or half-siblings) or no siblings.

To test the community connections hypothesis, we construct a dummy-variable measure of whether the child has experienced a residential move within the past two years and a measure of neighborhood-level monitoring based on the mother's report of whether her neighbors would tell her if they saw her child getting into trouble. The latter measure ranges from 1 to 5, with 5 indicating the highest level of neighborhood monitoring.

To assess the role of selection in producing observed differences in well-being across family structures, we construct several measures of the characteristics of the adolescent's biological mother, including her educational attainment, whether she is in fair or poor health (vs. good, very good, or excellent health), whether she usually wears her seat belt when riding in a car (a measure of risk-taking behavior), whether she is a current smoker, and whether she has consumed five or more alcoholic drinks on one occasion in the past month (a measure of binge-drinking behavior). We also construct measures of the mother's age at the adolescent's birth and whether the adolescent was low birth weight (less than 5 lbs., 8 oz.). The latter measure is often used as a proxy for the mother's socioeconomic status and access to prenatal care in the period preceding the birth (see Conley and Bennett 2000). All measures of mother's characteristics are based on her own self-reports in the parent interview.

Finally, we construct a set of control measures, including race, sex, age at interview, urban residence, and whether the adolescent was born in the United States. We also control for whether the adolescent reports ever having been romantically attracted to someone of the same sex, which is associated with emotional well-being among adolescents (Kitts 2005; Russell and Joyner 2001). Finally, we include the adolescent's age-standardized score on an abbreviated version of the Peabody Picture Vocabulary Test as a control variable. Theory suggests that school engagement ought to reduce the risk of delinquent behaviors (Sampson and Laub 1993), and this measure should be correlated with school performance but is arguably less likely to be endogenous to delinquency than other measures of school engagement, such as grades or attitude toward school.

ANALYTIC TECHNIQUES

We use linear regression for the analysis of depressive symptomatology and logistic regression for the analyses of seat belt use, unprotected sex, and drug selling. In the first stage of the analysis, we establish a baseline relationship between well-being and family structure, net only of the previously described control variables. We next add the set of hypothesized benefits of stepfamilies to the baseline specification, including improved economic and parenting resources. We then add the set of hypothesized costs of stepfamilies to the baseline specification, including family structure and residential instability and sibship complexity, and also estimate a model that includes the full set of hypothesized costs and benefits associated with stepfamilies. Finally, we add measures of mother's selective characteristics to the full model, to assess the extent to which selectivity can explain any observed associations between family structure and adolescent well-being. For reasons previously described, we highlight comparisons between groups of youth in single-mother families and stepfather families who share a common history of (non)divorce. Postdivorce single-mother families are treated as the omitted family structure category in all analyses, and supplementary Wald tests are used to assess the significance of differences between stepfather families and single-mother families formed after a nonmarital birth. Although this is not the focus of the current research, we also retain youth living with two biological parents in the analysis to maximize comparability with prior work.

RESULTS

We begin by descriptively examining family structure arrangements among adolescents. As shown in table 8.1, one-third of Add Health respondents living with a cohabiting or married stepfather entered those families after a nonmarital birth rather than after divorce (6 vs. 12 percent, respectively), and more than one-quarter of adolescent respondents living with a stepfather are living in a cohabiting rather than a married household (5 vs. 13 percent, respectively). Consistent with prior research, nonmarital childbearing and cohabitation are particularly important aspects of stepfamily experiences among black youths (Bumpass et al. 1995). Indeed, fully two-thirds of black adolescents living with a cohabiting or married stepfather entered their current family structure after a nonmarital birth rather than after divorce (14 vs. 7 percent), and close to half of these families involve a cohabiting rather than married mother (10 vs. 11 percent).

TABLE 8.1 Distribution of Family Structures by Race: National Longitudinal Study of Adolescent Health, wave 1

	ALL		WHITE ONLY		BLACK ONLY	
Family Structure/ History	Proportion	N	Proportion	N	Proportion	N
Two biological parents	0.66	4,882	0.71	4060	0.38	822
Divorce experienced						
Single mother	0.13	1,021	0.11	626	0.23	395
Cohabiting stepfamily	0.03	205	0.03	145	0.03	60
Married stepfamily	0.09	637	0.10	554	0.04	83
No divorce experienced						
Single mother	0.04	407	0.02	93	0.19	314
Cohabiting stepfamily	0.02	152	0.01	43	0.07	109
Married stepfamily	0.04	339	0.04	200	0.07	139
Total	1.00	7,643	1.00	5,721	1.00	1922

Note: Proportions are weighted, and frequency counts are unweighted.

Descriptive statistics for this study's other key independent and dependent variables are shown in table 8.2. There is much of interest here, but a few points are worth highlighting. First, among those living apart from their biological fathers, adolescents living in families formed after divorce tend to be more economically advantaged than those living in families formed after a nonmarital birth. For example, whereas approximately 27 percent of youth living with a single mother after divorce are in poverty (family-to-needs ratio<1), the same is true of 45 percent of youth living with a single mother without a preceding divorce. A youth in the latter group is also substantially more likely to live in a household where some form of public assistance was received in the past year, and is more likely to live with a mother who did not complete twelve years of schooling. Consistent with prior research, we also find generally higher levels of biological father involvement among those whose families formed after divorce rather than after a nonmarital birth. Yet not surprisingly, adolescents living in a single-parent family or stepfamily formed after divorce also tend to have experienced more family structure transitions than those living in these family types after a nonmarital birth, and are also more likely to have experienced a recent family structure transition.

The data in table 8.2 also reveal some evidence of advantage associated with living in a married-stepfather family rather than with a single mother. For example, within each divorce-history group, youth in stepfather families are considerably less likely than those in single-mother families to be in poverty and are more likely to have a parent home at key times of the day. Cohabiting stepfather families, however, tend to more closely resemble single-mother families than married-stepfather families with respect to these measures.

Yet we also see some evidence of potential disadvantage associated with both married- and cohabiting-stepfather families versus single-mother families, such as having experienced a greater number of family-structure transitions and having more complex sibship structures. For those with a history of divorce, however, youth living with a single mother are somewhat more likely to have experienced a recent family-structure transition than are those living with a married stepfather. We find initial support for the community-connections perspective primarily with respect to cohabiting-stepfather families. For this group, youth living with a stepfather are somewhat more likely to have experienced a recent move than are youth living with a single or married mother. Although mothers in married-stepfather families tend to report better health than do single mothers, other characteristics of biological mothers do not tell a consistent story

TABLE 8.2 Descriptive Statistics for Key Variables, by Family Structure: National Longitudinal Study of Adolescent Health, waves 1 and 2

			PRECEDING DIVORCE EXPERIENCED			NO PRECEDING DIVORCE EXPERIENCED		
Key Variables	Total	Two Biological Parents	Single Mother	Cohabiting Stepfamily	Married Stepfamily	Single Mother	Cohabiting Stepfamily	Married Stepfamily
			Potential stepfamily benefits *Family income-to-needs ratio*					
	0.117	0.054	0.272	0.330	0.062	0.449	0.411	0.143
o 1.9	0.172	0.139	0.279	0.260	0.184	0.210	0.303	0.188
o 3.9	0.370	0.399	0.294	0.276	0.413	0.157	0.175	0.404
	0.250	0.304	0.093	0.094	0.279	0.065	0.039	0.207
issing	0.091	0.104	0.062	0.040	0.062	0.119	0.072	0.057
ıblic assistance in past ear? (1=yes)	0.115	0.049	0.277	0.242	0.064	0.499	0.501	0.133
			Socialization/social control					
ırental presence	2.907	3.059	2.498	2.496	2.812	2.621	2.621	2.809
ımily rules	1.915	1.932	1.740	1.810	1.967	1.989	1.989	1.976
easoning parenting yle	4.113	4.127	4.063	4.084	4.113	4.076	4.076	4.105
Iother's involvement	3.737	3.730	3.898	3.665	3.911	3.422	3.422	3.337
iological father's ıvolvement	2.591	2.877	2.357	2.253	2.329	1.374	1.374	1.288
			Potential stepfamily difficulties *Stress/instability*					
otal number of union ransitions	0.649	0.039	1.788	2.701	2.353	0.897	1.882	1.159
Duration of family tability/union	12.489	15.432	5.079	3.534	6.708	11.479	6.251	10.116

Note: Table 8.2 continues on opposite page

TABLE 8.2 *(continued)*

Key Variables	Total	Two Biological Parents	PRECEDING DIVORCE EXPERIENCED			NO PRECEDING DIVORCE EXPERIENCED		
			Single Mother	Cohabiting Stepfamily	Married Stepfamily	Single Mother	Cohabiting Stepfamily	Marrie Stepfam
			Community connections					
Move in past 2 years? (1 = yes)	0.186	0.124	0.310	0.354	0.291	0.278	0.448	0.245
Neighborhood monitoring	3.946	3.935	3.848	3.949	4.029	4.077	3.926	4.115
			Sibship composition					
Simple (full siblings only)	0.682	0.814	0.550	0.485	0.347	0.372	0.368	0.292
Complex (includes step/ half siblings)	0.126	0.029	0.201	0.247	0.442	0.240	0.372	0.477
No siblings	0.192	0.157	0.250	0.268	0.211	0.388	0.260	0.231
			Selective characteristics of biological mother/child Mother's years of schooling					
< 12 years	0.313	0.081	0.251	0.194	0.107	0.147	0.090	0.261
12 years	0.340	0.348	0.381	0.329	0.295	0.378	0.344	0.318
13–15 years	0.313	0.296	0.371	0.375	0.351	0.277	0.276	0.339
= 16 years	0.244	0.275	0.227	0.100	0.215	0.144	0.092	0.138
Mother's age at child's birth (in years)	25.658	26.611	25.017	22.971	23.227	24.231	22.074	22.337
Low birthweight child (<5 lbs., 8oz.)	0.050	0.042	0.070	0.066	0.058	0.080	0.031	0.053
Mother's health is fair /poor	0.109	0.087	0.173	0.113	0.098	0.242	0.166	0.109
Mother does not usually wear seat belt	0.180	0.147	0.228	0.320	0.205	0.286	0.376	0.210
Mother smokes	0.305	0.236	0.455	0.606	0.367	0.401	0.573	0.438
Mother binge drinks	0.131	0.099	0.167	0.289	0.183	0.195	0.348	0.163

Variables	Total	Two Biological Parents	PRECEDING DIVORCE EXPERIENCED			NO PRECEDING DIVORCE EXPERIENCED		
			Single Mother	Cohabiting Stepfamily	Married Stepfamily	Single Mother	Cohabiting Stepfamily	Married Stepfamily
			Outcomes					
nptoms of depression past week (CES-D ore), Wave 1	10.155	9.432	10.904	10.934	11.738	12.533	13.211	11.705
rely / never wear seat t (1 = yes), Wave I	0.265	0.227	0.345	0.354	0.261	0.424	0.525	0.286
ld drugs in past year = yes), Wave 2*	0.064	0.052	0.092	0.108	0.096	0.090	0.147	0.040
d unprotected sex past year (1=yes), ave 2*	0.164	0.136	0.206	0.321	0.234	0.191	0.223	0.196
	7,643	4,882	1,021	205	637	407	152	339

ote: Descriptive statistics are adjusted for the sampling design of the Add Health. *Data restricted to Wave 2 spondents, as described in text (*n*=5,803).

regarding whether stepfather families should be associated with advantage or disadvantage for children, relative to living with a single mother.

The bottom panel of table 8.2 shows how patterns of youth well-being vary across family structures. These descriptive statistics suggest that the nature of the association between family structure and adolescent outcomes tends to vary across domains of well-being and across preceding state groups (divorce or nonmarital birth). For example, while symptoms of depression tend to be somewhat higher in married-stepfather families than in cohabiting-stepfather families or single-mother families formed after divorce, the reverse pattern holds among families formed after a nonmarital birth. Yet within both preceding state groups we see consistently lower levels of infrequent seat belts among youth in married-stepfather families than in single or cohabiting-stepfather families. We also see lower levels of drug selling among youth in married-stepfather families than cohabiting-stepfather families or single-mother families, but only when these families form after a nonmarital birth. Finally, for both preceding state groups, the risk of having unprotected sex appears to be greater in cohabiting-stepfather families than in either married-stepfather families or single-mother families.

MULTIVARIATE RESULTS

Symptoms of Depression

We begin the multivariate analysis with an investigation of depressive symptomatology. As shown in table 8.3, we initially regress CES-D score on family structure and the previously described set of control variables. In this baseline model specification (Model 1), living with a married stepfather rather than with a single mother after divorce is associated with approximately one additional symptom of depression in the past week. After a nonmarital birth, however, the estimated effect of living with a stepfather does not differ significantly from that for living with a single mother.

Once we adjust for the hypothesized benefits of stepfamilies, including increased economic and parenting resources, the gap in symptoms of depression associated with single-mother families versus married stepfather families becomes considerably larger (Model 2). In other words, we would expect the elevation in depression associated with living in a married-stepfather family rather than with a single mother to be even greater were remarriage not associated with economic and parenting benefits over single-mother families. Although this depression gap expands for both divorce history groups when potential stepfamily benefits are controlled, the difference between single-parent families and married stepfamilies is statistically meaningful only among youth who experienced a preceding divorce. We also see a direct relationship between having received public assistance in the past year and many aspects of parenting on youth emotional well-being.

In Model 3, we add measures of hypothesized costs of stepfamilies to the baseline specification (Model 1). Although the coefficient for married stepfamilies is no longer statistically significant from zero, the magnitude of the coefficient itself changes only a trivial amount (from 1.068 to 1.050). Model 3 does, however, suggest a direct relationship between residential mobility and depression, with a recent move in the past two years associated with a significant increase in depressive symptomatology.

Model 4 simultaneously adjusts for the hypothesized costs and benefits of stepfamilies. We again see evidence of higher levels of depression among youth in married stepfamilies than in single-mother families formed after divorce. Interestingly, among youth in postdivorce families, we also see significantly higher level of depression associated with living in a married than a cohabiting stepfamily. Finally, in Model 5 we ask whether important measures of selection can account for the differences in depression between youth in stepfamilies and those in single-parent families. The short answer is that they cannot, although several measures of mother's selective characteristics—including her educational background and subjective health status—are themselves significantly associated with offspring depression.

Unprotected Sex

We next consider the association between family structure and having had unprotected sex in the past year. These results are shown in table 8.4. In the model that includes only family structure and control variables (Model 1), we see a significantly higher risk of unprotected sex associated with cohabiting stepfamilies than single-mother families among youth who have experienced a preceding divorce. No contrasts between single-mother families and stepfather families are statistically meaningful, however, among youth in nonintact families formed without a preceding divorce. Once the hypothesized benefits of stepfamilies are controlled (Model 2), we see a significantly higher risk of unsafe sex emerge among youth in married stepfamilies than single-mother families formed after divorce. Model 3 suggests that at least some of this apparent disadvantage associated with postdivorce stepfamilies may be attributable to the stress and instability associated with family structure transitions themselves and to the complexity of sibling configurations. Comparing Model 4 to Model 5 further suggests that the selective characteristics of mothers also play a role in explaining the observed association between stepfamilies and the risk of unprotected sex. After these selective characteristics of biological mothers are controlled (Model 5), we see no remaining significant family structure contrasts. An elevated risk of unprotected sex among children without siblings was unanticipated, but perhaps reflects information sharing regarding contraception or sharing of actual contraceptive devices such as condoms among some biologically related siblings. This interesting finding warrants further examination in future research.

TABLE 8.3 Coefficients from Regression of Depressive Symptomatology on Family Structure and Key Independent Variables: National Longitudinal Study of Adolescent Health, 1995 (n =7,643)

Independent Variables	MODEL 1: BASELINE		MODEL 2: BASELINE + BENEFITS	
	Coeff.	Coeff./SE	Coeff.	Coeff./SE
Family structure/history				
Two biological parents	−0.953*	−2.927	0.056	0.189
Divorce experienced				
(Single mother)	—	—	—	—
Cohabiting stepfamily	−0.114	−0.173	−0.066	−0.099
Married stepfamily	1.068*	2.012	1.669*	3.260
No divorce experienced				
Single mother	0.979	1.751	0.482	0.883
Cohabiting stepfamily	1.962	1.942	1.450	1.615
Married stepfamily	0.841	1.163	1.029	1.564
Potential stepfamily benefits				
Family income-to-needs ratio				
<1	—	—	—	—
1 to 1.9	—	—	0.485	1.315
2 to 3.9	—	—	0.234	0.656
4+	—	—	−0.240	−0.610
Missing	—	—	−0.136	−0.315
Public assistance in past year? (1=yes)	—	—	1.531*	3.495

Note: Table 8.3 continues on next page

MODEL 3: BASELINE + COSTS		MODEL 4: FULL MODEL		MODEL 5: FULL MODEL + SELECTION	
Coeff.	Coeff./SE	Coeff.	Coeff./SE	Coeff.	Coeff./SE
–0.813	–1.460	0.124	0.252	0.054	0.106
—	—	—	—	—	—
–0.170	–0.260	0.000[1]	0.000	–0.055[1]	–0.085
1.050	1.808	1.808*	3.205	1.793*	3.217
1.028	1.759	0.453	0.808	0.370	0.634
1.824	1.836	1.363	1.551	1.353	1.493
0.893	1.185	1.084	1.555	1.104	1.528
—	—	—	—	—	—
—	—	0.499	1.351	0.602	1.646
—	—	0.254	0.712	0.595	1.668
—	—	–0.254	–0.647	0.304	0.771
—	—	–0.116	–0.270	0.038	0.087
—	—	1.531*	3.439	0.937*	2.059

(continued)

TABLE 8.3 *(continued)*

Independent Variables	MODEL 1: BASELINE		MODEL 2: BASELINE + BENEFITS	
	Coeff.	Coeff./SE	Coeff.	Coeff./SE
Socialization/social control				
Parental presence	—	—	–0.832*	–7.487
Family rules	—	—	0.294*	3.795
Reasoning parenting style	—	—	–1.499*	–10.562
Mother's involvement	—	—	–0.014	–0.204
Biological father's involvement	—	—	–0.285*	–5.315
	Potential stepfamily difficulties			
Stress/instability				
Total number of union transitions	—	—	—	—
Duration of family stability	—	—	—	—
Community connections				
Move in past 2 years? (1 = yes)	—	—	—	—
Neighborhood monitoring	—	—	—	—
Sibship composition				
Simple (full siblings only)	—	—	—	—
Complex (includes step-/half-siblings)	—	—	—	—
No siblings	—	—	—	—

Note: Table 8.3 continues on next page

MODEL 3: BASELINE + COSTS		MODEL 4: FULL MODEL		MODEL 5: FULL MODEL + SELECTION	
Coeff.	Coeff./SE	Coeff.	Coeff./SE	Coeff.	Coeff./SE
—	—	−0.825*	−7.407	−0.880*	−7.871
—	—	0.291*	3.742	0.291*	3.951
—	—	−1.497*	−10.576	−1.452*	−10.489
—	—	−0.016	−0.240	0.004	0.064
—	—	−0.288*	−5.183	−0.275*	−4.854
0.038	0.194	−0.135	−0.679	−0.138	−0.682
0.009	0.184	−0.013	−0.285	−0.011	−0.234
0.897*	3.207	0.776*	2.916	0.762*	2.992
−0.085	−0.725	−0.054	−0.460	−0.098	−0.841
—	—	—	—	—	—
0.029	0.077	−0.031	−0.082	−0.164	−0.417
−0.179	−0.636	0.124	0.444	−0.134	−0.463

(continued)

TABLE 8.3 (*continued*)

Independent Variables	MODEL 1: BASELINE		MODEL 2: BASELINE + BENEFITS	
	Coeff.	Coeff./SE	Coeff.	Coeff./SE
Mother's years of schooling				
< 12 years	—	—	—	—
12 years	—	—	—	—
13–15 years	—	—	—	—
> 16 years	—	—	—	—
Mother's age at child's birth (in years)	—	—	—	—
Low birth weight child (< 5 lbs., 8 oz.)	—	—	—	—
Mother's health is fair/poor	—	—	—	—
Mother does not usually wear seat belt	—	—	—	—
Mother smokes	—	—	—	—
Mother binge drinks	—	—	—	—

MODEL 3: BASELINE + COSTS		MODEL 4: FULL MODEL		MODEL 5: FULL MODEL + SELECTION	
Coeff.	Coeff./SE	Coeff.	Coeff./SE	Coeff.	Coeff./SE
—	—	—	—		
—	—	—	—	−0.873*	−2.084
—	—	—	—	−0.925*	−2.161
—	—	—	—	−1.511*	−3.233
—	—	—	—	0.040	1.743
—	—	—	—	0.450	0.964
—	—	—	—	1.911*	4.451
—	—	—	—	0.468	1.667
—	—	—	—	0.452	1.659
—	—	—	—	0.468	1.429

Note: Data are adjusted for the complex sampling design of the Add Health. All models also include control variables described in text.

* Coefficient differs significantly from zero at $p<.05$ level.

1. Postdivorce cohabiting-stepfamily coefficient differs significantly from postdivorce married-stepfamily coefficient.
2. "No divorce experienced" stepfamily coefficient (cohabiting or married) differs significantly from "no divorce" single-mother coefficient.
3. "No divorce experienced" cohabiting-stepfamily coefficient differs significantly from "no divorce" married-stepfamily coefficient.

TABLE 8.4 Coefficients from Logistic Regression of Any Unprotected Sex on Family Structure and Key Independent Variables: National Longitudinal Study of Adolescent Health, 1995 (n = 5,803)

Independent Variables	MODEL 1: BASELINE		MODEL 2: BASELINE + BENEFITS	
	Coeff.	Coeff./SE	Coeff.	Coeff./SE
Family structure/history				
Two biological parents	–0.350*	–2.900	–0.066	–0.490
Divorce experienced				
(Single mother)	—	—	—	—
Cohabiting stepfamily	0.646*	2.073	0.667	1.966
Married stepfamily	0.242	1.525	0.478*	2.751
No divorce experienced				
Single mother	–0.262	–1.087	–0.327	–1.302
Cohabiting stepfamily	0.113	0.328	0.006	0.015
Married stepfamily	0.015	0.068	0.131	0.535
Potential stepfamily benefits				
Family income-to-needs ratio				
<1	—	—	—	—
1 to 1.9	—	—	–0.183	–1.045
2 to 3.9	—	—	–0.366	–1.933
4+	—	—	–0.428*	–2.332
Missing	—	—	–0.246	–1.308
Public assistance in past year? (1 = yes)	—	—	0.147	0.885

Note: Table 8.4 continues on opposite page

MODEL 3: BASELINE + COSTS		MODEL 4: FULL MODEL		MODEL 5: FULL MODEL + SELECTION	
Coeff.	Coeff./ SE	Coeff.	Coeff./ SE	Coeff.	Coeff./ SE
–0.037	–0.177	0.217	1.082	0.160	0.797
—	—	—	—	—	—
0.510	1.621	0.556	1.656	0.508	1.513
0.084	0.507	0.344*	1.981	0.283	1.657
–0.186	–0.702	–0.271	–0.977	–0.333	–1.206
0.014	0.041	–0.080	–0.207	–0.162	–0.426
0.015	0.063	0.134	0.539	0.034	0.127
—	—	—	—	—	—
—	—	–0.180	–1.022	–0.188	–1.079
—	—	–0.349	–1.767	–0.299	–1.487
—	—	–0.446*	–2.314	–0.318	–1.481
—	—	–0.229	–1.201	–0.191	–0.980
—	—	0.132	0.793	0.050	0.288

(continued)

TABLE 8.4 (*continued*)

Independent Variables	MODEL 1: BASELINE		MODEL 2: BASELINE + BENEFITS	
	Coeff.	Coeff./ SE	Coeff.	Coeff./ SE
Socialization/social control				
Parental presence	—	—	–0.224*	–4.974
Family rules	—	—	–0.044	–1.427
Reasoning parenting style	—	—	–0.179*	–3.392
Mother's involvement		—	–0.008	–0.290
Biological father's involvement	—	—	–0.031	–1.001
Potential stepfamily difficulties				
Stress/instability				
Total number of union transitions	—	—	—	—
Duration of family stability	—	—	—	—
Community connections				
Move in past 2 years? (1 = yes)	—	—	—	—
Neighborhood monitoring	—	—	—	—
Sibship composition				
Simple (full siblings only)	—	—	—	—
Complex (includes step-/half-siblings)	—	—	—	—
No siblings	—	—	—	—

Note: Table 8.4 continues on opposite page

MODEL 3: BASELINE + COSTS		MODEL 4: FULL MODEL		MODEL 5: FULL MODEL + SELECTION	
Coeff.	Coeff./ SE	Coeff.	Coeff./ SE	Coeff.	Coeff./ SE
—	—	−0.226*	−4.917	−0.234*	−4.899
—	—	−0.041	−1.325	−0.037	−1.155
—	—	−0.180*	−3.481	−0.179*	−3.538
—	—	−0.009	−0.313	−0.005	−0.021
—	—	−0.025	−0.807	−0.019	−0.638
0.142*	2.175	0.119	1.805	0.086	1.246
0.007	0.349	0.005	0.289	0.009	0.469
0.175	1.338	0.162	1.261	0.109	0.834
−0.079	−1.527	−0.068	−1.310	−0.085	−1.673
—	—	—	—	—	—
0.343*	2.269	0.330*	2.046	0.297	1.879
0.231*	2.009	0.290*	2.541	0.311*	2.678

(continued)

TABLE 8.4 *(continued)*

Independent Variables	MODEL 1: BASELINE		MODEL 2: BASELINE + BENEFITS	
	Coeff.	Coeff./SE	Coeff.	Coeff./SE
	Selective characteristics of biological mother/child			
Mother's years of schooling				
<12 years	—	—	—	—
12 years	—	—	—	—
13–15 years	—	—	—	—
> 16 years	—	—	—	—
Mother's age at child's birth (in years)	—	—	—	—
Low birth weight child (<5 lbs., 8 oz.)	—	—	—	—
Mother's health is fair/poor	—	—	—	—
Mother does not usually wear seat belt	—	—	—	—
Mother smokes	—	—	—	—
Mother binge drinks	—	—	—	—

Note: Table 8.4 continues on opposite page

MODEL 3: BASELINE + COSTS		MODEL 4: FULL MODEL		MODEL 5: FULL MODEL + SELECTION	
Coeff.	Coeff./ SE	Coeff.	Coeff./ SE	Coeff.	Coeff./ SE
—	—	—	—		
—	—	—	—	0.007	0.046
—	—	—	—	–0.039	–0.233
—	—	—	—	–0.197	–0.822
—	—	—	—	–0.022*	–2.175
—	—	—	—	0.157	0.798
—	—	—	—	–0.065	–0.482
—	—	—	—	0.175	1.421
—	—	—	—	0.259*	2.313
—	—	—	—	0.067	0.410

Note: Data are adjusted for the complex sampling design of the Add Health. All models also include control variables described in text.

* Coefficient differs significantly from zero at $p < .05$ level.

1. Postdivorce cohabiting-stepfamily coefficient differs significantly from postdivorce married-stepfamily coefficient.
2. "No divorce experienced" stepfamily coefficient (cohabiting or married) differs significantly from "no divorce" single-mother coefficient.
3. "No divorce experienced" cohabiting-stepfamily coefficient differs significantly from "no divorce" married-stepfamily coefficient.

Infrequent Use of Seat Belts

We next turn to an examination of the association between stepfamilies and infrequent seat belt use, with results shown in table 8.5. When only family structure and controls are included in the model (Model 1), we see a significantly lower risk of infrequent seat-belt use among adolescents in married stepfamilies than in single-mother families. This pattern holds for both divorce history groups. For families formed after a nonmarital birth, however, we also see a particularly high risk of infrequent seat-belt use among youth in cohabiting stepfamilies. All of these differences, however, appear to be attributable to varying levels of economic and parenting resources across family structures (Model 2). One other finding in table 8.5 is particularly noteworthy: a longer period of stability in the current family structure is associated with a significantly reduced risk of infrequent seat belt use (Models 3 and 4). This association between duration of stability and seat belt use cannot be explained by the selective characteristics of biological mothers considered here (Model 5).

Drug Selling

Finally, we consider the association between stepfamilies and drug selling. These results are shown in table 8.6. We again see some apparent benefit of married stepfamilies relative to single-parent families, but now only among youth whose families formed without a preceding divorce (Model 1). The relative advantage associated with a stepfather family with respect to drug selling, however, does not extend to cohabiting stepfamilies. As seen in Model 2 through Model 5, we are not able to explain the apparent benefits associated with these married stepfather families with covariates currently included in the models. Future work on this topic might benefit from greater attention to the selectivity of families choosing marriage after a nonmarital birth as well as considering more information about adolescent social environments, including broader measurement of the economic characteristics of neighborhoods and schools.

DISCUSSION

The results of our research point to a complex relationship between stepfather families and the well-being of adolescents, with the nature of this association varying across domains of well-being. For example, we find relatively lower levels of emotional well-being and a greater risk of sexual risk-taking behavior among youth in married-stepfather families than among those in single-mother families, particularly for adolescents who experienced a preceding divorce. But our results also suggest that stepfather families are associated with some positive outcomes for young people. Indeed, youth in married-stepfather families are significantly more likely than those living with a single mother to regularly wear a seat belt when riding in a car, and among those not experiencing a preceding divorce, living with a married stepfather rather than with a single mother is associated with a reduced risk of selling drugs. It is important to keep in mind, however, that these results represent average effects associated with stepfather families and that considerable variability exists in youth well-being within all family structures.

We consider several mechanisms hypothesized to explain observed outcome differences between youth in stepfather families and those in single mother families. For example, we find relatively greater economic and parenting resources among youth living with a married stepfather than among those living with a single mother, and these benefits explain the married stepfamily advantage with respect to seat belt use. Even where associated with an overall reduction in youth well-being, as with symptoms of depression and sexual risk-taking behavior, stepfamilies still appear to convey some economic and parenting benefits. The apparent stepfamily advantage with respect to drug selling, however, is not attributable to these factors. Our results also point to negative effects associated with family structure transitions and with complexity in family living arrangements. For example, experiencing a larger number of family structure transitions or a complex sibship structure is associated with an elevated risk of having unprotected sex. A longer period of stability in the current family structure is associated with a reduced risk of infrequent seat belt use.

In addition to considering stepfamilies formed through marriage, we also examine stepfamilies formed through nonmarital cohabitation. Comparisons between cohabiting and married families are of particular interest to policymakers because they can provide suggestive evidence of how marriage per se—rather than the presence of two parental figures in the home—may influence the well-being of offspring. Consistent with prior work, our results do point to some meaningful differences in adolescent well-being associated with cohabitation rather than marriage. Relative advantage associated with married-stepfather families with respect to seat-belt use and drug selling, for

TABLE 8.5 Coefficients from Logistic Regression of Infrequent Seat-belt Use on Family Structure and Key Independent Variables: National Longitudinal Study of Adolescent Health, 1995 ($n = 7{,}643$)

Independent Variables	MODEL 1: BASELINE		MODEL 2: BASELINE + BENEFITS	
	Coeff.	Coeff./SE	Coeff.	Coeff./SE
Family structure/history				
Two biological parents	–0.471*	–4.399	–0.118	–1.009
Divorce experienced				
(Single mother)	—		—	
Cohabiting stepfamily	0.005	.025	–0.004	–0.018
Married stepfamily	–0.322*	–2.188	–0.018	–0.112
No divorce experienced				
Single mother	0.101	0.637	–0.029	–0.170
Cohabiting stepfamily	0.463[3]	1.960	0.311	1.380
Married stepfamily	–0.334[2]	–1.8	–0.179	–0.917
Potential stepfamily benefits				
Family income-to-needs ratio				
<1	—	—	—	—
1 to 1.9	—	—	–0.270*	–2.014
2 to 3.9	—	—	–0.581*	–3.892
4+	—	—	–0.943*	–6.178

Note: Table 8.5 continues on opposite page

	MODEL 3: BASELINE + COSTS		MODEL 4: FULL MODEL		MODEL 5: FULL MODEL + SELECTION	
	Coeff.	Coeff./SE	Coeff	Coeff./SE	Coeff.	Coeff./SE
	−0.183	−1.101	0.111	0.645	−0.050	−0.272
	—		—		—	
	−0.039	−0.186	−0.001	−0.006	0.159	−0.693
	−0.271	−1.843	0.101	0.656	−0.008	−0.052
	0.307	1.677	0.119	0.636	0.022	0.111
	0.501*[3]	2.004	0.212	1.496	0.233	0.966
	−0.180[2]	−0.845	−0.027	−0.125	−0.197	−0.901
	—	—	—	—	—	—
	—	—	−0.267*	−2.028	−0.165	−1.129
	—	—	−0.583*	−3.952	−0.363*	−2.200
	—	—	−0.949*	−6.266	−0.591*	−3.356
Missing			—	—	−0.422*	−2.514
Public assistance in past year? (1 = yes)			—	—	0.270*	2.117

(continued)

TABLE 8.5 (*continued*)

Independent Variables	MODEL 1: BASELINE		MODEL 2: BASELINE + BENEFITS	
	Coeff.	Coeff./SE	Coeff.	Coeff./SE
Socialization/social control				
Parental presence	—	—	–0.120*	–3.224
Family rules	—	—	–0.034	–1.532
Reasoning parenting style	—	—	–0.174*	–3.861
Mother's involvement	—	—	–0.073*	–3.329
Biological father's involvement	—	—	–0.037	–1.819
Potential stepfamily difficulties				
Stress/instability				
Total number of union transitions	—	—	—	—
Duration of family stability	—	—	—	—
Community connections				
Move in past 2 years? (1 = yes)	—	—	—	—
Neighborhood monitoring	—	—	—	—
Sibship composition				
Simple (full siblings only)	—	—	—	—

Note: Table 8.5 continues on opposite page

	MODEL 3: BASELINE + COSTS		MODEL 4: FULL MODEL		MODEL 5: FULL MODEL + SELECTION	
	Coeff.	Coeff./SE	Coeff	Coeff./SE	Coeff.	Coeff./SE
	—	—	−0.419*	−2.503	−0.267	−1.480
	—	—	0.272*	2.134	0.052	0.367
	—	—	−0.117*	−3.148	−0.148*	−3.710
	—	—	−0.034	−1.517	−0.042	−1.829
	—	—	−0.175*	−3.882	−0.201*	−4.029
	—	—	−0.071*	−3.158	−0.063*	−2.573
	—	—	−0.045*	−2.145	−0.041	−1.933
	−0.005	−0.099	−0.063	−1.292	−0.109*	−2.179
	−0.028*	−2.337	−0.033*	−2.738	−0.029*	−2.158
	0.062	0.634	0.024	0.239	0.001	0.012
	−0.021	−0.588	−0.024	−0.654	−0.030	−0.761
	—	—	—	—	—	—
Complex (includes step-/half-siblings)			—	—	—	—
No siblings			—	—	—	—

(continued)

TABLE 8.5 *(continued)*

Independent Variables	MODEL 1: BASELINE		MODEL 2: BASELINE + BENEFITS	
	Coeff.	Coeff./SE	Coeff.	Coeff./SE
Selective characteristics of biological mother/child				
Mother's years of schooling				
< 12 years	—	—	—	—
12 years	—	—	—	—
13–15 years	—	—	—	—
≥ 16 years	—	—	—	—
Mother's age at child's birth (in years)	—	—	—	—
Low birth weight child (< 5 lbs., 8 oz.)	—	—	—	—
Mother's health is fair/poor	—	—	—	—
Mother does not usually wear seat belt	—	—	—	—
Mother smokes	—	—	—	—
Mother binge drinks	—	—	—	—

Note: Table 8.5 continues on opposite page

MODEL 3: BASELINE + COSTS		MODEL 4: FULL MODEL		MODEL 5: FULL MODEL + SELECTION	
Coeff.	Coeff./SE	Coeff	Coeff./SE	Coeff.	Coeff./SE
–0.022	–0.153	–0.101	–0.767	–0.141	–0.985
–0.142	–1.379	0.002	0.015	–0.054	–0.497
—	—	—	—		
—	—	—	—	–0.381*	–3.383
—	—	—	—	–0.485*	–3.904
—	—	—	—	–0.641*	–3.723
—	—	—	—	–0.006	–0.780
—	—	—	—	0.221	1.259
—	—	—	—	1.625*	14.646
—	—	—	—	0.099	0.847
—	—	—	—	–0.012	–0.146
—	—	—	—	0.032	0.25

Note: Data are adjusted for the complex sampling design of the Add Health. All models also include control variables described in text.

* Coefficient differs significantly from zero at $p < .05$ level.

1. Postdivorce cohabiting-stepfamily coefficient differs significantly from postdivorce married-stepfamily coefficient.
2. "No divorce experienced" stepfamily coefficient (cohabiting or married) differs significantly from "no divorce" single-mother coefficient.
3. "No divorce experienced" cohabiting-stepfamily coefficient differs significantly from "no divorce" married-stepfamily coefficient.

TABLE 8.6 Coefficients from Logistic Regression of Drug Selling on Family Structure and Key Independent Variables: National Longitudinal Study of Adolescent Health, 1995 (n=5,803)

Independent Variables	MODEL 1: BASELINE		MODEL 2: BASELINE+ BENEFITS	
	Coeff.	Coeff./SE	Coeff.	Coeff./SE
Family structure/history				
Two biological parents	–0.645*	–3.792	–0.503	–2.406
Divorce experienced				
(Single mother)	—	—	—	—
Cohabiting stepfamily	.106	.321	0.073	0.212
Married stepfamily	–0.022	–0.094	0.046	0.190
No divorce experienced				
Single mother	0.113	0.363	0.002	0.007
Cohabiting stepfamily	0.546[3]	1.461	0.484[3]	1.292
Married stepfamily	–0.827*[2]	–2.260	–0.868*[2]	–2.277
Potential stepfamily benefits				
Family income-to-needs ratio				
<1	—	—	—	—
1 to 1.9	—	—	–0.302	–0.956
2 to 3.9	—	—	–0.253	–0.878
4+	—	—	0.019	–0.074
Missing	—	—	–0.064	–0.179
Public assistance in past year? (1=yes)	—	—	–0.071	–0.213

Note: Table 8.6 continues on opposite page

MODEL 3: BASELINE+ COSTS		MODEL 4: FULL MODEL		MODEL 5: FULL MODEL+ SELECTION	
Coeff.	Coeff./SE	Coeff.	Coeff./SE	Coeff.	Coeff./SE
−0.442	−1.679	−0.275	−0.971	−0.291	−0.981
—	—	—	—	—	—
0.037	0.110	0.024	0.067	−0.031	−0.085
−0.033	−0.135	0.030	0.115	−0.034	−0.133
0.191	0.557	0.111	0.332	0.098	0.305
0.487[3]	1.321	0.439[3]	1.191	0.382[3]	1.032
−0.772*[2]	−2.120	−0.823*[2]	−2.249	−0.872*[2]	−2.419
—	—	—	—	—	—
—	—	−0.281	−0.896	−0.289	−0.948
—	—	−0.213	−0.737	−0.199	−0.698
—	—	−0.052	0.198	0.119	0.432
—	—	−0.020	−0.055	0.039	0.109
—	—	−0.088	−0.263	−0.154	−2.419

(continued)

TABLE 8.6 *(continued)*

Independent Variables	MODEL 1: BASELINE		MODEL 2: BASELINE + BENEFITS	
	Coeff.	Coeff./SE	Coeff.	Coeff./SE
Socialization/social control				
Parental presence	—	—	–0.187*	–2.904
Family rules	—	—	–0.066	–1.004
Reasoning parenting style	—	—	–0.256*	–3.148
Mother's involvement	—	—	–0.064	0.603
Biological father's involvement	—	—	–0.071	–1.582
Potential stepfamily difficulties				
Stress/instability				
Total number of union transitions	—	—	—	—
Duration of family stability	—	—	—	—
Community connections				
Move in past 2 years? (1=yes)	—	—	—	—
Neighborhood monitoring	—	—	—	—
Sibship composition				
Simple (full siblings only)	—	—	—	—
Complex (includes step-/half-siblings)	—	—	—	—
No siblings	—	—	—	—

Note: Table 8.6 continues on opposite page

MODEL 3: BASELINE+ COSTS		MODEL 4: FULL MODEL		MODEL 5: FULL MODEL+ SELECTION	
Coeff.	Coeff./SE	Coeff.	Coeff./SE	Coeff.	Coeff./SE
—	—	–0.186*	–2.896	–0.193*	–3.073
—	—	–0.071	–1.098	–0.060	–0.903
—	—	–0.255*	–3.187	–0.262*	–3.317
—	—	0.031	0.563	0.030	0.554
—	—	–0.067	–1.472	–0.060	–1.336
0.007	0.056	–0.009	–0.068	–0.031	–0.241
–0.012	–0.628	–0.018	–0.876	–0.016	–0.746
0.369*	2.313	0.331*	2.049	0.291	1.756
0.053	0.682	0.068	0.864	0.067	0.838
—	—	—	—	—	—
0.043	0.182	0.079	0.324	0.062	0.244
0.031	0.166	0.012	0.061	0.063	0.306

(continued)

TABLE 8.6 *(continued)*

Independent Variables	MODEL 1: BASELINE		MODEL 2: BASELINE + BENEFITS	
	Coeff.	Coeff./SE	Coeff.	Coeff./SE
	Selective characteristics of biological mother/child			
Mother's years of schooling				
< 12 years	—	—	—	—
12 years	—	—	—	—
13–15 years	—	—	—	—
= 16 years	—	—	—	—
Mother's age at child's birth (in years)	—	—	—	—
Low birth weight child (<5 lbs., 8 oz.)	—	—	—	—
Mother's health is fair/ poor	—	—	—	—
Mother does not usually wear seat belt	—	—	—	—
Mother smokes	—	—	—	—
Mother binge drinks	—	—	—	—

Note: Table 8.6 continues on opposite page

MODEL 3: BASELINE+ COSTS		MODEL 4: FULL MODEL		MODEL 5: FULL MODEL+ SELECTION	
Coeff.	Coeff./SE	Coeff.	Coeff./SE	Coeff.	Coeff./SE
—	—	—	—		
—	—	—	—	0.106	0.442
—	—	—	—	0.177	0.747
—	—	—	—	0.216	0.758
—	—	—	—	–0.029*	–2.278
—	—	—	—	–0.206	–0.646
—	—	—	—	0.201	1.256
—	—	—	—	0.159	0.683
—	—	—	—	0.274	1.940
—	—	—	—	–0.258	–1.333

Note: Data are adjusted for the complex sampling design of the Add Health. All models also include control variables described in text.

* Coefficient differs significantly from zero at $p<.05$ level.

1. Postdivorce cohabiting-stepfamily coefficient differs significantly from postdivorce married-stepfamily coefficient.
2. "No divorce experienced" stepfamily coefficient (cohabiting or married) differs significantly from "no divorce" single-mother coefficient.
3. "No divorce experienced" cohabiting-stepfamily coefficient differs significantly from "no divorce" married-stepfamily coefficient.

example, does not extend to youth living with a cohabiting mother. It is important to keep in mind, however, that while cohabiting stepfamilies appear to bring fewer of the benefits of married stepfamilies—such as increased economic and parenting resources—they are also associated with more potential costs—such as having experienced a larger number of family structure transitions, more recent family structure transitions, and a relatively higher level of residential instability. With the exception of drug selling, relatively lower well-being among youth in cohabiting rather than married stepfamilies was largely attributable to these factors. Once adjusting for group differences in parenting and economic resources, we actually find lower levels of depression associated with postdivorce cohabiting than married stepfamilies. These findings contribute to growing evidence that differences in well-being between youth living with cohabiting and married parents result from more than legal status alone, and often relate to preexisting differences among families (see Smock and Manning 2004). Moreover, to the extent that parents consider their own children's best interests when deciding whether or not to marry a particular partner (who may or may not be the biological parent of their child, children, or all of their children in the case of multipartnered fertility), policies aiming to alter the outcome of marriage decisions as a route to improving child well-being should be considered with some caution.

Although it is important to document the nature of the association between family structure and youth well-being, it is also necessary to determine the extent to which family structure effects are causal as opposed to spuriously produced by preexisting characteristics of mothers and children who enter stepfamilies. Mothers' background characteristics such as education and poor health are associated with adolescent well-being, and they do contribute in a meaningful way to the elevated risk of having unprotected sex associated with living in a married stepfather family rather than with a single mother after divorce. Yet, even after adjusting for group differences in economic and parenting resources, these background factors cannot explain greater levels of depression observed among adolescents living in married-stepfather families rather than with a single mother after divorce. Nor can they explain the lower risk of selling drugs observed among youth living in a married stepfamily after a nonmarital birth rather than with a single or cohabiting mother. The number of background factors we examine is limited, however, and the majority of our measures reflect only mothers' characteristics at the time of the survey. A much larger array of background characteristics, measured at multiple points in time, should be considered in future research, as should the possibility that youth well-being may itself influence family structure. Greater attention is also needed to the characteristics of stepfathers themselves.

In conclusion, this research highlights important sources of diversity in stepfamily forms and offers an improved picture of the association between stepfamilies and adolescent well-being. Looking at multiple domains of well-being sheds light on the mechanisms through which family structure affects young people. For example, whereas the stress associated with family structure instability may be particularly important in the case of emotional outcomes such as depression, additional supervision in the home potentially provided by a stepparent may be more important in curbing some problem risk-taking behaviors. Future efforts to understand how the arrival of a stepfather influences youth well-being would likely benefit from taking such complexity into account. Additional work should also extend our understanding of well-being in stepfamilies to a greater number of racial and ethnic groups and to other stepfamily structures, including stepmother families and stepfamilies involving same-sex parents.

NOTES

This chapter was first prepared as a paper for presentation at the Evolving Family Marriage Conference, held at Cornell University April 7–8, 2006. This work was supported by a Scholars Award to the first author from the William T. Grant Foundation, the National Science Foundation (SES-0137182), and the Center for Advanced Study in the Behavioral Sciences. Any opinions, findings, and conclusions or recommendations expressed in this chapter are those of the authors. This research uses data from Add Health, a program project designed by J. Richard Udry, Peter S. Bearman, and Kathleen Mullan Harris, and funded by a grant P01-HD31921 from the National Institute of Child Health and Human Development, with cooperative funding from 17 other agencies. Special acknowledgment is due to Ronald R. Rindfuss and Barbara Entwisle for assistance in the original design. Persons interested in obtaining data files from Add Health should contact Add Health, Carolina Population Center, 123 W. Franklin Street, Chapel Hill, NC 27516–2524 (www.cpc.unc.edu/addhealth/contract.html).

1. Recent research raises questions about the generalizability of results from such sibling-based fixed effects models, however, which tend to compare outcomes between stepchildren and their half-siblings who are the biological children of both parents in the household. Ginther and Pollak (2004), for example, find educational outcomes for these two groups to be similar to one another, but significantly worse than those for youth living with two biological parents but without half-siblings in the household. Differences in the well-being of children living with both

biological parents in the two family types may reflect causal effects of half-siblings or other aspects of stepfamily life or may reflect preexisting selectivity in the characteristics of parents and children who enter stepfamilies.

2. Respondents who were in the twelfth grade at Wave 1 and not part of the genetic subsample were not selected to be interviewed at Wave 2 (Harris et al. 2003).
3. See Sweeney (2007) for a more detailed consideration of the association between stepfamilies and adolescent emotional well-being, including longitudinal assessments of depressive symptomatology.
4. A subset of the former cases involve youth whose mothers married someone other than their biological father before the child's birth, although the vast majority represent stepfamilies which formed after a nonmarital birth. The Add Health relationship history questions do not allow one to determine if marital transitions that occur in the year of the child's birth happened before or after the birth of the child. For the purposes of this analysis, these transitions are coded as not having been experienced by the child. Family structure measures were coded as missing when incomplete or inconsistent information was provided in the detailed relationship history, or information was inconsistent between the relationship history and reported marital status.
5. Hereafter we use "divorce" to refer to "divorce or separation."
6. Or responses of "s/he takes me to school" or "s/he brings me home from school," in the case of the two school-related measures.
7. The Add Health collects detailed information on the three most recent marriages or marriage-like relationships in the past eighteen years, and thus the timing of higher-order family-structure transitions experienced by some children is unknown. This omission should not pose a major problem for the current research, as less than 2 percent of sample members have a parent respondent who reports four or more marriage or marriage-like relationships in the past eighteen years (authors' tabulation). The Add Health also does not gather information on transitions from cohabitation to marriage, as each relationship is classified as being either "marriage" or "marriage-like." The influence of transitions from cohabitation to marriage on youth well-being is not well understood, and should be explored in future work using alternate data sources.
8. We also tested a quadratic specification of this measure in the multivariate models. In no case did adding the additional squared term for duration improve the fit of a model, and thus only results involving the more parsimonious linear measure of duration will be presented here.

REFERENCES

Amato, P. R. 1987. Family process in one-parent, stepparent, and intact families: The child's point of view. *Journal of Marriage and the Family* 49:327–337.

Amato, P.R., and B. Keith. 1991. Parental divorce and the well-being of children: A meta-analysis. *Psychological Bulletin* 110:26–46.

Anderson, E., S. Greene, E. M. Hetherington, and W. G. Clingempeel. 1999. The dynamics of parental remarriage: Adolescent, parent, and sibling influences. In E.M. Hetherington, ed., *Coping with divorce, single parenting, and remarriage: A risk and resiliency perspective*, 295–319. Mahwah, N.J.: Erlbaum.

Astone, N.M., and S. McLanahan. 1994. Family structure, residential mobility, and school dropout: A research note. *Demography* 31:575–584.

Brown, S.L. 2004. Family structure and child well-being: The significance of parental cohabitation. *Journal of Marriage and Family* 66:351–367.

Bumpass, L.L., R. K. Raley, and J. A. Sweet. 1995. The changing character of stepfamilies: Implications of cohabitation and nonmarital childbearing. *Demography* 32:425–436.

Cancian, M., and D. R. Meyer. 1998. Who gets custody? *Demography* 35:147–157.

Capaldi, D.M., and G. R. Patterson. 1991. Relation of parental transitions to boys' adjustment problems: I. A linear hypothesis. II. Mothers at risk for transitions and unskilled parenting. *Developmental Psychology* 27:489–504.

Chase-Lansdale, P.L. 1994. Policies for stepfamilies: Crosswalking private and public domains. In A. Booth and J. Dunn, eds., *Stepfamilies: Who benefits? Who does not?* 205–215. Hillsdale, N.J.: Erlbaum.

Chase-Lansdale, P.L., A. J. Cherlin, and K. E. Kiernan. 1995. The long-term effects of parental divorce on the mental health of young adults: A developmental perspective. *Child Development* 66:1614–1634.

Cherlin, A.J. 1978. Remarriage as an incomplete institution. *American Journal of Sociology* 84:634–650.

Conley, D., and N. G. Bennett. 2000. Is biology destiny? Birth weight and life chances. *American Sociological Review* 65:458–467.

Evenhouse, E., and S. Reilly. 2004. A sibling study of stepchild well-being. *Journal of Human Resources* 39:248–276.

Ganong, L.H., and M. Coleman. 2004. *Stepfamily relationships: Development, dynamics, and interventions*. New York: Kluwer Academic/Plenum.

Ginther, D.K., and R. A. Pollak. 2004. Family structure and children's educational outcomes: Blended families, stylized facts, and descriptive regressions. *Demography* 41:671–696.

Hagan, J., R. MacMillan, and B. Wheaton. 1996. New kid in town: Social capital and the life course effects of family migration on children. *American Sociological Review* 61:368–385.

Harris, K.M., G. J. Duncan, and J. Boisjoly. 2002. Evaluating the role of "nothing to lose" attitudes on risky behavior in adolescence. *Social Forces* 80:1005–1039.

Harris, K.M., F. Florey, J. Tabor, P. S. Bearman, J. Jones, and J. R. Udry. 2003. The National Longitudinal Study of Adolescent Health: Research Design. Retrieved August 22, 2007, from www.cpc.unc.edu/projects/addhealth/design.

Hetherington, E. M., and W. G. Clingempeel. 1992. Coping with marital transitions: A family systems perspective. *Monographs of the Society of Child Development* 57, nos. 2–3: 1–238.

Hetherington, E. M., and K. M. Jodl. 1994. Stepfamilies as settings for child development. In A. Booth and J. Dunn, eds., *Stepfamilies: Who benefits? Who does not?* 55–80. Hillsdale, N.J.: Erlbaum.

Hogan, D. P. 1994. Stepfamilies: Selectivity of high risk persons or risk state? In A. Booth and J. Dunn, eds., *Stepfamilies: Who benefits? Who does not?* 147–152. Hillsdale, N.J.: Erlbaum.

Kitts, R. L. 2005. Gay adolescents and suicide: Understanding the association. *Adolescence* 40:621–628.

Manning, W. D., and K. A. Lamb. 2003. Adolescent well-being in cohabiting, married, and single-parent families. *Journal of Marriage and Family* 65:876–893.

Martin, J. A., B. E. Hamilton, P. D. Sutton, S. J. Ventura, F. Menacker, and M. L. Munson. 2005. Births: Final data for 2003. *National Vital Statistics Reports*, 54, no. 2. Hyattsville Md.: National Center for Health Statistics.

McLanahan, S. 1997. Parent absence or poverty: Which matters more? In G. Duncan and J. Brooks-Gunn, eds., *Consequences of growing up poor*, 35–48. New York: Russell Sage Foundation.

McLanahan, S., and G. Sandefur. 1994. *Growing up with a single parent: What hurts, what helps?* Cambridge, Mass.: Harvard University Press.

Mekos, D., E. M. Hetherington, and D. Reiss. 1996. Sibling differences in problem behavior and parental treatment in nondivorced and remarried families. *Child Development* 67:2148–2165.

Morrison, D. R., and A. Ritualo. 2000. Routes to economic recovery after divorce: Are cohabitation and marriage equivalent? *American Sociological Review* 65:560–580.

Musick, K., and L. Bumpass. 1999. How do prior experiences in the family affect transitions to adulthood? In A. Booth, A. C. Crouter, and M. Shanahan, eds., *Transitions to adulthood in a changing economy: No work, no family, no future?* 69–102. Westport, Conn.: Praeger.

Needle, R. H., S. S. Su, and W. J. Doherty. 1990. Divorce, remarriage, and adolescent substance use: A prospective longitudinal study. *Journal of Marriage and the Family* 52:157–169.

Nelson, S., R. L. Clark, and G. Acs. 2001. Beyond the two-parent family: How teenagers fare in cohabiting couple and blended families. *New Federalism: National Survey of America's Families*, Series B, No. B-31. Washington, D.C.: Urban Institute.

Radloff, L. S. 1977. The CES-D scale: A self-report depression scale for research in the general population. *Applied Psychological Measurement* 1:385–401.

———. 1991. The use of the Center for Epidemiologic Studies Depression Scale in adolescents and young adults. *Journal of Youth and Adolescence* 20:149–166.

Raley, R. K., and E. Wildsmith. 2004. Cohabitation and children's family instability. *Journal of Marriage and Family* 66:210–219.

Russell, S. T., and K. Joyner. 2001. Adolescent sexual orientation and suicide risk: Evidence from a national study. *American Journal of Public Health* 91:1276–1281.

Sampson, R. J., and J. H. Laub. 1993. *Crime in the making: Pathways and turning points throughout life.* Cambridge, Mass.: Harvard University Press.

Seltzer, J. A. 1994. Consequences of marital dissolution for children. *Annual Review of Sociology* 20:235–266.

Seltzer, J. A., and S. M. Bianchi. 1988. Children's contact with absent parents. *Journal of Marriage and the Family* 50:663–677.

Smock, P. J., and W. D. Manning. 2004. Living together unmarried in the United States: Demographic perspectives and implications for family policy. *Law and Policy* 26:87–117.

South, S. J., K. D. Crowder, and K. Trent. 1998. Children's residential mobility and neighborhood environment following parental divorce and remarriage. *Social Forces* 77:667–693.

Sweeney, M. M. 2007. Stepfather families and the emotional well-being of adolescents. *Journal of Health and Social Behavior* 48:33–49.

Thomson, E., T. L. Hanson, and S. S. McLanahan. 1994. Family structure and child well-being: Economic resources vs. parental behaviors. *Social Forces* 73:221–242.

Thomson, E., S. S. McLanahan, and R. B. Curtin. 1992. Family structure, gender, and parental socialization. *Journal of Marriage and the Family* 54:368–378.

Thomson, E., J. Mosley, T. L. Hanson, and S. McLanahan. 2001. Remarriage, cohabitation, and changes in mothering behavior. *Journal of Marriage and the Family* 63:370–380.

U.S. Census Bureau. 1996. Income, poverty, and valuation of noncash benefits: 1994. *Current Population Reports*, Series P60–189. Washington, D.C.: GPO.

Wolfinger, N. H. 2000. Beyond the intergenerational transmission of divorce: Do people replicate the patterns of marital instability they grew up with? *Journal of Family Issues* 21:1061–1086.

Wood, D., N. Halfon, D. Scarlotta, P. Newacheck, and S. Nessim. 1993. Impact of family relocation on children's growth, development, school function, and behavior. *Journal of the American Medical Association* 270:1334–1338.

Wu, L. L. 1996. Effects of family instability, income, and income instability on the risk of a premarital birth. *American Sociological Review* 61:386–406.

Wu, L. L., and B. C. Martinson. 1993. Family structure and the risk of a premarital birth. *American Sociological Review* 58:210–232.

Parenting by Gay Men and Lesbians

NINE

Beyond the Current Research

GARY J. GATES AND ADAM P. ROMERO

News and entertainment media images of lesbians and gay men tend to portray them as predominantly white, wealthy, and urban. An analysis of American television broadcast media by the Gay and Lesbian Alliance Against Defamation (2007) found that images of the gay community primarily involved white gay men. The great diversity of the lesbian and gay community in the United States can be obscured not only in mainstream media, but also in academic research concerning gay and lesbian parenting. Such research is dominated by studies that focus on higher-income, well-educated, white lesbians.[1] Contrary to this trend, in this essay we analyze the characteristics of same-sex couples raising children identified in U.S. census data and show substantial geographic, racial, ethnic, and socioeconomic diversity among these families. As much as these analyses provide important pictures of gay and lesbian diversity and family diversity, they also challenge the academic community to broaden its scope substantially when studying lesbian and gay parenting. A broader, as well as more abundant, research effort is needed to better inform the public controversy associated with gay and lesbian relationships and parenting.

CURRENT RESEARCH ON GAY AND LESBIAN PARENTING

In their landmark study *American Couples* (1983), Philip Blumstein and Pepper Schwartz provided one of the first attempts to describe the characteristics and dynamics of both same-sex and different-sex couples. They recognized that understanding the dynamics of same-sex couples and their families contributes to a better understanding of all relationships and the social contexts in which those relationships exist. In assessing how gender and social norms impact relationships and childrearing, for example, studying same-sex couples can offer important insights into how relationships might form and thrive in the absence of gender difference between the partners as well as the social norms associated with the legal institution of marriage. The study of same-sex couples also allows for inquiry into the place, role, and importance of parental gender(s) to the health and well-being of children.

No authors have more carefully considered the literature regarding gay and lesbian parenting than sociologists Judith Stacey and Timothy Biblarz. Their groundbreaking analyses on whether and how sexual orientation might matter for parents and their children (Stacey and Biblarz 2001) remains one of the most comprehensive analyses of this subject. In a review of twenty-one studies spanning nearly twenty years, they convincingly argue that sexual orientation does not affect important dimensions of parenting and child well-being such as parental fitness, child psychological health, and the strength of parent-child relationships. But Stacey and Biblarz do not suggest that parental sexual orientation is irrelevant. In fact, they argue quite strongly that in a heterosexist society, sexual orientation does matter to parenting, because homophobia, sexism, heteronormativity, and attendant inequalities and discrimination make it matter. The authors also offer evidence that dimensions of child development associated with gender conformity and sexual development might be affected by the sexual orientation of parents. Specifically, children of gay parents may be more willing to question, if not challenge, traditional gender norms and may be more open to same-sex sexual attraction. However, one should be careful not to confuse sexual behavior with sexual orientation. While children of lesbian and gay parents may be more willing to entertain the idea of a same-sex sexual encounter, it is not at all clear that this ultimately affects the sexual orientation of the children. Findings from many studies demonstrate that sexual behavior and sexual orientation are not the same (Laumann et al. 1994; Mosher, Chandra, and Jones 2005).

Building on this work, Stacey and Biblarz (2006) again provide a thorough and updated review of literature on lesbian and gay parenting, but this time consider how this research can inform important debates about gender and parenting. Discussions of this issue often cite social science research findings that children do best when raised by their biological, married parents. Such assertions assume that parental gender is associated with distinctive parenting behaviors and children require a mix of both genders for optimal success. Research on same-sex couples with children can allow for a direct test of this theory for, as Stacey and Biblarz show, an appropriate consideration of parental gender requires a comparison of families with the same qualities (e.g., number of parents) except for the gender composition of the parents. In a comprehensive review of twenty-four studies, Stacey and Biblarz find that strengths typically associated with mother-father families appear at least to the same degree in families with two women parents, and likely also in those with two men.[2] Further, they argue that research confirms that compatible parents—regardless of gender, marital status, sexual identity, or biological parentage—provide advantages for children over single parents.[3] They even offer evidence that children born as a result of intentional parenting on the part of lesbian couples experience some advantages relative to children with different-sex parents. In fact, Stacey and Biblarz suggest that, based strictly on the published science, two women parent better on average than a woman and a man, or at least than a woman and man with a traditional division of family labor. Lesbian intentional coparents outperform married heterosexual pairs, even while denied the substantial social privileges of marriage, partly due to selection effects, and partly because women generally exceed heterosexual men in parenting interests and skills—two important indicators of parental quality.

However, even a cursory review of the research described above demonstrates that the studies have focused on a fairly narrow segment of lesbians and gay men who parent. Research subjects, especially in the research of the last decade and a half, are disproportionately white lesbians with relatively high levels of education and income. Further, as Stacey and Biblarz predict (2001), there appears to be a shift in research from a focus on unplanned to planned lesbian parenting. While the children in most of the early studies reviewed by Stacey and Biblarz were born within heterosexual marriages before one or both parents adopted a lesbian or gay identity, newer research focuses on lesbians who become parents through donor insemination. There are many important reasons for this focus, including the necessity to hold variables constant across samples in order to examine the effects, or lack thereof, of sexual orientation. Therefore, it is not our suggestion that this work is flawed or unimportant. Rather, our point is that the great diversity of gay and lesbian families requires a diverse and extensive research agenda if we are to fully understand the familial behaviors and patterns of lesbians and gay men.

WHAT DO CENSUS DATA TELL US ABOUT SAME-SEX PARENTING?

Perhaps the largest and most diverse source of information about same-sex couples and their families is the U.S. census. All data for the analyses described below are drawn from the 2000 decennial census, specifically, a combined 5 percent and 1 percent Public Use Microdata Sample (PUMS). The two PUMS samples represent independent draws from the responses to the long-form census, which contains detailed information about all members of the household. While we are able to identify and study same-sex couples with census data, as described below, because the census does not directly ask about sexual orientation or behavior, we cannot identify lesbians, gay men, and bisexuals who are single or who do not live with a partner. Nor can we identify any transgender individuals in the census because no questions are asked about gender identity or gender at birth compared to current gender.

When surveyed by the census, the householder/respondent defines his or her relationship to other members of the household. The respondent may choose among a roster of relationships, which fall into two broad categories: related persons (e.g., husband/wife, son/daughter, brother/sister), and unrelated persons (e.g., housemate/roommate, roomer/border, and other nonrelative). Since 1990, the U.S. Census Bureau has included an "unmarried partner" category to describe an unrelated household member's relationship to the householder. If the householder designates another adult of the same sex as his or her "unmarried partner" or "husband/wife," the household counts as a same-sex unmarried partner household. These same-sex couples are commonly understood to be primarily gay and lesbian couples (Black et al. 2000), even though, as noted, the census does not ask any questions about sexual orientation, sexual behavior, or sexual attraction—three common ways used to identify gay men and lesbians in surveys.

There are several selection bias and measurement error issues associated with the same-sex unmarried partner data. First, it is important to note that the sample is only a representation of couples. Their characteristics may differ substantially from those of single gay men and lesbians (Carpenter and Gates 2008; Badgett et al. 2008). Second, concerns about confidentiality may lead some same-sex couples to indicate a status that would not provide evidence of the true nature of their relationship. Other couples may believe that "unmarried partner" or "husband/wife" does not accurately describe their relationship. A study of undercount issues relating to same-sex unmarried partners in the 2000 census indicates that these were the two most common reasons that gay and lesbian couples chose not to designate themselves as unmarried partners (Badgett and Rogers 2003). It seems reasonable to believe that the census tends to capture same-sex couples who are more willing to acknowledge their relationship to the government and are potentially more "out" about their sexual orientation.

A measurement error issue also creates a potential bias in estimates. In the 1990 census, the Census Bureau decided that household records that included a same-sex "husband/wife" were miscoded. In most of those cases, the sex of the husband or wife was recoded, and the couple became a different-sex married couple in publicly released data (Black et al. 2000). This decision is reasonable if most of the same-sex husbands and wives were a result of the respondent checking the wrong sex for either himself or herself, or for his or her spouse. By contrast, for the 2000 census, officials decided to recode same-sex spouses as unmarried partners—rather than as different-sex spouses as was done in 1990—reasoning that some same-sex couples may consider themselves married, regardless of legal recognition.

This process inadvertently creates a measurement error issue. Some very small fraction of the different-sex couples likely makes an error when completing the census form and miscode the sex of one of the partners. Under the 2000 census editing procedures, all these miscoded couples would be included in the counts of same-sex unmarried partners. Because the ratio between different-sex married couples and same-sex couples is so large (roughly 90 to 1), even a small fraction of sex miscoding among different-sex married couples adds a sizable fraction of them to the same-sex unmarried-partner population, possibly distorting some demographic characteristics.

Black and colleagues (Black et al. 2003) propose a method for at least identifying the direction of the bias when considering various demographic characteristics of same-sex couples. Same-sex unmarried-partner households in which one member of the couple was identified as "husband/wife" make up the group at risk for this form of measurement error. There is no simple way to identify this group, but one way to isolate same-sex "spouses" is to consider the marital status variable allocation flag (a variable indicating that the original response had been changed). Census Bureau officials confirm that their editing procedures altered the marital status of any unmarried partners who said they were "currently married." (Changes in marital status occurred after editing all of the same-sex "husbands" and "wives" into the "unmarried partner" category.) A large portion of the same-sex unmarried partners who had their marital status allocated likely originally responded that they were "currently married" given that one of the partners was a "husband/wife." Same-sex partners who have not had their marital status variable allocated are likely free of significant measurement error. Using the procedure of Black and colleagues (2003), Carpenter and Gates (2004) show that the census's same-sex couple sample may suffer from some "contamination" with different-sex couples. As such, the analyses that follow include estimates among only same-sex partners who have not had their marital status allocated.

CHARACTERISTICS OF SAME-SEX COUPLES WITH CHILDREN

In 2000, the census counted 594,391 same-sex couples (Simmons and O'Connell 2003). By 2006, the number of same-sex couples increased by more than 30 percent to 779,867 (Gates 2007).[4] About a quarter of same-sex couples identified in the 2000 census are living with a child under age eighteen in the household (Gates and Ost 2004). Analyses of these same-sex couples and their children suggest that the existing research on gay and lesbian parenting has focused on a relatively narrow portion of lesbian and gay men who are raising children. For example, African American and Latina women in same-sex couples are more than twice as likely as their white counterparts to be raising a child (see figure 9.1). And African American and Latino men in same-sex couples are four times as likely to be raising children as are their white male counterparts. Fully 40 percent of individuals in same-sex couples raising children are nonwhite. By contrast,

Figure 9.1 Childrearing among individuals in same-sex couples, by sex and race/ethnicity (Census 2000)

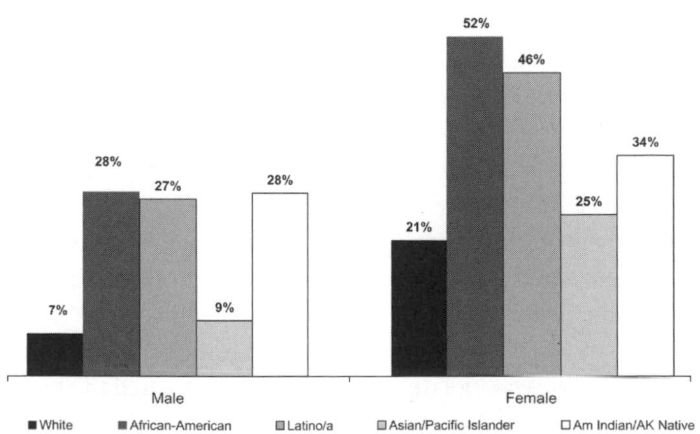

24 percent of all individuals in same-sex couples, with and without children, are nonwhite (Romero et al. 2007). Further, more than half of the children of same-sex couples are nonwhite.

Perhaps in part associated with the high levels of nonwhite childrearing among same-sex couples, census data also reveal that these couples are not particularly wealthy, especially when compared to different-sex married couples raising children. Across all racial and ethnic groups, same-sex couples raising children, both male and female, have lower median household incomes than married couples raising children. However, the household incomes of same-sex couples with children are higher than those of different-sex unmarried couples with children (see figure 9.2). It is particularly striking that same-sex male couples with children have lower household incomes than their different-sex married counterparts. One would expect that since men tend to earn more than women, households with two male incomes would produce higher household incomes than those with one male and one female income. But this is not the case, and it speaks to a broad economic disadvantage experienced by same-sex couples raising children.

A similar pattern holds if we consider the receipt of public assistance among couples with children, where the receipt of public assistance is a strong indicator of low to no earnings.[5] We observe that men and women in same-sex couples are more likely to have received public assistance than are married men and women among all racial and ethnic groups (see figure 9.3). The evidence suggests that across racial and ethnic groups same-sex couples raising children face economic disadvantages to a larger degree than do their married counterparts. Notably, women are more likely to

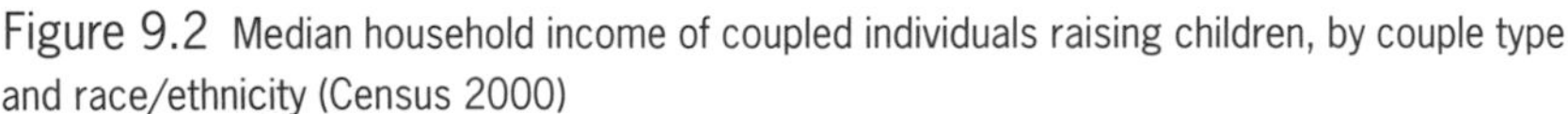

Figure 9.2 Median household income of coupled individuals raising children, by couple type and race/ethnicity (Census 2000)

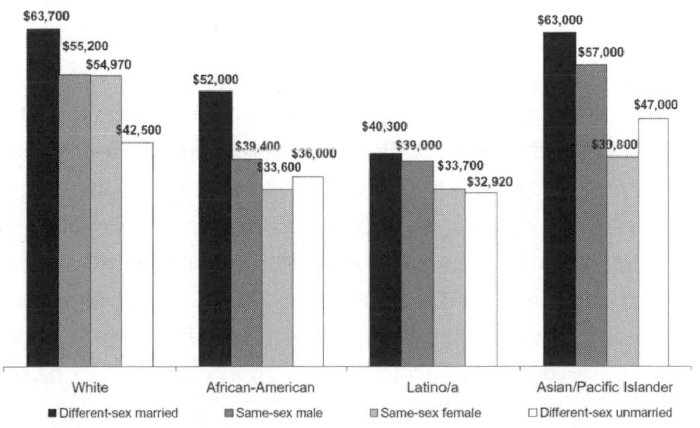

Figure 9.3 Receipt of public assistance by individuals in couples raising children, by couple type and race/ethnicity (Census 2000)

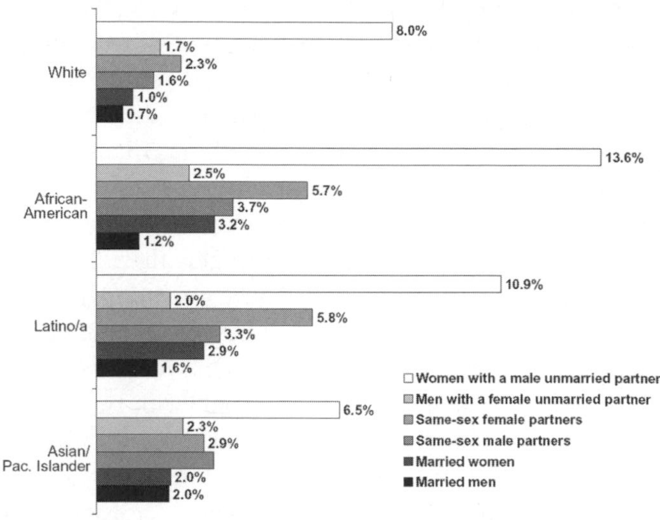

have received public assistance than men, and unmarried women partnered with men are substantially more likely than any of the other coupled individuals to receive public assistance.[6]

The location patterns of same-sex couples with children also suggest that many do not live in areas with large or relatively large gay populations and the accompanying social and legal support. Ranking states by the fraction of same-sex couples among all couples with children, states with socially, politically, and legally supportive climates for same-sex couples such as Vermont, California, New York, and Massachusetts all rank in the top ten; but so do more conservative states such as Nevada, Florida, Texas, and South Carolina (Gates and Ost 2004). More than two-thirds of children living in same-sex couple households live in states where second-parent adoption is not routinely available (Bennett and Gates 2004). Perhaps more surprising is that four in ten same-sex couples in Mississippi are raising children, making it the state where same-sex couples are most likely to have a child. Mississippi is followed by South Dakota, Alaska, South Carolina, and Louisiana. In general, same-sex couples who live in more socially and politically conservative areas are more likely than their counterparts living in more liberal areas to have children. It could very well be that lesbians and gay men tend to come out later in life if they live in areas with higher levels of stigma relating to homosexuality. As such, they are also more likely to have children prior to coming out.

We have already pointed out that there appears to be a trend in recent research toward a focus on intentional parenting among lesbians and gay men. While this is no doubt important, census data suggest that there still exists a large portion of lesbian and gay people who are raising children from prior heterosexual relationships. The census does not provide a clear mechanism for identifying the exact relationships among all members of a household. Instead, information is available only on the relationship between household residents and a single individual from the household who presumably filled out the form and serves as the reference person. A dependent can be identified as a "natural born child," "adopted child," or "stepchild," along with a variety of other relationships including grandchildren, siblings, and cousins. Children can also be designated as a "foster child" or as "unrelated."

Among children under the age of eighteen living with same-sex couples, the vast majority, more than 70 percent, are either the "natural born" child or a "stepchild" of the reference person. Only 7 percent are adopted, and 1.5 percent are foster children. An additional 5 percent are grandchildren, another 5 percent are other relatives such as siblings and cousins, and 10 percent are nonrelatives (at least in relation to the reference person). A portion of the 70 percent of children who are "natural born" or "stepchildren" are likely the product of reproductive technologies like donor insemination or surrogacy. Unfortunately, we have no way of estimating how common this practice is among same-sex couples or lesbian and gay people in general. However, given the expenses associated with these procedures and evidence regarding the economic disadvantage facing many of these couples, it seems likely that a large portion of these children are not the product of reproductive technology and came into this world via some type of heterosexual relationship.

One way to assess this argument is to consider the difference in the presence of children and the type of children present by whether or not the partners were previously married. Not surprisingly, men and women in same-sex couples who were previously married are nearly twice as likely as their never-married counterparts to have a child under eighteen in the home. Table 9.1 considers all same-sex couple households with children and shows the extent to which many of these households might include children from prior marriages. Recall that the children are designated by their relationship to the reference person. Among all same-sex couples with children, 8.4 percent include a stepchild and an additional 5.3 percent include other unrelated children (perhaps the children of the partner of the reference person).

TABLE 9.1 Same-sex Couples with Children, by Previous Marital Status and Type of Children in the Household, Census 2000 (by percentage)

	ALL SAME-SEX COUPLES	NEITHER EVER MARRIED	REFERENCE PERSON PREVIOUSLY MARRIED	PARTNER PREVIOUSLY MARRIED	BOTH PARTNERS PREVIOUSLY MARRIED
Any natural-born children	86.2	83.7	93.7	76.1	88.7
Any adopted children	11.7	16.4	6.2	14.1	6.2
Any stepchildren	8.4	6.2	4.5	19.7	11.6
Any grandchildren	2.5	1.5	2.5	1.3	5.3
Any foster children	0.4	0.4	0.7	0.3	0.1
Any other children	5.3	3.1	3.9	9.2	9.8

However, among households where the reference person was previously married and his or her partner was not, nearly 94 percent include a child designated as "natural born" (fully 10 percentage points higher than in couples where neither partner was ever married); only 4.5 percent of children are stepchildren and additional 4 percent are other unrelated children. But in the case where it is the partner who was previously married and the reference person was never married, nearly 20 percent include a stepchild, and an additional 9 percent include other unrelated children.

Ideally, it would be interesting to know something about the age of the child and duration of the same-sex couple in order to assess the extent to which children come from a prior relationship. While the census does not ask questions about relationship duration, it is possible to determine a subsample of same-sex couples (approximately 27 percent) who have been living in the same house together for at least five years. Approximately 12 percent of them have children under age eighteen in the home. Of that group, about 45 percent have a child under age five, suggesting that the child was perhaps an intentional decision on the part of the couple. Put differently, more than half of the children potentially precede the union of the couple. But there are substantial differences in that statistic depending on prior marital status. Among those where neither partner has been married, nearly two-thirds of them have a child under age five. But among those with a partner who was previously married, less than one-third have a child under age five, suggesting that a very large portion of those children could be from a relationship that preceded the cohabitation of the couple.

LEGAL AND POLICY IMPLICATIONS

Using U.S. census data, our analyses detailed and demonstrated significant demographic and economic diversity with respect to same-sex couples raising children. These insights not only provide interesting and important descriptions, but they also implicate federal, state, and local family law and policy.

Perhaps most glaring, census data reveal that the household incomes of same-sex parents tend to be substantially less than those of married parents: the median household income of same-sex couples with children is $46,200, or 22 percent lower than $59,600 for married parents; the mean household income of same-sex parents is $59,270, significantly less than $74,777 for married parents (Romero et al. 2007). Race and ethnicity—specifically that nonwhites' incomes tend to be lower than those of whites—appears to be playing a role in this disparity, for while 40 percent of parents in same-sex couples are nonwhite, 24 percent of married parents are nonwhite. However, even when same-sex and married parents are compared within racial and ethnic groups, same-sex parents' incomes tend to be less than married parents' incomes (Fig. 9.2). In a similar vein, census data also reveal that while 51 percent of same-sex parents own their home, 71 percent of married parents own their home (Romero et al. 2007).

Juxtaposition of these realities with the now well-known disadvantages gay and lesbian families face in legal and policy arenas (see Bennett 2002; Polikoff 2002) makes remedying those disadvantages even more urgent. Absent any form of relationship recognition at the federal level and in most states, same-sex couples cannot access an important collection of rights and benefits that the government provides to protect and support families and especially the dependents therein. According to the U.S. General Accounting Office (2004), more than a thousand benefits are linked to marital status at the federal level. Among those are tax advantages and discounts; spousal access to health, Social Security, military, and veteran benefits; immigration privileges; and the right to take unpaid leave from work to care for an ill spouse or parent of a spouse.[7] Further, disadvantage related to lack of relationship recognition for same-sex couples is likely exacerbated by the fact that many states' laws do not protect against sexual orientation discrimination in employment or public accommodations. And of the states that neither offer relationship recognition, nor provide for nondiscrimination, many are where same-sex couples are most likely to have children, including Mississippi, South Dakota, Alaska, South Carolina, and Louisiana.

But the diversity of same-sex families revealed in the census also suggests that securing civil marriage for same-sex couples is not the be-all and end-all for supporting lesbian and gay parents. For one, many gay and lesbian parents are not coupled or would choose not to marry. Further, given the disadvantage and discrimination African Americans and Latinos face in the labor market, we might expect marital patterns among African Americans and Latinos in same-sex couples to reflect those of African Americans and Latinos in different-sex couples. That is, we might expect African Americans and Latinos in same-sex couples to be less likely to marry—were they able—than their white counterparts. These concerns are not unfounded. In a study of California's domestic partnership program, Carpenter and Gates (2008) found that registered same-sex couples were more likely to be white and to have higher education and income levels than those in lesbian and gay couples who were not registered. In this regard, marriage for same-sex couples may actually serve to privilege white gay men and lesbians.[8] Significant political and financial resources have been funneled toward securing marriage rights for same-sex couples in the past decade. Yet without meaningful progress in other areas, such as employment discrimination, low wages, and educational opportunities, establishing legal recognition of same-sex couples may not have as great an impact as advocates would suggest. Recalling that 40 percent of individuals in same-sex couples raising children are nonwhite makes these points especially important.

That same-sex parents tend to have lower incomes than married parents also clarifies that public assistance provides an important resource for many lesbian and gay couples and their families. More than 3 percent of same-sex couples, or almost 24,000 same-sex couples, receive public assistance. Racial and ethnic dynamics are pronounced: while 2 percent of white individuals in same-sex couples with children report receiving public assistance, the comparable percentages for African American and Latino individuals in same-sex couples with children are nearly 5 percent. Public assistance is of heightened concern because reforms over the past decade have both diminished available assistance and explicitly incorporated heteronormative (and, as such, potentially gay stigmatizing) practices into program administration. For example, same-sex relationships are at risk of being marginalized (Cahill and Jones 2001; Smith 2007), if not demeaned, within and by welfare's marriage promotion campaigns and abstinence-only education, which typically posit that heterosexual marital relationships are the only safe and acceptable form of sexual intimacy and family core. In addition, as government increasingly turns to religious organizations to distribute resources and administer services, conflicts with regard to certain organizations' religious beliefs about homosexuality as sinful and immoral no doubt arise, as do concerns for those organizations' ultimate abilities to provide services to gay and lesbian families.

Census data show that a large number of children very likely come to same-sex couples via prior heterosexual relationships. Because many of those heterosexual relationships are dissolved in legal and administrative arenas, this finding has important legal and policy implications. One such implication involves child custody and visitation standards and procedures, which may incorporate prejudices and presumptions that can negatively affect custodial and visitation determinations for gays and lesbians. Most states have disclaimed per se rules restricting custody for gay and lesbian parents on the sole basis of sexual orientation, moving instead toward a more child-centered, evidentiary approach. However, even when the calculus focuses on the "best interests of the child," in some jurisdictions it is simply presumed that a parent's gay and lesbian sexual orientation or the presence of a same-sex partner is detrimental to a child's best interest. The "moral fitness" of a gay or lesbian parent may be called into question, or a judge might be concerned to protect a child from private biases against gay men and lesbians (Logue 2002). According to research by the Human Rights Campaign, 21 states and the District of Columbia have records that indicate sexual orientation is a neutral issue or nonissue, while the records are mixed or unclear in the remaining states.

CONCLUSION

Our analyses of census data provide new insights into the dynamics of parenting by same-sex couples. In particular, what is gained from such analysis—and what tends to be obscured in existing psycho-social research on gay and lesbian parenting—is a more thorough and nuanced understanding of a most basic point: the families of gays and lesbians are incredibly diverse, existing in a variety of forms and circumstances, often extending in very complex ways. Census data help us to better appreciate the significant ways in which race, ethnicity, class, gender, and sexual orientation may intersect and interact within the realm of family and, in particular, parenting. From the census, we also now know that a great many children come to same-sex couples—and by inference single gays, lesbians, and bisexuals too—through prior heterosexual, often marital, relationships.

Census data are far from a perfect tool to assess the nuances of same-sex couples' family lives, and they offer no evidence about lesbians and gay men who do not live with a same-sex partner. But they do illuminate some glaring gaps in the types of families who have been the primary subjects of research on childrearing among lesbians and gay men. The data offer evidence that to better understand the complexity of these families we must learn about a full range of characteristics, not only sexual orientation and gender. For example, many same-sex couples with children include non-white parents and children. We know virtually nothing about how the interplay of racial and ethnic cultural norms, juxtaposed with sexual orientation and gender composition, interact to affect parental behavior and child outcomes. Many of these families also include stepchildren from prior relationships. We know very little about how stepparenting plays out in families with same-sex parents and perhaps different-sex nonresidential coparents. In considering a long-term research agenda designed to better understand parenting and family formation of sexual minorities and their children, we must encourage social scientists to expand both the types of families studied and the conceptual and theoretical frameworks under which they frame their research.

The diversity of gay and lesbian families revealed in our analyses also implicates current family law and policy as well as the political debates about how to improve this law and policy to better support gay and lesbian families. We suggested that while civil marriage may be beneficial to many same-sex families, relationship recognition will neither cure all of the inequalities and disadvantages faced by gay and lesbian families, nor benefit all families. The diversity of same-sex couple families indicates that many stand to benefit greatly from progress in areas such as employment discrimination, low wages, public assistance, and child custody/visitation determinations. If nothing else, census data reveal that same-sex parents, and by extension the families of lesbian, gay, bisexual, and transgender people generally, exist within the broader contexts and patterns of society, affected not only by sexual orientation stigma, but also by other forms of disadvantage and prejudice.

NOTES

1. There are several reasons for this focus, one being the necessity to hold variables constant across samples (in order to examine the effects, or lack thereof, of sexual orientation on child development or parenting abilities), another being that limitations on researchers' economic and institutional resources cause them to use convenience samples that tend in the gay and lesbian community to attract higher-income, well-educated, white subjects.
2. There is very little research on gay men who intentionally father. However, Stacey and Biblarz find that studies do suggest that gay men, because of the motivation required of them to become a parent (for example, through adoption or surrogacy), are likely to score well on parenting skills and interest in parenting—two important indicators of parental quality.
3. The issue of marital status raises an interesting issue regarding the use of same-sex couples as a counterfactual. In most jurisdictions, same-sex couples cannot marry. This inability to marry could provide a mechanism for assessing if marriage (or compatibility, as Stacey and Biblarz suggest) actually fosters relationship and economic stability that could lead to better outcomes for couples and their children. However, it also could make it difficult to determine appropriate comparisons between same-sex couples and married different-sex couples since the same-sex couples are likely a mix of couples who structure their relationships more like married couples and those who are more akin to unmarried cohabiting couples. Census data provide evidence of this mixture. In many statistics that capture relationship stability and interdependence, same-sex couples fall in between their different-sex couple unmarried and married counterparts. For example, Gates (2006) shows that while only 18 percent of unmarried cohabiting different-sex couples report that they have lived in the same house together for the last five years, the comparable figure for same-sex couples is 28 percent, and for different-sex married couples the figure is nearly 59 percent. Similarly, home ownership rates for different-sex unmarried couples are 43 percent, 57 percent for same-sex couples, and 81 percent for married couples.
4. This increase likely reflects same-sex couples' growing willingness to disclose their partnerships on government surveys.
5. The census question regarding public assistance does not specify programs. Rather, the question asks if each member of the household received "any public assistance or welfare payments from the state or local welfare office." "Public assistance" for census purposes, however, does not include Supplemental Security Income, which is inquired about in a separate question.
6. Given that much public assistance is directed at children, it is to be expected that women would be more likely to receive public assistance than men since women tend to remain, across relationships, the primary caregiver of their biological children. It

is also unsurprising that women partnered with, but unmarried to, men are the most likely among these couple types to receive assistance for at least two reasons: first, marriage tends to reduce public assistance eligibility (Badgett et al. 2007); second, the women in different-sex unmarried couples are more likely than the men in those couples to be the biological parent.

7. In chapter 13 of this volume, Tamara Metz also highlights the link between marital status and eligibility for many publicly provided benefits.
8. Of course, marriage also serves to privilege couples over those not in a couple as well as those who decide not to marry (Fineman 1995; Polikoff 2005; chapter 12, this volume).

REFERENCES

Badgett, M. V. L., A. Baumle, S. Kravich, A. P. Romero, and R. B. Sears. 2007. The impact on Maryland's budget of allowing same-sex couples to marry. Williams Institute Policy Studies on the Impact of Extending Marriage to Same-Sex Couples, University of California, Los Angeles.

Badgett, M. V. L., G. J. Gates, and N. C. Maisel 2008. Registered domestic partnerships among gay men and lesbians: The role of economic factors. *Review of Economics of the Household* 6, no. 4.

Badgett, M. V. L., and M. A. Rogers. 2003. *Left out of the count: Missing same-sex couples in Census 2000*. Amherst, Mass.: Institute for Gay and Lesbian Strategic Studies.

Bennett, L. 2002. *The state of the family*. Washington, D.C.: Human Rights Campaign Foundation.

Bennett, L., and G. J. Gates. 2004. *The cost of marriage inequality to children and their same-sex parents*. Washington, D.C.: Human Rights Campaign Foundation.

Black, D., G. J. Gates, S. G. Sanders, and L. Taylor. 2000. Demographics of the gay and lesbian population in the United States: Evidence from available systematic data sources. *Demography* 37, no. 2: 139–154.

———. 2003. Same-sex unmarried partner couples in the 2000 census: How many are gay men and lesbians? Paper presented to the Population Association of America, Minneapolis.

Blumstein, P., and P. Schwartz. 1983. *American couples*. New York: William Morrow.

Cahill, S., and K. T. Jones. 2001. *Leaving our children behind: Welfare reform and the gay, lesbian, bisexual, and transgender community*. New York: Policy Institute of the National Gay and Lesbian Task Force.

Carpenter, C., and G. J. Gates. 2004. Benchmarking census same-sex unmarried partner data with other GLBT survey data. Paper presented to the Joint Statistical Meetings, Toronto.

———. 2008. Gay and lesbian partnership: Evidence from California. *Demography* 45, no. 3: 473–590.

Fineman, M. A. 1995. *The neutered mother, the sexual family, and other twentieth century tragedies*. New York: Routledge.

Gates, G. J. 2006. Characteristics and predictors of coresidential stability among couples. California Center for Population Research (UCLA) Online Working Paper Series, CCPR-69-06.

———. 2007. *Geographic trends among same-sex couples in the U.S. Census and the American Community Survey*. Los Angeles: Williams Institute.

Gates, G. J., and J. Ost. 2004. *The gay and lesbian atlas*. Washington, D.C.: Urban Institute.

Gay and Lesbian Alliance Against Defamation. 2007. *Network responsibility index, primetime programming 2006–2007*. New York: Gay and Lesbian Alliance Against Defamation.

Laumann, E. O., J. H. Gagnon, R. T. Mitchell, and S. Michaels. 1994. *The social organization of sexuality*. Chicago: University of Chicago Press.

Logue, P. M. 2002. The rights of lesbian and gay parents and their children. *Journal of the American Academy of Matrimonial Lawyers* 18:95–129.

Mosher, W. D., A. Chandra, and J. Jones. 2005. Sexual behavior and selected health measures: Men and women 15–44 years of age, United States, 2002. Advance data from *Vital and Health Statistics* 362, U.S. Department of Health and Human Services, Centers for Disease Control and Prevention National Center for Health Statistics.

Polikoff, N. 2002. Raising children: Lesbian and gay parents face the public and the courts. In J. D'Emilio, W. Turner, and U. Vaid, eds., *Creating change: Sexuality, public policy, and civil rights*, 305–335. New York: St. Martin's.

———. 2005. For the sake of all children: Opponents and supporters of same-sex marriage both miss the mark. *New York City Law Review* 8:573–598.

Romero, A. P., A. K. Baumle, M. V. L. Badgett, and G. J. Gates. 2007. *Census snapshot: The United States*. Los Angeles: Williams Institute.

Simmons, T., and M. O'Connell. 2003. Married-couple and unmarried-couple households Census *2000 Special Reports, CENSR-5*. Washington, D.C.: US Census Bureau.

Smith, A. M. 2007. *Welfare reform and sexual regulation*. New York: Cambridge University Press.

Stacey, J., and T. Biblarz. 2001. (How) does the sexual orientation of parents matter? *American Sociological Review* 66:159–183.

———. 2006. Gay parenthood and the redefinition of motherhood, fatherhood, and the politics of gender and family. Paper presented to the Conference on Marriage and Family: Complexities and Perspectives, Cornell University, Ithaca, N.Y.

U.S. General Accounting Office. 2004. *Defense of marriage act: Update to prior report* (GAO-04-353R). Washington, D.C.: GAO.

PART 3

Strengthening Marriage

TEN

Supporting Healthy Marriage

Designing a Marriage Education Demonstration and Evaluation for Low-Income Married Couples

VIRGINIA KNOX AND DAVID FEIN

In the decades since 1960, Americans have chosen to marry later, and more of their marriages have ended in separation or divorce. Although the trend toward later marriage has been fairly uniform by social class, the gap between higher rates of marital instability for economically disadvantaged couples and lower rates for nondisadvantaged couples has widened in recent decades (Martin 2002, 2006; Raley and Bumpass 2003). For this reason, and because poor women are much more likely to have births out of wedlock, children born to disadvantaged mothers now typically spend only half of their childhoods in families with two married parents (Bumpass and Lu 2000; Cherlin 2005).[1]

In response to these trends, when the Temporary Assistance to Needy Families (TANF) system was established in 1996, one of its four goals was to "encourage the formation and maintenance of two-parent families" (U.S. House of Representatives 2004). Five years later, the federal government took the additional step of launching a Healthy Marriage Initiative (HMI). Conducted by the Administration for Children and Families (ACF) within the U.S. Department of Health and Human Services, with substantial additional TANF funding under the 2005 Deficit Reduction Act, the HMI has provided grants to a range of state, local, and community-based service providers to fund activities aimed at providing couples the skills they need to form and sustain healthy marriages.[2] A particular focus of the HMI is *marriage education*, a voluntary preventive service aimed at providing interested couples with skills and information that may help them to develop and sustain successful marriages and relationships. Marriage education typically consists of a structured curriculum with multiple sessions taught by one or two facilitators. Marriage education falls within a broader class of preventive interventions called "relationship education" and has been adapted for married and unmarried couples, youth, or single adults.

An important component of ACF's Healthy Marriage Initiative has been a research agenda comprising a variety of research synthesis and evaluation projects, including several random assignment evaluations of the effectiveness of marriage education programs targeted to low-income couples. This chapter provides an overview of one of these evaluations—the Supporting Healthy Marriage evaluation (SHM)—the first large-scale, multisite test of marriage education programs for low-income married couples with children.

Although most existing marriage education curricula focus primarily on bolstering couples' communication skills, conflict resolution, emotional connection, and problem-solving skills, they vary along a number of dimensions, including theoretical underpinnings and approach to behavior change, the topics covered, intensity (length, hours/week), and modes of instruction.[3] SHM is testing a relatively intensive and comprehensive form of marriage education designed specifically for low-income families. Its yearlong program model packages a series of marriage education workshops with additional family support including case management, supportive services, and referrals to outside services as needed. The SHM team selected sites based on their experience providing marriage education or working with low-income families; interest in operating this particular program model; capacity to operate the program for several hundred participants; and interest in being part of a random assignment study. Thus, SHM is not a study of a randomly selected group of healthy-marriage programs around the country, but rather of a particular approach to marriage education.[4]

In addition to its relatively intensive program model, Supporting Healthy Marriage is distinguished by its target group—low-income couples who are married and have children. Low-income couples are the focus of the federal healthy marriage initiative because children in low-income families are particularly likely to experience family breakup and because their parents have previously had limited avenues for learning how to strengthen their marriages. Given its focus on married couples with children, SHM's unique contribution will be to assess whether such services can increase the quality and stability of existing marital relationships and thereby improve the well-being of children and their parents.

As described further in this chapter, the research team began the study by conceptualizing the processes that influence relationship quality and stability for low-income couples; developing hypotheses about how a marriage education program might affect the relationships of low-income couples; and ultimately, how changes in couples' relationship quality might affect the well-being of their children.[5] In this and subsequent phases of the study, we have drawn upon current research from a number of social science disciplines and have consulted closely with a wide range of practitioners and social scientists with expertise in research on the determinants of marital trajectories, intervention research about marriage education, and effective practices in working with low-income families.

In the initial stages of the project, the team concentrated on developing the program model and research design and recruiting sites able to run strong programs. Eight sites (with some sites spanning multiple organizations) are operating SHM programs around the country. Following a several-year period of program operations, data collection, and analysis, the project will issue an initial report on impacts on couples after twelve months of follow-up. In this chapter, we provide a broad introduction to the project. We describe first some of the demographic trends and prior research on marriage education providing the rationale for healthy-marriage interventions. Subsequent sections present the project's conceptual framework and program model. Last, we describe the major research questions investigated in SHM's implementation and impact analyses, the two major substudies of the project.

THE RESEARCH FOUNDATIONS OF THE SHM PROJECT

The Supporting Healthy Marriage project is motivated by three related but distinct bodies of research: Studies indicating that children in low-socioeconomic-status (SES) families spend less time in two-parent families (and that this gap for lower and higher income children continues to grow); studies suggesting that children benefit from growing up with two parents who are in a stable, low-conflict relationship; and random assignment evaluations demonstrating that at least for some target groups and some outcomes, marriage education interventions can have positive effects on couples and their children.

Trends in Marriage and Divorce

An important literature in recent years has examined differences in marriage and divorce by socioeconomic status. Married couples with low education levels are more likely to divorce (Fein 2004; Martin 2006), and when low-income married couples split up, their children are likely to become poor and dependent on public assistance (Behrman and Quinn 1994). Furthermore, socioeconomic inequality in children's access to two parents has increased in recent decades. Low-income individuals have become increasingly likely to have children before marrying, and, for those who marry, dissolution rates have remained very high while declining among better-off couples (Ellwood and Jencks 2004; Martin 2006; Raley and Bumpass 2003). If publicly funded interventions like SHM can promote marital quality and stability, they may be able to contribute to more equitable prospects for children.

Influences of Family Structure and Family Relationships on Child Well-Being

Reviews in other recent volumes have summarized past research on the effects of family structure on children's well-being (Amato 2005; Ribar 2004). Individual studies as well as meta-analyses have attempted to disentangle the effects on children of living in different types of households by comparing outcomes for children in a variety of family configurations. Additional research has attempted to uncover the potential causal contributions of specific experiences of children who live in different family structures. These several decades of nonexperimental studies have provided considerable evidence that children benefit when they have access throughout their childhoods to adequate financial resources, effective parenting, a stable household, and minimal exposure to parental conflict.

Over the past two decades, the evidence has strengthened that children who grow up with two parents who are in a stable relationship are more likely to receive the parenting and financial supports that promote their well-being (Amato 2000; McLanahan and Sandefur 1994). At the same time, there are many uncertainties about exactly what inputs matter most, the optimal role for public policy, and whether and why marital relationships may be particularly advantageous for children (Acs 2007; chapters 7 and 8, this volume).

Although carefully designed comparisons between children in different circumstances have contributed to our understanding of the processes by which families support children's development, nearly all of these prior studies are nonexperimental and vulnerable to potential bias due to parents' self-selection into different family structures and other circumstances (Ribar 2004). Thus, although the primary function of the SHM project is to test the effectiveness of marriage education for disadvantaged married couples, the experimental design of the SHM study also affords a unique opportunity to contribute to existing basic research: The proximate targets of the intervention (parents' handling of conflict, positive relationship qualities, and/or marital stability) will have been influenced by an exogenous influence—random assignment to either a group that receives marriage education or a group that does not. By analyzing both these proximate impacts of this intervention and the more distal effects on aspects of family life such as parents' mental health, parenting and coparenting, family income, and children's well-being, SHM has the potential to shed new light on the causal links between individual and family characteristics and child well-being that are difficult to identify definitively in a nonexperimental framework.

Effectiveness of Marriage Education Programs

A third important thread in prior research is a literature suggesting that psychoeducational interventions can be effective at improving couples' relationships. A common characteristic of these programs is their prevention outlook: At the same time that basic research on marriage was learning much about early communication and other behaviors associated with long-term relationship distress, practitioners were becoming increasingly convinced that marital therapy is likely to be only modestly successful given that couples often are seriously distressed by the time they seek help (Bradbury et al. 1998; Christensen 1999). Substantial enthusiasm thus greeted the idea that it might be possible to teach couples how to recognize and practice positive interaction and avoid negative exchanges while their relationships were still in good shape (Halford 2001; Halford et al. 2003; Markman and Floyd 1980; Silliman et al. 2002).

Until recently, this literature mainly comprised experiments involving small samples of mostly middle- and upper-class couples and conducted mainly by researchers and clinicians who developed the interventions. Meta-analyses of varying subsets of programs over the past two decades suggest that preventative psychoeducationally oriented programs on average have produced moderate positive effects on relationship satisfaction and communication (Butler and Wampler 1999; Carroll and Doherty 2003; Giblin, Sprenkle, and Sheehan 1985; Hawkins, Blanchard, and Fawcett 2007; Reardon-Anderson et al. 2005).

The earliest programs studied, such as the Couple Communication (Wampler 1990) and Relationship Enhancement (Guerney 1977) programs, focused on communication and problem-solving skills. A landmark 1985 meta-analysis of eighty-five studies (Giblin et al. 1985) found average effect sizes of .3 (men) and .5 (women) for relationship satisfaction and of .6 for communication skills (for both men and women).

A second generation of interventions broadened skills taught beyond communication and conflict resolution to include new insight into the role of couples' expectations and attitudes; emotions (both positive and negative); the meaning that might be derived from recurrent conflicts; and the importance of nurturing the positive side of the relationship, including fun, friendship, emotional supportiveness, and intimacy. The most widely disseminated of these is the Prevention and Relationship Enhancement Program (PREP; see Hahlweg et al. 1998; Halford, Sanders, and Behrens 2001; Markman and Hahlweg 1993; Stanley et al. 2001). Recent meta-analyses—which include second-generation evaluations in addition to earlier evaluations—have reported effect sizes roughly comparable to those reported in meta-analyses of earlier programs (Carroll and Doherty 2003; Hawkins et al. 2007; Reardon-Anderson et al. 2005).

Collectively, a series of sampling and technical limitations in these earlier studies makes it difficult to predict confidently the impacts of more intensive programs such as SHM developed for low-income couples. As mentioned, nearly all of the studies cited involved predominantly white, middle-class couples. Furthermore, though a good number of studies utilized experimental designs, many of them measured outcomes only for nonrandom subsamples of subjects originally assigned to experimental and comparison groups. Such selection occurred through a variety of mechanisms, such as researchers' decision to study only those treatment group members who participated in or completed the program and attrition when marriages dissolved or researchers could not locate original sample members (Carroll and Doherty 2003; Reardon-Anderson et al. 2005). Very few studies employed statistical techniques, such as regression adjustment, that might help control for such sources of imbalance in the designs. Finally, these evaluations tended to follow couples for only a very short time period—in many cases extending no more than several months after program completion—and rarely measured impacts on marital stability or child outcomes.

A third set of marriage education studies focused on couples experiencing stresses related to childrearing has begun to address some of these limitations. Common to this newer class of interventions is the notion that parents may be especially open to participating in marriage education if it is presented in a way that supports their roles as parents or addresses specific transition points in family life. Until recently, these studies again involved primarily middle-class couples, although they also tended to be based on somewhat larger samples, more careful designs, and longer follow-up.

The first important evaluation in this category, of a transition-to-parenthood program called Becoming a Family, used a group discussion format with skilled clinicians, and found effects on a range of outcomes, including positive effects on marital satisfaction (but not stability) at sixty-six months after random assignment (Cowan and Cowan 1992). More recently, the same investigators have reported impacts on marital satisfaction, parenting, and children's test scores and behavior in Schoolchildren and their Families, a study that recently completed a ten-year follow-up analysis (Cowan and Cowan 2006a). The ongoing Supporting Fathers' Involvement Study is finding impacts from a similar, discussion-based model for a mostly low-income Hispanic population (Cowan et al. 2006). Other higher-quality experiments reporting promising findings in this category include tests of the Bringing Baby Home program (Shapiro and Gottman 2005) and an adaptation of the Incredible Years that addressed relationships between parents coping with children with serious behavior problems (Webster-Stratton and Taylor 2001).

Thus, work to date provides many reasons to test more intensive, large-scale psychoeducational models and address the substantial deficit in knowledge about how marriage education may affect low-income couples. In the remainder of this chapter, we describe the conceptual model, program design, and evaluation approach for the Supporting Healthy Marriage demonstration, which is testing relatively intensive and comprehensive services in eight sites around the country.

CONCEPTUAL FRAMEWORK

A notable by-product of the federal marriage initiatives has been the emergence of a new multi-disciplinary perspective on how economic disadvantage affects couple relationships and related family processes. Previously, clinical and developmental psychologists had amassed a rich body of theory and evidence on couple relationship processes from fine-grained observational studies of small samples of largely white, upper-middle-class couples (Gottman and Notarius 2000). In contrast, sociologists and economists had used survey data to identify personal, family, and community demographic factors associated with a variety of family outcomes (Amato et al. 2003; Burstein 2007; Ellwood and Jencks 2004). Starting in the 1990s, social psychologists began to bridge these two perspectives by developing family process models integrating external factors and internal relationship dynamics (Conger, Reuter, and Elder 1999; Conger et al. 2002; Cutrona et al. 2003; Karney and Bradbury 1995). Spurred by the federal marriage initiatives, there more recently has been collaboration on interventions between experts in marriage interventions (who tend to be psychologists) and experts in antipoverty programs (who tend to be economists and sociologists). Such collaboration within the SHM project has been especially helpful in laying out a conceptual framework for marriage interventions for economically disadvantaged couples.

Key Elements of the SHM Framework

As shown in figure 10.1, the SHM conceptual framework represents the central aim of marriage programs as being to support "healthy marriage," a construct whose definition takes account of the way spouses interact, how they view the relationship, and whether they decide to stay together. Psychoeducational curricula seek to influence such outcomes by providing new insights, teaching new skills, and encouraging exploration of the values and expectations each partner brings to the relationship. To do so, they must work with, and sometimes against, many factors outside the relationship itself, including personal qualities of each partner and pressures and supports in the surrounding environment. If they are successful in supporting healthy marriage, programs ultimately seek to improve the well-being of individual adults—and especially of children.

Perhaps the thorniest question raised by this framework is how exactly projects like SHM should define and measure "success," in a field rife with multiple perspectives and empirical puzzles. Clinicians who work with troubled couples may see restoring some satisfaction with the relationship and some commitment to staying together as a major achievement. Prevention-

Figure 10.1 Conceptual framework for the Supporting Healthy Marriage Project

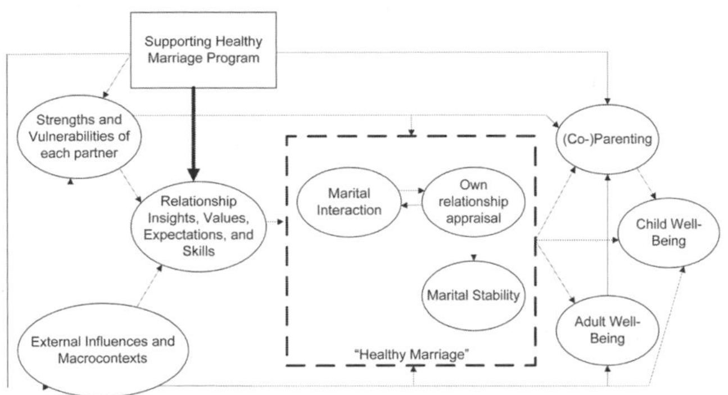

oriented psychologists, drawing on fine-grained predictive studies of initially satisfied couples, traditionally concentrated on developmental markers of relationship dysfunction, so that "success" involved helping couples avoid negative interactions that would threaten marital quality. More recently, psychologists have become more attentive to the idea that positive behaviors and sentiments may provide a powerful inoculation or buffer against potentially damaging experiences within relationships or outside stressors (Gottman and Notarius 2000; Halford et al. 2003). Given that there are a number of inconsistencies in the evidence on relationship attributes predicting satisfaction and stability over the long term (see Johnson et al. 2005 for discussion), it is tempting to simply say that a "successful" relationship is one that both partners see positively. It is insufficient to ignore the way couples actually interact, however, since perceptions do not always reflect relationship problems until it is too late (Fincham, Hall, and Beach 2006). A final approach—consistent with the concept of healthy behaviors in public health research—is one that defines marriages as healthy when they promote the individual well-being of both partners and their children.[6] This last approach requires a careful assessment of theory and evidence on aspects—and levels—of relationship functioning predictive of desired individual-level outcomes.

While experts have struggled to carefully define and measure marital success, federal policymakers have embraced the concept of a "healthy marriage" as the goal of the Healthy Marriage Initiative. A motivation in their doing so was to emphasize that the initiative was not intended solely to produce more marriages or longer-lasting marriages, but rather to promote more good marriages. As such, a description on the federal HMI website builds in a number of the markers mentioned above:

> There are at least two characteristics that all healthy marriages have in common. First, they are mutually enriching, and second, both spouses have a deep respect for each other.... [A healthy marriage] is a mutually satisfying relationship that is beneficial to the husband, wife and children (if present).... It is a relationship that is committed to ongoing growth, the use of effective communication skills and the use of successful conflict management skills. (US Department of Health and Human Services 2007).

Some recent efforts to operationalize this construct of healthy marriage similarly have proposed combinations of attributes found in prior research to be related to marital success (quality and stability) and to predict child and adult well-being. For example, one version developed by Child Trends based on reviews of the literature and expert input identifies the following ten elements of a healthy marriage: commitment between the partners; satisfaction; conflict resolution skills; lack of domestic violence; fidelity; interaction and time together; intimacy and emotional support; commitment to the children; and legal status and longevity (Moore et al. 2004). Similarly Stanley and his colleagues (Stanley 2007; Stanley, Markman, and Whitton 2002) propose that promoting a feeling of "safety" in relationships ought to be the unifying objective of marriage programs (they suggest four key dimensions of safety: physical, emotional, commitment, environmental).

To date, these varying efforts to identify coherent themes in the literature and expert opinion have been useful in setting general directions for policy and practice, but get us only partway toward an operational definition of healthy marriage for evaluation purposes. As described later in this chapter, the SHM research team will be gathering measures for a broad range of marital processes and outcomes identified in recent research so that we will be equipped to develop the strongest possible summary measures as we learn more about these processes for low-income couples. Accordingly, our heuristic framework simply depicts the broad dimensions of a potential definition of marital success in a very general way. As depicted in figure 10.1, spouses' relationship appraisals and their reciprocal association with marital interaction (Noller and Feeney 1998) are major (albeit not the only) determinants of whether couples stay together.

The framework posits that improvements in certain aspects of marital interaction, relationship appraisals, and stability will have a positive net effect on child and adult well-being (the right-hand side of figure 10.1).

Similar ecological models of family functioning and children's development have been proposed by a number of other investigators (e.g., Belsky 1984; Cowan et al. 1985; Cowan and Cowan 2006b; Cummings, Davies, and Campbell 2000; Heinicke 2002; Parke and Buriel 1998; Ribar 2004; Waite and Gallagher 2000).

Concerning child well-being, poorly handled conflict between parents can create emotional problems for children and provides children with poor models for their own relationships (Cummings and Davies 1994; Emery 1982; Gottman and Katz 1989; Hetherington et al. 1992; Morrison and Coiro 1999). Marital distress also can have negative effects on parenting by making it difficult to work together as a team in raising children (coparenting) and by creating distress that compromises each spouse's ability to parent effectively, leading to spillover of hostilities or withdrawal from relationships with children (Conger et al. 2002; Cowan and Cowan 2002; Hops 1992; Howes and Markman 1989; Cowan and McHale 1996). Finally, as mentioned earlier, by promoting marital stability, healthy marriages tend to increase both financial and parenting resources available to children over the long term (McBride and Rane 2001; Sigle-Rushton and McLanahan 2002).

Emerging Themes in Relationship Research

Having outlined our broad framework, it is helpful to identify some of the basic ideas from marriage research that underlie curricula used in SHM and other marriage education programs. A central goal of many marriage education programs is to improve the quality of marital interaction—the behaviors couples exchange when they are together and accompanying thoughts, feelings, and physiological responses. Prospective longitudinal studies have made substantial progress in identifying characteristics of interaction that predict long-term marital success and distress, though inconsistencies remain on a number of points (Johnson et al. 2005), and though there has been little study of low-income couples to test the degree to which similar relationship characteristics matter.

One important set of positive predictors includes expressions of positive affect, or emotions, and demonstrations of understanding and appreciation (see reviews by Gottman and Notarius 2000 and Halford et al. 2003). Positive expressions during interaction may be contingent (for instance, responses such as good humor or emotional validation that ease or defuse potentially difficult situations involving one or both spouses) or noncontingent (such as habits of attending to, showing appreciation, and developing a shared worldview regardless of what one's partner may say or do). Spouses in relationships that are high in positive affect are likely to attribute favorable motives to their partners' behaviors. Emotional intimacy—a feeling of closeness supported by trust and support in sharing feelings of vulnerability—is another form, or expression, of positive interaction (Cordova, Gee, and Warren 2005). Finally, the *amount* of time couples spend together in enjoyable activities is also related to marital success (Aron et al. 2000; Hill 1988; Presser 2000; White 1983).

The role of communication in marital outcomes remains somewhat uncertain, at least in part because the construct often has not been clearly defined. Since, in a sense, all interaction is communicative, useful research on communication per se requires a clear focus on a relatively narrow set of interactions (Snyder, Heyman, and Haynes 2008). For example, a substantial focus of prior research and marriage education curricula has been the narrower set of technical skills involved in the clear expression of thoughts, active listening, and demonstrating understanding or empathy as a listener. The research support for the effectiveness of particular communication techniques has been the subject of some debate (Gottman et al. 1998; Gottman et al. 2000; Johnson et al. 2005; Stanley, Bradbury, and Markman 2000).

Evidence is stronger on the negative effects of certain emotional expressions and sequences of behaviors. Observational studies consistently have found that expressions of hostility, contempt, sarcasm, rejection, and stonewalling early in marriage predict long-term difficulty, especially when observed in certain patterns (Gottman 1994; Gottman and Notarius 2000; Markman and Hahlweg 1993). One such pattern is "negative escalation," involving the reciprocation of increasingly intense negative affect, often triggered when one partner raises an issue in a negative manner ("harsh start-up"). Another pattern is repeated withdrawal and avoidance when one partner raises issues or makes a bid for attention. High-intensity negative affect often is accompanied, and further stimulated by, physiological arousal (increased adrenalin production, elevated heart rate, sweat) that "floods" thoughts and makes it difficult to deescalate consciously. Over the long term, such exchanges can lead to stable negative views of one's partner, leading to negative attributions of motives and responsibility (Fincham 2001), and ensuing heightening of relationship distress (Karney and Bradbury 2000).

Given the importance of such specific behaviors and patterns, marriage education curricula seek to teach couples about how relationships work and train them in specific skills that can give them some control over how they think, feel, and behave with each other. The SHM framework thus depicts relationship insights, values, expectations, and skills as the primary targets of marriage education programs. In the absence of intervention, these attributes are shaped by other factors such as experiences in one's family of origin; previous relationships as an adult; earlier experiences in the current relationship; and influences from friends, teachers, co-workers, and the mass media.

The Importance of Extrinsic Factors in Programs for Low-Income Couples

In addition to targeting these relationship mediators, SHM programs contain both curricula and services aimed directly at external challenges. At the left-hand side of figure 10.1, we introduce the concept that extrinsic influences can affect marriage outcomes (interaction, perceived quality, decisions to stay together) directly, as well as through effects on insights, skills, and values. A variety of personal strengths and vulnerabilities can come into play during marital interaction (which a more detailed causal diagram would indicate with an arrow pointing directly to interaction), including physical health, relatively stable personality traits such as neuroticism, depression and other mental illnesses, substance abuse, stress from various sources, cognitive resources, and values (Fein et al. 2007; Karney and Bradbury 1997, 2005).

Potentially consequential social contexts, a second broad category of extrinsic influences, include family and friendship networks, and work and community environments (Fein et al. 2007). In addition to their socializing influences, environments may affect personal strengths (e.g., social supports help individuals cope with stressful events) and vulnerabilities (e.g., job loss leads to depression). Environmental stressors, which may be greater for low-income couples, can affect relationship quality by inducing depression (Conger et al. 1999) or by diminishing partners' capacity to maintain a positive outlook on what transpires during interaction (Neff and Karney 2004). Contextual influences also can affect marital interaction and stability more directly (for example, family and friends may or may not urge a couple to stay together and work things out; public policies make it easier or harder to get a divorce).

Addressing extrinsic factors is especially important in marriage education programs for low-income couples, because these factors likely underlie greater difficulties in maintaining healthy relationships. Hence, whereas marriage education programs for middle-class couples could afford to focus mainly on the technical aspects of interaction between spouses, we hypothesize that there is a greater need for programs for low-income couples to address personal problems and environmental factors. To underscore this point, we provide a quick sketch of the SHM target population and the distinctive external stressors it faces.

As mentioned, the SHM target population is economically disadvantaged married adults who are living with one or more minor children or expecting a child. Program guidelines explain that programs generally should target couples with incomes below 200 percent of poverty, but do not require screening for income eligibility. Both spouses must volunteer to participate, and the couple should not be experiencing serious domestic violence issues. Staff members assess couples for domestic violence at intake, and for those enrolled, throughout program participation, using protocols developed in partnership with local domestic violence experts.

When the project began in 2003, virtually no research had focused on low-income married couples. Fresh tabulations of Current Population Survey data showed that eight million U.S. married couples had incomes below 200 percent of the federal poverty line and that six million of these couples were living with minor children (Fein 2004). A large fraction of these couples—37 percent—were Latinos, and only 8 percent were African Americans.[7] Only 65 percent of low-income husbands worked full-time, compared to 92 percent of those at or above three times the federal poverty level. There are a number of striking differences between low-income couples in different race-ethnicity groups: for example, 74 percent of low-income Latino husbands worked full-time, compared with 62 and 55 percent of low-income white and African American husbands, respectively. Only 39 percent of low-income Latino husbands had high-school degrees, compared with 79 and 78 percent of low-income white and African American husbands.

To assess external factors in marital distress, we analyzed data on 1,484 married couples in the bottom and top quintiles on an index of socioeconomic status in the National Survey of Families and Households (Fein et al. 2007). Analyses examined a wide range of hypothesized influences, organized into seven broad categories.[8] For each quintile, we first measured each factor's mean levels and correlations with marital happiness and stability and then measured its contribution to the gap in marriage outcomes between quintiles.

Findings showed differences by SES in mean levels of most characteristics. Differences between quintiles were especially large (at least .4 standard deviations) for: growing up in an intact family, health status, depressive symptoms, values supporting marriage, values supporting gender equality, the share of housework performed by husbands, participation in nonreligious organizations, and neighborhood socioeconomic status.

When mean levels differed between quintiles for factors associated with marriage outcomes, our analyses suggested that these factors helped to explain the net difference in average marital quality and stability between quintiles. In particular, regression decomposition analyses suggested that poorer physical health, substance abuse, and depression, along with lower levels of support for gender equality by husbands and less connectedness with social organizations among low-SES couples help to account for their lower levels of marital satisfaction and stability, compared with high-SES couples. Operating in the opposite direction (to favor the relationships of low-status couples) are: stronger promarriage values, a higher proportion of foreign-born, and lower work hours for wives and a higher prevalence of stepchildren of either parent (both positively associated with low-status wives' marital happiness).[9]

These exploratory comparisons do not establish the causes of economic differences in marriage outcomes, since they are based on cross-sectional comparisons and causal relationships could work in both directions. The results nonetheless suggest that future studies should assess more carefully the role of a variety of external circumstances and that, meanwhile, it may be worthwhile to address these factors in marriage programs for low-income couples. As described in the next section, the SHM model puts substantial emphasis on skills and services that may help couples cope with these types of external marriage stressors.

THE SHM PROGRAM MODEL

The goals of SHM programs are to help interested married couples learn how to maintain and improve their marital relationships and to have healthy long-lasting marriages, ultimately with the aim of improving the well-being of their children. To accomplish this, every SHM program includes three components: a core marriage education curriculum; extended marriage education activities that continue after the core sessions; and individual support for couples to help them participate in the program, to provide "coaching" or reinforcement of skills learned in the curriculum, and to link them with additional services in the community if needed.

To guide program development, the SHM team provided program guidelines that communicated essential principles and requirements for each component, but also gave curriculum developers and program operators substantial local flexibility in designing their programs. Two aspects of these program guidelines, and the program model itself, set the SHM program apart from many previous marriage education models. First, given the voluntary nature of the program, the guidelines particularly emphasized strategies to maximize participation by creating engaging services and removing as many barriers to participation as possible. Second, the program model is relatively intensive and comprehensive, with particular emphasis on strengthening programs' capacity to address the major external sources of marital distress for low-income couples that might limit couples' ability to attend and to apply the skills they have learned. As a starting point for understanding how we sought to accomplish these goals, it is helpful to have an idea of the kinds of organizations and supports involved in operating SHM programs.

Program Structure and Supports

When the SHM project began, few organizations were already providing marriage education services to low-income married couples at any scale. Thus, in the site-selection process we were looking for organizations that were interested in adding this brand new program to their existing menu of services. Some of them had experience working with low-income families but not in providing marriage education, while others had expertise providing marriage education to more general or middle-class populations. Other than capacity and interest, there were no restrictions on the kinds of organizations who could be SHM sites—sites could be new or existing organizations, public or private agencies, and run centrally in one area or by several agencies in multiple locations. The key requirements were the ability to develop and operate a program meeting SHM program guidelines, to recruit and sustain participation of a target number of eligible couples, and to support random assignment and data collection requirements associated with the experimental evaluation.

As mentioned, because recruitment and retention of low-income couples posed special challenges—most notably that of engaging both spouses in the program over a period of months—SHM guidelines put special emphasis on things sites should do to promote participation. Recommended programmatic measures included: locating the program in a pleasant environment; designing activities that are fun and motivating; making certain that the environment is welcoming to men; hiring warm, engaging staff; and making sure that couples leave each session with new skills that are immediately useful. The guidelines stressed the need for marketing materials to address likely attitudinal barriers arising from general unfamiliarity with a new kind of service, particularly the potential for confusion with marital therapy and perception that participation represented an admission of marriage problems. Programs also were to provide material supports to support attendance, such as child care, transportation, and participation incentives.

The Core Marriage Education Curriculum

The core of each SHM program is twenty-four to thirty hours of marriage education workshops provided in a group setting over several (typically two to four) months. While sites were allowed to choose from among different curricula, each curriculum was expected to cover six broad content areas, identified primarily because of evidence from prior research that they were potentially important influences on the quality of relationships for low-income couples. Program guidelines leave curriculum developers and sites substantial discretion in emphasis, organization, and pedagogic approaches to these topics. The first three areas represent traditional concerns of marriage education:

- *Understanding marriage.* This topic area addresses the assumptions, values, and levels of "relationship-mindedness" couples bring to their marriages. Material might explore expectations for responsibilities and roles, financial aspirations, time together, handling of anger and conflict, emotional intimacy, sexual exclusivity, or childrearing. This area also covers the benefits of healthy, lasting relationships for children and adults, and the role of commitment, sacrifice, and effort in healthy relationships.

- *Managing conflict.* Communication is a central skill in strong marital relationships. Good communication has a technical aspect (learning to express oneself clearly and to listen to one's spouse), as well as an emotional aspect (showing empathy and respect for other points of view). Material under this heading includes skills for identifying and controlling negative interaction styles, for clear and empathetic communication, and for structured approaches to problem solving.

- *Promoting positive connections between spouses.* The basis of a long-term healthy relationship often lies in developing deeper bonds of friendship and love. Under this topic area falls material on understanding and showing appreciation for each other's perspectives and dreams, spending enjoyable time together, creating shared goals, strengthening emotional connections, enhancing physical intimacy, and building mutual trust and commitment.

At the time SHM began, all three of these topic areas were covered in a variety of existing marriage education curricula. For SHM, curriculum developers were encouraged to tailor these topics for low-income couples by tying illustrations, anecdotes, and exercises explicitly to personal and environmental influences that might place greater stress on low-income couples' relationships, to help make instruction more vivid, relevant, and effective. For example, a discussion of how participants' own parents shared household responsibilities could be used to stimulate dialogue about expectations and desired changes in the division of labor in their current relationships. Or an exercise focused on helping couples plan for a night out together would ideally tackle financial, childcare, and other obstacles.

Unlike the first three curriculum content areas, the remaining three topics have not been widely included in marriage education curricula for middle-class couples. Reflecting the conceptual model described earlier, these content areas are designed to provide insights and skills pertinent to several broad external challenges:

• *Strengthening relationships beyond the couple.* Strong relationships with other family members and support networks are good for marriage and for personal well-being. Low-income couples are more likely to have had children from previous relationships and to have weaker connections to community organizations than their higher income counterparts. Relationships at work also may be more difficult, given the hierarchical and contingent nature of much low-wage employment. SHM curriculum guidelines encourage programs to explore how relationship skills might generalize to these relationships and structure group sessions and related activities to promote such strengthening. For example, curricula might encourage couples to identify current and potential sources of support or opportunities for social involvement, and identify steps to strengthen these connections.

• *Enhancing couples' ability to manage challenging external circumstances.* When couples experience stressful living conditions it is more difficult to find the time and emotional energy to sustain positive relationships. Challenges range from strains created by one spouse's mental health issues or substance abuse, to problems shared by both partners, such as financial stress or lack of safe, affordable housing. The guidelines emphasize the importance of this topic for helping couples become more sensitive to, and learn to respond to, the effects of stress on each other's behaviors (as a complement to the programs' supplemental services, which provide referrals to directly address some of these stressful conditions). Curricula may address coping skills, including providing emotional and instrumental support and solving problems together.

• *Strengthening parenting.* In addition to direct positive effects of exposure to healthy relationships between parents on child well-being, the SHM conceptual framework also reflects the possibility that the intervention could affect children through improved parenting skills. As a couples program, SHM is in a position to focus on skills that couples can use in parenting as a team, referred to by some as coparenting; for example, by sharing responsibilities and supporting each other in parenting decisions. Some curricula might also emphasize parenting issues specific to fathers and to children of varying ages.

In addition to adapting the *content* of marriage education, the SHM model embodies several key principles for making *instructional formats* more appropriate for economically disadvantaged couples. One key principle is to keep lecturing at a minimum in favor of interactive activities that are interesting and help participants build and practice their skills. For example, some programs structure their sessions to begin with a short presentation, followed by demonstration of a new skill by the facilitator, followed by an interactive exercise for each couple to practice. Other programs regularly use group discussions to generate new insights for the couples. The model assumes that the most effective curricula will maximize learning by using a mix of approaches, including in-person demonstrations and role modeling, videos, direct practice of new skills, coaching during this practice, and group discussion. The model also stresses the importance of using simple, culturally sensitive language; avoiding too much reading and writing; and repeating key themes throughout.

At the time the study began, there were few existing curricula that spanned all of these topics, were well documented in manuals, and used the range of recommended instructional formats. The team nonetheless felt that it was important to select and adapt well-established curricula, rather than create "model curricula" from scratch, since the former would be more readily disseminated if they were effective. Neither did we want to dictate that sites use a particular curriculum. The research team therefore reviewed numerous existing curricula to identify those that most comprehensively addressed the six topics of interest, with particular emphasis on curricula that had some evidence of effectiveness in prior research and a track record of being used with a variety of populations in different programmatic contexts. Based on this review, the SHM team worked with the developers of the PREP and Practical Application of Intimate Relationship Skills (PAIRS) curricula to produce adaptations that would meet the SHM curriculum guidelines and be available for SHM sites if they wished to use them. Sites were also invited to propose other curricula that would meet the SHM curriculum guidelines. Ultimately, sites proposed using two additional curricula—the Becoming Parents Program and Loving Couples, Loving Children, so that the eight SHM pilot sites are using four different curricula. The SHM team worked with the developers of these four curricula to guide what were in some cases extensive adaptations to meet the content and format guidelines described above.

Extended Marriage Education Activities

In the second SHM component, programs seek to engage participants in additional activities for a full year (about nine months beyond the core program). Providers are to design this component to be engaging, to provide varied activities that reinforce and integrate the skills and concepts learned in marriage education sessions, and to provide new information identified as a need by couples or facilitators. In addition to increasing program comprehensiveness, this component helps raise the probability that educational services will be available to couples as specific issues arise in their relationships.

SHM guidelines provide a series of examples of extended activities, but leave providers substantially free to design this component. Through one or more *booster sessions,* programs might provide opportunities to explore new issues or revisit material covered in the core curriculum. Or programs might provide opportunities for *one-on-one coaching or mentoring* from program staff or peers, perhaps during visits to couples' homes. *Group social events or community service activities* can be used to maintain and deepen bonds between participants and help them get to know local community agencies. Help organizing *date nights* reinforces the idea that it is good for couples to spend time on their relationships together and expands their repertoire of mutually enjoyable activities. Finally, *activities for the whole family* can help parents develop ideas and habits for spending quality time with their children—and possibly other relatives—or provide additional educational modules focusing on specialized aspects of family life.

Supplemental Services

Although the central emphasis in SHM is teaching relationship skills—including skills helping couples to weather external stresses successfully—the model recognizes that low-income couples often will have urgent needs for direct assistance. In addition to negatively affecting couples' relationships with each other and their children, these problems may also prevent them from attending marriage education sessions and distract them from practicing at home the skills they are learning. To respond to these needs, the SHM model thus also includes a supplemental services component.

Guidelines specify that programs should help couples gain access to a wide range of services and supports. Typically, access requires capacity to link couples to services in the community, such as physical or mental health services, substance abuse treatment, housing assistance, employment and training services, or childcare. Programs are encouraged to designate specialized staff members to function as family support coordinators. These staff typically play three roles, providing the types of outside referrals described here, providing and tracking participation supports such as child care or transportation vouchers, and providing one-on-one coaching with couples, to help reinforce the lessons learned during the marriage education workshops.

This chapter has described the research foundations and conceptualization of the SHM program model. Each site has used this model to develop a program that is consistent with its organizational culture and local needs. In addition, throughout the early program operations, the SHM team provided training and technical assistance to assist the sites in meeting these programmatic guidelines and developing their programs effectively. Future SHM implementation reports will describe how each component of the program was developed and operated in each site.

THE SHM STUDY DESIGN

The study is designed to achieve several goals. First, it will use a random assignment research design to test the effectiveness of the program model that we have described and to learn for which low-income families it works best and least well. Second, the study will describe how the programs operated in each site, both to shed light on patterns in program impacts and to provide lessons for future program operators. Third, because of the experimental research design, the project can provide unique scientific information about the causal links between family risk factors and couple and child outcomes.

Implementation Study

SHM represents a new type of public program that the federal government has only recently begun to provide at any scale. This early stage of program design and development across the country means that the implementation research to be conducted will play a critical role in informing future efforts at providing marriage-related services. As the research team documents how the programs are operated in each site, we will be explaining how a variety of community-based organizations begin to weave this new set of services into their program menus.

The main objective of the implementation research is to document how each site operated the program "on the ground." Knowing how the program was experienced by participants, as opposed to how it was designed on paper, provides critical context for interpreting the impacts achieved. It also provides practical information that future program operators will need to replicate the program, should it prove effective. How did each site define the mission of its program and how did their program operations reflect that perspective? What challenges did these early programs face and how did they resolve them? What methods did they use to recruit large numbers of couples into this voluntary program and keep them engaged in services over time? How did couples respond to this offer and to their experiences in the program? Did sites deliver the marriage education curricula as written, or did they make changes to these and other aspects of their programs in response to the needs of their local populations? Did programs develop innovative strategies for encouraging participation among fathers, parents with irregular work schedules, and other individuals who are typically more difficult to engage in group activities? Did these marriage education programs have any effect on services offered by the rest of the organization, or did they operate in isolation from the broader organization? Findings from the process study will begin to provide some basic information to this nascent field on challenges in, and promising practices for, providing marriage education to low-income couples. In so doing, we hope to explore broader lessons for providing voluntary services to disadvantaged families and for engaging fathers in social service settings that have historically focused primarily on serving mothers and children.

The results of the implementation research will be reported for each individual site, providing information needed to interpret variations in the impacts seen in different sites. The study is not designed to rigorously test how variations in site characteristics or program operating structures affect the impacts of the program. However, by documenting variations in program philosophies and operations, the implementation study does allow us to examine whether the patterns of impacts are consistent with particular hypotheses about how programs produce impacts on couples and families. Do the sites with the highest rates of participation and duration in the program consistently produce the greatest impacts on couple relationships? How are organizational and staff issues at the various sites related to the outcomes observed? Are there other variations in program operations that seem consistently to be associated with program impacts?

The implementation study will draw on both quantitative and qualitative data to document program operations. Data will include automated program tracking data to measure recruitment, participation patterns in marriage education groups, and individual or couple contacts with staff for the program group; twelve-month survey data to measure participation in a range of community services for both program and control groups; observations of marriage education classes in each site; observations of other staff-participant meetings and interactions; debriefings with curriculum developers, technical assistance providers, and managers in each site to understand the specific programmatic challenges faced by each site and any innovative solutions to those challenges; reviews of program documents; and interviews with program staff and participants.

Impact Study

As discussed earlier, the primary goal of SHM is to learn whether marriage education improves low-income married couples' relationships, helps them stay married, and benefits their children. In that light, the project will concentrate on two broad questions about the program's effects: Does the SHM intervention improve outcomes for low-income couples and their children? What family outcomes are affected?

The answer to these questions will flow from SHM's basic evaluation method: random assignment. The goal is for each participating program to randomly assign up to eight hundred couples to either a program group or a control group. Random assignment assures that systematic differences that later appear between the program and control groups can reliably be attributed to the marriage education services being studied rather than to preexisting differences. If sample sizes permit, the impact analysis will estimate the effects for each site as well as the pooled impacts across sites, since they are all operating within a common program framework.

The impact study will reflect as comprehensively as possible the multiple domains of family functioning that could be affected by the SHM program model, as hypothesized in the conceptual model in figure 10.1. These include couple relationship functioning or marital quality; marital duration and stability; the mental health and employment status of each individual spouse; family income; coparenting and parenting behavior; and child well-being. These potential program impacts will be measured at twelve and thirty months after random assignment—and possibly at sixty months if earlier findings reveal impacts.

The twelve-month survey will estimate outcomes considered most proximate to the intervention, particularly couple relationship quality and stability. As discussed earlier, measures of relationship quality will include those with negative as well as positive valence. As part of the twelve-month data collection effort, the research team also plans to collect videotaped direct observations of couple, coparenting, and parent-child interactions for a subset of the sample in each site. This aspect of the study draws on the techniques used in basic research on marriage to understand the patterns of interaction that predict couples' relationship satisfaction and stability. Much of this previous research has been conducted in university laboratories. Analogous to the growing use of in-home observations of parent-child relationships in large scale surveys and experiments, to our knowledge SHM is the first study to videotape structured interactions of couples in their homes as part of a large-scale multisite experiment.

Whereas self-reports provide an important portrait of couples' appraisals of their relationships, videotaped observations of couple interactions allow for direct assessment of specific patterns of communication and interaction. Independent observations are also capable of capturing aspects of couple and family interactions that are not readily captured by self-reports, in part because couples may not be aware of their nuanced interaction patterns. As with self-reports, we will record interactions that include both topics of disagreement as well as topics that elicit emotional support, reflecting current research on the importance of both positive and negative aspects of marital quality. In addition, the observational study will include parent-child interactions, providing an opportunity to measure effects of the intervention on coparenting and parenting, which have been found in some previous work to be an important mediator between marriage interventions and improvements in child well-being. Thus, the evaluation will provide a full picture of program effects covering outcomes in multiple domains measured using multiple methods and perspectives.

The thirty-month survey will provide longer-term follow-up of the same family outcomes, particularly marital outcomes, as measured on the twelve-month survey. In addition, it will include direct assessments of children's cognitive and behavioral development. Because improvements in parental relationships could theoretically produce different effects on children of different ages, if sample sizes allow, child well-being will be assessed for children whose ages at random assignment range from infancy to early adolescence.

Although the primary research question in SHM is to understand whether marriage education programs have any effect on marital relationships, the data collected will also provide some basis for understanding *how* the SHM program has any effects that are observed. As illustrated in the project's conceptual framework, impacts might occur through a number of pathways; by assessing impacts at different points in the model, we hope to shed light on how these interventions affect couples and families. Do we see impacts on individual spouses' attitudes, insights, or expectations about their marriage; in couples' communication and problem-solving skills; or in aspects of the relationships that are not as explicitly targeted by the curricula, such as couples' levels of commitment to their marriages? Do programs help couples to reduce negative interactions, to increase positive ones, or both? Have the programs reduced levels of exposure to chronic and acute stressors, as might occur directly, through supplemental services, or indirectly, through improved coping skills? When programs improve couples' ability to cope with external sources of stress, do we also see heightened improvements in marital satisfaction and stability? Answering some of these questions about the *kinds* of impacts achieved will help us understand how these programs might operate most effectively in the future.

A second critical set of mediators to explore concern how any impacts on marital relationships are ultimately associated with any impacts on child well-being. As shown in the conceptual model, we hypothesize that marriage education could affect children through improvements in their parents' mental health, marital quality, marital stability, coparenting behavior, or parenting behavior. Improvements in some or all of these areas by parents could lead children to have access to more positive relationship role models, to witness harmful conflict less frequently, to have better relationships with one or both of their parents, or to have access to greater family income. Each of these areas of parental behavior has been associated with improved child well-being, primarily in well-designed nonexperimental studies. SHM gives us the opportunity to observe whether an intervention that improves one or more of these outcomes for parents in turn produces improvements in child well-being.

We will also examine which types of families benefit the most or least from marriage education. It is possible that impacts of marriage education programs could vary depending on couples' characteristics at the time they entered the study. A survey administered at the time that couples enter the study will provide information on a range of individual and family characteristics that have been found to be associated with marital outcomes, and could, in turn, affect couples' responses to a marriage education intervention. These include, for example, the length of time couples have been married; couples' initial levels of marital satisfaction or distress; each spouse's level of commitment to the marriage; the mental health of each spouse; the number and characteristics of children; family income or education levels; family ethnic or racial characteristics; and the existence of significant external stressors such as unemployment or a family member with chronic health problems. The impact analysis can rigorously assess whether program impacts vary depending upon these family or individual characteristics by directly comparing the impacts achieved for different subgroups of families. Policymakers and practitioners could use this type of information to target future SHM-type services to couples and families for whom these services were most effective, while developing new strategies for serving subgroups of couples or families for whom these services were less effective.

CONCLUSION

The Supporting Healthy Marriage demonstration and evaluation will provide answers to important questions raised by the unfolding U.S. Healthy Marriage Initiative and, in the process, also address an array of broader policy concerns about low-income families and the implications of family instability for children. Findings should be of great interest for policy makers, researchers, and practitioners interested in the well-being of low-income families. No one study can answer every question. The SHM project is designed to test the effects of one approach to marriage education for one broad target population. Thus, findings will not address the effects of other possible approaches, of the "average" healthy marriage program, or of providing such services to other populations.

Nevertheless, because the SHM model is relatively comprehensive, science-based, and intensive compared with other marriage-strengthening programs, the results will provide an important benchmark for assessing the potential of such services to strengthen relationships among low-income couples. As described here, the SHM conceptual framework recognizes multiple sources of relationship strength and weakness, and the project's program model has followed this framework closely in adapting the content and delivery of marriage education services for low-income married parents. The study plan includes state-of-the art measurement of impacts through survey interviews and a large observational study of couple interaction. By such means, the project will gather detailed measures over a relatively long follow-up period. With its grounding in prior research and focus on conceptual antecedents and consequences of healthy marriage, the project will contribute to our understanding of whether these programs produced stronger marriages, of the pathways through which such strengthening may have occurred, and of the linkages between stronger marriages and the well-being of children and adults.

NOTES

We are indebted to Meghan McCormick for her research assistance, and to Elizabeth Peters, Claire Kamp Dush, Paul Amato, Carolyn Pape Cowan, Philip Cowan, Alan Hawkins, Benjamin Karney, David Ribar, Matthew Stagner, Scott Stanley, Nancye Campbell, Susan Jekielek, Barbara Goldman, and Charles Michalopoulos for comments on earlier drafts. By summarizing the design and conceptualization of the SHM demonstration and evaluation, this chapter reflects the contributions of a large team of collaborators at MDRC, Abt Associates, Child Trends, Optimal Solutions group, and a number of universities, as well as by our colleagues at the Office of Planning, Research, and Evaluation of the Administration of Children and Families, U.S. Department of Health and Human Services, which conceived and funded the project. The views expressed by the authors do not necessarily reflect the official policies of the Administration for Children and Families, nor does mention of trade names, commercial practices, or organizations imply endorsement by the U.S. government.

1. See chapter 12 in this volume for more detail on how marital experiences may differ in high-SES and low-SES families.
2. See chapter 4 in this volume for more information about state and federal healthy marriage efforts.
3. For a review of marriage education programs, see Dion 2005.
4. ACF has also commissioned two related large-scale evaluations. The Building Strong Families project (BSF) is a random assignment study of healthy marriage programs for unmarried adults who are expecting a child together (also known as "fragile families"). An additional study, the Community Healthy Marriage Initiative (CHMI), is assessing the effects of communitywide efforts to engage low-income couples in marriage education. More information on these studies and the Healthy Marriage Initiative can be found at www.acf.hhs.gov/healthymarriage.
5. The study is a collaboration among researchers at MDRC, Abt Associates, Child Trends, and Optimal Solutions Group. Academic scholars have also been integral members of the research team, with particularly extensive involvement over time by Carolyn Pape Cowan, Philip Cowan, and Thomas Bradbury.
6. An illustration is Halford, Kelly, and Markman's definition of healthy marriage, which emphasizes external referents and also contains a dose of cultural relativism: "A developing set of interactions between partners which promotes the individual well-being of each partner and their offspring, assists each partner to adapt to life stresses, engenders a conjoint sense of emotional and sexual intimacy between the partners, and which promotes the long-term sustainment of the relationship within the cultural context in which the partners live" (1997:8).
7. African Americans represent a small fraction of low-income married couples owing to relatively low rates of marriage and high rates of marital breakup (Fein 2004). Compared with other racial and ethnic groups, it thus is likely that low-income African Americans who are married represent a relatively select group of the overall population of low-income African Americans.
8. The seven categories were: personal strengths and vulnerabilities (growing up in an intact family, overall self-assessed health status, substance abuse, depression, stress); values and culture (importance of marriage, support for gender equality, race-ethnicity, whether foreign-born); marital history (previous marriages, premarital cohabitation, duration of marriage); family composition (number and ages of children, residential and nonresidential stepchildren, unintended births); home and market work (work hours, housework hours, husband's share of housework); social support and involvement (support in emergencies, social activity, involvement in religious and nonreligious organizations); and neighborhood characteristics (ratio of employed men to women, racial composition, socioeconomic index).
9. The analyses focused on factors associated with differences in the cross-section—that is, during a particular period (the early 1990s)—and the factors identified do not necessarily explain changes in the gap in marriage outcomes over time.

REFERENCES

Acs, G. 2007. Can we promote child well-being by promoting marriage? *Journal of Marriage and Family* 69, no. 5: 1326–1344.

Amato, P.R. 2000. Consequences of divorce for adults and children. *Journal of Marriage and the Family* 62:1269–1287.

———. 2005. The impact of family formation change on the cognitive, social, and emotional well-being of the next generation. *The Future of Children* 15, no. 2: 75–96.

Amato, P.R., D.R. Johnson, A. Booth, and S.J. Rogers. 2003. Continuity and change in marital quality between 1980 and 2000. *Journal of Marriage and Family* 65, no. 1: 1–22.

Aron, A., C.C. Norman, C. McKenna, and R.E. Heyman. 2000. Couples' shared participation in novel and arousing activities and experienced relationship quality. *Journal of Personality and Social Psychology* 78:273–284.

Behrman, R.E., and L.S. Quinn. 1994. Children and divorce: Overview and analysis. *The Future of Children* 4, no. 1: 4–14.

Belsky, J. 1984. The determinants of parenting: A process model. *Child Development* 55, no. 1: 83–96.

Bradbury, T.N., M.D. Johnson, E.E. Lawrence, and R.D. Rogge. 1998. Using basic research to craft effective interventions for marital dysfunction. In D.K. Routh and R.J. DeRubeis, eds., *The science of clinical psychology: Accomplishments and future directions*, 265–278. Washington, D.C.: American Psychological Association.

Bumpass, L., and T. Lu. 2000. Trends in cohabitation and implications for children's family contexts in the United States. *Population Studies* 54, no. 1: 29–41.

Burstein, N.R. 2007. Economic influences on marriage and divorce. *Journal of Policy Analysis and Management* 26:387–430.

Butler, M.H., and K.S. Wampler. 1999. A meta-analytic update of research on the Couple Communication Program. *American Journal of Family Therapy* 27:223–227.

Carroll, J.S., and W.J. Doherty. 2003. Evaluating the effectiveness of premarital prevention programs: A meta-analytic review of outcome research. *Family Relations* 52:105–118.

Cherlin, A.J. 2005. American marriage in the early twenty-first century. *The Future of Children* 15, no. 2: 33–55.

Christensen, A. 1999. Interventions for couples. *Annual Review of Psychology* 50:165–190.

Conger, R., L. Ebert-Wallace, Y. Sun, R. Simons, V. McLoyd, and G. Brody. 2002. Economic pressure in African American families: A replication and extension of the Family Stress Model. *Developmental Psychology* 38, no. 2: 179–193.

Conger, R.D., M.A. Reuter, and G.H. Elder Jr. 1999. Couple resilience to economic pressure. *Journal of Personality and Social Psychology* 76:54–71.

Cordova, J. V., C. G. Gee, and L. Z. Warren. 2005. Emotional skillfulness in marriage: Intimacy as a mediator of the relationship between emotional skillfulness and marital satisfaction. *Journal of Social and Clinical Psychology* 24:218–235.

Cowan, C. P., and P. A. Cowan. 1992. *When partners become parents: The big life change for couples*. New York: HarperCollins.

Cowan, C. P., P. A. Cowan, G. Heming, E. Garrett, W. S. Coysh, H. Curtis-Boles, et al. 1985. Transitions to parenthood: His, hers, and theirs. *Journal of Family Issues* 6:451–481.

Cowan, C. P., P. A. Cowan, M. K. Pruett, and K. Pruett. 2006. *The supporting father involvement study: The first public report*. Sacramento: California Department of Social Services.

Cowan, P. A., and C. P. Cowan. 2002. Interventions as tests of family systems theories: Marital and family relationships in children's development and psychopathology. *Development and Psychopathology* 14:731–759.

———. 2006a. Developmental psychopathology from a family systems and family risk factors perspective: Implications for family research, practice, and policy. In D. Cicchetti and D. J. Cohen, eds., *Developmental psychopathology*, 2nd ed., 1:530–587. New York: Wiley.

———. 2006b. The case for preventive intervention to strengthen couple relationships: Good for couples, good for children. Presentation at the Evolving Families Conference, Cornell University.

Cowan, P. A., and J. P. McHale. 1996. Coparenting in a family context: Emerging achievements, current dilemmas, and future directions. In J. P. McHale and P. A. Cowan, eds., *Understanding how family level dynamics affect children's development: Studies of two-parent families*, 74–91. San Francisco: Jossey-Bass.

Cummings, E. M., and P. Davies. 1994. *Children and marital conflict*. New York: Guilford.

Cummings, E. M., P. T. Davies, and S. B. Campbell. 2000. *Developmental psychopathology and family process*. New York: Guilford.

Cutrona, C. E., D. W. Russell, W. T. Abraham, K. A. Gardner, J. N. Melby, C. Bryant, and R. D. Conger. 2003. Neighborhood context and financial strain as predictors of marital interaction and marital quality in African American couples. *Personal Relationships* 10:389–409.

Dion, R. 2005. Healthy marriage programs: Learning what works. *Future of Children* 15, no. 2: 139–156.

Ellwood, D. T., and C. Jencks. 2004. The uneven spread of single-parent families: What do we know? Where do we look for answers? In K. Neckerman, ed., *Social inequality*, 3–77. New York: Russell Sage.

Emery, R. 1982. Interparental conflict and the children of discord and divorce. *Psychological Bulletin* 92:310–330.

Fein, D. J. 2004. Married and poor: Basic characteristics of economically disadvantaged married couples in the US. Retrieved February 21, 2008, from http://supportinghealthymarriage.org/publications/6/workpaper.html.

Fein, D. J., D. B. Gubits, L. A. Gennetian, and E. Yumoto. 2007. For poorer as for richer? Understanding differences in marital quality and stability. Paper presented at the 2007 Annual Meeting of the Population Association of America, New York.

Fincham, F. D. 2001. Attributions and close relationships: From balkanization to integration. In G. J. Fletcher and M. Clark, eds., *Blackwell handbook of social psychology*, 3–31. Oxford: Blackwell.

Fincham, F. D., J. Hall, and S. R. H. Beach. 2006. Forgiveness in marriage: Current status and future directions. *Family Relations* 55:415–427.

Giblin, P., D. Sprenkle, and R. Sheehan. 1985. Enrichment outcome research: A meta-analysis of premarital, marital and family interventions. *Journal of Marital and Family Therapy* 11:257–271.

Gottman, J. 1994. *What predicts divorce? The relationship between marital processes and marital outcomes*. Hillsdale, N.J.: Erlbaum.

Gottman, J., S. Carrére, C. Swanson, and J. A. Coan. 2000. Reply to "From basic research to interventions." *Journal of Marriage and the Family* 62:265–273.

Gottman, J. M., J. Coan, S. Carrere, and C. Swanson. 1998. Predicting marital happiness and stability from newlywed interactions. *Journal of Marriage and the Family* 60:5–22.

Gottman, J. M., and L. F. Katz. 1989. Effects of marital discord on young children's peer interaction and health. *Developmental Psychology* 25, no. 3: 373–381.

Gottman, J. M., and C. I. Notarius. 2000. Decade review: Observing marital interaction. *Journal of Marriage and the Family* 62:927–947.

Guerney, B. G., Jr. 1997. *Relationship enhancement*. San Francisco: Jossey-Bass.

Hahlweg, K., H. J. Markman, F. Thurmaier, J. Engl, and V. Eckert. 1998. Prevention of marital distress: Results of a German prospective longitudinal study. *Journal of Family Psychology* 12:543–556.

Halford, W. K. 2001. *Brief couple therapy*. New York: Guilford.

Halford, W. K., A. Kelly, and H. J. Markman. 1997. The concept of a healthy marriage. In W. K. Halford and H. J. Markman, eds., *Clinical handbook of marriage and couples interventions*, 118–135. Hoboken, N.J.: Wiley.

Halford, W. K., H. J. Markman, S. M. Stanley, and G. H. Kline. 2003. Best practices in couple relationship education. *Journal of Marriage and Family Therapy* 29:385–406.

Halford, K. W., M. R. Sanders, and B. C. Behrens. 2001. Can skills training prevent relationship problems in at-risk couples? Four-year effects of a behavioral relationship education program. *Journal of Family Psychology* 15:750–768.

Hawkins, A. J., V. L. Blanchard, and E. B. Fawcett. 2007. Is marriage and relationship education effective? A comprehensive meta-analysis. Poster presented at the Society for Prevention Research Annual Conference, Washington, D.C.

Heinicke, C. M. 2002. *The transition to parenting.* Mahwah, N.J.: Erlbaum.

Hetherington, E. M., W. G. Clingempeel, E. R. Anderson, J. E. Deal, S. M. Hagan, E. A. Hollier, and M. S. Linder. 1992. Coping with marital transitions: A family systems perspective. *Monographs of the Society for Research in Child Development* 57:2–3.

Hill, M. S. 1988. Marital stability and spouses' shared time: A multidisciplinary hypothesis. *Journal of Family Issues* 9:427–451.

Hops, H. 1992. Parental depression and child behaviour problems: Implications for behavioural family intervention. *Behaviour Change* 9:126–138.

Howes, P., and H. J. Markman. 1989. Marital quality and child attachment: A longitudinal study. *Child Development* 60:1044–1051.

Johnson, M. D., C. L. Cohan, J. Davila, E. Lawrence, R. D. Rogge, B. R. Karney, et al. 2005. Problem-solving skills and affective expressions as predictors of change in marital satisfaction. *Journal of Consulting and Clinical Psychology* 73, no. 1: 15–27.

Karney, B. R., and T. N. Bradbury. 1995. Assessing longitudinal change in marriage: An introduction to the analysis of growth curves. *Journal of Marriage and the Family* 57:1091–1108.

———. 1997. Neuroticism, marital interaction, and the trajectory of marital satisfaction. *Journal of Personality and Social Psychology* 72:1075–1092.

———. 2000. Attributions in marriage: State or trait? A growth curve analysis. *Journal of Personality and Social Psychology* 78:295–309.

———. 2005. Contextual influences on marriage: Implications for policy and intervention. *Current Directions in Psychological Science* 14:171–174.

Markman, H. J., and F. Floyd. 1980. Possibilities for the prevention of marital discord: A behavioral perspective. *American Journal of Family Therapy* 8, no. 2: 29–48.

Markman, H. J., and K. Hahlweg. 1993. The prediction and prevention of marital distress: An international perspective. *Clinical Psychology Review* 13:29–43.

Martin, S. P. 2002. *Delayed marriage and childbearing: Implications and measurement of diverging trends in family timing.* College Park: Maryland Population Research Center.

———. 2006. Trends in marital dissolution by women's education in the United States. *Demographic Research* 15:537–560.

McBride, B. A., and T. R. Rane. 2001. Father/male involvement in prekindergarten at-risk programs: An exploratory study. *Early Childhood Research Quarterly* 16:77–93.

McLanahan, S., and G. D. Sandefur. 1994. *Growing up with a single parent: What hurts? What helps?* Cambridge, Mass.: Harvard University Press.

Moore, K. A., S. M. Jekielek, J. Bronte-Tinkew, L. Guzman, S. Ryan, and Z. Redd. 2004. What is "healthy marriage?" Defining the concept. *Child Trends Research Brief* 2004–16: 1–11.

Morrison, D. R., and M. J. Coiro. 1999. Parental conflict and marital disruption: Do children benefit when high-conflict marriages are dissolved? *Journal of Marriage and the Family* 61:626–637.

Neff, L. A., and B. R. Karney. 2004. How does context affect intimate relationships? Linking external stress and cognitive processes within marriage. *Personality and Social Psychology Bulletin* 30:134–148.

Noller, P., and J. A. Feeney. 1998. Communication in early marriage: Responses to conflict, nonverbal accuracy, and conversational attributes. In T. Bradbury, ed., *The developmental course of marital dysfunction*, 11–44. Cambridge: Cambridge University Press.

Parke, R. D., and R. Buriel. 1998. Socialization in the family: Ethnic and ecological perspectives. In N. Eisenberg, ed., *Social, emotional, and personality development*, 5th ed., 3:463–552. New York: Wiley.

Presser, H. B. 2000. Nonstandard work schedules and marital instability. *Journal of Marriage and the Family* 62:93–110.

Raley, R. K., and L. L. Bumpass. 2003. The topography of the plateau in divorce: Levels and trends in union stability after 1980. *Demographic Research* 8:246–258.

Reardon-Anderson, J., M. Stagner, J. E. Macomber, and J. Murray. 2005. *Systematic review of the impact of marriage and relationship programs*. Washington, D.C.: Urban Institute.

Ribar, D.C. 2004. What do social scientists know about the benefits of marriage? A review of quantitative methodologies. Discussion Paper No. 998. Bonn, Germany: Institute for the Study of Labor. Retrieved February 19, 2008, from http://ftp.iza.org/dp998.pdf.

Shapiro, A. F., and J. M. Gottman. 2005. Effects on marriage of a psycho-communicative-educational intervention with couples undergoing the transition to parenthood. Evaluation at 1-year post intervention. *Journal of Family Communication* 5:1–24.

Sigle-Rushton, W., and S. McLanahan. 2002. Father absence and child wellbeing: A critical review. Princeton University Center for Research on Child Wellbeing Working Paper #02–20.

Silliman, B., S. M. Stanley, W. Coffin, H. J. Markman, and P. L. Jordan. 2002. Preventative interventions for couples. In H. A. Liddle, D. A. Santisteban, R. F. Levant, and J. H. Bray, eds., *Family psychology science-based interventions*, 123–145. Washington, D.C.: American Psychological Association.

Snyder, D. K., R. E. Heyman, and S. N. Haynes. 2008. Couple distress. In J. Hunsley and E. Mash, eds., *A guide to assessments that work*, 91–104. New York: Oxford University Press.

Stanley, S. M. 2007. Assessing couple and marital relationships: Beyond form and toward a deeper knowledge of function. In S. Hofferth and L. Casper, eds., *Handbook of measurement issues in family research*, 85–99. Mahwah, N.J.: Erlbaum.

Stanley, S. M., T. N. Bradbury, and H. J. Markman. 2000. Structural flaws in the bridge from basic research on marriage to interventions for couples. *Journal of Marriage and the Family* 62:256–264.

Stanley, S. M., H. J. Markman, L. M. Prado, P. A. Olmos-Gallo, L. Tonelli, M. St. Peters, B. D. Leber, M. Bobulinski, A. Cordova, and S. Whitton. 2001. Community based premarital prevention: Clergy and lay leaders on the front lines. *Family Relations* 50:67–76.

Stanley, S. M., H. J. Markman, and S. Whitton. 2002. Communication, conflict, and commitment: Insights on the foundations of relationship success from a national survey. *Family Process* 41:659–675.

U.S. Department of Health and Human Services, Administration for Children and Families. 2007. Healthy Marriage Initiative: Mission statement. Retrieved March 3, 2008, from www.acf.gov/healthymarriage/about/mission.html.

U.S. House of Representatives, Committee on Ways and Means. 2004. *2004 Green Book: Background material and data on program within the jurisdiction of the Committee on Ways and Means.* Washington, D.C.: GPO.

Waite, L. J., and M. Gallagher. 2000. *The case for marriage: Why married people are happier, healthier, and better off financially.* New York: Doubleday.

Wampler, K. S. 1990. An update of research on the Couple Communication Program. *Family Science Review* 3:21–40.

Webster-Stratton, C., and T. Taylor. 2001. Nipping early risk factors in the bud: Preventing substance abuse, delinquency, and violence in adolescence through intervention targeted at young children (0–8). *Prevention Science* 2:165–191.

White, L. K. 1983. Determinants of spousal interaction: Marital structure or marital happiness. *Journal of Marriage and the Family* 45:511–519.

ELEVEN

Differentiating Among Types of Domestic Violence

Implications for Healthy Marriages

MICHAEL P. JOHNSON

Beginning with the first large-scale surveys of family violence in the 1970s, family scholars and the general public have been amazed at how much violence is found in marriages in the United States and elsewhere. The first National Family Violence Survey in 1975 found that 16 percent of U.S. married couples acknowledged that one or both partners had been violent within the previous twelve months (Straus and Gelles 1990, 97), and the authors of that survey estimated that as many as two-thirds "have experienced such an incident at least once in the marriage" (Straus, Gelles, and Steinmetz 1980, 48). More recent surveys find similar or larger rates of violence in the United States and elsewhere. In a Canadian survey of cohabiting and married respondents, men reported one-year prevalence rates of husband-to-wife violence of 12.9 percent, and women reported wife-to-husband violence of 12.5 percent (Kwong, Bartholomew, and Dutton 1999). In samples of teenagers and young adults (dating, cohabiting, married), rates of physical violence toward partners are considerably higher than in general survey populations. For example, in a 1994 survey of a representative sample of twenty-one-year-old New Zealanders, 37.2 percent of women and 21.8 percent of men reported physical violence in the relationship (Magdol et al. 1997).

Surely, any level of partner violence is a sign of an unhealthy intimate relationship, and such an assumption is supported by considerable research. For example, Rogge and Bradbury's (1999) study of fifty-six newlywed couples found that level of violence reported in the first six months of the marriage was a much better predictor of separation or divorce four years later than were a number of widely used marital-communication variables. In terms of effects on individuals, Stets and Straus (1990) report that partner violence produces not only the injuries incurred directly from the violence but also increased days in bed due to illness and high levels of psychosomatic symptoms, stress, and depression.

However, there appears to be another side to this story. Physical violence does not *necessarily* lead to low marital satisfaction or stability. For example, one study of sixty-six married women found that physical victimization accounted for only 20 percent of the variance in marital satisfaction and 14 percent of the variance in marital stability (Arias, Lyons, and Street 1997). Data from the National Violence Against Women survey indicate that 74 percent of the married women who had experienced violence had never left their husbands (Johnson and Leone 2000). In terms of the effects on individuals, 31 percent of these married women were *below* the median level of depression for all married women in the sample, and 80 percent had experienced no injuries (Johnson and Leone 2000). Even more dramatically, the 1985 National Family Violence Survey data indicated that only 3 percent of women victims and less than .5 percent of male victims needed to see a doctor for injuries related to their marital violence (Stets and Straus 1990). Thus, although we may be able to agree that intimate partner violence is inherently unhealthy, there is evidently considerable variability in its effects on individuals and relationships. Recent work on types of intimate partner violence provides important insights into the nature of that variability.

TYPES OF DOMESTIC VIOLENCE

The global concept of domestic violence actually refers to a number of quite distinct phenomena that have different causes, different developmental trajectories, and different effects—and that therefore have different implications for healthy marriages and healthy marriage initiatives. The particular typology that I have developed (Johnson 2008) is organized around issues of relationship power and control. *Intimate terrorism*, the first of the three major types of intimate partner violence, involves a violent attempt to take complete control of or at least generally dominate the relationship. The second type, *violent resistance*, involves the use of violence to resist such a control attempt. The third, *situational couple violence*, is violence that is a product of particular conflicts or tensions within the relationship.[1]

As I discuss in more detail later, intimate terrorism may be more problematic to deal with in the context of healthy marriage interventions because it is more likely to have a strong negative impact on the relationship, it is generally less responsive to such interventions, and because participation in marriage education as a couple may actually pose a danger to the victim of intimate terrorism.

In this chapter I will briefly elaborate on these differences and discuss their implications for healthy marriage programs. Before I get to that, I want to make the general point that failures to acknowledge these differences have produced a number of major errors in the empirical literature on intimate partner violence. Two examples will illustrate the basic processes by which such errors are produced.

First, when researchers inadvertently aggregate different types of violence under one label, they produce data that are an "average" of the characteristics or correlates of the types that are aggregated. For example, a recent meta-analysis of the literature on the relationship between growing up in a violent home and subsequently becoming part of a violent marital relationship indicates quite small effects (Stith et al. 2000), calling into question what is often claimed to be one of the best-established phenomena in the literature of intimate partner violence, the so-called intergenerational transmission of violence. However, those who have conducted research investigating the intergenerational-transmission claim do not distinguish among types of violence, instead examining the effects of childhood experiences on any adult perpetration of intimate partner violence. This would not be a problem if the effects of childhood experiences on different types of adult violence were the same, but a recent study differentiating among the types finds that although childhood experiences of family violence are not strongly related to adult situational couple violence, they are strongly related to male intimate terrorism (Johnson and Cares 2004). The "average" violent relationship in survey research, dominated by situational couple violence, does not represent the relationship that is usually of most interest, the effect of childhood experiences on the likelihood of a man becoming a wife-beater—an intimate terrorist.

Second, sometimes research that deals with one type of intimate partner violence is used to draw conclusions about quite a different type. For example, in the late 1970s Suzanne Steinmetz (1977–78) used data from general survey samples that were dominated by situational couple violence as evidence about the nature of intimate terrorism, leading her to the incorrect conclusion that that there were as many battered husbands as battered wives.

This is the error that produced the decades-long and continuing debate over the gender symmetry of domestic violence (Johnson 2005). We need to attend to differences among types of intimate partner violence if we want to advance our understanding of such violence and to intervene effectively.

A TYPOLOGY OF INTIMATE PARTNER VIOLENCE

Intimate Terrorism

In intimate terrorism, the perpetrator uses violence in the service of gaining and holding general control over his or her partner.[2] The control that is the defining feature of intimate terrorism is more than the specific, short-term control that is often the goal of violence in other contexts. The mugger wants to control you only briefly in order to take your valuables and move on, hoping never to see you again. In contrast, the control sought in intimate terrorism is general and long-term. Although each particular act of intimate violence may have any number of short-term, specific goals, the violence is embedded in a larger pattern of coercive control that permeates the relationship.

Figure 11.1 is a widely used graphical representation of intimate partner violence deployed in the service of general control. This diagram and the understanding of domestic violence that lies behind it were developed over a period of years from testimony of battered women. This testimony convinced the staff of the Duluth Domestic Abuse Intervention Project that the most important characteristic of the violence they encountered was that it was embedded in a general pattern of coercive control. The Power and Control Wheel identifies eight nonviolent control tactics that accompany the violence of intimate terrorism: intimidation; emotional abuse; isolation; minimizing, denying, and blaming; use of children; asserting male privilege; economic abuse; and coercion and threats (Pence and Paymar 1993). Abusers do not necessarily use all of these tactics, but they do use a combination of the ones that they feel are most likely to work for them.

This powerful combination of violence with a general pattern of control is terrorizing because once a controlling partner has been violent, all of his other controlling actions take on the threat of violence. A look, a yell, a quiet warning, even an ostensibly benign request can have the emotional impact of a physical assault. Catherine Kirkwood (1993) describes it like this: "The women's descriptions of waiting for an attack, wondering about

Figure 11.1 The Power and Control Wheel

the intensity, searching their experience and resources for any method of diffusing the potential violence, all constitute a type of mental and emotional torture, and in fact their partners' behavior has been likened to the behaviour of captors who emotionally torture prisoners of war."

Such patterns of coercive control cannot, of course, be identified by looking at violent incidents in isolation. They can only be identified from more general information about the relationship—information about the use of multiple tactics to control one's partner, what Kirkwood calls a "web" of abuse (Kirkwood, 1993). This is the kind of violence that comes to mind when most people hear the term "domestic violence," and in heterosexual relationships it is largely male-perpetrated (Graham-Kevan and Archer 2003a, 2003b; Johnson 2001). It is more likely than the other types of intimate partner violence to produce injuries, long-term health effects, depression, posttraumatic stress, suicide, and homicide (Campbell 1995; Campbell and Lewandowski 1997; Golding 1999; Johnson, Conklin, and Menon 2002; Johnson and Leone 2005; Leone 2007; Leone et al. 2004).

In the context of this discussion of healthy marriage, however, it is also important to note that because coercive but nonviolent control tactics can be effective without the use of violence (especially if there has been a history of violence in the past), intimate terrorism does not *necessarily* manifest itself in high levels of violence. In fact, I have recently argued (Johnson 2008) for the recognition of "incipient" intimate terrorism (cases in which there is a clear pattern of power and control but in which there has as yet been no physical violence). Stark (2007) has argued, even more dramatically, that our focus should shift from the violence itself to the coercive control as a "liberty crime."

Violent Resistance

What is a woman to do when she finds herself terrorized in her own home? At some point, most women in such relationships do fight back physically. For some, this is an instinctive reaction to being attacked, and it happens at the first blow—almost without thought. For others, it does not happen until it seems the assaults will be endless if she does not do something to stop him—so she fights back. However, for most heterosexual women, the usual size difference between them and their partners ensures that violent resistance will not help and may make things worse, so they abandon violence and focus on other means of coping. For a few victims of intimate terrorism, eventually it seems that the only way out is to kill their partners (Richie 1996; Walker 1989).

The critical defining pattern of violent resistance is that the resistor, faced with an intimate terrorist, uses violence but not in an attempt to take general control over her partner or the relationship. Violence in the face of intimate terrorism may arise from any of a variety of motives (Swan and Snow 2002; Walker 1989). The resistor may (at least at first) believe that she can defend herself, that her violent resistance will keep her partner from attacking her further. That may mean that she thinks she can stop him right now, in the midst of an attack, or it may mean that she thinks that if she fights back often enough he will eventually decide to stop attacking her physically.

Even if she does not think she can stop him, she may feel that he should not be allowed to attack her without getting hurt himself. This desire to hurt him in return even if it will not stop him can be a form of communication ("What you're doing isn't right and I'm going to fight back as hard as I can") or it may be a form of retaliation or payback, along the lines of, "He's not going to do that without paying some price for it." In a few cases, she may seek serious retribution, attacking him when he is least expecting it and doing her best to do serious damage, even killing him. But there is another, more frequent motive for such premeditated attacks—escape. Sometimes, after years of abuse and entrapment, a victim of intimate terrorism may feel that the only way she can escape from this horror is to kill her tormenter (Browne 1987; O'Keefe 1997).

Situational Couple Violence

The first two types of intimate partner violence may be what most of us think of when we hear the term *domestic violence*, but the most common type of intimate partner violence does not involve any attempt on the part of either partner to gain general control over the relationship.[3] The violence is situationally provoked, as the tensions or emotions of a particular encounter lead someone to react with violence. Intimate relationships inevitably involve conflicts, and in some relationships one or more of those conflicts may escalate to violence. The violence may be minor and singular, with one argument at some point in the relationship escalating to the level that someone pushes or slaps the other, is immediately remorseful, apologizes and never does it again. Or it could be a chronic problem, with one or both partners frequently resorting to violence, minor or severe.

The motives for such violence vary. A physical attack might feel like the only way one's extreme anger or frustration can be expressed. It may even be intended to do serious injury as an expression of anger. It may primarily be an attempt to get the attention of a partner who does not seem to be listening. There can be a control motive involved, albeit not one that is part of a general pattern of coercive control. One partner may simply find that the argument is not going well for him or her, and decide that one way to win this is to get physical.

The separate violent incidents of situational couple violence may look exactly like those involved in intimate terrorism or violent resistance. The difference is in the general power and control dynamic of the relationship, not in the nature of any or all assaults. In situational couple violence there is no general pattern of exerting coercive control. It is simply that one or more disagreements have resulted in violence. The violence may even be frequent if the situation that provokes the violence is recurring, as when one partner frequently feels that the other is flirting and the confrontations over that issue regularly lead one or the other of them to lash out. And the violence may be quite severe, even homicidal. What makes it situational couple violence is that it is rooted in the events of a particular situation rather than in a relationship-wide attempt to control.

IMPLICATIONS FOR HEALTHY MARRIAGE

Violence and Marital Health

It seems so obvious that violence would be devastating to an intimate partnership that we are sometimes astonished that our surveys do not indicate that every violent spouse is a former spouse. However, when one acknowledges the different types of intimate partner violence described above, the devastating impact of violence on the marital relationship becomes less obvious. For example, data from a 1970s Pittsburgh study indicated that although 50 percent of women experiencing intimate terrorism are deeply dissatisfied with their marriage, the figure is only 13 percent for women experiencing situational couple violence (Johnson et al. 2002). Among married women interviewed for the 1995–96 National Violence Against Women Survey, only 7 percent of those experiencing situational couple violence from their husband had left him more than once, compared with 29 percent of those experiencing intimate terrorism (Johnson and Leone 2000, 2005).

However, the fact that the "average" impact of situational couple violence on a relationship is less than that of intimate terrorism should not lull us into thinking that situational couple violence is harmless. In the Pittsburgh study, 29 percent of the women experiencing situational couple violence had suffered at least one severe injury. We need to intervene as best we can in all types of intimate partner violence, but it is likely that our intervention strategies will need to be different for the different types.

Intervention Strategies

It is almost standard practice in the battered-women's movement to argue strongly against couples counseling as an intervention strategy for domestic violence. The reason is that intimate terrorism dominates the caseload at shelters and other agencies (such as the police, hospitals, and courts). For example, in the Pittsburgh data discussed earlier (Johnson 2001), intimate terrorism comprises 79 percent of the shelter sample and 68 percent of the court sample. As a consequence, the battered-women's movement has actually come to define domestic violence as intimate terrorism. For example, a typical brochure starts, "Most victims of domestic violence are women. They come from all backgrounds and neighborhoods. Domestic violence occurs within a family or intimate relationship as a way to control another person. Victims suffer physical injury, live in fear in their homes, and lose power over their lives" (Pennsylvania Coalition Against Domestic Violence 2002). In such cases there is a problem of purposeful, often brutal coercive control, not one of tensions and conflicts in the family or ineffective couple communication patterns. The standard couples-counseling approach of asking the couple to come together with a counselor to discuss honestly the problems in their relationship is likely not only to be ineffective, but also to put the victim in greater danger. However, couples-counseling strategies may be just what is needed in cases of situational couple violence. What we need are targeted strategies that take seriously the safety issues involved in intimate partner violence.

Of course, if we are going to tailor interventions to types of intimate partner violence, we will have to develop strategies for screening, strategies that are complicated by the fact that some types of error may put victims at risk of serous injury or death. Thus, we cannot approach measurement the way we might in a confidential survey. We need to use a strategy that studiously avoids the error of treating cases of intimate terrorism as if they were situational couple violence. Thus, my recommendation is that we initially assume that every case is a case of intimate terrorism, and that we focus foremost on safety planning. Although intake procedures might include a questionnaire assessment of type of violence as one source of information, these should be combined with more clinical approaches that rely on a team of advocates/clinicians who take into account both quantitative and qualitative information and who move slowly in the development of an intervention strategy. When the team is fairly confident that they are dealing with situational couple violence, some individual counseling could be introduced. Then, only if the information gleaned from the individual counseling continues to support the identification of the case as situational couple violence would it be appropriate to move to the more risky strategy of couples counseling.

Although I would argue that the great diversity among cases of situational couple violence calls for a great diversity of intervention strategies (Hamel 2005), and that individual cases would most likely call for multiple intervention tactics, it might be useful to identify three general classes of intervention. First, the clinician might identify the sources of conflict that produce arguments that escalate to violence, and then work with the couple to mitigate those problems. Some of the conflicts might arise from problems external to the couple, such as unemployment or other financial problems, and mitigation would include information regarding private or public agencies that provide financial aid or help with employment or training in the managing of marginal finances. Other conflicts might arise from actions of one member of the couple, actions that both agree are a problem, such as problem drinking or drug abuse, in which case the focus would be on helping the individual to overcome those problems.

Second, there might be individual personality problems that, rather than being a *source* of conflict, create difficulties with the resolution of conflicts that have other sources. Such individual problems as poor impulse control or anger management would call for interventions that focus on the individual. Finally, there would be cases in which the violence is primarily a function of couple-level processes that require work on skills such as conflict management or couple communication process.

As for violent resistance, there are two obvious strategies for intervention: dealing with the intimate terrorism of the partner and helping the victim to develop coping strategies that are less risky for her and her partner than is violent resistance. It is also important that interventions in violent resistance continue to be based in an empowerment model that is sensitive to the victim whose life has for some time been controlled by an intimate terrorist (Campbell 1998; Peled, Eisikovits, and Winstok 2000). This means working with the victim to provide the information and support that will allow her to develop safe strategies for eliminating the violence and control from her life, either within the relationship or by escaping from it.

Finally, what do we do about the intimate terrorist? Although the literature on intervention is filled with ostensibly contradictory data and debates about the effectiveness of arrest, mandated batterer education, and other strategies, I expect that considerable clarity could be achieved with attention to variations among types of violence. As I have noted, the Pittsburgh data suggest that the courts are dealing with a mix of cases of intimate terrorism, situational couple violence, and violent resistance. I expect that much of the contradictory data stems from the different mixes of these types in various assessment studies, and that the generally low success rates of various strategies is in part a function of the variable effectiveness of each strategy with respect to different types of violence. For example, the arrest literature suggests that arrest is more effective for some types of offenders than it is for others, but in that literature type of offender has generally been articulated in terms of social position, rather than type of violence (Buzawa 2003). Similarly, in the batterer-treatment literature there is evidence that different approaches are effective for different types of intimate terrorists. Saunders has shown that a feminist education approach is more effective with antisocial intimate terrorists than is a more psychodynamic intervention, whereas the psychodynamic approach is more effective with emotionally dependent intimate terrorists (Saunders 1996). Although no one has yet done such research using the more basic control types, there is some evidence for differential effectiveness of batterer intervention for different types of violence. One recent study of almost two hundred men court-mandated to a batterer-intervention program found that men involved in situational couple violence were the most likely (77 percent) to complete the program, with two groups of intimate terrorists falling far behind them at 38 percent and 9 percent completion (Eckhardt et al. 2008). Another study found that in a fifteen-month follow-up, only 21 percent of men involved in situational couple violence were reported by their partners to have committed further abuse, compared with 42 percent and 44 percent of the two groups of intimate terrorists (Clements et al. 2002). These preliminary findings suggest that targeted interventions that acknowledge differences among types of offenders might be a useful response to the complaints of both (1) the men who argue that they find feminist intervention approaches insulting (Raab 2000) and (2) the increasing number of women resisting intimate terrorism who find themselves in mandated treatment programs that are probably more appropriate for their partners than for them (Miller 2005).

EDUCATION AND PREVENTION

Most of the initiatives identified with the healthy-marriage movement involve education and prevention, and the implications of a typological approach to education are much the same as they are in the area of intervention. Healthy-marriage education needs to differentiate among the attitudes and skills that are likely to prevent each of the three major types of intimate partner violence. For intimate terrorism, the focus should be on mutual respect and equality, and perhaps on vigilance regarding the early warning signs that you are dealing with a partner who may not accord you that respect. For violent resistance, the focus would be on strategies for dealing with incipient intimate terrorism that would help the victim to address effectively the violence or escape from the relationship. For situational couple violence, the focus would be on dealing with the tensions of everyday life, managing anger, and developing effective communication skills.

The healthy-marriage movement is already well aware of these issues, and the distinctions discussed above are being incorporated into healthy-marriage programs in a variety of ways. First, one of the concerns of battered-women's advocates and of educators who work within the healthy-marriage model is that including intimate terrorists in marital-education programs might inadvertently increase the risks to their partners. As advocates have long argued, putting victims of intimate terrorism in the position of being asked to talk honestly about the nature of their relationship with their abuser may not only be ineffective but may also set them up for violence at home, as their abusers seek to reaffirm their control. As a result, the designers of these programs are struggling with issues of screening. Some healthy-marriage programs therefore screen out anyone who reports that they have experienced violence in their relationship. Others, acknowledging the differences among the types of violence discussed in this chapter, have taken other approaches. Some, assuming that intimate terrorists are not likely to be involved in voluntary marriage education programs in the first place, have concluded that screening is unnecessary (Stanley 2006). Others have opted for some means of screening out anyone who is experiencing intimate terrorism, while allowing victims of situational couple violence to continue in programs that address some of the causes of that violence in their relationship. The issues involved are complex. Is there some situational couple violence that poses the same risks as intimate terrorism? Is it relatively safe to address issues of marital conflict if the program is delivered only to individuals rather than couples? Does screening some people out deny them the very programs that might empower them to eliminate the violence in their lives, either by confronting it or by escaping it?

Second, issues of intimate partner violence enter into healthy-marriage curricula themselves at two points. Many healthy-marriage programs begin with the distribution and brief discussion of lists of local resources, including women's shelters and other domestic violence services. And at this early point in the curriculum, participants are sometimes warned about the dangers of taking such materials home if they are experiencing violence from their partners.

The next place that violence enters into the curriculum is in connection with definitions of healthy relationships and of the skills needed to maintain them. For example, one curriculum addresses the issue of partner violence in terms of "safety," which is presented as one of the defining elements of healthy relationships: "Three kinds of safety mark healthy relationships: emotionally safe and supportive, physically safe (no fear of intimidation and physical harm), and commitment safety (security about counting on one another to be there and be faithful)" (Stanley 2006).

This curriculum goes on, in the section on skills useful in any relationship, to address issues of violence in some depth, including making the distinction between intimate terrorism and situational couple violence.[4] In this curriculum, the distinction is made in the context of a discussion of dangerousness, with a checklist of "Signs of the Greatest Danger in a Relationship" that includes many of the elements of intimate terrorism, such as, "She's scared of her partner," "He tries to control what she does, who she sees, where she goes, the money she has and how she spends it," "He keeps her from working, or makes trouble for her at work and tries to keep her financially dependent on him," and "He tracks who she talks to, and how much contact she has with her friends, family and neighbors."

It is important that such lists do not imply that violence with other characteristics is *never* dangerous—and this is one of the issues that curriculum developers have struggled with. If the distinctions among types are presented as "hard" types, there is a danger that couples experiencing situational couple violence will minimize the risks or consequences of the violence in their relationship. It is important to make it clear that there are unhealthy consequences and danger involved in any violence in an intimate relationship. This curriculum and many others go on to present different strategies for eliminating the different types of violence from the relationship.

Finally, the curriculum addresses quite different approaches to managing the violence involved in intimate terrorism and situational couple violence, introducing as well some discussion of the inadvisability of violent resistance. Participants are taught about the different dynamics of the types of violence, the different prognoses for escalation or desistance, and the need for different means of intervening to eliminate or escape from the violence. The issues are complex, and different curricula address them in different ways, but it is encouraging that addressing issues of intimate partner violence and taking into account distinctions among types of such violence have become standard practice in healthy-marriage curricula.

CONCLUSION

Obviously, I think it is essential that we attend to differences among these basic types of intimate partner violence. All of them are dangerous, and all of them require our attention in prevention and intervention, but they develop differently, have different implications for relationships, and will require different strategies to address them as social and personal problems. We are still in the very early stages of introducing these distinctions into our research and into our thinking about intervention and prevention, and we still have a lot to learn. I know that my own thinking in this area has undergone major changes since I began this work fifteen years ago, and it continues to change as research on differences among the types is published and the early research results on the differential effects of intervention trickle in. It is clear, though, that research in this area can make major contributions to increased safety in our most intimate relationships.

NOTES

1. A fourth type, *mutual violent control*, comprises two intimate terrorists vying for control of their relationship. This type appears in very small numbers in some samples, and there is some debate about whether it is a true type or an artifact of the constraints of imperfect operationalization.
2. At this point I want to drop the term *domestic violence* because, although it has sometimes been used to refer to all of the types of intimate partner violence that I will identify, in the public mind (and that of many researchers as well) domestic violence is most clearly identified with one of those types, intimate terrorism. The term *intimate partner violence* avoids that confusion.
3. These sorts of estimates are always quite imprecise, but my best guess would be that three to four times more situational couple violence occurs than intimate terrorism in committed heterosexual relationships. The difference is probably even greater for heterosexual and same-sex dating relationships and for committed same-sex relationships.
4. Many of these healthy-marriage programs actually address healthy *relationships* and are relevant for and available to same-sex couples, couples who live together unmarried, couples who have a child together but are not romantically involved, or dating couples.

REFERENCES

Arias, I., C. M. Lyons, and A. E. Street. 1997. Individual and marital consequences of victimization: Moderating effects of relationship efficacy and spouse support. *Journal of Family Violence* 12, no. 2: 193–210.

Browne, A. 1987. *When battered women kill*. New York: Free Press.

Buzawa, E. S. 2003. *Domestic violence: The criminal justice response*. Thousand Oaks, Calif.: Sage.

Campbell, J. C. 1995. Prediction of homicide of and by battered women. In J. C. Campbell, ed., *Assessing dangerousness: Violence by sexual offenders, batterers, and child abusers*, 96–113. Thousand Oaks, Calif.: Sage.

———. 1998. Making the health care system an empowerment zone for battered women: Health consequences, policy recommendations, introduction, and overview. In J. C. Campbell, ed., *Empowering survivors of abuse: Health care for battered women and their children*, 3–22. Thousand Oaks, Calif.: Sage.

Campbell, J. C., and L. A. Lewandowski. 1997. Mental and physical health effects of intimate partner violence on women and children. *Psychiatric Clinics of North America* 20, no. 2: 353–374.

Clements, K., A. Holtzworth-Munroe, E. W. Gondolf, and J. C. Meehan. 2002. Testing the Holtzworth-Monroe et al. (2000) batterer typology among court-referred maritally violent men. Paper presented at the Association for the Advancement of Behavior Therapy annual meeting, Reno.

Eckhardt, C. I., A. Holtzworth-Munroe, B. Norlander, A. Sibley, and M. Cahill. 2008. Readiness to change, partner violence subtypes, and treatment outcomes among men in treatment for partner assault. *Violence and Victims* 23, no. 4: 446–477.

Golding, J. M. 1999. Intimate partner violence as a risk factor for mental disorders: A meta-analysis. *Journal of Family Violence* 14, no. 2: 99–132.

Graham-Kevan, N., and J. Archer. 2003a. Intimate terrorism and common couple violence: A test of Johnson's predictions in four British samples. *Journal of Interpersonal Violence* 18, no. 11: 1247–1270.

———. 2003b. Physical aggression and control in heterosexual relationships: The effect of sampling. *Violence and Victims* 18, no. 2: 181–196.

Hamel, J. 2005. *Gender inclusive treatment of intimate partner abuse: A comprehensive approach*. New York: Springer.

Johnson, M. P. 2001. Conflict and control: Symmetry and asymmetry in domestic violence. In A. Booth, A. C. Crouter, and M. Clements, eds., *Couples in conflict*, 95–104. Mahwah, N.J.: Lawrence Erlbaum.

———. 2005. Domestic violence: It's not about gender—or is it? *Journal of Marriage and Family* 67, no. 5: 1126–1130.

———. 2008. *A typology of domestic violence: Intimate terrorism, violent resistance, and situational couple violence*. Boston: Northeastern University Press.

Johnson, M. P., and A. Cares. 2004. Effects and non-effects of childhood experiences of family violence on adult partner violence. Paper presented at the National Council on Family Relations annual meeting, Orlando.

Johnson, M. P., V. Conklin, and N. Menon. 2002. The effects of different types of domestic violence on women: Intimate terrorism vs. situational couple violence. Paper presented at the National Council on Family Relations annual meeting, Houston.

Johnson, M. P., and J. M. Leone. 2000. The differential effects of patriarchal terrorism and common couple violence: Findings from the National Violence Against Women survey. Paper presented at the Tenth International Conference on Personal Relationships, Brisbane, Australia.

———. 2005. The differential effects of intimate terrorism and situational couple violence: Findings from the National Violence Against Women Survey. *Journal of Family Issues* 26, no. 3: 322–349.

Kirkwood, C. 1993. *Leaving abusive partners: From the scars of survival to the wisdom for change*. Newbury Park, Calif.: Sage.

Kwong, M. J., K. Bartholomew, and D. G. Dutton. 1999. Gender differences in patterns of relationship violence in Alberta. *Canadian Journal of Behavioural Science* 31, no. 3: 150–160.

Leone, J. M. 2007. Suicide ideation among African American victims of intimate terrorism and situational couple violence. Paper presented at the National Council on Family Relations annual meeting, Pittsburgh.

Leone, J. M., M. P. Johnson, C. M. Cohan, and S. Lloyd. 2004. Consequences of male partner violence for low-income, ethnic women. *Journal of Marriage and Family* 66, no. 2: 471–489.

Magdol, L., T. E. Moffitt, A. Caspi, D. L. Newman, J. Fagan, and P. A. Silva. 1997. Gender differences in partner violence in a birth cohort of 21-year-olds: Bridging the gap between clinical and epidemiological approaches. *Journal of Consulting and Clinical Psychology* 65, no. 1: 68–78.

Miller, S. L. 2005. *Victims as offenders: The paradox of women's violence in relationships*. New Brunswick, N.J.: Rutgers University Press.

O'Keefe, M. 1997. Incarcerated battered women: A comparison of battered women who killed their abusers and those incarcerated for other offenses. *Journal of Family Violence* 12, no. 1: 1–19.

Peled, E., Z. Eisikovits, G. Enosh, and Z. Winstok. 2000. Choice and empowerment for battered women who stay: Toward a constructivist model. *Social Work* 45, no. 1: 9–25.

Pence, E., and M. Paymar. 1993. *Education groups for men who batter: The Duluth model*. New York: Springer.

Pennsylvania Coalition Against Domestic Violence. 2002. Are you or is anyone you know a battered woman? Retrieved March 17, 2006, from www.pcadv.org.

Raab, S. 2000. Men explode. *Esquire* 134, no. 3: 244–248.

Richie, B. 1996. *Compelled to crime: The gender entrapment of battered black women.* New York: Routledge.

Rogge, R. D., and T. N. Bradbury. 1999. Till violence does us part: The differing roles of communication and aggression in predicting adverse marital outcomes. *Journal of Consulting and Clinical Psychology* 67, no. 3: 340–351.

Saunders, D. G. 1996. Feminist-cognitive-behavioral and process-psychodynamic treatments for men who batter: Interactions of abuser traits and treatment model. *Violence and Victims* 4, no. 4: 393–414.

Stanley, S. 2006. Personal communication.

Stark, E. 2007. *Coercive control: The entrapment of women in personal life.* New York: Oxford University Press.

Steinmetz, S. K. 1977–78. The battered husband syndrome. *Victimology* 2, nos. 3–4: 499–509.

Stets, J. E., and M. A. Straus. 1990. Gender differences in reporting marital violence and its medical and psychological consequences. In M. A. Straus and R. J. Gelles, eds., *Physical violence in American families: Risk factors and adaptation to violence in 8,145 families*, 151–165. New Brunswick, N.J.: Transaction Press.

Stith, S. M., K. H. Rosen, K. A. Middleton, A. L. Busch, K. Lundeberg, and R. P. Carlton. 2000. The intergenerational transmission of spouse abuse: A meta-analysis. *Journal of Marriage and the Family* 62, no. 3: 640–654.

Straus, M. A., and R. J. Gelles. 1990. How violent are American families? Estimates from the National Family Violence resurvey and other studies. In M. A. Straus and R. J. Gelles, eds., *Physical violence in American families: Risk factors and adaptations to violence in 8,145 families*, 95–112. New Brunswick, N.J.: Transaction Press.

Straus, M. A., R. J. Gelles, and S. K. Steinmetz. 1980. *Behind closed doors: Violence in the American family.* Garden City, N.Y.: Doubleday.

Swan, S. C., and D. L. Snow. 2002. A typology of women's use of violence in intimate relationships. *Violence Against Women* 8, no. 3: 286–319.

Walker, L. E. 1989. *Terrifying love: Why battered women kill and how society responds.* New York: Harper & Row.

PART 4

The Future of Marriage

TWELVE

The Growing Importance of Marriage in America

STEVEN L. NOCK

Current trends indicate that marriage in the future will be less central as a defining event in the life course of adults than it is in the present. Marriage will increasingly compete with cohabitation as an alternative form of intimate family life, and increasing numbers of adults will live alone. The overall fraction of adults who are currently married will decline (U.S. Census Bureau 2007a; chapter 4, this volume). My purpose is to explain how these trends may elevate the importance of marriage for those who do select it. To the extent that fewer individuals are married at any point in time, the symbolic importance of marriage increases. The symbol of marriage has potentially important significance in the labor market. If marriage implies valuable traits about individuals, then those who are married may enjoy benefits that their unmarried counterparts do not. Additionally, as alternatives to marriage (e.g., cohabitation, singleness) grow in popularity, then marriage increasingly serves to sort individuals based on the personal attributes associated with various living arrangements. I conclude that men and women who marry are each likely to benefit by this sorting. However, there are plausible reasons to suspect that the beneficial consequences of marriage for women may be less than for men (or even negative in some cases).

My framework relies on *economic signaling theory* to explain how marriage distinguishes the married from others. By considering marriage a sign of otherwise unknowable personal traits, we learn how it may matter to employers, the state, and others. My work, which considers marriage to be a social institution, offers a framework to identify the content of the marital signal. This content, when perceived by others, is the value of marriage. I am attempting to unite signaling and institutional theories of marriage. The result is a partial explanation for why married people are treated differently than their unmarried counterparts. I focus on marriage as a signal in the labor market primarily because signaling theory considers risk reduction. Marriage confers value in other settings (e.g., tax policy, criminal law, social status) that are beyond the scope of this chapter.

About six of ten Americans (62 percent) aged 25 to 64 were currently married in 2006 (U.S. Census Bureau 2006b). In 1984, the corresponding percentage was 73 percent (U.S. Census Bureau 1985). Marriage rates have been declining for several decades and for many reasons (later age at marriage, high unwed birth rates, increasing incidence of cohabitation, high divorce rates). Regardless of the reasons marriage is delayed, disrupted, or foregone, the result is that being married is an increasingly distinctive status because a growing fraction of people are *not* (chapter 15, this volume). Among those about whom little is known (particularly younger adults and those without established employment histories), credentials such as marriage or a college education provide minimal evidence of important characteristics. Married workers (especially men) have higher earnings than their unmarried counterparts (Bartlett and Callahan 1984; Gorman 2000; Hill 1976; Korenman and Neumark 1991). The evidence for women is complicated by the fact that married women are more likely than unmarried women to have children. There is a larger wage penalty associated with motherhood than there is a wage gain associated with marriage for women. When multivariate analyses control for the typical determinants of wages (e.g., education, age, experience) and for the number of children, married women earn more than their unmarried counterparts unless they have children (Waite 1995). Those with children have lower wages, except for black married mothers, who enjoy a wage gain for marriage and motherhood (U.S. Census Bureau 2007b). Though there is still debate about why marriage has such differing effects for the two sexes, the explanation I offer contributes to our understanding of how marriage contributes to income inequalities.

To put the demographic change in the incidence of marriage in perspective, consider another important status characteristic, graduation from college. In 2006, 28 percent of Americans over twenty-five had a four-year college degree. In 1984, 19 percent had that level of educational attainment (U.S. Census Bureau 2007c). The increase in college graduates is of about the same magnitude as the decrease in married adults over the past couple of decades.

HOW MARRIAGE MATTERS

Marriage has been argued to produce benefits for individuals in at least three basic ways (Becker 1981; Becker, Landes, and Michael 1977). First, there are wholly *external factors* that influence the value of marriage regardless of the particular individuals involved. These have their source completely outside the particular relationship of two people. Every married couple enjoys such benefits. For example, state and federal domestic relations and tax laws assign different obligations on the basis of marital status. But, as I will show, most such benefits originate outside the law. Second, there are *marriage-specific benefits* (and possible costs) that develop in a relationship over time. One obvious example is the division of tasks that arises in most married households. To the extent that marriage contributes to the development of such specialization, efficiencies arise. Of course, such efficiencies may mean that one spouse contributes fewer hours to paid labor. If so, her or his value in the market may decline as skills atrophy. Finally, there are *partner-specific benefits* that depend on the particular individual and her or his spouse for their value. For example, sensitivities, tastes, habits, and hobbies are developed over the course of time in a marriage. These unique partner-specific features of the relationship depend on the particular combination of personalities involved.

My concern in this chapter is about the first type of benefits, those that originate outside of the particular marital relationship. How, in other words, does marriage, per se, matter? Alternatively, how are married individuals treated differently *because* they are married? This means that I do not address issues of love or affection despite the fact that these emotions are central. However, they are not unique to marriage.

THE DISTINCTIVE FEATURES OF MARRIAGE

Marriage generates benefits in ways cohabitation cannot. While often similar in terms of the ongoing relationship, the most important differences are in how people enter and exit. More specifically, the two differ in whether entry and exit are governed by *rituals, rules, and social recognition*.

Almost all marriages (even those preceded by cohabitation) are formed through a *public* act involving the mutual exchange of promises before an official authorized to conduct marriages. Entry into a marriage requires a license and some form of procedure. Except in unusual circumstances, the law of all states requires that marriages be solemnized by mutual exchanges of intent to be married before an official authorized to perform the wedding. Three in four (73 percent) marriages begin with a public ceremony of some type, with an average of 184 guests, at an average (2005) cost of $26,800 (Wedding Report 2006). The costly marriage ceremony has been shown to be an indicator (or signal) of conformity to conventional marriage and social norms (Kalmijn 2004). The ceremony itself is important, but the clearly marked transition is apparent (to the couple, at least) even absent a public ceremony (for instance, in many second marriages). After the wedding, there is little question about the new status of the couple: they are husband and wife. To family, friends, and the couple, the ritual is significant in marking a social and legal change of status.

In contrast, cohabitation typically evolves from less serious relationships. There are seldom any public declarations of a milestone in the relationship. According to Manning and Smock, cohabitation is regarded as a hiatus from being single (Manning and Smock 2005; see also chapter 6, this volume). There is little to suggest that strong cultural guidelines are involved in the entry to cohabitation. Neither are there any legal requirements to enter a cohabiting union.

Beyond its public significance, rituals contribute to the creation of an *identity* (or sense of presence) with something larger than the individual (Durkheim 1915; Gluckman and Gluckman 1977). The wedding ceremony is typically only the first ritual for married couples. Anniversaries or other ceremonies teach individuals that "this is the way our family is" (Wolin and Bennett 1984:401; see also Reiss 1981). Social science and the law acknowledge the value of a *shared family identity* for stabilizing a marriage. Unlike any individual asset, a shared family identity is a joint product. Anything that jeopardizes the relationship, therefore, threatens this invention. To the extent the shared sense of family is important to individuals, an incentive to maintain it is created. Though the disciplines differ in emphasis and terminology, all focus on the powerful stabilizing effect of perceived threats to family identity (in psychology, *constraint commitment* [Stanley and Markman 1992]; in social psychology, *barriers* [Levinger 1976]; in economics, *marital specific capital* [Becker 1981]; and in law, *consortium* [Krause and Meyer 2003]). There is no evidence that cohabiting unions involve rituals that would contribute to such identities, at their outset or later.

Divorce is the most obvious legal distinction between marriage and cohabitation. It is also the most important difference. In law, divorce is the most important component of domestic relations regulations. Divorce laws are a legal form of insurance that safeguards the interests of children and the adults involved (Scott 2000). At the time of dissolution, divorce laws stipulate specifically the terms of that exit. By getting married, each partner consents to important limits on their future behaviors and claims on some types of property. In both fault and no-fault divorces, there are rules about property distributions, claims on retirement benefits, and the value of less tangible property such as professional degrees. There are also rules about future support requiring the valuation of "compensatory" payments, "spousal support," and (in fault actions) alimony. Unless the couple is able to arrive at a mutually accepted settlement of such issues, the court will apply state law and principle to arrive at a settlement (Wadlington and O'Brien 2007). Knowing that property rights are conditioned by their marriage, partners are aware that their decision or their partner's decision to terminate the relationship has predictable consequences through the application of law (even if they are unaware of the specific terms). In other words, by getting married, each partner has accepted the potential role of the state in enforcing enduring obligations.

This cannot be said about cohabiting in the United States. Rather, states have attempted to deal with the problems that arise upon dissolution of informal unions by recourse to various contract laws. Written agreements between cohabiting partners have been declared enforceable in some jurisdictions. In others, such agreements are not legally binding. The American Law Institute (ALI), which drafts model laws and tries to have them adopted by states, recommends that domestic partners ("two persons of the same or opposite sex, not married to one another, who for a significant period of time share a primary residence and a life together as a couple") be given a fair division of property and the equivalent of alimony ("compensatory payments") at the time of dissolution. Though controversial, this appears to be the general direction of domestic relations law at the moment, though still on a case-by-case basis rather than by established legal principle (American Law Institute 2003, chapter 5; Friedman 2004:90–91). Cohabitation is likely to gain increasing legal standing because individuals in such unions are requesting such protection. For the near future, however, only marriage will have formal default exit rules to protect the interests of all parties at the time of dissolution.

Why would individuals be willing to specialize in household tasks, knowing that such specialization is risky (Becker 1981)? Without some assurance of a return, few would make this kind of risky future-oriented investment (Landes 1978). Only marriage guarantees such a return on investments because only the marriage contract is governed by default exit rules. There are no default rules about compensating a partner when a cohabiting union ends.

Beyond the legal issues of entry and exit rules, it is more challenging to characterize the differences and similarities of marriages and cohabiting unions. Social scientists have explored many dimensions of the two types of relationships. They have studied transitions from cohabitation into marriage, the attitudes and demographic traits of cohabiting individuals, the division of household tasks, and the variety of relationship types that social scientists characterize as cohabiting unions (see Seltzer 2000 and Smock 2000 for reviews). The informal rules governing such relationships are still largely unexplored. Do cohabiting couples insist on sexual fidelity? Do they pool financial resources in the name of efficiency? Are obligations for children structured in predictable ways? What is owed to the other partner when a relationship ends? How are such obligations enforced?

Marriage and cohabitation in the United States differ in how they are regarded by friends, relatives, employers, the state, and other people, a theme central to my basic argument. This is so even if the particular individuals involved in them may sometimes experience the relationships similarly. This means that the two types of unions are culturally different. They mean different things in our society. The reason is because common understandings of what a relationship is indicate that there are social norms about it. Marriage, in short, is a social institution (Nock 1998).

Marriage is a social institution because conventional expectations are associated with it, such as customary ways to be a good husband or wife. Many of these norms are quite formal (religious or legal), but most are little more than conventional expectations. Other people expect husbands and wives to do things differently from when they were not married. When children are born, the husband will automatically be assumed (socially and legally) to be the father and his responsibilities and obligations to his children will begin immediately. By getting married, partners announce to others that they accept an obligation to be faithful, to give and receive help in times of sickness, and to endure hardships. It is more difficult for a married than for an unmarried person to break such promises because they are part of our laws, religions, and definitions of morality. Society enforces these ideals both formally and informally. Nothing of the sort can yet be said about any other type of intimate relationship between two adults with the possible exception of same-sex civil unions. But while such unions are almost identical to marriages in law, we have no evidence about whether other people regard them in the same way they understand heterosexual marriages.

Cohabiting couples often resemble married couples in the organization of their households and the exchange of help. And there is good evidence that the routine daily lives of the two types of couples will continue to grow in similarity (Smock 2000). But a key difference between them is the role others play in their affairs. Cohabitation offers individuals much more freedom than marriage does *because* there are no widely accepted and approved expectations about the relationship. Unmarried partners decide how they will arrange their relationships—how to deal with the other's parents, for example. They decide whether money is pooled or held in separate accounts. Sexual fidelity may, or may not, be a dominant expectation. The parents of a cohabiting couple will also need to create a relationship without much guidance. Is the cohabiting couple to be treated as a married pair in matters of inheritance or intergenerational help and assistance? In such small ways, cohabiting couples and their associates create their own relationships. Married couples also face decisions like these, but spouses typically have a pattern to follow. For most matters of domestic life, the social institution of marriage offers guidance.

There is no direct method to determine the extent to which marriage is, and cohabitation is not, institutionalized. But public opinion is surely a very large part of any social institution. Indirect evidence on the institutionalization of marriage is found in public opinion. Every administration of the national General Social Survey has repeated a question first asked in 1972: "What is your opinion about a married person having sexual relations with someone other than the marriage partner—is it always wrong, almost always wrong, wrong only sometimes, or not wrong at all?" In 2004, eight in ten (80.8 percent) Americans responded that it was always wrong. Ten years earlier (1994), an almost identical percentage (78.5 percent) said the same thing. Interestingly, American's views about other forms of sexual expression have liberalized notably. In 1994, seven in ten Americans (70.0 percent) felt that sex between adults of the same sex was always wrong. In 2004, the percentage had dropped to 64.3 percent. Similar but smaller changes are seen in matters of premarital sex as well. In short, while Americans are becoming less united in opposition to some forms of sexual expression, they remain in strong agreement when condemning extramarital sex. Simply, fidelity in marriage is a strong norm, even if it is not strictly required by law—for instance, adultery is not criminalized in some states, and elsewhere is almost never enforced (Wadlington and O'Brien 2007).

Similar agreement is found in opinions about divorce. Americans generally believe that divorce should be difficult. The General Social Survey includes the question: "Should divorce in this country be easier or more difficult to obtain than it is now?" In 2004, only a quarter (25.4 percent) stated that divorce should be easier than it is now. Ten years earlier, the comparable percentage was the same (23.1 percent). In both periods, about half of Americans (53.6 percent in 2004, 49.5 percent in 1994) said that divorce should be harder to obtain, with the balance saying that the laws should stay as they are. This most important legal aspect of marriage, therefore, enjoys very strong normative support among adults in America, and half of adults believe divorce should be even harder to obtain.

Given a focus on entry and exit rules, we could say that any relationship of two adults that is normatively governed by entry and exit rules is a marriage, whether or not it is legally regarded as such. This is the traditional definition of the institution for most of human history (Cott 2000; Glendon 1989). Historically, of course, marriages did not permit unions of same-sex couples, but this general definition would include them if entry and exit norms developed for those unions. If such rules developed among cohabiting couples (and, indeed, the law indicates that this is happening regarding exit, as it has in other countries), then cohabitation would be marriage as I am defining it.

The national debate now taking place about same-sex marriages illustrates some of the common understandings of the institution of marriage. Though Massachusetts and Connecticut have legalized marriage between two people of the same sex, the more general trend is to create comparable legal statuses that are not called marriage but civil unions. And while civil unions and civil marriages may be equal in law (in the state in which they are created), they are clearly not regarded that way in culture. Legislatures that are willing to enact equal status civil unions for same sex couples are unwilling to create homosexual marriages. But it is not just a word that distinguishes the two—it is the meaning of that word (see chapter 13, this volume). There is considerable debate within both the gay and straight communities about the word and its meaning. And there may be legal differences as well; for example, will a state that allows same-sex marriage recognize civil unions created in another?

Both sides agree that marriage means "more" than civil unions (Rauch 2004). The fact that the name of the relationship has played such a role in this national debate illustrates clearly how marriage is an institution while no other form of intimate relationship yet is. In fact, there is no vernacular word to use when describing one's unmarried partner or the relationship involved whether it is a same-sex or opposite sex union (my friend? my fiancé? my partner?).

MARRIAGE AS A SIGNAL

Economic signaling theory originated with the work of Michael Spence in the early 1970s (Spence 1974). Spence was interested in the problem of uncertainty in markets. For example, an employer in search of workers faces serious problems of uncertainty. How can such uncertainty be managed when no directly relevant information is available? When applicants for jobs have no prior record of accomplishment in such occupations or no evidence of skills and traits desired, how can an employer know if a particular candidate will be productive? The answer, according to Spence, is that the employer will rely on indirect information—or signals—to reduce the uncertainty involved in hiring.

Of the many possibly relevant indirect sources of information available about a person, many are ascribed (at birth) characteristics or otherwise beyond personal control. For example, one's sex, age, and race are not at the individual's discretion. They are therefore not signals, even if others distinguish on their basis. Signals are *observable* characteristics attached to the individual that are subject to *manipulation*. Sociologists would recognize them as achieved characteristics (Spence 1973). Education is the classic example used to explain signals. An individual can adjust her education by attending or completing college. But doing so involves certain costs, what Spence refers to as *signaling costs*. Such costs are central to the theory for they replace (or represent) the costs and benefits of more reliable (yet unknowable) information.

The theory of signaling depends on the relationship between the costs of signaling and productivity. If there is no such correlation, then everyone will invest equally in the signal (for instance, a college degree), so they cannot be distinguished by it. Spence suggests that signaling costs are negatively related to productivity. In the case of education, therefore, it is less costly (in psychological effort, time, money, or opportunities, for example) for the more productive individual to obtain a college degree. So long as employers believe that there is some level of education at which expected productivity is high enough to warrant hiring the applicant, then individuals will respond by sorting themselves into those who will obtain the requisite level (at affordable signaling costs) and those who will not or cannot because the cost is too high. If, in the long run, the employer's expectations are confirmed (or not disconfirmed) then equilibrium will be established in which employers demand certain levels of education in return for an offered wage, and applicants capable of certain productivity are able to afford the signaling costs required to obtain such levels of education. As Spence summarizes, "An alterable characteristic like education, which is a potential signal, becomes an actual signal if the signaling costs are negatively correlated with the individuals' unknown productivity" (Spence 1973:367). Note that the theory does not assert that education (in this case) actually makes an individual productive. On the contrary, education simply must correlate with productivity. If it actually were productive in proportion to its costs, then everyone would invest heavily in education, and it would cease to have a signaling function.

From the employer's perspective, education matters because it is an indication of productivity. The employer is willing to pay more for educated workers so long as doing so reduces the risks of hiring unproductive workers. The central (and probably unanswerable) question about signals such as education is whether they stand for the traits that an employer wants, or whether they actually make a person more productive. The employer does not care, of course, so long as her expectations are not disconfirmed. And empirically, one cannot really adjudicate this question because both existing and acquired traits of value (to the employer) are unobservable in almost all cases.

Marriage is also selective of individuals with traits that are valuable in the market. In 1984, William Bishop published the first application of signaling theory to marriage (Bishop 1984). Since then, several economists and legal scholars have elaborated the perspective (Brinig 2000; Rowthorn 2002; Scott and Scott 1998; Treblicock 1999). The initial focus of signaling theory applied to marriage was on the value transmitted by one individual to another potential spouse (that is, a search theory). Individuals seeking a committed relationship must find some effective way to signal this intention to one another. Beginning with the assumption that marriage involves costs (mainly in forgone opportunities with other romantic partners, but also in limits on future behaviors generally), Bishop asked how the uncertainty involved in selecting a partner might be reduced.

Bishop reasoned that three objectives influence a person's orientation toward marriage. First, the individual wants a social/sexual partner. Second, he wants the power to decide the length or the term of the relationship because being abandoned ("dropped") has significant costs (emotional distress, costs of searching for a new partner, and so on). Third, most people want sexual loyalty from their partner. The value of a signal in this case of partner search is in how it informs each preference. Bishop developed an argument about how prior relationships (especially divorce), children from earlier relationships, and other knowable information provided information about the quality of a match. Basically, he outlined a search model that relies on various signals. He asked: how do signals reduce uncertainty when searching for a potential spouse?

His answer is that the voluntary acceptance of enforceable constraints on future behavior (that is, willingly agreeing to be bound by the exit rules from marriage) can be an efficient way of signaling private information to others. Additionally, the willingness to accept the legally binding contract of marriage reduces the chances that minor events will result in dissolution (since divorce is, in fact, costly). "Thus, the marriage contract is like a product guarantee. The contract itself shields the other party against risk, and the fact that someone is willing to sign such a contract provides information about this person's intentions and expectations" (Rowthorn 2002:139). The argument I am sketching is that marriage may signal potential employers in the same way Bishop argued it signals potential spouses.

What then, does marriage signal in today's world? Minimally, at least two things: commitment and sexual exclusivity. But marriage may also be a signal of many other personal and relational characteristics known to be correlated with it, including better physical and mental health, lower mortality, lower rates of violence, and higher productivity in jobs. If marriage is a signal of such traits as sexual exclusivity and commitment, is it also a valuable signal to others (not to potential spouses only)? Does marriage have market value as a type of credential?

In fact, marriage often serves as a signal to the rest of the world. As originally developed by Spence, a reliable signal is costly. That signaling cost stands for certain traits assumed about individuals. A range of decisions can be based on marital status: a spouse has the right to immigrate, can file a joint tax return, can qualify for pension benefits from a partner, enjoys lower insurance rates, and so forth. Often, such distinctions are based on actuarial risks. For example, married people enjoy better health and lower rates of crime, and they tend to live longer (Waite 1995). Insurers use marriage as a signal of health, accordingly. So long as the insurer's expectations are not disconfirmed by this practice, then it will continue.

Those who cannot or will not subscribe to constraints on future behaviors, fidelity, and commitment may see marriage as too costly and opt, instead, for cohabitation, at least for the moment. The result is that those signaling costs distinguish married and unmarried people.

Marriage conveys information to employers and others in the same indirect manner higher education does. The details of such a signal are not yet fully understood. But it is very clear that public officials (federal and state governments), private firms, and ordinary individuals react to the status of being married in predictable ways. But what signals does marriage convey, and more importantly, what behaviors, benefits, or expectations follow? What gives marriage market value? This question is easily answered because marriage is an institution. Marriage signals and the norms associated with the status are similar.

MARRIAGE AS A SOCIAL INSTITUTION

The core of any social institution is agreement among members of society about the norms that govern people in the roles of that social structure. In the matter of marriage, this means that the institution consists of various beliefs (that is, norms) about what a married man or woman should and should not do.

The vows taken by married partners are more than personal promises because they are enforceable. Laws, religion, and customs bolster this contract. So do relatives and friends. Through their marriages, husbands and wives become connected to new kin (and friends of new kin). The nature of kinship ties that result from marriage differs from that in more casual relationships because the former typically involve extensive obligations—a key normative dimension of marriage and kinship. In times of need, one may call upon relatives and expect that assistance will be given. The enduring nature of kinship obligations means that such debts persist and bind relatives together in an ongoing relationship.

By considering public opinion, law, demographic patterns, and religious doctrine, I have showed that Americans are broadly united in their views about the following marriage norms (see Nock 1998 for details):

1. Marriage is a free choice, based on love.

2. Marriage presumes individual maturity and independence (contractual ability, residential independence, etc.).

3. Marriage presumes heterosexuality, even in a regime permitting same-sex marriage.

4. Men must provide support; working is not optional for husbands, even if it is for wives.

5. Married partners are sexually faithful.

6. Parenthood—married spouses are presumed to become parents.

Since most Americans share them, these expectations can also be understood as the signals of marriage. It is still an empirical question whether assumptions about maturity, independence, commitment to employment, fidelity, and parenthood (not to mention heterosexuality) are relevant in important labor-market decisions where uncertainty must be reduced. My belief is that they are. Employers, for example, may differentially reward married workers by offering spousal benefits (for example, health insurance) without appearing to discriminate on the basis of marital status. They may discriminate in hiring by subtle preferences for married adults supporting a family. In hiring, there is some evidence of prejudice against mothers (Correll, Benard, and Paik 2007).

The norms of marriage provide a clue to the elements that influence individual spouses. But how might the norm of fidelity matter to someone other than a spouse? Or the expectation that spouses be parents? A few illustrations of how marital norms influence behaviors follow as hypotheses for future research.

Consider the norm of maturity and independence associated with marriage in America (although possibly not in some other countries). The expectation that married individuals will live independently, echoed in their actual behaviors, creates an expectation by others that married people will make efforts to maintain independence—working regularly, budgeting appropriately, and the like. Living arrangements illustrate this pattern clearly. Newly married couples in America typically establish a new residence, often miles from either set of parents. Only 0.4 percent of married couples in the United States live with a parent. Very few married couples receive significant financial assistance from parents on a routine basis, and parental assistance drops off rather quickly after a child gets married (Hogan, Eggebeen, and Clogg 1993).

Likewise, the norm that husbands must work is strongly supported by research showing that men's income and labor-force attachments increase following marriage. Men with favorable expected earnings are more likely to marry and less likely to divorce. Economists Sanders Korenman and David Neumark (1991) examined employment records that included performance evaluations and other indicators of productivity. They found that married men had higher performance ratings than unmarried men and that their higher productivity was largely responsible for their higher earnings. Married men are assumed to be dedicated to working and earning in the name of their families.

The norm of fidelity is a signal of trustworthiness. Married individuals are assumed to be able to make such an important promise and keep it. This norm is so important that it was traditionally bolstered by law, such that adultery was universally an accepted "fault" that justified divorce. Though no longer so strongly supported by law, sexual fidelity in marriage remains a central normative expectation.

The expectations about parenting in marriage also have broad implications, especially for men. Married fathers are probably regarded as more willing to accept responsibility. Marital paternity differs from the nonmarital variety primarily in the public statement it makes about a man. While married and unmarried fathers may each enjoy comparable custody rights and obligations, in reality they do not. Unmarried men who do not live with the mothers of their children may seem uninterested in assuming the social and legal role of father to their children. This sentiment may also be true of married men. However, the very large difference between the two is the automatic attribution of enduring and enforceable obligations for married men. A married man's role as social and legal father to his children is automatically conferred by marriage (Schneider and Brinig 2000, chapter 11).

Expectations about parenthood may work against married women. Employers are less likely to hire female married applicants with children than female married applicants without children. There is some evidence that the opposite is true for men (Correll, Benard, and Paik 2007). If employers expect that a married woman will become a mother, this would lead to poorer outcomes in job seeking. Here, the norms of marriage operate in opposite directions for the two sexes.

A NOTE ON GENDER AND RACE

More generally, does marriage have the same signaling value for men and women, or people of different racial and ethnic groups? The answer depends on whether marriage selects each sex or race similarly. It also depends on whether the signals of marriage have the same content for the different sexes and racial and ethnic groups. Do the same types of men and women marry? And do the same types of men and women postpone or forgo marriage? To the extent that attractive alternatives to marriage exist, then we would expect greater selectivity into marriage (or the alternatives).

Women's alternatives to getting married have increased because of higher education and employment. There is considerable debate about whether such economic opportunities have contributed to declining marriage rates and marital stability; this is the so-called independence effect (Casper and Bianchi 2002). The focus in this debate is whether a woman's economic independence might contribute to her unwillingness to endure or enter a poor-quality marriage. Women with higher skills and earnings potential, therefore, are predicted to have lower marriage rates and higher divorce rates. Empirical evidence to support such predictions, however, is quite mixed and contradictory. In fact, college-educated women now have higher marriage rates and lower divorce rates than women without college degrees (Goldstein and Kenney 2001; Martin 2006). Women's economic alternatives to depending on a husband for economic support may translate into delayed or forgone marriage. But the empirical evidence suggests otherwise.

Educational attainment and the likelihood of marriage are correlated in America. The primary question is whether either has value net of the other. From the perspective of the potential applicant for a job, it is likely that education was obtained in pursuit of the signals it sends (or, more simply, in pursuit of a good job). Marriage, however, is unlikely to have been entered into for such reasons. Therefore, the signaling costs of education and those of marriage are very different in purpose, even if the signals are similar in content.

Since employers rely on many signals in hiring decisions other than education (such as "integrity tests," drug tests, résumé checking, and lie-detector tests), marriage is likely to augment anything else used, inasmuch as the employer's obtaining the information is so inexpensive, even if illegal. Even if marriage and education convey similar signals, there is no reason to expect that employers will not use both when available. That is, marriage and education will each matter at the margins at a minimum. More importantly, to the extent that employers come to regard marriage as a more reliable signal than other more costly forms of information, its value will increase. Whether marriage grows in importance as a primary source of unknowable information is an empirical question yet to be answered (or asked). But to the extent that marriage becomes less common, its signaling value will grow in importance.

To the extent that cohabitation delays or serves as an alternative to marriage, too, selection into an informal union is also (for a large fraction of couples) selection out of marriage. We can compare couples in the two types of relationships to learn about selection into them. Research of this sort has shown that cohabiting individuals (both male *and* female) tend to be less traditional in their views and behaviors. They are more egalitarian in the division of household tasks, for example. They are less likely to embrace traditional norms of lifelong marriage and are more accepting of divorce (Casper and Bianchi 2002). Significantly, cohabitation is more common among those with lower incomes and educational attainments (Bumpass and Lu 2000). In general, cohabitation appears to be a lifestyle that appeals to those who are uncertain about making a commitment to another partner.

When asked for the reasons people would cohabit rather than marry, both sexes gave very similar answers in the late 1980s: cohabitation requires less personal commitment, is more sexually satisfying than dating, allows one to share living expenses, requires less sexual faithfulness, allows couples to be certain about compatibility before marriage, allows greater independence than marriage, and so on (Bumpass, Sweet, and Cherlin 1991; see also chapter 6, this volume). Such expectations, in other words, are the norms currently associated with cohabitation.

Based on available evidence, it is reasonable to assume that cohabitation is now a popular alternative form of intimate relationship. Either as a prelude or as a more or less permanent alternative to marriage, both sexes elect to cohabit when they are uncertain about commitment (their own or their partner's), compatibility, fidelity, and independence. For many who go on to marry, cohabitation is probably best understood as a search model. Either way, this alternative is likely to delay marriage. And to the extent that the decision to cohabit reflects individual characteristics that others view as lower trustworthiness (less sexual exclusiveness) or lower commitment (greater independence), then cohabitations will be more likely to include such individuals, while marriages will be more likely to include the opposite types of people. For those who transition into marriage, this speculation would imply that marriages preceded by cohabitation would unite individuals with higher risks of problematic relationships and higher chances of divorce. There is evidence that this is so (Casper and Bianchi 2002; Kamp Dush, Cohan, and Amato 2003). Such divorces would remove those individuals from the ranks of the married, further distinguishing the two groups.

The overall result of increasing cohabitation, then, is that married individuals will be considered more committed, more trustworthy, and more approving of the very basic and broad norms of marriage outlined earlier. This would imply that as cohabitation grows in popularity, the signal of marriage will become increasingly reliable evidence of those traits. And given what we know, it should do so similarly for both sexes except, possibly, in the matter of parenthood.

It is more challenging to speculate on the signaling aspect of marriage among those of different races. While marriage rates have declined overall, they have done so more notably among African Americans since the mid-twentieth century. Eighty-five percent of African Americans born in the late 1940s are estimated to have married by age 65 (versus 95 percent of whites), while 64 percent of those born in the 1960s are married (versus 93 percent of whites) (Goldstein and Kenney 2001). No one really knows why, although there have been many attempts to explain this trend. Undoubtedly there are many factors that have influenced it, and signaling can only be part of the explanation. But how can it be a part of the story? At least two possibilities exist.

First, there may be little or no advantage to marriage for blacks in the market. Employers, for example, may discriminate uniformly on the basis of race, negating any possible advantage that might otherwise exist for a marriage signal. Alternatively, marriage may mean very different things for blacks and whites. The argument I have developed about how marriage might signal value presumes that the norms (and meaning) of marriage are fairly uniform throughout society. Alternatively, it assumes that the signaling costs of marriage are similar (for example, forgoing others and making lifelong commitments). But it may be that marriage has very different meanings for those of different racial or ethnic groups. Cultural beliefs and history may have led to the creation of different institutions of marriage that are not uniform. The meaning of marriage may have changed unevenly in society (see chapter 14, this volume).

It seems undeniable that the meaning of marriage has changed significantly in the past century. This is especially so in regard to issues of gender. But it may also be true that marriage is coming to be seen as something fundamentally different among some racial and ethnic subgroups. The broad norms outlined earlier represent common themes found in public opinion, law, and religious writings. But they may not be shared among all subgroups in our society. As Kathryn Edin and Maria Kefalas (2005) suggest, marriage is highly valued among low-income single mothers. But it is viewed as something one postpones until other matters are resolved, most important of them getting a good job. By this logic, one marries after obtaining a good standard of living, and not as a means for doing so. Marriage is seen as a capstone event rather than a foundation for achievement. Childbearing cannot be postponed indefinitely, so having children before marriage is a logical response to this view of the meaning of marriage. To the extent that this is true, marriage may not sort individuals in the way I have suggested. If widespread agreement exists among some racial or ethnic groups that marriage is unrelated to childbearing, for example, then married and unmarried men are less likely to be seen as differing in their willingness to assume responsibility.

CONCLUSION: WHY MARRIAGE SIGNALS MATTER

Research on who marries whom consistently shows that the sorting and matching process unites similar individuals. In regard to race and ethnicity, for instance, the percentage of those married endogamously ranges from 95 percent for blacks, to 75 percent for Asians, 65 percent for Hispanics, and 45 percent for American Indians, but only 25 percent for European ethnic groups (Italian, Polish, and so on). High rates of endogamy are also recorded for most mainline religious denominational memberships. All such forms of endogamy, however, are declining over time (Kalmijn 1998).

In contrast, educational similarity is very high and has actually increased in the past sixty years. Today, educational matching in marriage is distinguished by the presence or absence of a college degree. Increasingly, those with college degrees marry only those with college degrees. Likewise, intermarriages between high-school dropouts and those with more education are increasingly rare (Schwartz and Mare 2005).

Marriage resembles a college degree in its signals. If we can determine why a college degree conveys meaning about productivity, then we can better understand how and why marriage does.

A college degree is important in marriage matches because it is an interpersonal signal of important and desired traits to partners. Now that there are viable and attractive alternatives to marriage, marriage searches that sort couples on educational attainment also sort them on the important marriage norms. The connection between the symbolic value of marriage and education implies that marriage would be less common among the less educated, and so it is. It also implies that the less educated would be more likely to cohabit rather than marry, and so they do. In other words, marriage should increasingly function as a base of social distinction, just as a college degree does. Consider why the education and marriage signals are similar.

First, a college degree offers proof that one can sustain commitment. Those who complete college have incurred enormous costs in pursuit of their degrees. The ability to do so may be minimal evidence of productivity to employers. And survey results suggest that it is also evidence of earnings potential to currently unmarried men and women. But it is also strong evidence of a temperament that can endure despite occasional failures and setbacks. It minimally signals an ability to make and honor a promise or commitment. In this way, it also may signal trustworthiness.

A college degree is also clear evidence of a prospective (future-looking) temporal orientation. Completion of higher education signals a demeanor capable of deferred gratification (the ability to wait for things you want). It is obvious in everyday life that people have some standard by which they decide if a larger reward is worth waiting for. Many people buy short-term certificates of deposit instead of long-term CDs because the payoff for the latter is delayed, even though the rate of return is higher. This is the "discount rate," the rate at which something's subjective value declines over time. A person planning for the future would choose to wait to get more return in the future. A person not planning for the future would prefer immediate though lower returns. All else being equal, a college degree reflects a willingness to forgo current consumption at the current rate of return to education. The ability to plan for the future and postpone immediate rewards is minimal evidence of maturity.

Like a college degree, marriage is likely to become an increasingly powerful signal because it indicates those same important traits about people that are in high demand in the economic marketplace. As fewer elect to marry, the signal increases in value due to its scarcity relative to its demand. Marriage signals a willingness to honor promises made (that is, commitments). Marriage signals a person's willingness to defer gratification in the name of present sacrifices. And marriage signals minimal evidence of trustworthiness (Oppenheimer 1988). To the extent that marriage signals those values sought by employers, we would expect to see growing inequality between the married and the unmarried in a market economy. Abundant evidence suggests that this is the case. The bases of social inequality will increasingly include marital status because the status is an increasingly important signal.

Legal distinctions based on marital status are now challenged as inequitable. For example, Tamara Metz argues that if marriage were essentially separated from law (she calls this "deinstitutionalizing marriage") there would be greater liberty, equality, and stability of marriages. Individuals could contract for the basic dimensions of caregiving relationships (see chapter 13, this volume). Allen Parkman also suggests that individuals be permitted to contract the primary dimensions of marital relationships before entering them (Parkman 2000). Indeed, Elizabeth and Robert Scott refer to marriage and marriage-like arrangements as "relational contracts" (1998). The primary point of such arguments is that default laws associated with marital status inevitably deny certain privileges to some individuals. If they could arrange their own affairs more in the manner they wish, such invidious distinctions would disappear or diminish.

We must consider whether the inequalities associated with marital status are the result of law and public policy. And we must ask whether modifying state marriage laws will lead to more equality. I believe that the best answer to both questions is no—or at least not much.

First, it is unlikely that many Americans who want to marry would abandon "traditional" marriage simply because it was redefined in law. Even in those few American states that continue to recognize consensual, "common-law" marriage, the overwhelming majority of individuals elect the conventional form. The law is a rather incomplete instrument in the matter of marriage as an American institution because the institution of marriage is only partially formed by law. It may be influenced by law in some ways, of course, especially default-divorce law. Social and religious norms, however, are the primary pillars of the marriage institution. Were we to alter the entrance rules for marriage but retain the exit rules, it is unlikely that the social institution of marriage would change significantly, but the legal benefits and obligations associated with marriage would become more widely available. We know how contentious such an effort would be from our experience with same-sex marriage. But this strategy does not require that much change in our marriage culture except our laws.

Second, the benefits of marriage are not largely legal. As I have argued here, married people benefit from the assumptions made about them—the belief that they are more productive, trustworthy, and dedicated individuals. The primary benefits of marriage, that is, originate from others, not from the state (not to deny that there are legal benefits and obligations attached to being married).

The basic point I have made in this chapter is that the market generates distinctions based on marital status because those willing to marry are viewed as more valuable. This has little to do with the law. Indeed, it contradicts the law. Like the market, countless other social forces are involved in creating distinctions among people that reflect their marital and parental statuses. Those who wish to reduce inequalities associated with marital status should be modest in their expectations about the impact of legal change on the institution of American marriage.

I believe that the future of marriage depends on the future of cohabitation and other alternative living arrangements. If cohabitation remains a poorly defined, nonlegal arrangement, then all evidence points to the growing importance of marriage as more elect to cohabit. On the other hand, if current legal trends continue, default exit rules similar to those now found in marriage will emerge for cohabitations. This will require some strategy, of course, to determine that such a union existed. To do this, entry rules will be established. If entry and exit rules emerge for cohabitation, then the arrangement would become marriage, at least in the legal sense. If comparable social norms emerge, then cohabitation would be largely indistinguishable from marriage. In that case, marriage would become less important.

My reading of the evidence is that the legal changes are happening much slower than the behavioral changes. Cohabiting is growing more popular, while legal efforts to regulate it are developing much slower. And there is little to suggest that social norms are developing about cohabiting relationships. For the foreseeable future, therefore, we should expect to see marriage grow in importance because of the increase in cohabitation.

NOTE

Special thanks to Elizabeth Peters, Claire Kamp Dush, Seth Sanders, Daphne Spain, Margaret Brinig, Chris Einolf, Ryan Gruters, Paul Kingston, and W. Bradford Wilcox for helpful comments and suggestions on this chapter.

REFERENCES

American Law Institute. 2003. *Principles of the law of family dissolution: Analysis and recommendations.* Philadelphia: American Law Institute.

Bartlett, R. L., and C. Callahan III. 1984. Wage determination and marital status: Another look. *Industrial Relations* 23, no. 1: 90–96.

Becker, G. S. 1981. *A treatise on the family.* Chicago: University of Chicago Press.

Becker, G. S., E. M. Landes, and R. T. Michael. 1977. An economic analysis of marital instability. *Journal of Political Economy* 85:1141–1187.

Bishop, W. 1984. Is he married? Marriage as information. *University of Toronto Law Journal* 34:245–262.

Brinig, M. F. 2000. *From contract to covenant.* Cambridge, Mass.: Harvard University Press.

Bumpass, L., and H. H. Lu. 2000. Trends in cohabitation and implications for children's family contexts in the United States. *Population Studies, 54,* 19–41.

Bumpass, L. L., J. A. Sweet, and A. J. Cherlin. 1991. The role of cohabitation in declining rates of marriage. *Journal of Marriage and the Family* 53:338–355.

Casper, L., and S. M. Bianchi. 2002. *Continuity and change in the American family.* Thousand Oaks, Calif.: Sage.

Correll, S. J., S. Benard, and I. Paik. 2007. Getting a job: Is there a motherhood penalty? *American Journal of Sociology* 112, no. 5 (March): 1297–1338.

Cott, N. 2000. *Public vows: A history of marriage and the nation.* Cambridge, Mass.: Harvard University Press.

Durkheim, E. 1915. *The elementary forms of the religious life: A study in religious sociology.* Trans. Joseph Ward Swain. New York: Macmillan.

Edin, K., and M. Kefalas. 2005. *Promises I can keep: Why poor women put children before marriage.* Berkeley: University of California Press.

Friedman, L. M. 2004. *Private lives: Families, individuals, and the law.* Cambridge, Mass.: Harvard University Press.

Glendon, M. A. 1989. *The transformation of family law: State, law, and family in the United States and Western Europe.* Chicago: University of Chicago Press.

Gluckman, M., and M. Gluckman. 1977. On drama, games, and athletic contests. In S. Moore and B. Myerhoff, eds., *Secular ritual,* 227–243. Amsterdam: Van Gorcum.

Goldstein, J. R., and C. T. Kenney. 2001. Marriage delayed or marriage forgone? New cohort forecasts of first marriage for U.S. women. *American Sociological Review* 66, no. 4: 506–519.

Gorman, E. H. 2000. Marriage and money: The effect of marital status on attitudes toward pay and finances. *Work and Occupations* 27, no. 1: 64–88.

Hill, M. S. 1976. The wage effects of marital status and children. *Journal of Human Resources* 14, no. 4: 579–595.

Hogan, D. P., D. J. Eggebeen, and C. C. Clogg. 1993. The structure of intergenerational exchanges in American families. *American Journal of Sociology* 98, no. 6 (May): 1428–1458.

Kalmijn, M. 1998. Intermarriage and monogamy: Causes, patterns, trends. *Annual Review of Sociology* 24:395–421.

———. 2004. Marriage rituals as reinforcers of role transitions: An analysis of weddings in The Netherlands. *Journal of Marriage and the Family* 66, no. 3: 582–594.

Kamp Dush, C. M., C. L. Cohan, and P. R. Amato. 2003. The relationship between cohabitation and marital quality and stability: Changes across cohorts? *Journal of Marriage and Family* 65:539–549.

Korenman, S., and D. Neumark. 1991. Does marriage really make men more productive? *Journal of Human Resources* 39:282–307.

Krause, H. D., and D. D. Meyer. 2003. *Family law: In a nutshell.* 4th ed. St. Paul, Minn.: West Group.

Landes, E. 1978. Economics of alimony. *Journal of Legal Studies* 7:35–63.

Levinger, G. 1976. A social psychological perspective on marital dissolution. *Journal of Social Issues* 32:21–47.

Manning, W., and P. J. Smock. 2005. Measuring and modeling cohabitation: New perspectives from qualitative data. *Journal of Marriage and Family* 67:989–1002.

Martin, S. P. 2006. Trends in marital dissolution by women's education in the United States. *Demographic Research* 15:537–560.

Nock, S. 1998. *Marriage in men's lives.* New York: Oxford University Press.

Oppenheimer, V. K. 1988. A theory of marriage timing. *American Journal of Sociology* 94, no. 3: 563–591.

Parkman, A. 2000. *Good intentions gone awry: No-fault divorce and the American family.* New York: Rowman & Littlefield.

Rauch, J. 2004. *Gay marriage: Why it is good for gays, good for straights, and good for America.* New York: Times Books.

Reiss, D. 1981. *The family's construction of reality.* Cambridge, Mass.: Harvard University Press.

Rowthorn, R. 2002. Marriage as a signal. In A. W. Dnes and R. Rowthorn, eds., *The law and economics of marriage and divorce*, 132–156. Cambridge: Cambridge University Press.

Schneider, C. E., and M. F. Brinig. 2000. *An invitation to family law: Principles, process, and perspectives.* 2nd ed. St. Paul, Minn.: West Group.

Schwartz, C., and R. D. Mare. 2005. Trends in educational assortative marriage from 1940 to 2003. *Demography* 42, no. 4: 621–646.

Scott, E. S. 2000. Social norms and the legal regulation of marriage. *Virginia Law Review* 86, no. 8 (November): 1901–1970.

Scott, E. S., and R. Scott. 1998. Marriage as a relational contract. *Virginia Journal of Law* 76:9–94.

Seltzer, J. A. 2000. Families formed outside of marriage. *Journal of Marriage and the Family* 62:1247–1268.

Smock, P. J. 2000. Cohabitation in the United States: An appraisal of research themes, findings, and implications. *Annual Review of Sociology* 26:1–20.

Spence, M. A. 1973. Job market signaling. *Quarterly Journal of Economics* 87, no. 3 (August): 355–374.

———. 1974. *Market signaling: Informational transfer in hiring and related screening processes.* Cambridge, Mass.: Harvard University Press.

Stanley, S. M., and H. J. Markman. 1992. Assessing commitment in personal relationships. *Journal of Marriage and the Family* 54:595–608.

Trebilcock, M. J. 1999. Marriage as a signal. In F. H. Buckley, ed., *The fall and rise of freedom of contract*, 245–255. Durham, N.C.: Duke University Press.

U.S. Census Bureau. 1985. Marital status and living arrangements: March 1984. *Current population reports*, P-20, no. 399, Table 1.

———. 2006a. Marital status of people 15 years and over, by age, sex, personal earnings, race, and Hispanic origin, 2006. www.census.gov/population/socdemo/hh-fam/cps2006/tabA1-all.csv.

———. 2006b. Current population survey reports. Table A2: America's families and living arrangements.

———. 2007a. Projections of the marital status of the population by age and sex: 1995, 2000, 2005, and 2010, Series 1, 2, and 3. Table 7: National households and families projections.

———. 2007b. *Annual social and economic supplement: Tables.* PINC-02.

———. 2007c. Educational attainment: Historical tables (Table A2). www.census.gov/population/socdemo/education/cps2006/tabA-2.xls.

Wadlington, W., and R. C. O'Brien. 2007. *Family law in context.* 2nd ed. Eagan, Minn.: Foundation.

Waite, L. J. 1995. Does marriage matter? *Demography* 32, no. 4: 483–507.

Wedding Report. 2006. www.theweddingreport.com.

Wolin, S. J., and L. A. Bennett. 1984. Family rituals. *Family Process* 23, no. 3: 401–420.

THIRTEEN

The Future of Marriage and the State

A Proposal

TAMARA METZ

In light of changing social practices, declining consensus about what marriage and family are, or ought to be, and furious political debates these facts engender, what should government do? The previous chapters present a detailed picture of what *is*, of how we Americans arrange our family and marital lives, of how this is changing, and hypotheses about causes and effects of these changes. In this chapter, I address that political question: What *should* government do? What policy toward marriage and families best balances our often-competing commitments to liberty, equality, and stability? To answer this question, I first define "family" and, in broad terms, sketch the demands of liberty, equality and stability applied to legal institutions and public policy concerning family. From these starting points, I assess the current system and recommend reform. I propose that we disestablish marriage as a legal institution, and, in its place, create an intimate caregiving union (ICGU) status, a legal status tailored to protecting both marital and nonmarital families. Current policy, at the core of which is an arrangement I call the *establishment of marriage*, fails families, weakens marriage and threatens our basic political commitments to liberty and equality.[1] Disestablishing marriage and creating an intimate caregiving union status would do better by all of these concerns.

DEFINITIONS AND GUIDING PRINCIPLES

I define "families" as those unions within which the labor of intimate care is given, taken, and received (Levy 2005; Kittay 1999; Tronto 1993). To highlight the inclusiveness of this definition, I also use the terms "intimate caregiving union," "functional families," and "networks of intimate care." Intimate care is that essential (that is, life-sustaining and nurturing) variety of care exchanged in relationships involving utter or provisional dependency/interdependency. It is typically characterized by the unmonitored, noncontractual, and rarely strictly reciprocal exchange of diverse and often incommensurable "goods" (e.g., psychological, social, spiritual, physical, financial and material goods) (Tronto 1993; Kittay 1999).[2] Gary Gates and Adam Romero (see chapter 9) and Rachel Dunifon (see chapter 5), along with other family scholars, describe myriad relationships that fall into this category of "functional families" (McClain 2006; Stacey 2003). These include (de facto) parent-child or (de facto) parents and children; husband and wife; long-term, cohabitating heterosexual and homosexual lovers and partners; "lesbigay" units (Stacey 2003); nonsexually intimate adult units or groups;[3] adult siblings; and adult children and aging parents.

Crucially, though intimate care is uniquely consonant with human attachment, particularity, diversity, and freedom, it is also rife with risk (Elshtain 1982; Fineman 1995; Kittay 1999; Tronto 1993). As economist Nancy Folbre (2001) explains, in our political-economic system this type of work often carries a penalty and thus generates vulnerability.[4] Because this labor is (even ideally) unpaid, unmonitored, and not strictly reciprocal, caring for vulnerable people generates its own physical and material vulnerability, what Fineman (1995) calls "derivative dependency." That relationships of intimate care between unequals (for example, parent and child) involve risk for both the dependent, who is vulnerable to noncare and abuse, and the caregiver, who gives without promise of like return, may seem obvious.[5] But caregiving is also risky among equals. Though return of some sort is typically expected, the unmonitored, unpredictable, and often incommensurable nature of caregiving means that even between able-bodied, able-minded adults caregiving involves serious material and physical risk. Because the risk involved in intimate care generates systematic vulnerabilities and serious disincentives, any society that wishes this work to be done well and its benefits and burdens distributed justly (within and among families), must offer a degree of insurance against these risks.[6] As the entity charged with the task and tools of protecting citizens from physical harm and securing a framework for the just distributions of the costs and benefits of political life, the state is appropriate source of this insurance (Kittay 1999; Okin 1989; Rawls 1971, 1993).

I take it that commitments to liberty, equality, and stability should guide government policy. Broadly, freedom from undue intrusion; freedom to live according to one's own view of what is good, rights to property, privacy, speech, thought, and association; and the deep diversity that flowers with their protection fall under the heading, "liberty." Equality includes formal and substantive equality among and within families. In the present discussion, "stability" refers to conditions under which networks of intimate care are able to engage in their characteristic and essential labor reliably and justly. Crucially, these commitments often conflict: for example, freedom of association weighs in favor of letting people define family for themselves, and yet, in order to support families—a demand of stability—the state must define "family" and therefore limit the freedom of its citizens. The basic challenge of our public policy is finding the right balance in these conflicts. The presumption that the state should remain neutral with respect to matters that do not impinge on the physical and material well-being of citizens has long been central to the liberal democratic approach to negotiating these inevitable conflicts (see Cornell 1998; Locke 1988; Mill 1970, 1997; Rawls 1971, 1993; Shklar 1989). With respect to family life, this approach recommends that the physical and material well-being of families, not marriage per se, be the measure of our family policy.

CURRENT POLICY AND THE ESTABLISHMENT OF MARRIAGE

In the United States today, marriage is established. To say this is to highlight two facts. First, as chapters 5, 7, 9, 10, 12, and 14 in this volume demonstrate, marriage is the favored family form of our public policy (Metz 2007; Fineman 1995; Duggan 1994, 2004; Card 1996). The state *privileges* the marital family in designing and dispersing legal benefits aimed at protecting and supporting networks of intimate care. Legal kinship presumptions (e.g., paternity presumption when a birth occurs within marriage), frameworks for dissolving families, (e.g., settled divorce procedures),[7] and material bonuses for engaging in family life under the marital veil (e.g., the spousal benefits of social security) evince this practice.[8] This is not, of course, to say that other family forms are roundly ignored or excluded from government policies. TANF benefits target nonmarried, single-parent households and food stamps are available regardless of marital status. Still, as a rule the marital family is the preferred form. Government efforts after the

1996 welfare reform to support poor families by strengthening their marriages are perhaps the most striking example of this fact.[9]

Second, the state exercises final say over the content and public use of the marital label, and thus serves an integral role in the meaning side of marriage. By the meaning side of marriage, I mean the diverse sociocultural significance attached to and expressed by marriage. This unique, extralegal, social significance, I will argue, explains the difference between marital status and an instrumental status such as registered domestic partner. Although the state is lenient with most extralegal use of the marital label, it can and does exercise final control over the public, even nonlegal use of the term "marriage." Take the case of polygamist Tom Green, who ended up in jail for violating Utah's laws against plural marriage *despite* the fact that he and his "spiritual wives" scrupulously avoided seeking legal recognition for their unions (*Utah v. Green* 2001).[10] Green, it seems, was prosecuted for misusing even the extralegal marital label. Government wields control of "marriage" over and against all other public authorities—religious and secular—and in doing so serves as *the* predominant authority in the reproduction not just of a legal status but also of a comprehensive social institution. In sum, to call marriage established is to draw attention to the integral place of marriage in state policy and to the central role assumed by the state in defining (a particular version of) marriage.

SHORTCOMINGS OF CURRENT POLICY

The legal privilege that marriage enjoys violates our guiding political commitments: it fails families, weakens marriage, and threatens both equality and liberty. It does so as the result of two sets of problems: the first stems from the use of marriage to identify families worthy of government protection and support. I call these the target problems. The second concerns the role the state assumes when it wields final control over the public meaning and use of the marital label. I call these the authority problems.

Target Problems

When government uses marriage as the privileged model of family, two undesirable consequences follow. First, as a matter of policy, an array of families with which the state should be concerned (but who are not defined by marriage) are unduly disadvantaged or excluded from its protective purview. If it is the case that the state has a key role to play insuring the labor of intimate care, then from our commitments to equality, liberty, and stability it follows that the state must recognize and support all unions within which it is a central activity—that is, families of all types. Thus, as it is currently crafted, state family policy fails families, and violates liberty and equality because, very simply, it misses its mark. When marital status is the primary avenue for a flow of legal benefits, many families are left out or unduly disadvantaged (Fineman 1995; Metz 2007; Smith 2007).[11] In most jurisdictions legal presumptions—concerning, for instance, inheritance and adoption—crafted to support the special commitments and risks of families are tied to marital status. In these instances, single-parent and same-sex families and groups of nonsexually intimate caregivers (siblings or postmarriage collectives, for example) are seriously disadvantaged. The state thus violates the principle of equality, of treating similarly situated citizens—in this case, intimate caregivers—alike. Moreover, because its protections serve some families more fully than others, this policy threatens equality among families and within families (between primary caregivers and others). Primary caregivers in families supported by the state have the insurance of settled dissolution and inheritance policies to reduce the risk of their labor. This is not so for such caregivers in nonmarital families.

By missing the appropriate target of family policy, the establishment of marriage interferes with liberty in many ways. It violates what we might call freedom of marital expression when it prosecutes fundamentalist Mormons for using the label but not prosecuting non-Mormons engaged in functionally similar relationships. More importantly, this arrangement violates liberty by limiting social insurance against the risks of intimate care; because intimate care done well and fairly depends on this insurance, when it is withheld, the freedom of intimate association is threatened. Think of same-sex adoptive parents whose joint parenthood is not presumed, or unmarried long-term couples for whom joint home ownership is more expensive or riskier (if they opt not to pay lawyers to resolve the legal complications of their ownership). Both examples illustrate how people who wish to arrange their intimate caregiving lives outside the marital norm do not, under current policy, have the same range of freedom to do so.

The second target problem that arises from the establishment of marriage is that of skewed public discourse: the focus on marriage distracts us from the matter of real import, and directs us toward the impossible task of defining marriage. The matter of real concern ought to be the costs and benefits, distribution and needs of actual intimate caregiving arrangements. Does the paid labor force accommodate those who provide intimate care to children or elderly parents? When it does not, who "pays" and how? Women? Children? Underpaid public care providers? If the costs and benefits of care are to be acknowledged and justly distributed, they cannot remain hidden behind the veil of marriage. If the penalty for engaging in the essential labor of intimate care is to be relieved, its existence must be acknowledged in our public-policy debates. Government policy that focuses on marriage distracts us from these concerns.

At the same time, such policy directs our attention toward the impossible task of arriving at a widely shared, nontrivial definition of marriage. It is not surprising that citizens cannot agree on a substantive definition of marriage; the integral ties to deeply divergent worldviews are what make marriage so important to people. These ties explain the difference between marital status and civil union.[12] Even when marriage and civil union provide citizens with the same legal benefits (which they rarely do), they always *mean* different things.[13] The legal status of marriage draws on the reservoir of meaning attached to often incommensurable visions of the institutions that exist outside the law. And for this reason, we can hardly expect citizens to agree on a single definition of marriage.

That citizens cannot agree upon a definition is not problematic—as far as government policy is concerned. The state does not need take sides in *this* disagreement. What government must do is take sides on what counts as intimate care. This question will, of course, provoke controversy. But compared to the controversy surrounding marriage, an open debate about what counts as a network of intimate care will be more fruitful and fairer. Such a debate will be more fruitful because the focus will be limited to questions about function and material concerns and away from larger disagreements about marriage. Discussions will thus be less infused with profoundly irreconcilable questions of religious or other comprehensive moral beliefs. By honing the focus of the debates, we increase our chances of finding common ground. To the extent that the discussion focuses on intimate caregiving of all sorts, it is also likely that the resulting policy would be more effective and fairer.

Many reject the claim that deserving families are unduly disadvantaged by marriage-centered family policy (Blankenhorn 2007; Elshtain 1982; Galston 1996a, 1996b; Shell 2004; Waite and Gallagher 2000). While they agree that the material well-being of families must be the driving concern of the state, they argue that because of the proven benefits of marriage, public policy should channel people into its folds.[14] Government cannot be perfectly neutral with respect to all choices, and must not be where the safety and well-being children and caregivers are at issue. This pro-establishment camp argues that the benefits of crafting laws and regulations to discourage the formation of extra-marital families far outweigh the costs. Some, whom I call pro-establishment conservatives, go a step further and argue that marriage should be reserved for hetero-monogamous couples (Blankenhorn 2007; Defense of Marriage Act 1996; Shell 2004).

There is another version of the pro-establishment position more fully committed to freedom of familial choice and equality within and among families. I call this the progressive pro-establishment position (McClain 2006; Shanley 2004). Defenders of this view hold that families of all forms deserve government support, but they contend that the problem with current policy is not its marriage-centricity but rather the too-narrow definition of marriage. Same-sex marriage advocates and feminist scholars such as Mary Lyndon Shanley (2004) and Linda McClain (2006) argue that the legal status must be made available to couples who are "functionally equivalent" to heterosexual couples who may now assume the status (Stacey 2003). Feminist proponents of this position pair their defenses of expanding marriage with a serious concern for inequality within and among all types of intimate caregiving unions, and thus advocate for enhanced public support for all functional families, marital or not. Still, they expressly reject the call by a growing number of scholars for the abolition of marriage as a legal category (Fineman 1995; Duggan 1994, 2004; Card 1996; Warner 1999; Metz 2007). The state should use marriage as a tool in its family policy because, they claim, it is especially well suited to providing intimate caregiving unions with the recognition, protection, and support they need (McClain 2006; Shanley 2004).

The pro-establishment progressives point to two features of marriage in defending the reformed establishment of marriage. Marriage, they argue, is especially well suited to the task of supporting intimate caregiving because it is a public status, and not simply a contract. As a status, marriage provides a mechanism with which society (via the state) can insure against the risks of intimate care without egregiously limiting choice within the union, undermining norms of unmonitored reciprocity, or bolstering existing inequalities (McClain 2006; Minow and Shanley 1996; Shanley 2004). Contract, in contrast, may facilitate individual choice, but as Pateman (1988) argues, it merely reproduces existing power relations; given the pervasiveness of gender inequality and the inequalities inherent in intimate care, this is problematic. Furthermore, contract requires that terms be delineated and held into the unforeseeable future. Thus, it threatens the norms of unpredictable and changing reciprocity that ideally characterize intimate relations. Contract is an inadequate tool for state protection of intimate caregiving unions, even when they involve only able adults (and no utter dependents).

Pro-establishment progressives argue convincingly that status—a predetermined bundle of rights and responsibilities—can provide protection from egregious inequality, by building equality protections into its terms, without violating privacy or undermining norms of noncontractual reciprocity. For example, in exchange for the benefit of being able to share material resources without taxation or monitoring, couples agree—in most states in the United States—to a presumed equitable division of material assets should they dissolve their union (Lehman and Phelps 2005). Status can also provide presumptive protection against state regulation of parenting practices without fully cordoning off the family from the demands of justice.[15] Thus, status is the best mechanism for the state to simultaneously secure families against the risks of intimate care, support the norms of unmonitored reciprocity, and protect a significant degree of privacy. On this point, the pro-establishment progressives are convincing.

Yet they do not, as they assume, therefore make a case for marriage. All of the virtues they attribute to marital status in terms of protecting intimate care unions can be easily obtained with an instrumental status such as the proposed ICGU status. That marriage is a status does not, therefore, justify its establishment.

The second feature that pro-establishment progressives claim makes marriage an important focus of family policy is that marriage is not just any status, it is a special status, what I call a *constitutive* status. This status has the power to transform both those who accept it and those who confer it, from the inside out. In its groundbreaking decision, the Massachusetts Supreme Judicial Court wrote, "Civil marriage is at once a deeply personal commitment to another human being and a highly public celebration of the ideals of mutuality, companionship, intimacy, fidelity, and family" (*Goodridge* 2003). Commentator Jonathan Rauch elaborates: "Marriage does much more than ratify relationships . . . it fortifies relationships by embedding them in a dense web of social expectations" (Rauch 2007). Echoing Rauch, Shanley (2004) describes marriage as "a special bond and public status . . . a relationship that transcends the individual lives of the partners" in which the "public has a legitimate interest."

There is no doubt that, as these commentators claim, "marriage" carries special social significance and that any legal status so labeled participates in this resource. The state's definition and use of the marital label draws upon reservoirs of meaning and norms that exist outside the law. Further, for many people this extra value affects belief and behavior. As writers as diverse as Augustine, Hegel, Rauch, and Shanley argue, in the right circumstances marriage has the power to transform individuals from the inside out, to change their basic self-understandings, and to integrate them on the deepest levels with their spouses and their community. This, I propose, is at the heart of the logic of the version of marriage that has dominated American legal, social, and political traditions (Metz 2007). The pro-establishment camp is right that marriage is more than any instrumental legal status. Where its proponents go wrong is in their assumptions about value and effects of government involvement in and use of this status and the extra value it carries.

Here we arrive at the second set of problems with the establishment of marriage: the authority problem.

The Authority Problem

What both the conservative and progressive pro-establishment positions fail to appreciate are the serious and unnecessary costs—to marriage, families, liberty, and equality—of state involvement in the reproduction of and reliance on the constitutive purposes and effects of marriage. When government serves as the controlling public authority vis-à-vis marriage it assumes the role of what I call *ethical authority*, for which it neither is nor ought to be suited. The establishment of marriage casts the state in a role that it fills poorly, and risks violating the type of neutrality necessary for the state to secure liberty and equality in a diverse polity such as ours. For all of these reasons, the establishment of marriage weakens families.

To illustrate my point, let us return to Shanley's (2004) claim, echoed throughout public discourse, from judicial decisions to politician's podiums, that marriage is "a special bond and public status . . . a relationship that transcends the individual lives of the partners." This seems a fair first-cut description of what distinguishes marriage from, say, civil union. Still, if we wish to know whether the state's control and use of the status is good or necessary we need to ask how the public status of marriage affects the transcendence to which Shanley refers, and what this potential assumes about the conferring authority? Like most in the progressive pro-establishment camp, Shanley gives us little to go on.[16] Conservatives tend to say a bit more (see Blankenhorn 2007; Rauch 2004; Schneider 1999). Schneider, for instance, describes marriage law as the paradigmatic example of how the state uses its instrumental tool—law—to draw upon the forces of religion and culture to secure its aims. The legal status of marriage alters belief through its association with these extralegal institutions. But just how deeply engaged in which of the competing religious and cultural versions of marriage must the state be in order to elicit these special powers? The worry is that the state must engage too intimately, and thus violate limits necessary to secure liberty and equality in a diverse society.

One way to read Schneider's claim is that the relation between marriage law and the transformative power it elicits is merely coincidental. That the state's use of the "m word" elicits deeply religious and cultural associations for many people is but a side effect of its use of a technically instrumental status (Opinions 2004). This explanation squares with our commitments to a limited, sometimes neutral state, but it does not make much sense. If the association is coincidental, then why is there such heated opposition to changing the legal definition? Why the fear that changing the legal definition will fundamentally alter marriage? Steven Nock's very plausible description of one popular understanding of marriage (see chapter 12) does not help much on this count, for he does not identify a meaning unique to marriage. If it does not already, civil union will, no doubt, with time come to signal long-term commitment to intimacy and care.

The more plausible explanation of what the pro-establishment defenders assume is that when the state recognizes and regulates marriage as such, it participates as an integral player in the production or reproduction of a particular version of the social institution of marriage. As a matter of history and institutional logic, marriage not only ratifies but also "fortifies relationships" (Rauch 2007) by conveying what we can call *constitutive* or *ethical recognition*—the moral approval and the complex normative account of the relationship it names. Think of what many understand to be happening when a couple stands in front of its community—whether a collection of hippies in a northern California redwood grove or a traditional congregation in a Catholic church—and accepts the marital status bestowed by that community. The community's conferral and the couple's acceptance of marital status are understood as acts intended to alter the way each sees and relates to the other.

Note what this assumes about the relation between the community that confers the label and the recipients. The conferring authority must represent and defend a comprehensive story about the relationships (between the individuals in the couple, and the couple and the community) it labels and represents. The public performance of these accounts transforms by enacting, celebrating, and calling for public defense of the shared understandings they express. Think of bar mitzvah or baptismal status: they are conferred with the aim of altering beliefs, to integrate individuals into the norms and beliefs that define the community. By calling on the ethical authority of a community of shared worldviews, these statuses alter self-understandings. In short, if marriage is fundamentally different from civil union because of its power to transform beliefs and especially, self-understanding—a popular and plausible claim—then when the state fills the role of controlling public authority it assumes the role of ethical authority. This in turn rests on the existence of a community of comprehensive belief.

We can now see why it is especially appropriate to speak of marriage as established. Just as the "establishment of religion" refers to the state's involvement in defining, inculcating and reproducing a particular religious worldview and institution, so the "establishment of marriage" highlights the state's integral role in reproducing and relying on belief in a particular, institutional form of intimate life and its tie to the community. The comparison to religion highlights the second fact not appreciated by pro-establishment advocates, even the progressives: when it fills the role of primary controller of marriage, the state fails on two counts (beyond the equality issue discussed above). It fails liberty. The role of the public authority in marriage is not merely incidental. It is integral to the transformative potential of marriage. As the primary public authority in marriage, the state engages in a role, the basic purpose of which is to alter the self-understandings of those who assume and those who honor the label. In this position, the state intrudes on the realm of belief, and thus it violates one of the most basic liberal mechanisms for protecting liberty. For good reason, the role of the ethical authority is far more familiar to us from the realm of religion than that of politics. By design the liberal state is more distant, neutral, and uninvolved with the beliefs of its citizens than the picture just sketched. The familiar idea behind the limited state is that freedom consists, in large part, in individuals being free from interference to live according to their own design. Marriage asks for and depends on much more from its regulating authority than what the liberal state can or should try to give.

In this role the state also fails marriage and by extension all families who depend on its special powers to bolster their existence. The liberal state is ill suited to serve as an ethical authority, and so when it functions as the public authority of greatest significance vis-à-vis marriage, the state actually threatens marriage by undermining the force of its constitutive sway. Again, the example of bar mitzvah status is helpful. We would doubt both the effectiveness of the status and the justice of the action were the state to start doling out bar mitzvah status. To effect its psychosocial transformation, the status must come from a community of shared religious belief and from Jewish religious leaders, as representatives of the community of belief that gives the status meaning. For the state to try to fill this role would rightly be seen as inappropriate—a violation of even the least restrictive variety of state neutrality—and, crucially, ineffective.

THE CASE FOR DISESTABLISHING MARRIAGE AND CREATING ICGU STATUS

If marriage requires constitutive recognition from an ethical authority, yet the liberal democratic state cannot (and should not try to) effectively provide such recognition, what is to be done? Must we choose between a healthy marital institution and liberal commitments and institutional arrangements? My answer is no. The suggestion implicit in the comparison to religion—that there may be good reason for the state to withdraw from its pivotal role in controlling marital status—is compelling. Disestablishing marriage would mean that the state would withdraw from its current role in defining and controlling marriage; it would not confer marital status or use "marriage" as a category for dispersing benefits or assigning legal obligations. Marital status would be left to voluntary associations, religious, ethical, and cultural entities that wield ethical authority more effectively and justly than does the state.

In place of marriage, we could create ICGU status. In many ways, it would look like marital status today (Metz 2007). It would afford legal recognition from which would flow various legal presumptions (lines of rights and responsibilities), protection from certain types of intrusion, and material benefits (tax advantages and the like). As with marital status now,

ICGU status would be defined, conferred, and if necessary, dissolved by the state. Unlike marriage, however, ICGU status would be expressly tailored to protecting intimate care in its various forms. So, for example, the status would reflect assumptions of longevity and resource sharing. To protect the norms of unmonitored reciprocity and to protect caregivers, at dissolution property would be divided to achieve substantive postdissolution equality. Crucially, ICGU status would be designed with instrumental not constitutive purposes in mind. Any special expressive significance attached to ICGU status would be incidental.

These reforms would address both the target and the authority problems of our current family policy and thus better balance our commitments to liberty, equality and stability. They would shift the focus of public policy and discussion from marriage to intimate care. Exposing the real costs and benefits of caregiving would increase the chances that public support would be well crafted. For example, workplace policy would reflect the needs of intimate caregivers by providing for ample leave and flexible schedules. Policies would also be better targeted. Kinship presumptions would be, for example, as readily available to sexually intimate unions as to nonsexually intimate unions. Replacing marriage as the primary means for supporting intimate caregiving with a narrowly focused instrumental status would increase the chances that *all* actual caregivers would be served equally by the law. Further, by exposing and more effectively addressing the realities of the derivative vulnerabilities and gender inequalities often created by current intimate caregiving arrangements, the changes would benefit gender equality.

Freedom of intimate association would also benefit under the proposed regime. In the American constitutional tradition, for instance, marriage has long served to justify protection of this freedom (*Bowers v. Hardwick* 1986; Cornell 1998; *Griswold v. Connecticut* 1965; *Loving v. Virginia* 1967; *Zablocki v. Redhail* 1978). Doing away with the marital category would be one crucial step in dislodging marriage from its seat as the reigning proxy for relationships that need and deserve such protection. The move would help highlight the fact that all human beings—married or not, heterosexual, homosexual, single, paired, sexual or celibate—need a space within which to imagine and enact their social intimate lives. Further, just as the nonestablishment of religion insures that a citizen's right to vote cannot depend on her religious affiliation, so too the disestablishment of marriage would guarantee that government-provided benefits for intimate caregiving would not hinge on an individual's public acceptance of a particular vision of marriage. Disentangling marriage from government support of intimate caregiving would therefore solve the target problem of current policy.

Disestablishing marriage and creating an ICGU status would also address the authority problem. Government authority, unique though circumscribed as it is, would concern itself with basic physical and material security of citizens, and not with their beliefs. On the most basic level, releasing "marriage" from the hands of government would protect a unique kind of expression. Unlike under the current regime where citizens can be prosecuted for unsanctioned use of the marital title—as was polygamist Tom Green—under the proposed regime, citizens who wished to call themselves married could do so without fear of state punishment (*Utah v. Green* 2001). As with bar mitzvah status, nongovernmental authorities would confer the label. While it would carry no legal weight, marriage would still carry its constitutive potential. Call this the freedom of marital expression.

Conversely, by vacating its current place vis-à-vis marriage, the state would free up space for authorities better suited to dealing in the constitutive recognition in which marriage trades. If I am right about the extra value of marital status, then *state* control is not essential to its realization. On the contrary, the constitutive potential of marriage depends on power that the state does not and ought not attempt to possess: ethical authority. The key to effective ethical authority in marriage is that there is a shared understanding that the conferrer possesses the authority to bestow and wield the resulting responsibility that their shared vision of marriage entails. Nonstate entities—associations of civil society—represent just such potential authorities. Such an authority might, for some people, be a religious leader. For others an ethical authority might be the head of a cultural group or the esteemed representative of one's family.[17] So, by releasing "marriage" from state control into the arms of these entities, the nonestablishment of marriage places control of a constitutive status into the hands of those best suited for wielding it effectively, and therefore marriage is likely to benefit.

In addition, under the proposed regime, acquiring marital status would be the ticket to the ethical recognition of a community of shared understandings and not to a vast array of legal and material benefits. Changing the benefits would change the motivations for seeking the status. As many same sex couples do already, couples would acquire marital status when they wanted meaningful recognition from a community that held ethical sway in their lives (Campton 2004; Goodstein 2004). Moreover, shifting control of marital status to voluntary groups in civil society would increase the likelihood that marital status would be assumed in the context of a community of shared understandings about marriage. This improved fit between the couple's understanding of marriage and that of their conferring community could also bolster the transformative force of marital status. By shifting control of marriage to cultural authorities and their diverse—and, admittedly, not always liberal accounts of marriage—a point to which I return shortly, the proposed regime would benefit marriage by invigorating the constitutive force of the status.

My proposal is likely to elicit numerous objections. Here I address two. The first concerns equality: if marriage is left to associations of civil society, do we not run the risk of pushing further from public scrutiny the inequality and oppression often shrouded behind the conjugal veil? For instance, would not disestablishing marriage effectively allow polygamy and therefore promote gender inequality? This worry invites three responses: First, were marriage disestablished, some groups would openly sanction polygamous marriage, and undoubtedly gender inequality would flourish in many of these unions. These groups might assume ICGU status. They would, therefore, gain support and protection from the state. Crucially, however, they would receive support by virtue of their willingness to enter into the civil status, with its protection and responsibilities for caregiving activities. In this sense, my proposal promotes gender inequality no more than do current regimes that permit but do not ostensibly promote traditional (gendered) marriage.[18] Second, gender equality would benefit under the proposed regime because the increased recognition of and support for caregiving would insure that even women who opted for traditional gendered marriages would be less vulnerable as a result of gendered division of power and labor within their families. Public policies would be crafted to protect all intimate caregivers; those who opt to care full-time might, for instance, receive financial support from the government. Less radically, unpaid labor would be factored into postdivorce settlements. Still, the critic might say, by increasing the power of potentially illiberal communities the proposal promises to increase their sway over the way people *think* and therefore, behave, and this is no small power. To this, I offer a third response: we must balance liberty, equality, and stability. Even with this very real danger, I believe that the proposed model does a better job balancing these commitments. It increases liberty by limiting the objects and intent of state action without relinquishing influence over the most significant sources of inequality and instability (especially the material and physical risks assumed by primary caregivers).

The second objection contends that mine is a rather incoherent "anything goes" policy. This worry is misplaced. Both marriage and ICGU status reflect value judgments. In defining and conferring either status, the state is acting in a way that reflects particular political commitments. There are compelling liberal reasons for the state to recognize, protect, and support intimate caregiving. The case against state control of marriage is not that it reflects a substantive commitment, but rather that it entangles the state in an institution, the primary purpose of which is to alter self-understanding in ways that go beyond what it necessary to the legitimate public welfare concerns of the state. I agree with these critics that "marriage" matters: it carries a unique value, beyond the material and legal benefits that attach to it, even beyond the generic expressive goods that comes with any legally privileged position. To ignore this extra value is naïve and detrimental for marriage, equality, liberty, and fairness. But marriage is not the only or even the best means by which stable caregiving relationships can be understood and protected. It is, for the potential benefits to those who are moved by marriage, an institution that should be afforded public support and protection. From civil society, marriage can receive its constitutive recognition. From the state, marriage and all other caregiving relationships can and should receive instrumental support. Disestablishing marriage and creating an ICGU would best balance our often-competing commitments to liberty, equality, and stability.

NOTES

I would like to thank Shannah Metz and Amanda Ufheil-Somers for research assistance and the editors of this volume for their generous feedback on this chapter.

1. I borrow this term from Nancy Cott (2000). I am not the first recent scholar to recommend that we abolish marriage as a legal category. Feminist legal theorist Martha Fineman and queer theorists such as Claudia Card, Lisa Duggan, and Michael Warner are pioneers on this count. And our company grows. For the details of what disestablishment would take away from our legal framework, Fineman's (1995) description is one of the best. I add to this argument in at least two ways. First, where Fineman works within the American legal tradition, I make the case from within the broader tradition of liberal political thought and practice. Second, I defend ICGU as an essential alternative to the current policy. On this point, Fineman and I diverge significantly.

2. Here I draw on Joan Tronto's more general definition of care, as the kind of activity that contributes to the maintenance of the world we inhabit. More precisely: care is an ongoing activity that involves four phases: caring about (recognition), taking care of (assuming responsibility), caregiving (direct meeting of needs), and care receiving (object of care responds) (Tronto 1993). In contrast to nondependent intimate relationships, such as (typical, noncaregiving) friendships or sexual liaisons, typical intimate caregiving relationships involve deeper and often diverse (material, emotional, physical, and psychological) interdependencies. In contrast to nonintimate care, which may involve utter dependency but is basically public, intimate caregiving is basically private: it is largely unmonitored by outside parties, is motivated primarily by noncontractual ties, and rarely involves systematic financial exchange.
3. See the *New York Times* article on widowed women pooling resources and living together (Gross 2004). The question of whether groups of sexually intimate adults and their children should be considered intimate caregiving units is, in my view, quite simple. If they provide intimate care as described, then the answer is yes. Polygamous units may also be intimate caregiving units. I shall defend the possibility that these units receive support from the state. They are not, however, common enough to be included in this list. In any case, polygamous units are too provocative to include without explanation.
4. See also Tronto 1993.
5. Of course, caregiving also produces unique, priceless rewards that most caregivers would not quickly give up. Unfortunately—to paraphrase the Harvard janitorial union—one cannot eat these kinds of rewards.
6. Since human survival and flourishing rely on care, any time one human being exists and interacts with another, we know that care has already been exchanged. This means, as theorists of care argue, that the real political and ethical questions with regard to care are not whether it happens, but how: by whom, to whom, in what manner, and with what support? Here I follow numerous theorists of care, among them Tronto, Folbre, and Fineman.
7. The exclusivity and value of this benefit was recently highlighted when the Rhode Island Supreme Court refused to allow a same-sex couple, married under Massachusetts law, to divorce in a Rhode Island court.
8. See, for example, Kennedy 1988. For further elaboration see Card 1996; Duggan 1994, 2004; Fineman 1995; Metz 2007; and Warner 1999.
9. See chapters 4 and 10 in this volume for descriptions of these programs. See also: Healthy Marriage Initiative, Administration for Children and Families. Available at www.acf.hhs.gov/healthymarriage/index.html.
10. This contrasts with those who give no public title to their (multiple) sexual and childbearing unions but are left, in practice and in technical legal terms, in most

states, free to do as they choose. Though twenty-three states criminalize adultery, few actually enforce these laws and legal scholars note a legal trend in the direction of decriminalizing adultery. See Falco 2004:743–46; Green 1989 (discussing enforcement of adultery statutes); Posner and Silbaugh 1996:98.

11. Martha Fineman persuasively shows that when the state uses marital status as the primary avenue through which to support caregiving, it significantly disadvantages many actual caregivers. Social-welfare policies aimed at discouraging unwed single motherhood are powerful examples of this dynamic. Not only do such policies perpetuate the view that single motherhood is bad in itself, but they actually make it more difficult to be a successful single mother (Fineman 1995:100–142).
12. It is precisely for this reason that the Vermont decision to create a parallel status scheme—marriage for straights and civil union for gays, on the basis of equal protection logic—is simply but revealingly incoherent. The strange aversion in many judicial rulings to admitting or fully elaborating, embracing this fact reflects unresolved tensions in traditions of liberal thought and practice with respect to the relationship between marriage and the state (see Metz 2007).
13. In chapter 12 in this volume, Steven Nock sketches one way in which the social significance of marriage is changing. What he does not address are alternative ways that people might express elements of the message he attributes to marriage. For instance, I suspect that with time civil union will carry for many similar connotations of responsibility and commitment.
14. One influential book on the subject argues that it makes people healthier, happier, and wealthier (Waite and Gallagher 2000).
15. See, e.g., Smith 2007 for an account of the ills of unprotected privacy of poor families.
16. See Metz 2007 for an extended discussion of the history of this particular silence in liberal theory and practice.
17. For those skeptical about the claim that informal, secular groups will produce ethical authorities capable of conferring effective constitutive recognition, see Lehmann-Haupt 2003.
18. Perhaps the best description of the dangers of traditional, gendered marriage is to be found in Okin 1989. Chapter 3 in this volume also analyzes marriage and gender inequality.

REFERENCES

Blankenhorn, D. 2007. *The future of marriage*. New York: Encounter.

Bowers v. Hardwick. 1986. 478 U.S. 186.

Campton, T. 2004. At a gay synagogue, a rabbi isn't fazed by legalities. *New York Times*, March 21.

Card, C. 1996. Against marriage and motherhood. *Hypatia* 11, no. 3: 1–23.

Coontz, S. 2005. *Marriage: A history.* New York: Viking Penguin.

Cornell, D. 1998. *At the heart of freedom: Feminism, sex, and equality.* Princeton: Princeton University Press.

Cott, Nancy. 2000. *Public vows: A history of marriage and the nation.* Cambridge, Mass.: Harvard University Press.

Defense of Marriage Act of 1996. 1996. Public Law No. 104–199, 110, Stat. 2419.

Duggan, L. 1994. Queering the state. *Social Text* 39:1–14.

———. 2004. Holy matrimony! *The Nation* 278, no. 10: 14–19.

Elshtain, J. 1982. Feminism, family, and community. *Dissent* 29:442–449.

Falco, M.C. 2004. The road not taken: Using the eighth amendment to strike down criminal punishment for engaging in consensual sexual acts. *North Carolina Law Review* 82:723–758.

Fineman, M.A. 1995. *The neutered mother, the sexual family and other twentieth century tragedies.* New York: Routledge.

Folbre, N. 2001. *The invisible heart: Economics and family values.* New York: New Press.

Galston, W. 1996a. Divorce American style. *The Public Interest* 124:12–17.

———. 1996b. Reinstitutionalization of marriage: Political theory and public policy. In D. Popenoe, J.B. Elshtain, and D. Blankenhorn, eds., *Promises to keep: The decline and renewal of marriage in America*, 271–290. Lanham, Md.: Rowman & Littlefield.

Goodridge v. Department of Public Health. 2003. 440 Mass. 309.

Goodstein, L. 2004. Gay couples seek unions in god's eyes. *New York Times*, January 20.

Green, R. 1989. Griswold's legacy: Fornication and adultery as crimes. *Ohio Northern University Law Review* 16:545–549.

Griswold v. Connecticut. 1965. 381 U.S. 479.

Gross, J. 2004. Older women team up to face future together. *New York Times*, February 27.

Kennedy, S. 1988. Ruling Clouds Inheritance of Rentals. *New York Times*, March 20.

Kittay, E.F. 1999. *Love's labor: Essays on women, equality and dependency.* New York: Routledge.

Lehman, J., and S. Phelps, eds. 2005. *West's encyclopedia of American law.* Detroit: Thomson/Gale.

Lehmann-Haupt, R. 2003. Need a minister? How about your brother? *New York Times*, January 12.

Levy, T. M. 2005. At the intersection of intimacy and care: Redefining the family through the lens of a public ethic of care. *Politics and Gender* 1, no. 1: 65–95.

Locke, J. 1988. *Two treatises of government.* Ed. P. Laslett. Cambridge: Cambridge University Press.

Loving v. Virginia. 1967. 388 U.S. 1.

McClain, L. 2003. Intimate affiliation and democracy: Beyond marriage? *Hofstra Law Review* 32:379–421.

———. 2006. *The place of families: Fostering capacities, equality and responsibility.* Cambridge, Mass.: Harvard University Press.

Metz, T. 2007. The liberal case for disestablishing marriage. *Contemporary Political Theory* 6:196–217.

Mill, J. S. 1997. On liberty. In A. Ryan, ed., *Mill: Texts and Commentaries*, 41–131. New York: Norton.

Mill, J. S., and H. T. Mill. 1970. The subjection of women. In A. Rossi, ed., *Essays on sex equality*, 123–242. Chicago: University of Chicago Press.

Minow, M., and M. L. Shanley. 1996. Relational rights and responsibilities: Revisioning the family in liberal political theory and law. *Hypatia* 11, no. 1: 4–29.

Okin, S. M. 1989. *Justice, gender and the family.* New York: Basic Books.

Opinions of the Justices to the Senate. 2004. 440 Mass. 1201.

Pateman, C. 1988. *The sexual contract.* Stanford, Calif.: Stanford University Press.

Posner, R. A., and K. B. Silbaugh. 1996. *A guide to America's sex laws.* Chicago: University of Chicago Press.

Rauch, J. 2004. *Gay marriage: Why it is good for gays, good for straights, and good for America.* New York: Henry Holt.

———. 2007. Family reunion: The case against the case against gay marriage. *Democracy: A Journal of Ideas.* www.democracyjournal.org.

Rawls, J. 1971. *A theory of justice.* Cambridge, Mass.: Harvard University Press.

———. 1993. *Political liberalism.* New York: Columbia University Press.

Schneider, C. E. 1999. The channelling function in family law. In M. F. Brinig, C. E. Schneider, and L. E. Teitelbaum, eds., *Family law in action: A reader*, 406–515. New York: Oxford University Press.

Shanley, M. L. 2004. *Just marriage.* New York: Oxford University Press.

Shell, S. 2004. The liberal case against gay marriage. *The Public Interest* 156:3–15.

Shklar, J. 1989. Liberalism of fear. In N. Rosenblum, ed., *Liberalism and the moral life*, 3–20. Cambridge, Mass.: Harvard University Press.

Smith, A. M. 2007. *Welfare reform and sexual regulation.* New York: Cambridge University Press.

Stacey, J. 2003. Toward equal regard for marriages and other imperfect intimate affiliations. *Hofstra Law Review* 32:331–348.

Tronto, J. 1993. *Moral boundaries: A political argument for an ethic of care.* New York: Routledge.

Utah v. Green. 2001. WL 422825 (Utah App.).

Waite, L. J., and M. Gallagher. 2000. *The case for marriage.* New York: Doubleday.

Warner, M. 1999. *The trouble with normal.* Cambridge, Mass.: Harvard University Press.

Zablocki v. Redhail. 1978. 434 U.S. 374.

Why Won't African Americans Get (and Stay) Married? Why Should They?

FOURTEEN

SHIRLEY A. HILL

The extent to which African American families conform to mainstream family ideologies was the focus of much scholarly debate throughout the twentieth century, with the prevalence of single-mother families being at the center of that debate. Early research explained single-mother families as a legacy of slavery and offered a class analysis of black families that characterized them matriarchal, dysfunctional, and a barrier to socioeconomic mobility. This work, however, was thoroughly challenged during the civil-rights era of the 1960s as revisionist scholars studied the family lives of enslaved black people (Blassingame 1972; Gutman 1976) and drew parallels between the family systems of precolonial Africans, slaves, and contemporary African American families (Nobles 1974). Social historians studying enslaved families argued that two-parent families were and had always been the statistical norm among African Americans, even during slavery, and that persistent racism was more responsible for single-mother families than slavery (Gutman 1976). This broader scholarship led those who were studying contemporary African American families to shift their focus from their deficiencies to their cultural strengths, often highlighting the adaptive strategies (e.g., extended families) that had enabled them survive slavery, economic exclusion, and institutional racism (Allen 1978; Billingsley 1968; 1972; Stack 1974).

This cultural-strengths framework still informs much research on African American families, but it is not without critics. More recent researchers, for example, have contested the notion that two-parent families were the norm among enslaved African Americans, asserting that this assumes a universality in their family experiences that simply did not exist. Instead, social-structural factors produced a diversity of family forms among slaves (Dunaway 2003; Franklin 1997). The decline in the quality of life for low-income African American families during the 1980s, as seen in weaker extended family ties, a decrease in marriage, and the rise in nonmarital childbearing and welfare dependency, also seemed to assert the primacy of social-structural forces, namely the rise of the postindustrial economy (Wilson 1978), in shaping families. Cultural theorists were at a loss to explain why the cultural traditions that had enabled black families to survive centuries of slavery and racial oppression were so weakened by economic restructuring. Moreover, the historic focus on the strengths of *families* had never offered much analysis of African American *marriages*, yet by the 1990s black women were the *least* likely to marry and the *most* likely to become single mothers.

Between 1930 and 1944, black men married at an earlier age than white men (23.3 compared to 24.3) (Koball 1998). Heather Koball notes that during this era black men, mostly as tenant-farmers, were more likely to be employed full-time than white men and benefited from the labor of their wives and children. But even more important, she argues, was the fact that their life options were constrained by their low levels of education and concentration in the poor, rural South. Despite this high rate of marriage, very little is known about the quality and resilience of African American marriages during this era, but it is likely that both cultural traditions (e.g., female-centered families) and structural forces (e.g., racism, economic hardship, northward migration) converged to heighten their risk of marital separation and divorce (Frazier 1957; Marks 1989).

By 1945 a racial crossover in marriage had occurred, with blacks marrying later and less often than whites (Koball 1998). By the 1950s, 88 percent of African American and 95 percent of white American women entered marriage (Cherlin 2008). The marriage decline continued at an accelerated rate for African Americans in the ensuing decades. During the 1970s, the rate of marriage among women under the age of twenty fell for all racial groups, but much more dramatically for African American women (Fitch and Ruggles 2000). Moreover, the rate of nonmarriage among African American women more than doubled between 1970 and the 1990s, rising from 17 to 40 percent. By the late 1990s, only about 15 percent of black women between the ages of twenty and twenty-four had married, compared to one-third of white women; by the age of forty, 93 percent of white women had married, compared to only 65 percent of black women (Cherlin

2008; Huston and Melz 2004). Thus, marriage rates among African American women reached a historic low during the latter decades of the twentieth century, sparking concern over the welfare of children and the impact of social-welfare policies on families.

In this chapter, I begin with a historical overview of African American marriages that shows how centuries of slavery compromised African marriage traditions, yet precluded African Americans from embracing American traditions. As noted, the extent to which enslaved black families formed two-parent families has now become a matter of some debate; however, it seems clear that most sought to legalize their marital unions after slavery was abolished. Their ability to reap the benefits of marriage, however, was curtailed by racist policies and dominant gender ideologies, thus undermining the viability of their marriages and perpetuating a strong tradition of single-mother and extended families. Next, I show how social scientists have characterized African American families, arguing that theorists have often ignored marriage and the demands of the traditional marriage contract, which were inconsistent with the cultural traditions and economic resources of African Americans. I explore how the intersection of race, gender, and class inequalities continue to affect African American families and relationships adversely, and I conclude with a look at the future of marriage for African Americans.

MARRIAGE AMONG AFRICAN AMERICANS: A HISTORICAL PERSPECTIVE

Although marriage and families are universal institutions that are often seen as the bases for societal stability, the rules and norms that govern these institutions are a product of differing cultural ideologies and economic forces. In West African societies, marriage was often arranged and polygamous and, given the importance placed on fertility, was sometimes preceded by the birth of children (Cherlin 2008). Both American and African marriages embraced patriarchal traditions, but the implications of male authority were muted in African societies by the economic roles of women, the primacy of the mother-child relationship, female-centered kin relationships, and the fact that blood relationships were often seen as more important than marital relationships (Caldwell 1996; Young 1970) Thus, Africans brought to the United States their own marital and family traditions, some of which were destroyed by the demands of slavery (e.g., polygamy), while others were reinforced by slavery (e.g., female work roles, extended families). Enslaved blacks undoubtedly merged West African and American family traditions in ways that enabled them to survive, but faced formidable obstacles to conforming fully to either family system. For example, the marriages of enslaved blacks had no legal sanction and were often unstable, and slavery coerced and controlled their labor and lives in ways that undermined family life. Black families were often defined as mothers and their children. Equally arduous labor was required for men and women, and men, even when present in families, were neither the primary providers nor heads of their families. These factors made it impossible for marriage to become thoroughly institutionalized among African Americans, but also freed them from rigid gender norms and the notion that love, sexuality, and family had to be centered in a legally sanctioned marriage contract (Hill 2005).

Emancipation had a destabilizing effect on African American families, often resulting in starvation, migration, marital separation, and the desertion of spouses and children. During the Civil War, armies invaded and disrupted plantation life, setting thousands of black people adrift and leading many to abandon their spouses and children (Frazier 1957). Resisting the loss of cheap labor, white southerners sometimes refused to allow black soldiers returning from war to claim their wives and children (Landry 2000), and some states passed laws allowing whites to "indenture" (or re-enslave) the children of black couples who were unmarried or unemployed (Scott 1985). As racism intensified, African American men lost many of the skilled jobs they had held during slavery. Frequently charged with crimes like vagrancy and rape, they increasingly faced the prospects of being lynched, incarcerated, or forced into labor contracts (Booker 2000). As Booker has explained, many southerners argued that slavery had a civilizing influence on black people, but without it they were regressing to their primitive state, such as giving in to their natural tendency toward sexual immorality.

Amid myths of dangerous, unbridled sexuality among African Americans, a campaign was waged to legalize their marital unions, with marriage described as elevating "freedpeople to a new level of civilization" (Giddings 1984; Higginbothan 1993; Schwalm 1997). Former slaves were sometimes forced to legalize fairly casual sexual relationships; Frankel, for example, found a 1870 Mississippi law declaring all African American couples "who have not married, but are now living together, cohabiting as man and wife, shall be taken and held, for all purposes in the law, as married" (Frankel

1999). The legalization of marriage was also urged for economic reasons—the need to reorganize the labor of black people for the sharecropping system.

Evidence suggests that the majority of African Americans married after slavery ended; however, a significant minority remained single and/or formed single-mother families. There was, for example, much regional variation in marriage rates. Dabel found that two-thirds of free black women living in New York City between 1850 and 1870 did not marry (Dabel 2002); perhaps they were live-in domestics or had fewer potential marriage partners, since most blacks lived in the South. Indeed, in earlier research (Hill 2005, 2006), I have argued that while most African Americans married after slavery ended, there was also a nonmarriage ethos among a significant minority of black women, since the costs of being married outweighed the benefits. For example, many had developed a tradition of self-reliance during slavery, could perform labor that was still in demand, and were participants in female-centered kin networks that were not easily abandoned in favor of marriage. But even those who married did not necessarily adhere to mainstream family ideologies or abandon black cultural traditions such as relying extended families and fostering children to other families. The latter may account for the fact that Steven Ruggles found that in 1850 nearly half of all free black children lived with one or neither of their parents, and by the 1880s (a few years after slavery was abolished) parental absence was five times more common among blacks than whites (Ruggles, 1994).

Northward migration further diminished marital stability among African Americans, as many migrants failed to gain the economic foothold they had expected. The tradition of working wives was simply transferred from rural to urban areas (Landry 2000), where the tendency of white families to insist on live-in maids threatened the ability of African American women to prioritize caring for their own families (Marks 1989). Efforts to create married couple families were also countered by growing rates of unemployment among African American men during the 1950s (Billingsley 1992), the same decade that marriage rates began to decline. In fact, the birthrate among single African American women tripled between 1940 and 1957 (Franklin 1997), which suggests that nonmarital parenting, although neither normative nor the ideal, was not strongly stigmatized among blacks. Still, the growing concentration of single-mother families in urban areas and on welfare rolls made them more visible and controversial, thus setting the stage for twentieth-century debates about African American families.

THEORIZING AFRICAN AMERICAN FAMILIES

The early sociological study of families was guided by the theoretical premises of structural functionalism, which saw the breadwinner-homemaker family model as ideal for social mobility in the rapidly industrializing economy. Centuries of slavery and racism had made it difficult for most African Americans to form such families; yet racist thinking often led scholars to explain the "deficiencies" in black families using theories of biological inferiority. Even those at the Chicago School of Sociology, which was known for its focus on the primacy of social and environmental forces, sometimes fell sway to the belief that different human populations were "endowed with different *biologically transmitted* cultural capacities" (Hall 2002). Among those opposing such reasoning was E. Franklin Frazier, an influential black scholar who argued that African American families had been shaped by social structural forces. Like other liberal scholars of the era, Frazier essentially offered a class analysis of African American families.

The Class (or Social Deficit) Perspective

Early twentieth-century sociologists focused heavily on processes of assimilation among racial-ethnic minorities who were moving into urban areas, and most sought to refute biological theories of racial inequality by emphasizing the impact of social structural forces on families. Thus, they often highlighted the similarities between middle-class black and white families that had assimilated into mainstream society, but provided dire portrayals of poor black families that had been unable to do so, especially those headed by single mothers (Davis and Havighurst 1946; Kardiner and Ovesey 1951). Frazier also emphasized class diversity among African American families (Frazier 1957), and he thought slavery had destroyed their African culture and was responsible for fostering single-mother families. He argued that single-mother (or matriarchal) families among African Americans had often worked well in the South, but they impeded socioeconomic mobility in a rapidly modernizing society. Never doubting the premises of the dominant theory of his era, structural-functionalism, or the merits of assimilating into the dominant culture, Frazier saw single-mother families as a legacy of slavery and two-parent, patriarchal families as ideal. This theme resonated with most African American activists and leaders throughout the 1950s; however, when reiterated in the Moynihan

Report, it became the catalyst for a new genre of research on black families (Moynihan 1965).

The Cultural (or Family Strength) Perspective

The revolutionary era of the 1960s and 1970s produced research that was more critical of hegemonic family, marital, and gender ideologies, and of the social deficit perspective on African American families. The Moynihan Report, although it emphasized that there was significant class diversity among African Americans, was seen during the civil-rights era as attributing the blame for black economic disadvantage to single-mother families rather than racism. The report was widely criticized among activists and scholars, including feminists who bristled at the notion of patriarchal families as inherently superior to those headed by women. In their efforts to refute depictions of African American families as pathological and matriarchal, it became common to valorize the strength and family support networks of single mothers (Stack 1974) and argue that black married couples had created egalitarian relationships (Scanzoni 1977).

Two important themes emerged in the field of African American families studies among these revisionist scholars. First, social historians—in work that ultimately tended to "humanize" slave owners and "masculinize" the study of black families—argued that strong, stable, two-parent families were the norm among enslaved African Americans (Gutman 1976). According to revisionist researchers, enslaved black men exercised considerable authority over their families; indeed, "slaves created impressive norms of family life, including as much of a nuclear family norm as the conditions allowed," and slave owners "rarely if ever denied the moral content of the [marriage] relationship" between slaves (Genovese 1974). More recent scholars have challenged this work by emphasizing the diversity of experiences among enslaved African Americans, even describing revisionist accounts of family life under slavery as being nothing more than "Disney scripts" (Dunaway 2003).

Second, revisionist scholars rejected the idea that African cultural traditions had been destroyed by slavery. Walter Allen, for example, argued that African American families are best described as "culturally variant" rather than "culturally deviant" (Allen 1978), and Robert Hill described their cultural traditions as including religiosity, extended kin networks, the primacy of blood over marital relationships, multiple parentage, and flexible or egalitarian gender roles (Hill 1972). The premise that African American families were simply culturally different from white families and that most were supported by extended family networks deflected some of the criticism of single-mother families and sparked a virtual cottage industry of studies on the nature, extent, and consequences of their extended family networks.

But the cultural perspective also inadvertently fostered a monolithic depiction of *the* black family as governed by an immutable set of cultural traditions, and failed to offer many insights into African American marriages. In addition, it was at a loss to explain the decline of poor families and their traditions during the post–civil rights era, when, arguably, opportunities for African Americans had expanded. Meanwhile, the political discourse on culture among low-income African Americans had begun to focus on the urban underclass and their lack of family values, with some arguing that escalating rates of nonmarriage and single-mother families were the direct result of generous welfare policies (Murray 1984).

Criticism of the "urban underclass" helped reignite the class perspective on African American families, with William J. Wilson arguing that the rise of the postindustrial economy had severely diminished the employment prospects of young men and produced significant class polarization among African Americans (Wilson 1978). Wilson theorized that class had become more important than race in predicting the life chances of African Americans, and linked the decline in marriage to growing joblessness among men. His narrow focus on the employment-marriage connection, however, failed to place the marriage dilemma of African Americans in historical context or acknowledge the impact of multiple forms of social inequality on marriage.

AFRICAN AMERICAN MARRIAGES: A CONTEMPORARY PERSPECTIVE

Scholarly inquiry into the demise of marriage has produced a host of studies showing that attitudinal support for marriage among African Americans has remained strong; indeed, blacks often express greater support for traditional ideals about sexuality, marriage, and family than do white Americans. Despite living lives that contradict their expressed ideals, African Americans are as likely as white Americans to idealize marriage (Edin 2000; Harknett and McLanahan 2004) and are less accepting of nonmarital sex, cohabitation, and divorce than whites (Huston and Melz 2004). How, then, does one explain the discrepancy between their support for marriage and their lived experiences? I argue that marriage has traditionally been based on social norms and ideologies that were at odds with the cultural traditions and economic resources of African Americans, and thus has never been as firmly institutionalized among black people. I use an intersectionality framework to show that class, race, and gender inequalities have made and continue to make it difficult for many African Americans to conform to mainstream marital expectations, and that these structural inequalities have fostered their participation in cultural patterns (such as nonmarriage and single motherhood) that contradict their professed ideals. Neither cultural nor structural theorists have adequately dealt with the intersection of these inequalities, and thus have offered at best partial explanations of the marriage decline.

The traditional marriage contract is rooted in notions of patriarchy, female subordination, distinct roles for men and women, the protection of property, and the production of legitimate children—all of which were negated for African Americans for centuries by the dictates of slavery. Slavery, as noted earlier, demanded diversity and flexibility in the family arrangements of black people, depending on factors such as the type of economy, region, size of the plantation, and solvency of the slave owner (Dunaway 2003; Franklin 1997). At best, slavery nearly always undermined the economic basis for male authority in families, fostered female independence, prevented blacks for owning much property, and defined families primarily as mothers and their children. Most evidence suggests that a majority of African Americans married and formed two-parent families after slavery ended. Clearly, however, a significant minority either remained single (Hill 2005, 2006) or lived in informal or cohabiting relationships (Frankel 1999), at least partly because it was difficult for them to reap the benefits and privileges of married life. For example, most former slaves entered the sharecropping system that demanded the labor of men and women, and that criticized black women who tried to exempt themselves from such work as "aspiring to a model of womanhood that was considered inappropriate for them" (Dill 1988). This labor system made it difficult for black men to claim head-of-household status based on economic provisioning or for wives to prioritize caring for their children and homes. Marriage neither exempted women from productive labor nor substantially improved their standards of living, yet those who married sometimes found their husbands eager to assert patriarchal power in their families—a factor blamed for high rates of domestic violence and marital separation among the newly freed slaves (Franklin 1997). Indeed, mainstream gender expectations, economic marginalization, and racism continued to make it difficult for African Americans to create stable marriages.

THE INTERSECTION OF CLASS, GENDER, AND RACIAL INEQUALITY

Intersectionality refers to understanding the "interconnectedness of ideas and the social structures in which they occur, and the intersecting hierarchies of gender, race, economic class, sexuality, and ethnicity" (Collins 1999). In applying this concept to the study of marriage, I focus on how structural factors shape cultural ideas and how multiple forms of inequality affect the challenges of marrying and staying married. For example, class matters a great deal as a factor in whether people will get and stay married: researchers have consistently found that higher income and educational attainment predict marriage and marital stability (Cherlin 2008). The rate of poverty among African Americans remains twice as high as that of white Americans, and much of that poverty is related to joblessness among black men (Wilson 1978). Low-income women, although struggling alone to make ends meet, are unwilling to marry men who cannot contribute much to their economic support (Edin 2000). Moreover, joblessness and poverty help push young African American men from mainstream society, and in their pursuit for manhood and respect many embrace behaviors (e.g., violence, hypersexuality) (Anderson 1999) that do not bode well for marriage and often lead to criminal behavior. Indeed, Western and Beckett (1999) have argued the racially motivated sentencing has made the penal system a major strategy in regulating the labor market, with more than 1.6 million people (disproportionately male and black) incarcerated by the late 1990s.

Economic restructuring has lessened the demand for unskilled labor, but racism in the labor market also undercuts the economic position of African Americans. Data from the Bureau of Labor Statistics reveal that among men twenty-five years of age or older in 2005, black men (7.6 percent) were more than twice as likely as white men (3.5 percent) to be unemployed. Moreover, African American men are discriminated against by employers for numerous reasons (Wilson 1987), including the notion that they simply lack the "soft skills" that are now in demand, such as "skills, abilities and traits that pertain to personality, attitude and behavior rather than formal or technical knowledge" (Moss and Tilly 1996). As Moss and

Tilly have noted, employers often describe black men as being unmotivated, defensive, and hostile. Similar stereotypes undermine the ability of black women to find work. They are twice as likely as white women to be unemployed, and employers often stereotype them as unreliable single mothers (Browne and Kennelly 1995).

Neither the end of legalized racial segregation nor the gains made since the civil-rights era have eliminated racism or racial inequality; white Americans still endorse a spate of racist assumptions about African Americans and their families (Bobo, Kluegel, and Smith 1997). Racism and racial exclusion adversely affect the feelings of African Americans about their place in society and their quality of life. Hughes and Thomas, for example, found racial disparities in life quality between black and white Americans, and they argued that racism produces identity problems and a sense of rage and resentment among African Americans. Even when age and social class were considered, "African Americans were less satisfied, less happy, more mistrustful, more anomic, had less happy marriages, and rated their physical health worse than whites" (Hughes and Thomas 1998). This sense of being disrespected and disvalued in the larger society can adversely affect the quality of intimate relationships and the likelihood of marriage.

Persistent class and race inequalities intersect with and shape gender ideologies, making it difficult for African Americans to conform to traditional gender expectations or embrace the evolving ideal of gender-egalitarian marriages. For example, their long tradition of work and socioeconomic gains makes it difficult for many African American women to "marry up," or even marry men whose educational and economic position is comparable to their own. Although African American men earn more than black women, mostly because they hold male-typed jobs and more high-paying professional positions, the gains since the 1950s have been greater for black women. African American women, for example, are more likely than men to hold managerial and professional jobs (albeit in areas such as social work and teaching), more likely to have bachelor and especially graduate degrees, and more likely to feel integrated into the values of the dominant culture. This has created an important status gap between black women and men—and numerous books and movies that suggest the problem could be solved if middle-class black women would accept and marry working- or lower-class black men (Hill 2005). But class matters in forming viable marriages and marrying men of a lower class or status may help explain why black women feel less benefited by marriage than white women (Goodwin 2003). Indeed, the ideology of "marrying up" also affects low-income women, who are concerned about the loss of respectability associated with marrying poor and often jobless men (Edin 2000).

These structural inequalities foster cultural practices and behaviors that militate against marriage and marital success. Economic exclusion and persistent racial inequality, for example, ultimately creates an "oppositional culture that devalues work, schooling, and marriage" (Massey and Denton 1993). The courtship practices of young African American men who lack decent jobs or respect in mainstream society are often characterized by deceit, violence, and a general disrespect for women (Anderson 1990). The skewed gender ratio of men to women favors men and shapes their attitudes toward marriage and women; for example, Harknett and McLanahan found that "when men are in short supply, partner quality and relationship quality tend to be worse, and parents place less emphasis on the two-parent, male breadwinner norm" (Harknett and McLanahan 2004). African American men who marry tend to bring to their relationships more conservative gender beliefs than white men (Blee and Tickamyer 1995) and, despite being more accepting of employed wives, their marriages are characterized by more work-family conflicts, especially when the wife has a career (Bridges and Orza 1996). Gender traditions also persist in the division of domestic work: African American men spend only about half as much time doing housework as their partners (John and Shelton 1997). Overall, black couples are less satisfied in their marriages than white couples; they report sharing fewer activities and experiencing more conflict and distrust (Harknett and McLanahan 2004).

THE MARRIAGE DECLINE: CAN (SHOULD) IT BE REVERSED?

The strongest arguments for marriage is that married couples have higher levels of health and well-being than singles, that marriage reduces poverty, and that children fare better in two-parent families. For these reasons, the 1996 Personal Responsibility and Work Opportunity Act (PRWOA) declared that marriage "is the foundation of a successful society" and "is an essential institution that promotes the interests of children" (Jayakody and Cabrera 2002). Proponents of marriage contend that married people are happier, healthier, and wealthier than single people (Waite and Gallagher 2000). Still, the extent to which this applies to African American couples is debatable. As indicated earlier, there is a racial gap in marital satisfaction, with married African American couples experiencing more conflict and distrust in their relationships than white couples. Although their lower level of marital satisfaction cannot be explained away by noting class differences between blacks and whites, it is undoubtedly exacerbated by the fact that African Americans are more likely to be in the working and lower classes, where divorce and domestic violence are more common. Staying in unhappy marriages correlates with adverse health outcomes, such as elevated levels of psychological distress and poor health (Hawkins and Booth 2005). There is also evidence that marital unhappiness takes a greater toll on the health of wives than of husbands, with unhappy wives having high levels of depression and substance abuse (Coontz 2005).

From an economic standpoint, black married couple families fare better than single-mother families, although their 2001 median household income ($55,618) was much less than that of white married couple families ($71,155) (Conrad and King 2005). Linda Waite has found that several factors reduce the economic benefits of marriage for African Americans, such as lower wage gap between black men and women, the lower returns black women receive for investing in their husband's earnings, and the expense of raising children, who are more likely to be present in the homes of black couples (Waite 1995). For lower-income couples, where the prospects of unemployment, divorce, and domestic violence are high, the economic benefits of marriage may prove even more meager. D. T. Lichter and colleagues report that poverty rates would still be more than twice as high among African American women if they had the same family background and rates of marriage and unwed childbirth as white women (Lichter, Graefe, and Brown 2003). They also found that among economically disadvantaged black women, marriage is associated with downward educational mobility, and those who marry and divorce have higher rates of poverty than those who never married.

Although the growth in single-mother families has leveled off in recent years, nearly 41 percent of American children live in such families, with African American children (53 percent) more likely to do so than white children (22 percent) (Sigle-Rushton and McLanahan 2004). Children benefit from having the emotional and financial support of their fathers; indeed, many studies have shown that children living with single mothers, regardless of their race or social class, are more likely than those living with two biological parents to experience academic failure, behavioral and psychological problems, delinquency, and illegal drug use (Ellwood and Jencks 2004; Sigle-Rushton and McLanahan 2004). Still, single-mother families and extended family relationships are more institutionalized among African Americans and may have fewer adverse consequences for black children. A study comparing male adolescents living in white and black single-mother families found that lack of involvement with fathers elevated the risk of problematic behaviors only for white sons—at least partially because they were more likely to live in *divorced* single-mother families and were more likely to have lost a father with whom they had a relationship (Thomas, Farrell, and Barnes 1996). For African Americans, the risks of single-mother families may be more the result of the demise of extended family relationships and higher rates of poverty and extreme poverty; for example, in 2001 the median household income for black single mothers was less than $21,000, compared to $29,650 for white single mothers (Conrad and King 2005).

So, should African Americans get married? There are clearly benefits to be gained from marriage, although most evidence suggests that those benefits are not as great for blacks as for whites. But given the diminishing support single mothers are receiving from the state and their extended families, marriage may become more appealing. Moreover, there is strong ideological support for marriage among African Americans; the majority would like to get married, and they equate marriage with respectability, endorsing more traditional marital, gender, and sexual norms that white Americans. Still, a gap has always existed for African Americans between their endorsement of mainstream family values and their lived experiences. As I have argued, many African Americans have historically lacked the economic and cultural resources to conform to the traditional marriage contract, which was based on male-domination, gendered roles, and property. Today, these institutional aspects of marriage have now given way to marriage as a personal relationship based on gender equality and emotional satisfaction (Amato 2004). Such marital expectations should, at least arguably, make it easier for African Americans to achieve marital success, since the emphasis on economics has declined. Still, these new marital expectations are more likely to be embraced by middle-class couples, and African Americans have primarily been in the working and lower classes, where traditional values are more apparent. For example, as Landry has pointed out, employed wives have always been acceptable among African Americans, but "[it] remained for the upper-middle-class black wives to elevate the *acceptable* to the *desirable* in the early decades of the twentieth century" (Landry 2000).

CONCLUSION

In this chapter, I have argued that multiple forms of social inequality, both historically and currently, have created an important gap between the marital ideals of African Americans and the resources needed to live those ideals. This has made marriage seem less attainable, and thus has fostered cultural alternatives to marriage, such as high rates of single-mother families and nonmarital cohabitation. Mainstream marital traditions, for example, have supported patriarchal marriages headed by men earning the family wage, but exempted African American men from such jobs. These marital traditions have also been based on the primacy of marriage-centered families, but African Americans have often had to rely on extended families networks in order to survive. It has also been traditionally based on a gender division of labor that makes women economic dependents by placing them in the home, yet since slavery African American women have always combined productive and domestic work. Thus, despite high levels of attitudinal support for marriage among black Americans, dominant marital traditions have been at odds with their experiences. In this sense, marriage has never been fully institutionalized among African Americans.

Multiple social inequalities are responsible for the erosion of marriage among African Americans during the twentieth century, and addressing those inequalities is the key to restoring marriage as a vital institution. For example, workshops have sprung up to teach African American men the value of being involved in their children's lives, but less has been done to bring them into the economic mainstream or enhance their employment skills or educational achievement—both of which are important if they are to participate consistently in family life. Similarly, both politicians and religionists who trumpet the value of marriage and two-parent families have not always acknowledged the gender inequities in those arrangements, which women increasingly refuse to tolerate. Welfare-related marriage-promotion programs have more leverage over poor, young mothers than they do the fathers, and some research suggests that such programs place the responsibility on mothers to "swallow their rage and grievances against men" and bring them into the cultural mainstream of marriage (Huston and Melz 2004). Failing to resolve basic gender issues, though, will not lead to successful marriages. Finally, marriages have changed for all Americans over the past few decades, with more employed wives, more dual-income families, more economic independence, and more couples unwilling to stay in marriages that are emotionally unsatisfying. These changes in marriage have made issues such as gender equity in the home, adequate childcare, and family-friendly practices by employers key factors in the maintenance of families.

REFERENCES

Allen, W.R. 1978. The search for applicable theories of black family life. *Journal of Marriage and the Family* 40, no. 1: 117–129.

Amato, P.R. 2004. Tension between institutional and individual views of marriage. *Journal of Marriage and Family* 66 (November): 959–965.

Anderson, E. 1990. *Streetwise: Race, class, and change in an urban community.* Chicago: University of Chicago Press.

———. 1999. *Code of the street: Decency, violence, and the moral life of the inner city.* New York: Norton.

Billingsley, A. 1968. *Black families in white America.* Englewood Cliffs, N.J.: Prentice-Hall.

———. 1992. *Climbing Jacob's ladder: The enduring legacy of African-American families.* New York: Simon & Schuster.

Blassingame, J.W. 1972. *The slave community: Plantation life in the antebellum south.* New York: Oxford University Press.

Blee, K.M., and A. R. Tickamyer. 1995. Racial differences in men's attitudes about women's gender roles. *Journal of Marriage and the Family* 57, no. 1: 21–30.

Bobo, L., J. R. Kluegel, and R. A. Smith. 1997. Laissez-faire racism: The crystallization of a kinder, gentler, antiblack ideology. In S.A. Tuch and J.K. Martin, eds., *Racial attitudes in the 1990s: Continuity and change,* 15–42. Westport, Conn.: Praeger.

Booker, C.B. 2000. *"I will wear no chain!" A social history of African American males.* Westport, Conn.: Praeger.

Bridges, J.S., and A. M. Orza. 1996. Black and white employed mothers' role experience. *Sex Roles* 35, nos. 5–6: 337–385.

Browne, I., and I. Kennelly. 1995. Stereotypes and realities: Images of black women in the labor market. In I. Brown, ed., *Latinas and African American women at work: Race, gender, and economic inequality,* 302–326. New York: Russell Sage.

Caldwell, J.C. 1996. The demographic implications of West African family systems. *Journal of Comparative Family Studies* 27:331–352.

Cherlin, A.J. 2008. *Public and private families: An introduction.* New York: McGraw Hill.

Collins, P.H. 1999. Moving beyond gender: Intersectionality and scientific knowledge. In M.M. Ferree, J. Lorber, and B.B. Hess, eds., *Revisioning gender,* 261–284. Thousand Oaks, Calif.: Sage.

Conrad, C.A., and M. C. King. 2005. Single-mother families in the black community: Economic context and policies. In C.A. Conrad, J. Whitehead, P. Mason, and J. Stewart, eds., *African Americans in the U.S. Economy*, 163–174. Lanham, Md.: Rowman & Littlefield.

Coontz, S. 2005. *Marriage, a history: From obedience to intimacy, or how love conquered marriage*. New York: Viking Penguin.

Dabel, J.E. 2002. African American women and household composition in New York City, 1827–1877. In J.L. Conyers Jr., ed., *Black cultures and race relations*, 60–72. Chicago: Burnham.

Davis, A., and R. J. Havighurst. 1946. Social class and color differences in child-rearing. *American Sociological Review* 2:698–710.

Dill, B.T. 1988. Our mothers' grief: Racial ethnic women and the maintenance of families. *Journal of Family History* 13, no. 4: 415–431.

Dunaway, W.A. 2003. *The African American family in slavery and emancipation*. New York: Cambridge University Press.

Edin, K. 2000. What do low-income single mothers say about marriage? *Social Problems* 47, no. 1: 112–113.

Ellwood, D.T., and C. Jencks. 2004. The spread of single-parent families in the United States since 1960. In D.P. Moynihan, T.M. Smeeding, and L. Rainwater, eds., *Future of the family*, 25–65. New York: Russell Sage Foundation.

Fitch, C.A., and S. Ruggles. 2000. Historical trends in marriage formation: The United States 1850–1990. In L.J. Waite, Bachrach, M. Hindin, E. Thomson, and A. Thornton, eds., *The ties that bind: Perspectives on marriage and cohabitation*. New York: Aldine de Gruyter.

Frankel, N. 1999. *Freedom's women: Black women and families in Civil War–era Mississippi*. Bloomington: Indiana University Press.

Franklin, D.L. 1997. *Ensuring inequality: The structural transformation of the African-American family*. New York: Oxford University Press.

Frazier, E.F. 1957. *The Negro in the United States*. New York: Macmillan.

Genovese, E.D. 1974. *Roll, Jordan, roll: The world the slaves made*. New York: Pantheon.

Giddings, P. 1984. *When and where I enter: The impact of black women on race and sex in America*. New York: Bantam.

Goodwin, P.Y. 2003. African American and European American women's marital well-being. *Journal of Marriage and the Family* 65 (August): 550–560.

Gutman, H.G. 1976. *The black family in slavery and freedom, 1750–1925*. New York: Pantheon.

Hall, R.L. 2002. E. Franklin Frazier and the Chicago school of sociology. In J.E. Teele, ed., *E. Franklin Frazier and the black bourgeoisie*, 47–67. Columbia: University of Missouri Press.

Harknett, K., and S. S. McLanahan. 2004. Racial and ethnic differences in marriage after the birth of a child. *American Sociological Review* 69 (December): 790–811.

Hawkins, D., and A. Booth. 2005. Unhappily ever after: Effects of long-term, low-quality marriages on well-being. *Social Forces* 84, no. 1: 451–471.

Higginbothan, E. B. 1993. *Righteous discontent: The women's movement in the black Baptist church, 1880–1920*. Cambridge, Mass.: Harvard University Press.

Hill, R. B. 1972. *The strengths of black families*. New York: Emerson Hall.

Hill, S. A. 2005. *Black intimacies: A gender perspective on families and relationships*. Walnut Creek, Calif.: AltaMira.

———. 2006. Marriage among African Americans: A gender perspective. *Journal of Comparative Family Studies* 37, no. 3: 421–440.

Hughes, M., and M. E. Thomas. 1998. The continuing significance of race revisited: A study of race, class and quality of life in America, 1972 to 1996. *American Sociological Review* 63 (December): 785–795.

Huston, T. L., and H. Melz. 2004. The case for (promoting) marriage: The devil is in the details. *Journal of Marriage and Family* 66 (November): 943–958.

Jayakody, R., and N. Cabrera. 2002. What are the choices for low-income families? Cohabitation, marriage, and remaining single. In A. Booth and A. C. Crounter, eds., *Just living together: Implications of cohabitation on families, children, and social policy*, 85–95. Mahwah, N.J.: Erlbaum.

John, D., and B. A. Shelton. 1997. The production of gender among black and white women and men: The case of household labor. *Sex Roles* 36, nos. 3–4: 171–193.

Kardiner, A., and L. Ovesey. 1951. *The mark of oppression: Explorations in the personality of the American Negro*. New York: Meridian.

Koball, H. 1998. Have African American men become less committed to marriage? Explaining the twentieth century racial cross-over in men's marriage timing. *Demography* 35, no. 2: 251–258.

Landry, B. 2000. *Black working wives: Pioneers of the American family revolution*. Berkeley: University of California Press.

Lichter, D. T., D. R. Graefe, and J. B. Brown. 2003. Is marriage a panacea? Union formation among economically disadvantaged unwed mothers. *Social Problems* 50, no. 1: 60–86.

Marks, C. 1989. *Farewell—we're good and gone: The great black migration*. Bloomington: Indiana University Press.

Massey, D. S., and N. A. Denton. 1993. *American apartheid: Segregation and the making of the underclass*. Cambridge, Mass.: Harvard University Press.

Moss, P., and C. Tilly. 1996. "Soft" skills and race: An investigation of black men's employment problems. *Work and Occupations* 23, no. 3: 252–276.

Moynihan, D. P. 1965. *The Negro family: The case for national action*. Washington, D.C.: Office of Policy Planning and Research.

Murray, C. 1984. *Losing ground: American social policy, 1950–1980*. New York: Basic Books.

Nobles, W. W. 1974. Africanity: Its role in black families. *Black Scholar* 5, no. 9: 10–17.

Ruggles, S. 1994. The origins of African-American family structure. *American Sociological Review* 59 (February): 136–151.

Scanzoni, J. 1977. *The black family in modern society: Patterns of stability and security*. Chicago: University of Chicago Press.

Schwalm, L. A. 1997. *A hard fight for we: Women's transition from slavery to freedom in South Carolina*. Urbana: University of Illinois Press.

Scott, R. J. 1985. The battle over the child: Child apprenticeship and the freedmen's bureau in North Carolina. In N. R. Hiner and J. M. Hawes, eds., *Growing up in America: Children in historical perspective*, 193–207. Chicago: University of Chicago Press.

Sigle-Rushton, W., and S. McLanahan. 2004. Father absence and child well-being: A critical review. In D. P. Moynihan, T. M. Smeeding, and L. Rainwater, eds., *Future of the family*, 116–155. New York: Russell Sage Foundation.

Stack, C. 1974. *All our kin: Strategies for survival in a black community*. New York: Harper & Row.

Thomas, G., M. P. Farrell, and G. M. Barnes. 1996. The effects of single-mother families and nonresident fathers on delinquency and substance abuse in black and white adolescents. *Journal of Marriage and the Family* 58 (November): 884–894.

U.S. Department of Labor, Bureau of Labor Statistics. Household data and annual averages. Retrieved January 25, 2008, from www.bls.gov/cps/cpsaat24.pdf.

Waite, L. 1995. Does marriage matter? *Demography* 32, no. 4: 483–507.

Waite, L., and M. Gallagher. 2000. *The case for marriage: Why married people are happier, healthier, and better off financially*. New York: Doubleday.

Western, B., and K. Beckett. 1999. How unregulated is the U.S. labor market? The penal system as a labor market institution. *American Journal of Sociology* 104, no. 4: 1030–1060.

Wilson, W. J. 1978. *The declining significance of race: Blacks and changing American institutions*. Chicago: University of Chicago Press.

———. 1987. *The truly disadvantaged*. Chicago: University of Chicago Press.

Young, V. H. 1970. Family and childhood in a southern Negro community. *American Anthropologist* 72, no. 2: 269–288.

Race, Immigration, and the Future of Marriage

FIFTEEN

DANIEL T. LICHTER AND WARREN A. BROWN

Growing racial and ethnic diversity and increasing economic inequality in American society have reinforced family change and shifting cultural values. Indeed, some social observers now claim that the family and economic trajectories of America's children—those growing up with two biological married parents and those living with unmarried parents—are rapidly diverging (Lichter, Qian, and Crowley 2007; McLanahan 2004). Today, as in the past, the children of America's haves and have-nots are often defined along racial lines. And, unfortunately, the economic hardships and early-life experiences of minority children ultimately find full expression in adulthood, when they assume (or not) productive adult roles and start families of their own. Disadvantaged children, including racial and ethnic minorities growing up in poor single parent and cohabiting families, are at risk of leading unstable family lives as adults. Current family patterns are thus self-reinforcing, while giving demographic impetus to accelerated changes in marriage and family life in the future.

In this chapter, we examine current and future patterns of marriage and family structure in America's rapidly growing minority and immigrant populations. Our basic assumption is that the future of "the family" is really a story of America's *families*. We argue here that accelerating racial and ethnic diversity in marriage patterns will be a primary engine of family change. Indeed, the family is buffeted in myriad ways by changes in America's ethnic and racial makeup. The so-called traditional nuclear family—with its male breadwinner and female homemaker—arguably is a social construction that is applied reflexively to America's white majority population, but that constitutes a declining share of the U.S. population.[1] Roughly 40 percent of America's children today are racial or ethnic minorities or have immigrant parents (Hernandez 2004). The future of America's families ultimately will be shaped by *these* children as they enter adulthood, marry or not, and bear and rear children of their own. This statistical fact is too often overlooked in recent prognostications about the future of American families (see Walker 2004). The key questions are clear. Will America's burgeoning immigrant and minority children, as adults, embrace the diverse cultural family forms and traditions they experienced while growing up? Or, instead, will they become "Americanized," adopt the family patterns of the non-Hispanic white majority, or perhaps even experience "downward" assimilation into a permanent underclass, where family disruption, nonmarital fertility, and single parenthood are the norm and reinforce intergenerational poverty and racial inequality?

In this chapter, we have three specific objectives. First, we begin by highlighting growing racial and ethnic diversity in marriage and family living arrangements. Second, we evaluate the demographic implications of growing racial and cultural diversity for the future of the family. We provide new marital status projections of the U.S. population in 2050 that account for America's changing racial and ethnic composition. Third, we highlight several alternative demographic scenarios about the future of marriage in the United States that make population forecasts difficult. In the end, our goal is to shift the current discussion from its singular focus on the "deinstitutionalization" of traditional marriage and family life (Cherlin 2004; Nock 2002) to a new emphasis on the "reinstitutionalization" of American marriage, which is expressed in increasingly myriad ways that effectively serve traditional functions of mate selection, childbearing, and childrearing. Particular attention will be given to new immigrant groups that are likely to remake America's future while also reshaping ongoing debates on the thesis of family decline, cultural and economic assimilation, and the "American way of life."

AMERICA'S NEW FAMILY MOSAIC

Recent government estimates suggest that roughly 1 million new immigrants move into the United States each year (Martin and Midgley 2006). Nearly one-half of all immigrants come from Latin America—mostly from Mexico. Another 30 percent come from Asia. Immigration has both a primary and secondary impact on American society. Immigration's most immediate and primary impact is on the growth of racial and ethnic minorities in United States. The white majority is declining. Indeed, U.S. Census Bureau reports indicate that between 1990 and 2006, the percentage of non-Hispanic whites in the U.S. population declined from 80 to 66 percent. A large secondary effect resides in the age makeup of the new immigrant population—its youthful age profile—and the potential for high fertility and rapid population growth as today's minority adolescents and young adults enter the family-building stage of the life course. In the absence of economic and cultural incorporation of new immigrant groups, America's racial and ethnic diversity will go hand in hand with growing diversity in its patterns of mate selection, fertility, and family form.

What do we know about marriage among America's racial and ethnic minority populations? Overall, the percent of ever-married U.S. women, aged 15–54, remained relatively constant at about 72 percent between 1980 and 2000 (see figure 15.1; Lichter and Qian 2004). What changed over this twenty-year period is the *timing* of marriage. Young adults are delaying marriage. In 1980, for example, 52 percent of women aged 20–24 had ever married, compared with only 33 percent in 2000. Most whites nevertheless ultimately marry. In both 1980 and 2000, 95 percent had ever married by age 50–54 (although a large share did not stay married). Racial and ethnic differences are large, however. Among blacks, for example, the percentage ever married declined from 58 to 51 percent, and the percentage married by 20–24 dropped by one-half, from 33 percent to 17 percent between 1980 and 2000. Roughly two-thirds of Hispanics ages 15–54 had ever married in both 1980 and 2000, but the percentage of 20–24 year olds ever marrying dipped from 55 to 42 percent over this period. The percentages of Hispanic women who marry early exceed those of whites and are much higher than those of America's blacks. For Asians, the percentage of those aged 15–54 who had ever married dropped only slightly over 1980–2000 (from 71 to 68 percent). But Asians, like other minorities, retreated rapidly from early marriage over this period. The percentage of those aged 20–24 who had ever married declined from 39 to 23.[2]

Of course, measures of the prevalence and timing of marriage are but crude indicators of changing family patterns. Nonmarital childbearing as a share of all births increased dramatically over the past several decades—from 5.6 percent in 1960 to 38.5 percent in 2006 (Hamilton, Martin, and Ventura 2007; Ventura and Bachrach 2000). More than 1.6 million children were born outside of marriage in 2006—a record number.[3]

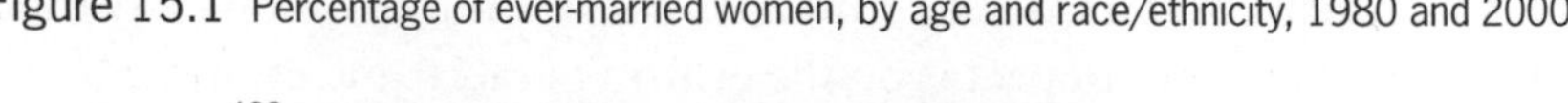
Figure 15.1 Percentage of ever-married women, by age and race/ethnicity, 1980 and 2000

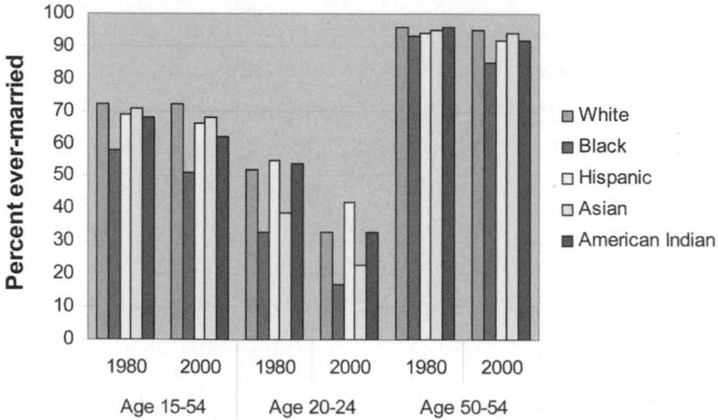

Cross-sectional racial and ethnic differences in out of wedlock childbearing are often extreme (see table 15.1). Moreover, recent cohort-life-table estimates by Wu (2008) suggest that the share of women born in 1965–1969 with a nonmarital birth by age 30 was 19.6 percent among whites, 31 percent among Hispanics, and 61.2 percent among blacks. Along with high rates of divorce (which have persisted at about 50 percent over the past thirty years), current rates of out-of-wedlock childbearing are giving impetus to growing shares of children who live in single parent families or who have ever lived with divorced or never-married mothers. As with marriage rates, patterns of divorce, nonmarital fertility, and single parenthood vary substantially across racial and ethnic groups (see chapter 5, this volume; Raley and Sweeney 2007). Recent estimates from the National Center for Health Statistics indicate that nearly 70 percent of African American children are born to single mothers (Hamilton, Martin, and Ventura 2006). These numbers contrast sharply with non-Hispanic whites (25.4 percent), Hispanics (47.9 percent), and Asians (16.2 percent). Divorce rates among Asians are also very low in comparison to divorce rates among whites and Hispanics, but especially in comparison to blacks, who continue to experience very high and increasing rates of divorce (Sweeney and Philips 2004).

The "retreat from marriage" and other family changes over the past forty years have been especially dramatic among African Americans (Ellwood and Jencks 2004). They represent a relatively stable but increasingly heterogeneous share of America's population. Indeed, the growing im-

TABLE 15.1 Fertility and Nonmarital Births, 2005, by Race and Hispanic Origin of Mother

RACE OF MOTHER	BIRTH RATE	TOTAL FERTILITY RATE[1]	PERCENTAGE OF BIRTHS TO UNMARRIED MOTHER
All races	14	2,054	36.8
Non-Hispanic white	11.5	1,843	25.4
Non-Hispanic black	15.7	2,019	69.5
American Indian or Alaska Native	14.2	1,749	63.3
Asian or Pacific Islander	16.5	1,890	16.2
Hispanic	23	2,877	47.9

1. Per 1000 women of reproductive age
Source: Hamilton, Martin, and Ventura 2006

migrant population from the West Indies and Africa exhibits much different family and fertility patterns from native-born African Americans, and those immigrants often distance themselves socially and physically from their native-born counterparts (Batson, Qian, and Lichter 2005; Waters and Jimenez 2005). This example suggests that the black family today is no monolith in the new era of rapid immigration (Kent 2007). But our more general point remains: It is impossible to accurately forecast the future of marriage and families—and the implications for children—without fully acknowledging America's growing racial and ethnic diversity, which is fueled by new immigration, especially from Latin America and Asia.

DIVERSITY AND AMERICA'S FUTURE

Recent projections prepared by the U.S. Census Bureau (2004) dramatically illustrate the magnitude of future changes in America's ethnic and racial composition. The Census Bureau projects that the non-Hispanic white population, as a percentage of total population, will decline from 69 percent in 2000 to 50 percent in 2050. Hispanics will constitute roughly 25 percent of the population in 2050, double the percentage today. The Asian population over this same period will increase threefold, from about 11 million to 33 million. Still, in 2050, the Asian population will constitute only about 8 percent of the U.S. population. The black population over the same period will grow hardly at all—from 13 to 15 percent of the total population.

Stated more starkly, the U.S. population is expected to increase by 130 million between 2000 and 2050. Of this total population increase, less than 15 million, or only 12 percent, will be due to growth in the non-Hispanic white population. The rest will be made up of today's minority populations. Changing demography will thus bear heavily on America's future families—what they look like and how well they function. For example, Hispanics will account for roughly two-thirds of the projected population increase over 2000–2050. From a strictly demographic standpoint, marriage and the American family will be reshaped in complex and unpredictable ways by the massive new Hispanic immigration and high fertility. Family patterns will also depend on future immigration policy—whether it becomes more restrictive, whether the criteria for entry (such as family reunification) change, and whether the flood of undocumented workers is cut off or better regulated.

At a minimum, understanding the future impact of immigration and growth on the U.S. population requires a new appreciation of Hispanic and Asian families. In particular their socioeconomic status and skills, diversity across generations and national-origin groups, prospects for economic, cultural, and political incorporation, and (changing) linkages between economic mobility and family change and stability will all affect the future of the family. At the same time, we recognize that it has become increasingly difficult to justify using the native-born non-Hispanic white population as a model or standard for evaluating marriages or families in America. Indeed, if past is prologue, non-Hispanic white families—by virtue of their retreat from marriage and changing fertility patterns—will represent a rapidly changing "standard" for intergroup comparisons and will have a declining impact on conventional marriage and family statistics that define public policy debates about America's future.

Family scholars and the public policy community cannot hope to understand the American family without some understanding of America's changing racial and ethnic mosaic, now and in the future (see Wu and Li 2005). Oropesa and Landale (2004), however, suggest that growth of the Hispanic population through immigration will have only small demographic impacts on the marital-status distribution of the population in

2050. A simple demographic exercise confirms their point. By taking the projected age-sex-race composition of the U.S. population in 2050 and applying the current age-sex-race-specific marital-status distribution, we can project the marital-status composition of the population in 2050. For our purposes, we use the national population projections provided by the U.S. Census Bureau (2004), along with age-sex-race-specific marital-status distributions from the 2006 American Community Survey (U.S. Census Bureau 2007). An assumption here, of course, is that marriage and divorce rates will not change in the future for each age-sex-race group. This demographic exercise nevertheless provides a useful heuristic devise for evaluating—in simple mathematical terms—the demographic implications of changing racial composition on the family if today's marriage patterns persist indefinitely.

On balance, our projections indicate that the net effects of changing age-sex-race composition are small. Changes between 2006 and 2050 in the demographic composition of the population will, in fact, have only a small net effect on the percentage married. In 2006, 50.1 percent of the population was married. In 2050, if current age-sex-race-specific marriage rates remain constant, the percentage married will be 49.3 percent. The percentage of the never-married population (age 15 and older) declines only slightly over this period, from 31 to 28 percent. What changes most rapidly over this forty-four-year period is the percentage of widows, which will increase from 6.2 percent in 2006 to 10.4 percent in 2050. But this largely reflects aging and mortality rather than increasing racial or ethnic diversity. Clearly, changes in the demographic composition of the population have little built-in momentum for the continuing retreat from marriage.

A key limitation of these projections, of course, is that they do not consider the countervailing patterns across racial groups, which may contribute to small *net* impacts on the marital status distribution. Table 15.2 provides marital-status projections for each race and ethnic group. Racial and ethnic differences are large. Our projected changes in the age and sex composition of minorities will not substantially affect characteristic differentials (for instance, the small percentage of married blacks compared with married whites, Asians, and Hispanics). At the same time, our projections confirm that the racial composition of married people will change significantly. In 2006, nearly 70 percent of all married persons were non-Hispanic white. In 2050, 54.4 percent of married persons will be non-Hispanic white. In 2006, Hispanics (of any race) represented only 11.8 percent of the married population. This will increase to 22.5 percent in 2050.

TABLE 15.2 Persons by Race/Ethnicity and Marital Status, 2006 and 2050

	ALL RACIAL/ETHNIC CATEGORIES		WHITE ALONE, NON-HISPANIC	
	2006	2050	2006	2050
Marital status (number)				
Total persons aged 15+	253,535	344,396	163,715	174,414
Married	127,026	169,879	88,333	92,453
Widowed	15,600	35,666	11,611	20,796
Divorced	26,202	33,576	18,352	18,152
Separated	6,040	8,849	2,557	2,429
Never married	78,666	96,427	42,862	40,684
Marital status (percentage)				
Total persons aged 15+	100	100	100	100
Married	50.1	49.3	54.0	53.0
Widowed	6.2	10.4	7.1	11.9
Divorced	10.3	9.7	11.2	10.4
Separated	2.4	2.6	1.6	1.4
Never married	31.0	28.0	26.2	23.3

Note: Table 15.2 continues on opposite page

Clearly, we cannot hope to understand patterns of mate selection, marital scripts, fertility, and kin relationships in the future without a much better understanding of the diverse new groups that will make up the U.S. married population.

Our focus here on marital-status distributions is appropriate for obvious reasons: Marriage is the demographic driver of changes in many other key indicators of family and economic change, such as fertility rates, nonmarital fertility ratios, divorce, single parenting and children's living arrangements, and poverty and inequality. As we have shown here, however, projected changes in the racial and ethnic composition of the U.S. population will give demographic impetus to only small changes in the marital status composition of the population. Perhaps more significantly, demographic trends will lead to large changes in the racial composition of marital couples (and their functional and structural characteristics).

BLACK ALONE		ASIAN ALONE		ALL OTHER RACES[2]		HISPANIC, ANY RACE	
2006	2050	2006	2050	2006	2050	2006	2050
28,129	48,374	10,696	27,778	19,435	15,639	31,560	78,090
8,699	15,653	6,376	16,656	8,615	6,924	15,003	38,192
1,802	5,432	461	2,538	639	1,007	1,087	5,893
3,224	5,795	527	1,428	1,647	1,402	2,452	6,799
1,366	2,325	144	398	742	597	1,231	3,099
13,037	19,169	3,188	6,757	7,792	5,710	11,787	24,107
100	100	100	100	100	100	100	100
30.9	32.4	59.6	60.0	44.3	44.3	47.5	48.9
6.4	11.2	4.3	9.1	3.3	6.4	3.4	7.5
11.5	12.0	4.9	5.1	8.5	9.0	7.8	8.7
4.9	4.8	1.3	1.4	3.8	3.8	3.9	4.0
46.3	39.6	29.8	24.3	40.1	36.5	37.3	30.9

1. The U.S. Census Bureau population projections do not report on persons categorized as Hispanic, Asian, Black, or Other Races. Therefore, these categories overlap, and their sum exceeds the total population by 6.3 percent in 2006 and 2.1 percent in 2050.
2. This category includes American Indian and Alaska Native alone, Native Hawaiian and Other Pacific Islander alone, and Two or More Races.

Source: U.S. Census Bureau 2007.

DEINSTITUTIONALISM OR REINSTITUTIONALISM OF THE FAMILY?

Population forecasts rarely come true.[4] We acknowledge that statistical links between marriage and various family outcomes are not immutable; they are likely to change in unpredictable ways. Indeed, over the recent past, the historical rise in the nonmarital fertility ratio suggests an unprecedented uncoupling of marriage from fertility (Hamilton, Martin, and Ventura 2006; Wu and Li 2005). Patterns of marriage and childbearing among different racial and ethnic groups will undoubtedly change, often in unforeseen ways. Shifts in the meaning or value of marriage and family also are unlikely to be the same for all economic and cultural groups (Raley and

Sweeney 2007; Thornton, Axinn, and Xie 2007). Marriage and family life will be reshaped by differential rates of economic and cultural incorporation for different racial and ethnic immigrant groups into mainstream society.

The fundamental question for the future therefore is straightforward: Will family patterns and processes among America's racial and ethnic minorities "converge" to the white majority population, which itself is changing rapidly—even deinstitutionalizing—while also becoming a smaller majority share of the population with perhaps less cultural impact on other groups? By deinstitutionalization, Cherlin (2004) refers to the waning or even extinction of old patterns: patriarchal gender relations, traditional patterns of mate selection (for example, premarital abstinence and courtship practices), marital fidelity and life-long marriage, and stable nuclear families as a context for childbearing and childrearing. At the same time, marriage and family life arguably are undergoing a process of *reinstitutionalization*. This, in our view, does not mean a return to more marriage, less cohabitation, less out-of-wedlock childbearing, and higher fertility. Reinstitutionalization simply means that the rules that govern romance, mate selection, family building, marital interaction (such as who does the household chores and who makes the important decisions), and the normative sequencing of family-life-course events are being recreated or reshaped in new ways to serve traditional functions (replenishment of population, kinship systems and inheritance, and socialization of children).

The reinstitutionalization of marriage and family life may thus take many forms, and these will undoubtedly differ widely across racial and economic groups depending upon the degree of cultural incorporation into society. In our view, what is different from the past is that deinstitutionalization of old family forms and processes is occurring simultaneously with the reinstitutionalization of new ones, which have yet to be fully revealed. This means that the normative context of marriage and family life in the future is likely to be highly segmented (and institutionalized) along distinct racial, cultural, and economic lines. In our view, there is no such thing as the deinstitutionalization of marriage, unless deinstitutionalization is defined narrowly to refer to sweeping secular processes (such as declining fertility) that crosscut all of society and its constituent populations. In fact, Steven Nock argues in chapter 12 of this volume that marriage as an institution is growing more important rather than less important in American society.

From this perspective, we can envision several alternative demographic scenarios for the future. Each will likely render inaccurate the aforementioned marital-status projections (table 15.2), but in very different ways. One demographic scenario, for example, is that the acculturation processes will inevitably bring immigrant and minority patterns of marriage and family formation into line with the Anglo majority. Oropesa and Landale (2004) acknowledge that the generational succession of Hispanic immigrants will likely change significantly over the next half-century. For example, Suro and Passell (2003) estimate large increases in the share of second-generation and third-generation Hispanics after 2020. The share of first-generation Hispanics will decline from roughly 40 percent in 2000 to 25 percent in 2050. America's second-generation (38.1 percent) and third-generation (47.4 percent) Hispanics have much lower percentages of married persons than first-generation Hispanics (63.3 percent) (Oropesa and Landale 2004).[5] Under this demographic scenario, the pronuptiality patterns characteristic of first-generation Hispanics—high marriage rates and high fertility—will be replaced with new patterns (perhaps those of non-Hispanic whites) over successive immigrant generations. Simply put, the marriages and families of their children and grandchildren may increasingly mimic their native-born Anglo counterparts.

The likely effects of generational succession on American family life also will depend on the changing mix of national origin groups. Racial and immigrant minorities start in many different places. America's Hispanic and Asian populations are culturally and economically heterogeneous—perhaps increasingly so. For example, if Cuban Americans had the same mix of generation and age as non-Hispanic whites, the percent married (61.1 percent) would exceed the percent for non-Hispanic whites (57.4 percent). On the other hand, these adjusted marriage rates are lower among Mexicans (54.1 percent), Puerto Ricans (45.3 percent), and Central/South Americans (49.5 percent) (Oropesa and Landale 2004). Lichter and Qian (2004) also show that the households of Asian Indians are much more likely than Filipinos (20 versus 8 percent) to comprise working fathers and nonworking mothers (the so-called "traditional" American family). Asians in general are much more likely than Hispanics overall to be living alone. For example, 32 percent of Japanese American households are headed by persons living alone (Lichter and Qian 2004). By comparison, only 9 percent of Mexican American households are headed by single people. The lesson for the future seems clear: Any long-term demographic impacts of Hispanic and Asian population growth and immigration on U.S. marriage patterns will depend, at least in part, on the changing mix of Hispanics and Asians with different national origins, which, on its face, is difficult to forecast with any certainty.

A second alternative demographic scenario emphasizes the effects of intermarriage and racial mixing (Oropesa and Landale 2004). That is, the future of American family life will be reshaped by changing patterns of intermarriage between different racial and ethnic groups. Intermarriage with native-born whites reflects economic and cultural incorporation of minority groups; intermarriage rates typically increase when the social distance between partners of different racial or ethnic groups declines (Qian and Lichter 2007; Sassler 2005). To be sure, growing racial and ethnic diversity creates potentially large cultural barriers and fragmented social networks, including increasingly segmented marriage markets. But racial intermarriage—to the extent that it exists and grows—also breeds new associational ties between racial and ethnic groups (McPherson, Smith-Lovin, and Cook 2001). Interracial couples act as associational brokers or bridges between friends and families of different races. As such, they putatively link diverse family traditions and cultural repertoires. In our view, the long-term growth of intermarriage rates acts to break down group boundaries and promotes assimilation and acculturation on many different dimensions. This is not an asymmetrical process. There is a kind of iterative harmonization between groups that reflects the reciprocal influences of intergroup interaction. The children of interracial couples stir the ethnic melting pot by diluting ethnic and racial identity and bridging racial groups (Bratter 2007). The implication is clear: Accounts of the future of marriage must acknowledge the central role of intermarriage.

The problem today is that it is difficult to forecast intermarriage rates. Intermarriage rates with whites are high among Asians and Hispanics, but they also have declined over the past decade for first time in recent memory (Qian and Lichter 2007). Technically speaking, new demographic opportunities for intermarriage will by definition increase with growing racial and ethnic diversity in America. But it is much less clear whether attitudes or preferences to marry interracially will change, especially if immigration fuels increases in the pool of potential marriage partners for members of the same race or ethnic group. Whether intermarriage rates increase or decrease and whether they will be different for different racial or immigrant groups clearly will affect the trajectory of overall family change in the United States. For example, black-white intermarriage rates historically have been very low, especially in comparison to intermarriage rates between whites and either Asians or Hispanics. On the other hand, the new immigration of Afro-Caribbeans and Africans into the United States apparently has not provided a new or expanding pool of potential marriage partners for native-born blacks. Intermarriage rates among different black subpopulations is very low (Batson, Qian, and Lichter 2006).

A third demographic scenario suggests that the future of the family depends on intergenerational mobility and economic incorporation among America's racial and immigrant minorities. Increasingly, marriage is viewed as a "luxury good" that is out of the reach of low-income groups, including many racial and minority groups (Burstein 2007; Elwood and Jencks 2005). Over the past twenty years, the statistical relationship between education (as a proxy for income) and marriage switched from negative to positive (Lichter and Qian 2004). The implication seems clear: Convergence of racial and ethnic minorities to some kind of American middle-class family ideal will depend, at least in part, on patterns of upward economic mobility and declining racial inequality. In this regard, it is hard to predict the future. Racial and ethnic inequality in America remains large and is slow to change (Lichter, Qian, and Crowley 2007). For example, non-Hispanic whites at the twentieth income percentile have incomes that are 66 percent higher than the poverty income thresholds in 2000. Among Hispanic children, incomes at the twentieth income percentile are 21 percent lower than the poverty income thresholds. Moreover, during the 1990s, the median family-size adjusted incomes of Hispanic children were about 35 percent lower than the average incomes for the United States overall. The children of Asian and Hispanic immigrants also had much lower incomes than the children of their native-born counterparts.

The fact that recent rates of upward intergenerational mobility have favored whites over minorities means that any convergence in marriage and family life among racial and ethnic minorities also is likely to be slow. Intergenerational mobility among minorities may even have diverged recently from whites. Isaacs (2007) recently showed that about two-thirds of the white children of middle-income parents tended to exceed their parents in income. In contrast, the majority (69 percent) of black children of middle-income parents—defined as the middle quintile—fell below their parents' income when they reached adulthood. These estimates suggest that black-white differences in marriage and family life are likely to diverge rather than converge, even as America's majority white population retreats from marriage (if measured by later ages at marriage and declining first-marriage and remarriage rates). Similarly, the absence of economic incorporation among Hispanic immigrants (which may drive other forms of economic and cultural assimilation) may usher in an accelerated "retreat" from the pronuptiality norms and family tendencies typically associated with most Latino populations (except Puerto Ricans, who are more similar to African Americans) (Oropesa and Landale 2004).

Clearly, these three alternative demographic, social, and economic scenarios have different implications for the future of marriage and family life. The common thread among them, however, is clear. Given expected shifts in the generational composition of the large immigrant groups (especially Mexicans), declining intermarriage rates with whites, and large racial and ethnic differences in economic status and upward generational mobility, it is hard to imagine some kind of racial or ethnic convergence to a white middle-class norm. Instead, we foresee the possibility of a new kind of segmented reinstitutionalization of marriage and family life and, by implication, much greater cultural diversity and economic balkanization in American society.

THE FUTURE OF MARRIAGE: WHAT'S NEXT?

What is the future of marriage? Some answers were presumably contained in the November 2004 issue of *Journal of Marriage and Family*, which provided a "symposium on marriage and the future" (Walker 2004). The most interesting aspect of this forum was not what was discussed but how little the topic of race or ethnicity was considered. Few of the authors acknowledged how American family life is now being reshaped in new ways by the infusion of growing minority populations through unprecedented immigration (for an exception, see Oropesa and Landale 2004). Straight-line assimilation theory suggests that length of residence in the United States or the replacement of one immigrant generation with another will ultimately transform the minority population; they will be "Americanized." And to be an American has traditionally meant to stay in school, find a job, get married, and have children—in that order. But this normative sequencing of life-course stages has never been inviolate and has never been experienced similarly across racial or ethnic groups (for discussion, see Wu and Li 2005).

As we have argued here, the future of the family will be one of great diversity, fragmentation, and potential balkanization as groups simultaneously distinguish themselves from one another while both adopting the changing patterns of the majority white population and reinforcing family change overall. More generally, the rhetoric of family decline is no longer appropriate. It is being replaced by a new appreciation of diverse families that reflect changing racial and ethnic patterns of legal and informal marriage, fertility, and gender relations. The idea that we can conveniently summarize the typical family experiences of average Americans, both now and in the future, by calculating aggregate rates of marriage and fertility, seems increasingly arcane. In the case of marriage and family life, statistical averages may obfuscate as much as illuminate.

NOTES

Comments from the editors, Michael Jones-Correa, Sharon Sassler, and Larry Wu are greatly appreciated. All opinions are ours.

1. Only 11 percent of all non-Hispanic white families in 2000 comprised a working husband and stay-at-home mother (Lichter and Qian 2004). The percentage among Hispanic and Asian families was slightly higher—about 15 percent—but was much lower among blacks (about 5 percent).
2. By ages 30–34, however, the percentage of Asians who had ever married catches up with their non-Hispanic white counterparts (Lichter and Qian 2004).
3. Recent estimates suggest that about one-half of these children, however, live with both biological parents who are cohabiting (Sigle-Rushton and McLanahan 2002). Many of these couples ultimately marry, but perhaps an even larger share of cohabiters break up, subsequently repartner, and then bear additional children (Lichter, Qian, and Mellott 2006). Young mothers with children from multiple partners are less likely than other women to marry or stay married.
4. The forecast itself may stimulate new policies or change behaviors in ways that alter the future.
5. These generational differences largely reflect age differences born of past Hispanic immigration and fertility. Third-generation Hispanics are much older than first- and second-generation Hispanics and, as a result, are more likely to have married.

REFERENCES

Batson, C. D., Z. C. Qian, and D. T. Lichter. 2006. Interracial and intraracial patterns of mate selection among America's diverse black populations. *Journal of Marriage and Family* 68:658–672.

Bratter, J. 2007. Will "multiracial" survive to the next generation? The racial classification of children of multiracial parents. *Social Forces* 86:821–849.

Burstein, N.R. 2007. Economic influences on marriage and divorce. *Journal of Policy Analysis and Management* 26:387–429.

Cherlin, A. J. 2004. The deinstitutionalization of American marriage. *Journal of Marriage and Family* 66:848–461.

Ellwood, D. T., and C. Jencks. 2004. The spread of single-parent families in the United States since 1960. In D. P. Moynihan, T. M. Smeeding, and L. Rainwater, eds., *The future of the family*, 25–65. New York: Russell Sage Foundation.

Hamilton, B. E., J. A. Martin, and S. J. Ventura. 2006. Births: Preliminary data for 2005. Retrieved December 4, 2007, from www.cdc.gov/nchs/products/pubs/pubd/hestats/prelimbirths05/prelimbirths.

———. 2007. Births: Preliminary data for 2006. Retrieved December 9, 2007, from www.cdc.gov/nchs/data/nvsr/nvsr56/nvsr56_07.pdf.

Hernandez, D. J. 2004. Demographic change and the life circumstances of immigrant families. *Future of Children* 14:17–47.

Isaacs, J. 2007. *Economic mobility of black and white families*. Washington, D.C.: Brookings Institution.

Kent, M. M. 2007. Immigration and America's black population. *Population Bulletin* 62:1–16.

Lichter, D. T., and Z. Qian. 2004. Marriage and family in a multiracial society. *The American people: Census 2000 series*. New York: Russell Sage Foundation.

Lichter, D. T., Z. Qian, and M. L. Crowley. 2007. Poverty and economic polarization among children in racial minority and immigrant families. In D. R. Crane and T. B. Heaton, eds., *Handbook of families and poverty*, 119–146. Los Angeles: Sage Publications.

Lichter, D. T, Z. Qian, and L. M. Mellott. 2006. Marriage or dissolution? Union transitions among poor cohabiting women. *Demography* 43:223–240.

Martin, P., and E. Midgley. Immigration: Shaping and reshaping America. *Population Bulletin* 61, no. 4: 1–64.

McLanahan, S. 2004. Diverging destinies: How children are faring under the second demographic transition. *Demography* 41:607–627.

McPherson, M., S. Smith-Lovin, and J. M. Cook. 2001. Birds of a feather: Homophily in social networks. *Annual Review of Sociology* 27:415–444.

Nock, S. L. 2002. The social costs of de-institutionalizing marriage. In A. J. Hawkins, L. D. Wardle, and D. O. Coolidge, eds., *Revitalizing the institution of marriage for the twenty-first century*, 1–13. Westport, Conn.: Praeger.

Oropesa, R. S., and N. S. Landale. 2004. The future of marriage and Hispanics. *Journal of Marriage and Family* 66:901–920.

Qian, Z., and D. T. Lichter. 2007. Social boundaries and marital assimilation: Interpreting trends in racial and ethnic intermarriage. *American Sociological Review* 72:68–94.

Raley, R. K., and M. M. Sweeney. 2007. What explains race and ethnic variation in cohabitation, marriage, divorce, and nonmarital fertility? CCPR working paper series 26–07. Los Angeles: California Center for Population Research.

Sassler, S. 2005. Gender and ethnic differences in marital assimilation in the early twentieth century. *International Migration Review* 39:608–636.

Sigle-Rushton, W., and S. McLanahan. 2002. The living arrangements of new unmarried mothers. *Demography* 39:415–433.

Suro, R., and J. Passel. 2003. *The rise of the second generation: Changing patterns in Hispanic population growth*. Washington, D.C.: Pew Hispanic Center.

Sweeney, M. A., and J. A. Phillips. 2004. Understanding racial differences in marital disruption: Recent trends and explanations. *Journal of Marriage and Family* 66:639–650.

Thornton, A., W. G. Axinn, and Y. Xie. 2007. *Marriage and cohabitation*. Chicago: University of Chicago Press.

U.S. Census Bureau. 2004. U.S. interim projections by age, sex, race, and Hispanic origin. Retrieved Mar. 18, 2004, from www.census.gov/ipc/www/usinterimproj.

———. 2007. American Community Survey (ACS) 2006: Public Use Microdata Sample (PUMS), 2007.

Ventura, S. J., and C. A. Bachrach. 2000. Nonmarital childbearing in the United States. National Vital Statistics Reports, 48, no. 16. Washington, D.C.: U.S. Department of Health and Human Services.

Walker, A. 2004. A symposium on marriage and the family. *Journal of Marriage and Family* 66:843–847.

Waters, M. C., and T. R. Jimenez. 2005. Assessing immigrant assimilation: New empirical and theoretical challenges. *Annual Review of Sociology* 31:105–125.

Wu, L. 2008. Cohort estimates of nonmarital fertility among US women. *Demography* 45:193–207.

Wu, L., and J-C. A. Li. 2005. Historical roots of family diversity: Marital and childbearing trajectories of American women. In R. A. Setterstein Jr., F. F. Furstenberg Jr., and R. G. Rumbaut, eds., *On the frontier of adulthood: Theory, research, and public policy*, 110–149. Chicago: University of Chicago Press.

Contributors

Paul Amato is distinguished professor of sociology and demography at Pennsylvania State University. His research focuses on marital quality, the causes of divorce, and the effects of marital conflict and divorce on children. He has published four scholarly books and more than one hundred book chapters and journal articles. In 1994, 2000, and 2002, he received the Reuben Hill Award from the National Council on Family Relations for the best article published during the previous year to combine research and theory on the family.

Cara Bergstrom-Lynch is assistant professor of sociology at Eastern Connecticut State University. Her research and teaching focus on lesbian and gay parenthood and family building. She holds a PhD and MA from the University of Michigan and a BA from Wellesley College. Her work has appeared in *Journal of Comparative Family Studies* and *Early Child Development and Care.*

Warren Brown is Senior Public Service Associate and Director of the Applied Demography Program, a partnership between the University of Georgia's Carl Vinson Institute of Government and the State of Georgia Office of Planning and Budget. This initiative provides current demographic data and detailed projections about Georgia's population to state and local decision makers for strategic planning purposes.

Rachel Dunifon is an associate professor of policy analysis and management at Cornell University, with a PhD in human development and social policy from Northwestern University. Much of her research examines family structure and the well-being of children, focusing specifically on race differences in the role of single parenthood, as well as on the role of grandparents in the lives of children. Other research focuses on how welfare reform and other policies have influenced child well-being and parenting behaviors, as well as how the conditions of the low-wage labor market influence children.

Paula England is professor of sociology at Stanford University. Her research and teaching focus on gender and class inequality at work and in the family. She is the author of *Comparable Worth* (1992) and *Households, Employment, and Gender* (1986, with George Farkas). From 1994 to 1996 she was editor of the *American Sociological Review*. She was the 1999 recipient of the American Sociological Association's Jessie Bernard Award for career contributions to the study of gender.

David Fein is a senior associate at Abt Associates. He has led a wide range of research projects focusing on welfare reform, poverty, family formation, and the intersections of these subjects. He currently directs the Innovative Strategies for Increasing Self-Sufficiency (ISIS) demonstration and heads Abt's work on the Supporting Healthy Marriage (SHM) demonstration. He holds a BA in history from Oberlin College, an MA in demography from Georgetown University, and a PhD in sociology and demography from Princeton University.

Gary J. Gates is a senior research fellow at the Williams Institute, UCLA School of Law. He coauthored *The Gay and Lesbian Atlas* (2004) and focuses his research on the demographic, geographic, and economic characteristics of the gay and lesbian population. Gates holds a PhD from the Heinz School, Carnegie Mellon University. He also holds a master of divinity degree from St. Vincent Seminary and a bachelor's degree in computer science from the University of Pittsburgh at Johnstown.

Shirley A. Hill is professor of sociology at the University of Kansas, where she teaches classes on families, medical sociology, social inequality, and qualitative methods. Her research has focused on access to health care and family caregiving (*Managing Sickle Cell Disease in Low-Income Families*, 2003), child socialization (*African American Children: Socialization and Development in Families*, 1999), and how race, class, and gender affect families and intimate relationships (*Black Intimacies: A Gender Perspective on Families and Relationships*, 2005).

Michael P. Johnson is associate professor emeritus of sociology, women's studies, and African and African American Studies at Pennsylvania State University. His current research, summarized in *A Typology of Intimate Partner Violence: Intimate Terrorism, Violent Resistance, and Situational Couple Violence* (2008), focuses on the implications of differentiating among types of violence in intimate relationships. Recent papers are available at his Web site at www.personal.psu.edu/mpj.

Claire M. Kamp Dush is an assistant professor in human development and family science and a faculty affiliate of the Initiative in Population Research at Ohio State University. She completed her PhD in human development and family studies at Pennsylvania State University in 2005 and was an Institute for the Social Sciences postdoctoral fellow at Cornell University. Her research centers on understanding relationship quality and stability longitudinally, and examining how relationship experiences shape individual development.

Virginia Knox codirects the policy area on Family Well-Being and Children's Development at MDRC, overseeing studies examining the effectiveness of economic supports and services for low-income children and families. She is currently the project director and principal investigator for the Supporting Healthy Marriage project. The author of numerous published reports and papers, Knox holds a doctorate in public policy from Harvard University.

Daniel T. Lichter is Ferris Family Professor in the Department of Policy Analysis and Management at Cornell University and director of the Bronfenbrenner Life Course Center. He has published widely on topics related to welfare policy and the changing family, including studies of children's changing living arrangements and poverty, cohabitation and marriage among unwed mothers, and welfare incentive effects on the family. He currently sits on several advisory boards and is former editor of *Demography.*

Bobbi S. Low is professor of resource ecology in the School of Natural Resources, University of Michigan, and a faculty associate at Institute for Social Research and the Center for Study of Complex Systems. Her research interests center on behavioral ecology and life history theory. Her interdisciplinary interests have lead to two books, *Why Sex Matters* (2000) and *Institutions, Ecosystems, and Sustainability* (with Elinor Ostrom, Bob Costanza, and James Wilson, 2000), as well as numerous papers.

Wendy D. Manning is professor of sociology, director of the Center for Family and Demographic Research, and codirector of the National Center for Marriage Research at Bowling Green State University. Her research examines how family members define and understand their obligations to each other in an era of increasingly diverse and complex family relationships. Manning has examined the meaning of cohabitation, fertility in cohabiting unions, the stability of cohabiting unions, transitions to marriage, and implications of cohabitation for child well-being.

Tamara Metz is assistant professor of political science and humanities at Reed College. Her fields of interests include history of Western political thought, liberalism and its critics, feminist and postmodern theory, and theories of law. Current research concerns families and care in diverse, liberal democracies, and freedom in the age of Prozac.

Steven Nock was professor of sociology and psychology at the University of Virginia until his death in 2008. He earned his PhD at the University of Massachusetts–Amherst in 1976. His work focuses on the causes and consequences of change in the American family, investigating issues of privacy, unmarried fatherhood, cohabitation, commitment, divorce, and marriage.

H. Elizabeth Peters is professor of policy analysis and management and director of the Cornell Population Program at Cornell University. Her professional career has focused on issues in family economics and family policy, specifically examining the effects of public policies such as divorce laws, taxes, and welfare reform on family formation and dissolution decisions, inter- and intrahousehold transfers, and family investments in children. Her research has been widely published in journals of economics, demography, and sociology.

Adam P. Romero is law clerk to Judge Margaret McKeown of the Ninth Circuit U.S. Court of Appeals and former Peter Cooper Fellow at the Williams Institute, UCLA School of Law. His scholarly research concerns the significance of family in society, especially as related to family failure. He is coeditor of the collection *Feminist and Queer Legal Theory: Intimate Encounters, Uncomfortable Conversations* (2009). He holds a JD from Yale Law School, where he was awarded the Kelley Prize and a Coker Fellowship. He received his AB from Cornell University, graduating summa cum laude.

Pamela J. Smock is professor of sociology and women's studies and research professor at the Population Studies Center at the University of Michigan, Ann Arbor. A family demographer, she focuses on the causes and consequences of family patterns and change, engaging their intersections with economic, racial/ethnic, and gender inequalities. She has published on topics such as cohabitation, the economic consequences of divorce and marriage, nonresident fatherhood, child support, remarriage, and the motherhood wage penalty.

Megan Sweeney is associate professor of sociology at the University of California, Los Angeles. Her research interests focus on the determinants and consequences of family transitions in the United States, with a particular emphasis on variation over historical time, across subpopulations, and over the life course. Her current work includes an investigation of the emotional, physical, and behavioral well-being of children and adolescents living in stepfamilies.

Arland Thornton is professor of sociology and research professor at the Population Studies Center and Survey Research Center of the University of Michigan. His research focuses on marriage, family, and social change in several settings, including Argentina, China, Egypt, Nepal, Taiwan, and the United States. His books include *Reading History Sideways: The Fallacy and Enduring Impact of the Developmental Paradigm on Family Life* (2005), *International Family Change: Ideational Perspectives* (2008), and *Marriage and Cohabitation* (2007).

Tami M. Videon is assistant professor at Rutgers University. She earned her PhD in sociology from Rutgers University. Much of her research investigates the determinants of adolescent well-being. Her work has appeared in *Journal of Adolescent Health*, *Journal of Family Issues*, *Journal of Health and Social Behavior*, and *Journal of Marriage and Family*.

Hongbo Wang received his PhD in sociology from the University of California, Los Angeles. He is currently a postdoctoral fellow at the Harris

School of Public Policy Studies of the University of Chicago. He is interested in family influences on child development and later life outcomes, immigrant adaptation, demography, and social stratification in China. His current work involves econometric analysis of roles of personality traits, coupled with cognitive ability, for health and behavioral outcomes.

Index